UKRAINIAN
VOCABULARY

ENGLISH-UKRAINIAN

The most useful words
To expand your lexicon and sharpen
your language skills

9000 words

Ukrainian vocabulary for English speakers - 9000 words

By Andrey Taranov

T&P Books vocabularies are intended for helping you learn, memorize and review foreign words. The dictionary is divided into themes, covering all major spheres of everyday activities, business, science, culture, etc.

The process of learning words using T&P Books' theme-based dictionaries gives you the following advantages:

- Correctly grouped source information predetermines success at subsequent stages of word memorization
- Availability of words derived from the same root allowing memorization of word units (rather than separate words)
- Small units of words facilitate the process of establishing associative links needed for consolidation of vocabulary
- Level of language knowledge can be estimated by the number of learned words

T&P Books Publishing
www.tpbooks.com

ISBN: 978-1-78071-815-6

This book is also available in E-book formats.
Please visit www.tpbooks.com or the major online bookstores.

UKRAINIAN VOCABULARY
for English speakers

T&P Books vocabularies are intended to help you learn, memorize, and review foreign words. The vocabulary contains over 9000 commonly used words arranged thematically.

- Vocabulary contains the most commonly used words
- Recommended as an addition to any language course
- Meets the needs of beginners and advanced learners of foreign languages
- Convenient for daily use, revision sessions, and self-testing activities
- Allows you to assess your vocabulary

Special features of the vocabulary

- Words are organized according to their meaning, not alphabetically
- Words are presented in three columns to facilitate the reviewing and self-testing processes
- Words in groups are divided into small blocks to facilitate the learning process
- The vocabulary offers a convenient and simple transcription of each foreign word

The vocabulary has 256 topics including:

Basic Concepts, Numbers, Colors, Months, Seasons, Units of Measurement, Clothing & Accessories, Food & Nutrition, Restaurant, Family Members, Relatives, Character, Feelings, Emotions, Diseases, City, Town, Sightseeing, Shopping, Money, House, Home, Office, Working in the Office, Import & Export, Marketing, Job Search, Sports, Education, Computer, Internet, Tools, Nature, Countries, Nationalities and more ...

T&P BOOKS' THEME-BASED DICTIONARIES

The Correct System for Memorizing Foreign Words

Acquiring vocabulary is one of the most important elements of learning a foreign language, because words allow us to express our thoughts, ask questions, and provide answers. An inadequate vocabulary can impede communication with a foreigner and make it difficult to understand a book or movie well.

The pace of activity in all spheres of modern life, including the learning of modern languages, has increased. Today, we need to memorize large amounts of information (grammar rules, foreign words, etc.) within a short period. However, this does not need to be difficult. All you need to do is to choose the right training materials, learn a few special techniques, and develop your individual training system.

Having a system is critical to the process of language learning. Many people fail to succeed in this regard; they cannot master a foreign language because they fail to follow a system comprised of selecting materials, organizing lessons, arranging new words to be learned, and so on. The lack of a system causes confusion and eventually, lowers self-confidence.

T&P Books' theme-based dictionaries can be included in the list of elements needed for creating an effective system for learning foreign words. These dictionaries were specially developed for learning purposes and are meant to help students effectively memorize words and expand their vocabulary.

Generally speaking, the process of learning words consists of three main elements:

- Reception (creation or acquisition) of a training material, such as a word list
- Work aimed at memorizing new words
- Work aimed at reviewing the learned words, such as self-testing

All three elements are equally important since they determine the quality of work and the final result. All three processes require certain skills and a well-thought-out approach.

New words are often encountered quite randomly when learning a foreign language and it may be difficult to include them all in a unified list. As a result, these words remain written on scraps of paper, in book margins, textbooks, and so on. In order to systematize such words, we have to create and continually update a "book of new words." A paper notebook, a netbook, or a tablet PC can be used for these purposes.

This "book of new words" will be your personal, unique list of words. However, it will only contain the words that you came across during the learning process. For example, you might have written down the words "Sunday," "Tuesday," and "Friday." However, there are additional words for days of the week, for example, "Saturday," that are missing, and your list of words would be incomplete. Using a theme dictionary, in addition to the "book of new words," is a reasonable solution to this problem.

The theme-based dictionary may serve as the basis for expanding your vocabulary.

It will be your big "book of new words" containing the most frequently used words of a foreign language already included. There are quite a few theme-based dictionaries available, and you should ensure that you make the right choice in order to get the maximum benefit from your purchase.

Therefore, we suggest using theme-based dictionaries from T&P Books Publishing as an aid to learning foreign words. Our books are specially developed for effective use in the sphere of vocabulary systematization, expansion and review.

Theme-based dictionaries are not a magical solution to learning new words. However, they can serve as your main database to aid foreign-language acquisition. Apart from theme dictionaries, you can have copybooks for writing down new words, flash cards, glossaries for various texts, as well as other resources; however, a good theme dictionary will always remain your primary collection of words.

T&P Books' theme-based dictionaries are specialty books that contain the most frequently used words in a language.

The main characteristic of such dictionaries is the division of words into themes. For example, the *City* theme contains the words "street," "crossroads," "square," "fountain," and so on. The *Talking* theme might contain words like "to talk," "to ask," "question," and "answer".

All the words in a theme are divided into smaller units, each comprising 3–5 words. Such an arrangement improves the perception of words and makes the learning process less tiresome. Each unit contains a selection of words with similar meanings or identical roots. This allows you to learn words in small groups and establish other associative links that have a positive effect on memorization.

The words on each page are placed in three columns: a word in your native language, its translation, and its transcription. Such positioning allows for the use of techniques for effective memorization. After closing the translation column, you can flip through and review foreign words, and vice versa. "This is an easy and convenient method of review – one that we recommend you do often."

Our theme-based dictionaries contain transcriptions for all the foreign words. Unfortunately, none of the existing transcriptions are able to convey the exact nuances of foreign pronunciation. That is why we recommend using the transcriptions only as a supplementary learning aid. Correct pronunciation can only be acquired with the help of sound. Therefore our collection includes audio theme-based dictionaries.

The process of learning words using T&P Books' theme-based dictionaries gives you the following advantages:

- You have correctly grouped source information, which predetermines your success at subsequent stages of word memorization
- Availability of words derived from the same root (lazy, lazily, lazybones), allowing you to memorize word units instead of separate words
- Small units of words facilitate the process of establishing associative links needed for consolidation of vocabulary
- You can estimate the number of learned words and hence your level of language knowledge
- The dictionary allows for the creation of an effective and high-quality revision process
- You can revise certain themes several times, modifying the revision methods and techniques
- Audio versions of the dictionaries help you to work out the pronunciation of words and develop your skills of auditory word perception

The T&P Books' theme-based dictionaries are offered in several variants differing in the number of words: 1.500, 3.000, 5.000, 7.000, and 9.000 words. There are also dictionaries containing 15,000 words for some language combinations. Your choice of dictionary will depend on your knowledge level and goals.

We sincerely believe that our dictionaries will become your trusty assistant in learning foreign languages and will allow you to easily acquire the necessary vocabulary.

TABLE OF CONTENTS

T&P Books' Theme-Based Dictionaries   4
Pronunciation guide   15
Abbreviations   17

BASIC CONCEPTS   18
Basic concepts. Part 1   18

1. Pronouns   18
2. Greetings. Salutations. Farewells   18
3. How to address   19
4. Cardinal numbers. Part 1   19
5. Cardinal numbers. Part 2   20
6. Ordinal numbers   21
7. Numbers. Fractions   21
8. Numbers. Basic operations   21
9. Numbers. Miscellaneous   22
10. The most important verbs. Part 1   22
11. The most important verbs. Part 2   23
12. The most important verbs. Part 3   24
13. The most important verbs. Part 4   25
14. Colors   26
15. Questions   27
16. Prepositions   27
17. Function words. Adverbs. Part 1   28
18. Function words. Adverbs. Part 2   30

Basic concepts. Part 2   32

19. Weekdays   32
20. Hours. Day and night   32
21. Months. Seasons   33
22. Time. Miscellaneous   35
23. Opposites   36
24. Lines and shapes   38
25. Units of measurement   39
26. Containers   40
27. Materials   41
28. Metals   41

HUMAN BEING
Human being. The body

	HUMAN BEING	43
	Human being. The body	43

29. Humans. Basic concepts — 43
30. Human anatomy — 43
31. Head — 44
32. Human body — 45

Clothing & Accessories — 46

33. Outerwear. Coats — 46
34. Men's & women's clothing — 46
35. Clothing. Underwear — 47
36. Headwear — 47
37. Footwear — 47
38. Textile. Fabrics — 48
39. Personal accessories — 48
40. Clothing. Miscellaneous — 49
41. Personal care. Cosmetics — 50
42. Jewelry — 51
43. Watches. Clocks — 51

Food. Nutricion — 52

44. Food — 52
45. Drinks — 54
46. Vegetables — 55
47. Fruits. Nuts — 55
48. Bread. Candy — 56
49. Cooked dishes — 57
50. Spices — 58
51. Meals — 58
52. Table setting — 59
53. Restaurant — 60

Family, relatives and friends — 61

54. Personal information. Forms — 61
55. Family members. Relatives — 61
56. Friends. Coworkers — 62
57. Man. Woman — 63
58. Age — 64
59. Children — 64
60. Married couples. Family life — 65

Character. Feelings. Emotions — 67

61. Feelings. Emotions — 67

62. Character. Personality 68
63. Sleep. Dreams 69
64. Humour. Laughter. Gladness 70
65. Discussion, conversation. Part 1 71
66. Discussion, conversation. Part 2 72
67. Discussion, conversation. Part 3 73
68. Agreement. Refusal 74
69. Success. Good luck. Failure 75
70. Quarrels. Negative emotions 75

Medicine 78

71. Diseases 78
72. Symptoms. Treatments. Part 1 79
73. Symptoms. Treatments. Part 2 80
74. Symptoms. Treatments. Part 3 81
75. Doctors 82
76. Medicine. Drugs. Accessories 82
77. Smoking. Tobacco products 83

HUMAN HABITAT 84
City 84

78. City. Life in the city 84
79. Urban institutions 85
80. Signs 87
81. Urban transportation 88
82. Sightseeing 89
83. Shopping 89
84. Money 90
85. Post. Postal service 91

Dwelling. House. Home 93

86. House. Dwelling 93
87. House. Entrance. Lift 94
88. House. Electricity 94
89. House. Doors. Locks 94
90. Country house 95
91. Villa. Mansion 96
92. Castle. Palace 96
93. Apartment 97
94. Apartment. Cleaning 97
95. Furniture. Interior 97
96. Bedding 98
97. Kitchen 98
98. Bathroom 100
99. Household appliances 100
100. Repairs. Renovation 101

101. Plumbing   101
102. Fire. Conflagration   102

HUMAN ACTIVITIES   104
Job. Business. Part 1   104

103. Office. Working in the office   104
104. Business processes. Part 1   105
105. Business processes. Part 2   106
106. Production. Works   107
107. Contract. Agreement   109
108. Import & Export   109
109. Finances   110
110. Marketing   110
111. Advertising   111
112. Banking   112
113. Telephone. Phone conversation   113
114. Mobile telephone   113
115. Stationery   114
116. Various kinds of documents   114
117. Kinds of business   115

Job. Business. Part 2   118

118. Show. Exhibition   118
119. Mass Media   119
120. Agriculture   120
121. Building. Building process   121
122. Science. Research. Scientists   122

Professions and occupations   124

123. Job search. Dismissal   124
124. Business people   124
125. Service professions   126
126. Military professions and ranks   126
127. Officials. Priests   127
128. Agricultural professions   128
129. Art professions   128
130. Various professions   129
131. Occupations. Social status   130

Sports   132

132. Kinds of sports. Sportspersons   132
133. Kinds of sports. Miscellaneous   133
134. Gym   134

135.	Hockey	134
136.	Football	134
137.	Alpine skiing	136
138.	Tennis. Golf	136
139.	Chess	137
140.	Boxing	137
141.	Sports. Miscellaneous	138

Education — 140

142.	School	140
143.	College. University	141
144.	Sciences. Disciplines	142
145.	Writing system. Orthography	142
146.	Foreign languages	144
147.	Fairy tale characters	145
148.	Zodiac Signs	145

Arts — 146

149.	Theater	146
150.	Cinema	147
151.	Painting	148
152.	Literature & Poetry	149
153.	Circus	150
154.	Music. Pop music	150

Rest. Entertainment. Travel — 152

155.	Trip. Travel	152
156.	Hotel	153
157.	Books. Reading	153
158.	Hunting. Fishing	155
159.	Games. Billiards	156
160.	Games. Playing cards	156
161.	Casino. Roulette	157
162.	Rest. Games. Miscellaneous	157
163.	Photography	158
164.	Beach. Swimming	159

TECHNICAL EQUIPMENT. TRANSPORTATION — 161
Technical equipment — 161

165.	Computer	161
166.	Internet. E-mail	162
167.	Electricity	163
168.	Tools	164

Transportation   167

169.	Airplane	167
170.	Train	168
171.	Ship	169
172.	Airport	170
173.	Bicycle. Motorcycle	171

Cars   173

174.	Types of cars	173
175.	Cars. Bodywork	173
176.	Cars. Passenger compartment	175
177.	Cars. Engine	175
178.	Cars. Crash. Repair	176
179.	Cars. Road	177
180.	Traffic signs	178

PEOPLE. LIFE EVENTS   180
Life events   180

181.	Holidays. Event	180
182.	Funerals. Burial	181
183.	War. Soldiers	182
184.	War. Military actions. Part 1	183
185.	War. Military actions. Part 2	184
186.	Weapons	186
187.	Ancient people	187
188.	Middle Ages	188
189.	Leader. Chief. Authorities	190
190.	Road. Way. Directions	190
191.	Breaking the law. Criminals. Part 1	192
192.	Breaking the law. Criminals. Part 2	193
193.	Police. Law. Part 1	194
194.	Police. Law. Part 2	195

NATURE   197
The Earth. Part 1   197

195.	Outer space	197
196.	The Earth	198
197.	Cardinal directions	199
198.	Sea. Ocean	199
199.	Seas' and Oceans' names	200
200.	Mountains	201
201.	Mountains names	202
202.	Rivers	203
203.	Rivers' names	203

204. Forest   204
205. Natural resources   205

The Earth. Part 2   207

206. Weather   207
207. Severe weather. Natural disasters   208
208. Noises. Sounds   208
209. Winter   209

Fauna   211

210. Mammals. Predators   211
211. Wild animals   211
212. Domestic animals   213
213. Dogs. Dog breeds   214
214. Sounds made by animals   214
215. Young animals   215
216. Birds   215
217. Birds. Singing and sounds   216
218. Fish. Marine animals   217
219. Amphibians. Reptiles   218
220. Insects   218
221. Animals. Body parts   219
222. Actions of animals   220
223. Animals. Habitats   220
224. Animal care   221
225. Animals. Miscellaneous   221
226. Horses   222

Flora   224

227. Trees   224
228. Shrubs   225
229. Mushrooms   225
230. Fruits. Berries   225
231. Flowers. Plants   226
232. Cereals, grains   227
233. Vegetables. Greens   228

REGIONAL GEOGRAPHY   230
Countries. Nationalities   230

234. Western Europe   230
235. Central and Eastern Europe   232
236. Former USSR countries   233
237. Asia   234

238.	North America	236
239.	Central and South America	237
240.	Africa	238
241.	Australia. Oceania	238
242.	Cities	239
243.	Politics. Government. Part 1	240
244.	Politics. Government. Part 2	242
245.	Countries. Miscellaneous	243
246.	Major religious groups. Confessions	244
247.	Religions. Priests	245
248.	Faith. Christianity. Islam	245

MISCELLANEOUS

248

249.	Various useful words	248
250.	Modifiers. Adjectives. Part 1	249
251.	Modifiers. Adjectives. Part 2	252

MAIN 500 VERBS

255

252.	Verbs A-C	255
253.	Verbs D-G	257
254.	Verbs H-M	260
255.	Verbs N-S	262
256.	Verbs T-W	265

PRONUNCIATION GUIDE

Letter	Ukrainian example	T&P phonetic alphabet	English example

Vowels

A a	акт	[ɑ]	shorter than in park, card
E e	берет	[e], [æ]	pet, absent
Є є	модельєр	[ɛ]	man, bad
И и	ритм	[ɪ]	big, America
I i	компанія	[i]	shorter than in feet
Ї ї	поїзд	[ji]	playing, spying
O o	око	[ɔ]	bottle, doctor
У у	буря	[u]	book
Ю ю	костюм	[juː], [ju]	cued, cute
Я я	маяк	[jɑ]	young, yard

Consonants

Б б	бездна	[b]	baby, book
В в	вікно	[w]	vase, winter
Г г	готель	[ɣ]	between [g] and [h]
Ґ ґ	ґудзик	[g]	game, gold
Д д	дефіс	[d]	day, doctor
Ж ж	жанр	[ʒ]	forge, pleasure
З з	зброя	[z]	zebra, please
Й й	йти	[j]	yes, New York
К к	крок	[k]	clock, kiss
Л л	лев	[l]	lace, people
М м	мати	[m]	magic, milk
Н н	назва	[n]	name, normal
П п	приз	[p]	pencil, private
Р р	радість	[r]	trilled [r]
С с	сон	[s]	city, boss
Т т	тир	[t]	tourist, trip
Ф ф	фарба	[f]	face, food
Х х	холод	[h]	huge, hat
Ц ц	церква	[ts]	cats, tsetse fly
Ч ч	час	[tʃ]	church, French

Letter	Ukrainian example	T&P phonetic alphabet	English example
Ш ш	шуба	[ʃ]	machine, shark
Щ щ	щука	[ɕ]	sheep, shop

Combinations with the soft sign (Ь ь)

ь	камінь	[ʲ]	soft sign - no sound
ль	медаль	[ʎ]	daily, million
нь	мішень	[ɲ]	canyon, new
сь	восьмий	[s]	soft [s]
ть	швидкість	[t]	tune, student
ъ	ім'я	[ʺ]	hard sign - no sound

ABBREVIATIONS
used in the vocabulary

ab.	-	about
adj	-	adjective
adv	-	adverb
anim.	-	animate
as adj	-	attributive noun used as adjective
e.g.	-	for example
etc.	-	et cetera
fam.	-	familiar
fem.	-	feminine
form.	-	formal
inanim.	-	inanimate
masc.	-	masculine
math	-	mathematics
mil.	-	military
n	-	noun
pl	-	plural
pron.	-	pronoun
sb	-	somebody
sing.	-	singular
sth	-	something
v aux	-	auxiliary verb
vi	-	intransitive verb
vi, vt	-	intransitive, transitive verb
vt	-	transitive verb
m	-	masculine noun
f	-	feminine noun

BASIC CONCEPTS

Basic concepts. Part 1

1. Pronouns

I, me	я	[ja]
you	ти	[tɪ]
he	він	[win]
she	вона	[wo'na]
we	ми	[mɪ]
you (to a group)	ви	[wɪ]
they	вони	[wo'nɪ]

2. Greetings. Salutations. Farewells

Hello! (fam.)	Здрастуй!	['zdrastuj]
Hello! (form.)	Здрастуйте!	['zdrastujtɛ]
Good morning!	Доброго ранку!	['dɔbroɣo 'raŋku]
Good afternoon!	Добрий день!	['dɔbrɪj dɛɲ]
Good evening!	Добрий вечір!	['dɔbrɪj 'wɛʧir]
to say hello	вітатися	[wi'tatɪsʲa]
Hi! (hello)	Привіт!	[prɪ'wit]
greeting (n)	вітання (n)	[wi'taɲja]
to greet (vt)	вітати	[wi'tatɪ]
How are you?	Як справи?	[jak 'sprawɪ]
What's new?	Що нового?	[ɕo no'wɔɣo]
Bye-Bye! Goodbye!	До побачення!	[do po'batʃɛɲja]
See you soon!	До швидкої зустрічі!	[do ʃwid'kɔjɪ 'zustriʧi]
Farewell! (to a friend)	Прощавай!	[proɕa'waj]
Farewell (form.)	Прощавайте!	[proɕa'wajtɛ]
to say goodbye	прощатися	[pro'ɕatɪsʲa]
So long!	Бувай!	[bu'waj]
Thank you!	Дякую!	['dʲakuju]
Thank you very much!	Щиро дякую!	['ɕɪro 'dʲakuju]
You're welcome	Будь ласка.	[budʲ 'laska]
Don't mention it!	Не варто подяки	[nɛ 'warto po'dʲakɪ]
It was nothing	Нема за що.	[nɛ'ma za ɕo]

Excuse me! (fam.)	Вибач!	['wɪbatʃ]
Excuse me! (form.)	Вибачте!	['wɪbatʃtɛ]
to excuse (forgive)	вибачати	[wɪbɑ'tʃɑtɪ]

to apologize (vi)	вибачатися	[wɪbɑ'tʃɑtɪsʲa]
My apologies	Моє вибачення.	[mo'ɛ 'wɪbatʃɛnjɑ]
I'm sorry!	Вибачте!	['wɪbatʃtɛ]
to forgive (vt)	пробачати	[probɑ'tʃɑtɪ]
please (adv)	будь ласка	[budʲ 'lɑskɑ]

Don't forget!	Не забудьте!	[nɛ zɑ'budʲtɛ]
Certainly!	Звичайно!	[zwɪ'tʃɑjno]
Of course not!	Звичайно ні!	[zwɪ'tʃɑjno ni]
Okay! (I agree)	Згоден!	['zɣɔdɛn]
That's enough!	Досить!	['dɔsɪtʲ]

3. How to address

mister, sir	Пан	[pɑn]
ma'am	Пані	['pɑni]
miss	Дівчино	['diwtʃɪno]
young man	Хлопче	['hlɔptʃɛ]
young man (little boy)	Хлопчику	['hlɔptʃɪku]
miss (little girl)	Дівчинко	['diwtʃɪŋko]

4. Cardinal numbers. Part 1

0 zero	нуль	[nuʎ]
1 one	один	[o'dɪn]
2 two	два	[dwɑ]
3 three	три	[trɪ]
4 four	чотири	[tʃo'tɪrɪ]

5 five	п'ять	[pʰjatʲ]
6 six	шість	[ʃistʲ]
7 seven	сім	[sim]
8 eight	вісім	['wisim]
9 nine	дев'ять	['dɛwʰjatʲ]

10 ten	десять	['dɛsʲatʲ]
11 eleven	одинадцять	[odɪ'nɑdtsʲatʲ]
12 twelve	дванадцять	[dwɑ'nɑdtsʲatʲ]
13 thirteen	тринадцять	[trɪ'nɑdtsʲatʲ]
14 fourteen	чотирнадцять	[tʃotɪr'nɑdtsʲatʲ]

15 fifteen	п'ятнадцять	[pʰjat'nɑdtsʲatʲ]
16 sixteen	шістнадцять	[ʃist'nɑdtsʲatʲ]
17 seventeen	сімнадцять	[sim'nɑdtsʲatʲ]

| 18 eighteen | вісімнадцять | [wisimˈnɑdtsʲatʲ] |
| 19 nineteen | дев'ятнадцять | [dɛwˈjatˈnɑdtsʲatʲ] |

20 twenty	двадцять	[ˈdwɑdtsʲatʲ]
21 twenty-one	двадцять один	[ˈdwɑdtsʲatʲ oˈdɪn]
22 twenty-two	двадцять два	[ˈdwɑdtsʲatʲ dwɑ]
23 twenty-three	двадцять три	[ˈdwɑdtsʲatʲ trɪ]

30 thirty	тридцять	[ˈtrɪdtsʲatʲ]
31 thirty-one	тридцять один	[ˈtrɪdtsʲatʲ oˈdɪn]
32 thirty-two	тридцять два	[ˈtrɪdtsʲatʲ dwɑ]
33 thirty-three	тридцять три	[ˈtrɪdtsʲatʲ trɪ]

40 forty	сорок	[ˈsɔrok]
41 forty-one	сорок один	[ˈsɔrok oˈdɪn]
42 forty-two	сорок два	[ˈsɔrok dwɑ]
43 forty-three	сорок три	[ˈsɔrok trɪ]

50 fifty	п'ятдесят	[pʰjatdɛˈsʲat]
51 fifty-one	п'ятдесят один	[pʰjatdɛˈsʲat oˈdɪn]
52 fifty-two	п'ятдесят два	[pʰjatdɛˈsʲat dwɑ]
53 fifty-three	п'ятдесят три	[pʰjatdɛˈsʲat trɪ]

60 sixty	шістдесят	[ʃizdɛˈsʲat]
61 sixty-one	шістдесят один	[ʃizdɛˈsʲat oˈdɪn]
62 sixty-two	шістдесят два	[ʃizdɛˈsʲat dwɑ]
63 sixty-three	шістдесят три	[ʃizdɛˈsʲat trɪ]

70 seventy	сімдесят	[simdɛˈsʲat]
71 seventy-one	сімдесят один	[simdɛˈsʲat odɪn]
72 seventy-two	сімдесят два	[simdɛˈsʲat dwɑ]
73 seventy-three	сімдесят три	[simdɛˈsʲat trɪ]

80 eighty	вісімдесят	[wisimdɛˈsʲat]
81 eighty-one	вісімдесят один	[wisimdɛˈsʲat oˈdɪn]
82 eighty-two	вісімдесят два	[wisimdɛˈsʲat dwɑ]
83 eighty-three	вісімдесят три	[wisimdɛˈsʲat trɪ]

90 ninety	дев'яносто	[dɛwʰjaˈnɔsto]
91 ninety-one	дев'яносто один	[dɛwʰjaˈnɔsto oˈdɪn]
92 ninety-two	дев'яносто два	[dɛwʰjaˈnɔsto dwɑ]
93 ninety-three	дев'яносто три	[dɛwʰjaˈnɔsto trɪ]

5. Cardinal numbers. Part 2

100 one hundred	сто	[sto]
200 two hundred	двісті	[ˈdwisti]
300 three hundred	триста	[ˈtrɪsta]
400 four hundred	чотириста	[ʧoˈtɪrɪsta]
500 five hundred	п'ятсот	[pʰjaˈtsɔt]

600 six hundred	шістсот	[ʃisˈtsɔt]
700 seven hundred	сімсот	[simˈsɔt]
800 eight hundred	вісімсот	[wisimˈsɔt]
900 nine hundred	дев'ятсот	[dɛwʰjaˈtsɔt]

1000 one thousand	тисяча	[ˈtɪsʲatʃa]
2000 two thousand	дві тисячі	[dwi ˈtɪsʲatʃi]
3000 three thousand	три тисячі	[trɪ ˈtɪsʲatʃi]
10000 ten thousand	десять тисяч	[ˈdɛsʲatʲ ˈtɪsʲatʃ]
one hundred thousand	сто тисяч	[sto ˈtɪsʲatʃ]
million	мільйон (m)	[miʎˈjon]
billion	мільярд (m)	[miˈʎjard]

6. Ordinal numbers

first (adj)	перший	[ˈpɛrʃɪj]
second (adj)	другий	[ˈdruɣɪj]
third (adj)	третій	[ˈtrɛtij]
fourth (adj)	четвертий	[tʃɛtˈwɛrtɪj]
fifth (adj)	п'ятий	[ˈpʰjatɪj]

sixth (adj)	шостий	[ˈʃostɪj]
seventh (adj)	сьомий	[ˈsʲɔmɪj]
eighth (adj)	восьмий	[ˈwosʲmɪj]
ninth (adj)	дев'ятий	[dɛwʰʲjatɪj]
tenth (adj)	десятий	[dɛˈsʲatɪj]

7. Numbers. Fractions

fraction	дріб (m)	[drib]
one half	одна друга	[odˈna ˈdruɣa]
one third	одна третя	[odˈna ˈtrɛtʲa]
one quarter	одна четверта	[odˈna tʃɛtˈwɛrta]

one eighth	одна восьма	[odˈna ˈwosʲma]
one tenth	одна десята	[odˈna dɛˈsʲata]
two thirds	дві третіх	[dwi ˈtrɛtih]
three quarters	три четвертих	[trɪ tʃɛtˈwɛrtih]

8. Numbers. Basic operations

subtraction	віднімання (n)	[widniˈmanja]
to subtract (vi, vt)	відняти	[widˈnʲatɪ]
division	ділення (n)	[ˈdilɛnja]
to divide (vt)	ділити	[diˈlɪtɪ]
addition	додавання (n)	[dodaˈwanja]

to add up (vt)	додати	[do'datı]
to add (vi, vt)	додавати	[doda'watı]
multiplication	множення (n)	['mnɔʒenja]
to multiply (vt)	множити	['mnɔʒıtı]

9. Numbers. Miscellaneous

digit, figure	цифра (f)	['ʦıfra]
number	число (n)	[ʧıs'lɔ]
numeral	числівник (m)	[ʧıs'liwnık]
minus sign	мінус (m)	['minus]
plus sign	плюс (m)	[plys]
formula	формула (f)	['fɔrmula]

calculation	розрахунок (m)	[rozra'hunok]
to count (vt)	рахувати	[rahu'watı]
to count up	підраховувати	[pidra'howuwatı]
to compare (vt)	зрівнювати	['zriwnywatı]

How much?	Скільки?	['skiʎkı]
sum, total	сума (f)	['suma]
result	результат (m)	[rɛzuʎ'tat]
remainder	залишок (m)	['zalıʃok]

a few …	декілька	['dɛkiʎka]
few, little (adv)	небагато …	[nɛba'ɣato]
the rest	решта (f)	['rɛʃta]
one and a half	півтора	[piwto'ra]
dozen	дюжина (f)	['dyʒına]

in half (adv)	навпіл	['nawpil]
equally (evenly)	порівну	['pɔriwnu]
half	половина (f)	[polo'wına]
time (three ~s)	раз (m)	[raz]

10. The most important verbs. Part 1

to advise (vt)	радити	['radıtı]
to agree (say yes)	погоджуватися	[po'ɣoʤuwatısʲa]
to answer (vi, vt)	відповідати	[widpowi'datı]
to apologize (vi)	вибачатися	[wıba'ʧatısʲa]
to arrive (vi)	приїжджати	[prıjı'ʒatı]
to ask (~ oneself)	запитувати	[za'pıtuwatı]
to ask (~ sb to do sth)	просити	[pro'sıtı]

to be (vi)	бути	['butı]
to be afraid	боятися	[bo'jatısʲa]
to be hungry	хотіти їсти	[ho'titı 'jistı]

to be interested in …	цікавитися	[ʦiˈkawitisʲa]
to be needed	бути потрібним	[ˈbuti potˈribnim]
to be surprised	дивуватись	[diwuˈwatisʲ]
to be thirsty	хотіти пити	[hoˈtiti ˈpiti]

to begin (vt)	починати	[potʃiˈnati]
to belong to …	належати	[naˈlɛʒati]
to boast (vi)	хвастатися	[ˈhwastatisʲa]
to break (split into pieces)	ламати	[laˈmati]

to call (for help)	кликати	[ˈklikati]
can (v aux)	могти	[moɣˈti]
to catch (vt)	ловити	[loˈwiti]
to change (vt)	поміняти	[pomiˈɲati]
to choose (select)	вибирати	[wibiˈrati]

to come down	спускатися	[spusˈkatisʲa]
to come in (enter)	входити	[ˈwhɔditi]
to compare (vt)	зрівнювати	[ˈzriwnywati]
to complain (vi, vt)	скаржитися	[ˈskarʒitisʲa]

to confuse (mix up)	помилятися	[pomiˈʎatisʲa]
to continue (vt)	продовжувати	[proˈdɔwʒuwati]
to control (vt)	контролювати	[kontrolyˈwati]
to cook (dinner)	готувати	[ɣotuˈwati]

to cost (vt)	коштувати	[ˈkɔʃtuwati]
to count (add up)	лічити	[liˈtʃiti]
to count on …	розраховувати на …	[rozraˈhowuwati na]
to create (vt)	створити	[stwoˈriti]
to cry (weep)	плакати	[ˈplakati]

11. The most important verbs. Part 2

to deceive (vi, vt)	обманювати	[obˈmanywati]
to decorate (tree, street)	прикрашати	[prikraˈʃati]
to defend (a country, etc.)	захищати	[zahiˈɕati]
to demand (request firmly)	вимагати	[wimaˈɣati]

to dig (vt)	рити	[ˈriti]
to discuss (vt)	обговорювати	[obɣoˈworywati]
to do (vt)	робити	[roˈbiti]
to doubt (have doubts)	сумніватися	[sumniˈwatisʲa]
to drop (let fall)	упускати	[upusˈkati]

to exist (vi)	існувати	[isnuˈwati]
to expect (foresee)	передбачити	[pɛrɛdˈbatʃiti]
to explain (vt)	пояснювати	[poˈjasnywati]
to fall (vi)	падати	[ˈpadati]
to find (vt)	знаходити	[znaˈhɔditi]

to finish (vt)	закінчувати	[zɑˈkintʃuwɑtɪ]
to fly (vi)	летіти	[lɛˈtitɪ]
to follow … (come after)	іти слідом	[iˈtɪ ˈslidom]
to forget (vi, vt)	забувати	[zɑbuˈwɑtɪ]
to forgive (vt)	прощати	[proˈɕɑtɪ]

| to give (vt) | давати | [dɑˈwɑtɪ] |
| to give a hint | натякати | [nɑtʲɑˈkɑtɪ] |

to go (on foot)	йти	[jtɪ]
to go for a swim	купатися	[kuˈpɑtɪsʲɑ]
to go out (from …)	виходити	[wɪˈhɔdɪtɪ]
to guess right	відгадати	[widɣɑˈdɑtɪ]

to have (vt)	мати	[ˈmɑtɪ]
to have breakfast	снідати	[ˈsnidɑtɪ]
to have dinner	вечеряти	[wɛˈtʃɛrʲɑtɪ]
to have lunch	обідати	[oˈbidɑtɪ]

to hear (vt)	чути	[ˈtʃutɪ]
to help (vt)	допомагати	[dopomɑˈɣɑtɪ]
to hide (vt)	ховати	[hoˈwɑtɪ]
to hope (vi, vt)	сподіватися	[spodiˈwɑtɪsʲɑ]
to hunt (vi, vt)	полювати	[polyˈwɑtɪ]
to hurry (vi)	поспішати	[pospiˈʃɑtɪ]

12. The most important verbs. Part 3

to inform (vt)	інформувати	[informuˈwɑtɪ]
to insist (vi, vt)	наполягати	[nɑpoʎɑˈɣɑtɪ]
to insult (vt)	ображати	[obrɑˈʒɑtɪ]
to invite (vt)	запрошувати	[zɑpˈroʃuwɑtɪ]
to joke (vi)	жартувати	[ʒɑrtuˈwɑtɪ]

to keep (vt)	зберігати	[zbɛriˈɣɑtɪ]
to keep silent	мовчати	[mowˈtʃɑtɪ]
to kill (vt)	убивати	[ubɪˈwɑtɪ]
to know (sb)	знати	[ˈznɑtɪ]
to know (sth)	знати	[ˈznɑtɪ]

to laugh (vi)	сміятися	[smiˈjɑtɪsʲɑ]
to liberate (city, etc.)	звільняти	[zwiʎˈɲɑtɪ]
to like (I like …)	подобатися	[poˈdɔbɑtɪsʲɑ]
to look for … (search)	шукати	[ʃuˈkɑtɪ]
to love (sb)	кохати	[koˈhɑtɪ]

to make a mistake	помилятися	[pomɪˈʎɑtɪsʲɑ]
to manage, to run	керувати	[kɛruˈwɑtɪ]
to mean (signify)	означати	[oznɑˈtʃɑtɪ]
to mention (talk about)	згадувати	[ˈzɣɑduwɑtɪ]

| to miss (school, etc.) | пропускати | [propus′katı] |
| to notice (see) | помічати | [pomi′ʧatı] |

to object (vi, vt)	заперечувати	[zapɛ′rɛʧuwatı]
to observe (see)	спостерігати	[spostɛri′ɣatı]
to open (vt)	відчинити	[widʧı′nıtı]
to order (meal, etc.)	замовляти	[zamow′ʎatı]
to order (mil.)	наказувати	[na′kazuwatı]
to own (possess)	володіти	[wolo′ditı]

to participate (vi)	брати участь	[′bratı ′uʧastʲ]
to pay (vi, vt)	платити	[pla′tıtı]
to permit (vt)	дозволяти	[dozwo′ʎatı]
to plan (vt)	планувати	[planu′watı]
to play (children)	грати	[′ɣratı]

to pray (vi, vt)	молитися	[mo′lıtısʲa]
to prefer (vt)	воліти	[wo′litı]
to promise (vt)	обіцяти	[obi′ʦʲatı]
to pronounce (vt)	вимовляти	[wımow′ʎatı]
to propose (vt)	пропонувати	[proponu′watı]
to punish (vt)	покарати	[poka′ratı]

to read (vi, vt)	читати	[ʧı′tatı]
to recommend (vt)	рекомендувати	[rɛkomɛndu′watı]
to refuse (vi, vt)	відмовлятися	[widmow′ʎatısʲa]
to regret (be sorry)	жалкувати	[ʒalku′watı]

to rent (sth from sb)	наймати	[naj′matı]
to repeat (say again)	повторювати	[pow′torywatı]
to reserve, to book	резервувати	[rɛzɛrwu′watı]
to run (vi)	бігти	[′biɣtı]

13. The most important verbs. Part 4

to save (rescue)	рятувати	[rʲatu′watı]
to say (~ thank you)	сказати	[ska′zatı]
to scold (vt)	лаяти	[′lajatı]
to see (vt)	бачити	[′baʧıtı]
to sell (vt)	продавати	[proda′watı]
to send (vt)	відправляти	[widpraw′ʎatı]

to shoot (vi)	стріляти	[stri′ʎatı]
to shout (vi)	кричати	[krı′ʧatı]
to show (vt)	показувати	[po′kazuwatı]
to sign (document)	підписувати	[pid′pısuwatı]
to sit down (vi)	сідати	[si′datı]
to smile (vi)	посміхатися	[posmi′hatısʲa]
to speak (vi, vt)	розмовляти	[rozmow′ʎatı]
to steal (money, etc.)	красти	[′krastı]

to stop (please ~ calling me)	припиняти	[prɪpɪ'ɲatɪ]
to stop (for pause, etc.)	зупинятися	[zupɪ'ɲatɪs'a]
to study (vt)	вивчати	[wɪw'tʃatɪ]
to swim (vi)	плавати	['plawatɪ]
to take (vt)	брати	['bratɪ]
to think (vi, vt)	думати	['dumatɪ]
to threaten (vt)	погрожувати	[poɣ'rɔʒuwatɪ]
to touch (with hands)	торкати	[tor'katɪ]
to translate (vt)	перекладати	[pɛrɛkla'datɪ]
to trust (vt)	довіряти	[dowi'r'atɪ]
to try (attempt)	пробувати	['prɔbuwatɪ]
to turn (~ to the left)	повертати	[powɛr'tatɪ]
to underestimate (vt)	недооцінювати	[nɛdoː'tsinywatɪ]
to understand (vt)	розуміти	[rozu'mitɪ]
to unite (vt)	об'єднувати	[obʰ'ɛdnuwatɪ]
to wait (vt)	чекати	[tʃɛ'katɪ]
to want (wish, desire)	хотіти	[ho'titɪ]
to warn (vt)	попереджувати	[popɛ'rɛdʒuwatɪ]
to work (vi)	працювати	[pratsy'watɪ]
to write (vt)	писати	[pɪ'satɪ]
to write down	записувати	[za'pɪsuwatɪ]

14. Colors

color	колір (m)	['kolir]
shade (tint)	відтінок (m)	[wid'tinok]
hue	тон (m)	[ton]
rainbow	веселка (f)	[wɛ'sɛlka]
white (adj)	білий	['bilɪj]
black (adj)	чорний	['tʃɔrnɪj]
gray (adj)	сірий	['sirɪj]
green (adj)	зелений	[zɛ'lɛnɪj]
yellow (adj)	жовтий	['ʒɔwtɪj]
red (adj)	червоний	[tʃɛr'wɔnɪj]
blue (adj)	синій	['sɪnij]
light blue (adj)	блакитний	[bla'kɪtnɪj]
pink (adj)	рожевий	[ro'ʒɛwɪj]
orange (adj)	помаранчевий	[poma'rantʃɛwɪj]
violet (adj)	фіолетовий	[fio'lɛtowɪj]
brown (adj)	коричневий	[ko'rɪtʃnɛwɪj]
golden (adj)	золотий	[zolo'tɪj]
silvery (adj)	сріблястий	[srib'ʎastɪj]

beige (adj)	бежевий	[ˈbɛʒɛwɪj]
cream (adj)	кремовий	[ˈkrɛmowɪj]
turquoise (adj)	бірюзовий	[biryˈzɔwɪj]
cherry red (adj)	вишневий	[wɪʃˈnɛwɪj]
lilac (adj)	бузковий	[buzˈkɔwɪj]
crimson (adj)	малиновий	[maˈlɪnowɪj]

light (adj)	світлий	[ˈswitlɪj]
dark (adj)	темний	[ˈtɛmnɪj]
bright, vivid (adj)	яскравий	[jɑskˈrɑwɪj]

colored (pencils)	кольоровий	[kolɜˈrɔwɪj]
color (e.g., ~ film)	кольоровий	[kolɜˈrɔwɪj]
black-and-white (adj)	чорно-білий	[ˈtʃɔrno ˈbilɪj]
plain (one-colored)	однобарвний	[odnoˈbarwnɪj]
multicolored (adj)	різнобарвний	[riznoˈbarwnɪj]

15. Questions

Who?	Хто?	[hto]
What?	Що?	[ɕo]
Where? (at, in)	Де?	[dɛ]
Where? (to)?	Куди?	[kuˈdɪ]
From where?	Звідки?	[ˈzwidkɪ]
When?	Коли?	[koˈlɪ]
Why? (What for?)	Навіщо?	[naˈwiɕo]
Why? (reason)	Чому?	[tʃoˈmu]

What for?	Для чого?	[dʎɑ ˈtʃoɣo]
How? (in what way)	Як?	[jɑk]
What? (What kind of ...?)	Який?	[jaˈkɪj]
Which?	Котрий?	[kotˈrɪj]

To whom?	Кому?	[koˈmu]
About whom?	Про кого?	[pro ˈkɔɣo]
About what?	Про що?	[pro ɕo]
With whom?	З ким?	[z kɪm]

| How many? How much? | Скільки? | [ˈskiʎkɪ] |
| Whose? | Чий? | [tʃij] |

16. Prepositions

with (accompanied by)	з	[z]
without	без	[bɛz]
to (indicating direction)	в	[w]
about (talking ~ ...)	про	[pro]
before (in time)	перед	[ˈpɛrɛd]

in front of …	перед	['pɛrɛd]
under (beneath, below)	під	[pid]
above (over)	над	[nɑd]
on (atop)	над	[nɑd]
from (off, out of)	з	[z]
of (made from)	з	[z]
in (e.g., ~ ten minutes)	за	[zɑ]
over (across the top of)	через	['ʧɛrɛz]

17. Function words. Adverbs. Part 1

Where? (at, in)	Де?	[dɛ]
here (adv)	тут	[tut]
there (adv)	там	[tɑm]
somewhere (to be)	десь	[dɛsʲ]
nowhere (not anywhere)	ніде	[niˈdɛ]
by (near, beside)	біля	['biʎɑ]
by the window	біля вікна	['biʎɑ wikˈnɑ]
Where (to)?	Куди?	[kuˈdɪ]
here (e.g., come ~!)	сюди	[syˈdɪ]
there (e.g., to go ~)	туди	[tuˈdɪ]
from here (adv)	звідси	['zwidsɪ]
from there (adv)	звідти	['zwidtɪ]
close (adv)	близько	['blɪzʲko]
far (adv)	далеко	[dɑˈlɛko]
near (e.g., ~ Paris)	біля	['biʎɑ]
nearby (adv)	поряд	['porʲɑd]
not far (adv)	недалеко	[nɛdɑˈlɛko]
left (adj)	лівий	['liwɪj]
on the left	зліва	['zliwɑ]
to the left	ліворуч	[liˈworuʧ]
right (adj)	правий	['prɑwɪj]
on the right	справа	['sprɑwɑ]
to the right	праворуч	[prɑˈworuʧ]
in front (adv)	спереду	['spɛrɛdu]
front (as adj)	передній	[pɛˈrɛdnij]
ahead (look ~)	уперед	[upɛˈrɛd]
behind (adv)	позаду	[poˈzɑdu]
from behind	ззаду	['zzɑdu]
back (towards the rear)	назад	[nɑˈzɑd]

middle	**середина** (f)	[sɛˈrɛdɪna]
in the middle	**посередині**	[posɛˈrɛdɪni]
at the side	**збоку**	[ˈzbɔku]
everywhere (adv)	**скрізь**	[skrizʲ]
around (in all directions)	**навколо**	[nawˈkɔlo]
from inside	**зсередини**	[zsɛˈrɛdɪnɪ]
somewhere (to go)	**кудись**	[kuˈdɪsʲ]
straight (directly)	**напрямки**	[naprʲamˈkɪ]
back (e.g., come ~)	**назад**	[naˈzad]
from anywhere	**звідки-небудь**	[ˈzwidkɪ ˈnɛbudʲ]
from somewhere	**звідкись**	[ˈzwidkɪsʲ]
firstly (adv)	**по-перше**	[po ˈpɛrʃɛ]
secondly (adv)	**по-друге**	[po ˈdruɣɛ]
thirdly (adv)	**по-третє**	[po ˈtrɛtɛ]
suddenly (adv)	**раптом**	[ˈraptom]
at first (adv)	**спочатку**	[spoˈʧatku]
for the first time	**уперше**	[uˈpɛrʃɛ]
long before …	**задовго до …**	[zaˈdɔwɣo do]
anew (over again)	**заново**	[ˈzanowo]
for good (adv)	**назовсім**	[naˈzowsim]
never (adv)	**ніколи**	[niˈkɔlɪ]
again (adv)	**знову**	[ˈznɔwu]
now (adv)	**тепер**	[tɛˈpɛr]
often (adv)	**часто**	[ˈʧasto]
then (adv)	**тоді**	[toˈdi]
urgently (quickly)	**терміново**	[tɛrmiˈnɔwo]
usually (adv)	**звичайно**	[zwɪˈʧajno]
by the way, …	**до речі**	[do ˈrɛʧi]
possible (that is ~)	**можливо**	[moʒˈlɪwo]
probably (adv)	**мабуть**	[maˈbutʲ]
maybe (adv)	**може бути**	[ˈmɔʒɛ ˈbutɪ]
besides …	**крім того, …**	[krim ˈtoɣo]
that's why …	**тому**	[toˈmu]
in spite of …	**незважаючи на …**	[nɛzwaˈʒajuʧɪ na]
thanks to …	**завдяки …**	[zawdʲaˈkɪ]
what (pron.)	**що**	[ɕo]
that (conj.)	**що**	[ɕo]
something	**щось**	[ɕosʲ]
anything (something)	**що-небудь**	[ɕo ˈnɛbudʲ]
nothing	**нічого**	[niˈʧoɣo]
who (pron.)	**хто**	[hto]
someone	**хтось**	[htosʲ]
somebody	**хто-небудь**	[hto ˈnɛbudʲ]

nobody	ніхто	[nih'tɔ]
nowhere (a voyage to ~)	нікуди	['nikudɪ]
nobody's	нічий	[ni'ʧɪj]
somebody's	чий-небудь	[ʧɪj 'nɛbudʲ]

so (I'm ~ glad)	так	[tak]
also (as well)	також	[ta'kɔʒ]
too (as well)	також	[ta'kɔʒ]

18. Function words. Adverbs. Part 2

Why?	Чому?	[ʧo'mu]
for some reason	чомусь	[ʧo'musʲ]
because …	тому, що …	[to'mu ɕo]
for some purpose	навіщось	[na'wiɕosʲ]

and	і	[i]
or	або	[a'bɔ]
but	але	[a'lɛ]
for (e.g., ~ me)	для	[dʎa]

too (~ many people)	занадто	[za'nadto]
only (exclusively)	тільки	['tiʎkɪ]
exactly (adv)	точно	['tɔʧno]
about (more or less)	приблизно	[prɪb'lɪzno]

approximately (adv)	приблизно	[prɪb'lɪzno]
approximate (adj)	приблизний	[prɪb'lɪznɪj]
almost (adv)	майже	['majʒɛ]
the rest	решта (f)	['rɛʃta]

each (adj)	кожен	['kɔʒɛn]
any (no matter which)	будь-який	[budʲ ja'kɪj]
many, much (a lot of)	багато	[ba'ɣato]
many people	багато хто	[ba'ɣato hto]
all (everyone)	всі	[wsi]

in return for …	в обмін на …	[w 'ɔbmin na]
in exchange (adv)	натомість	[na'tɔmistʲ]
by hand (made)	вручну	[wruʧ'nu]
hardly (negative opinion)	навряд чи	[naw'rʲad ʧɪ]

probably (adv)	мабуть	[ma'butʲ]
on purpose (adv)	навмисно	[naw'mɪsno]
by accident (adv)	випадково	[wɪpad'kɔwo]

very (adv)	дуже	['duʒɛ]
for example (adv)	наприклад	[nap'rɪklad]
between	між	[miʒ]
among	серед	['sɛrɛd]

| so much (such a lot) | стільки | ['stiʎkɪ] |
| especially (adv) | особливо | [osob'lɪwo] |

Basic concepts. Part 2

19. Weekdays

Monday	понеділок (m)	[ponɛ'dilok]
Tuesday	вівторок (m)	[wiw'tɔrok]
Wednesday	середа (f)	[sɛrɛ'da]
Thursday	четвер (m)	[tʃɛt'wɛr]
Friday	п'ятниця (f)	['pʰjatnɪts⁽ʲ⁾a]
Saturday	субота (f)	[su'bota]
Sunday	неділя (f)	[nɛ'diʎa]

today (adv)	сьогодні	[sɜ'ɣɔdni]
tomorrow (adv)	завтра	['zawtra]
the day after tomorrow	післязавтра	[pisʎa'zawtra]
yesterday (adv)	вчора	['wtʃora]
the day before yesterday	позавчора	[pozaw'tʃora]

day	день (m)	[dɛɲ]
working day	робочий день (m)	[ro'botʃij dɛɲ]
public holiday	святковий день (m)	[swʲat'kɔwɪj dɛɲ]
day off	вихідний день (m)	[wɪhid'nɪj dɛɲ]
weekend	вихідні (pl)	[wɪhid'ni]

all day long	весь день	[wɛsʲ dɛɲ]
next day (adv)	на наступний день	[na nas'tupnɪj dɛɲ]
two days ago	2 дні тому	[dwa dni 'tomu]
the day before	напередодні	[napɛrɛ'dɔdni]
daily (adj)	щоденний	[ɕo'dɛnɪj]
every day (adv)	щодня	[ɕod'na]

week	тиждень (m)	['tɪʒdɛɲ]
last week (adv)	на минулому тижні	[na mɪ'nulomu 'tɪʒni]
next week (adv)	на наступному тижні	[na nas'tupnomu 'tɪʒni]
weekly (adj)	щотижневий	[ɕotɪʒ'nɛwɪj]
every week (adv)	щотижня	[ɕo'tɪʒna]
twice a week	два рази на тиждень	[dwa 'razɪ na 'tɪʒdɛɲ]
every Tuesday	кожен вівторок	['kɔʒɛn wiw'tɔrok]

20. Hours. Day and night

morning	ранок (m)	['ranok]
in the morning	вранці	['wrantsi]
noon, midday	полудень (m)	['poludɛɲ]

in the afternoon	після обіду	[ˈpisʎa oˈbidu]
evening	вечір (m)	[ˈwɛtʃir]
in the evening	увечері	[uˈwɛtʃɛri]
night	ніч (f)	[nitʃ]
at night	уночі	[unoˈtʃi]
midnight	північ (f)	[ˈpiwnitʃ]

second	секунда (f)	[sɛˈkunda]
minute	хвилина (f)	[hwɪˈlɪna]
hour	година (f)	[ɣoˈdɪna]
half an hour	півгодини (pl)	[piwɣoˈdɪnɪ]
quarter of an hour	чверть (f) години	[tʃwɛrtʲ ɣoˈdɪnɪ]
fifteen minutes	15 хвилин	[pʲjatˈnadtsʲatʲ hwɪˈlɪn]
24 hours	доба (f)	[doˈba]

sunrise	схід (m) сонця	[shid ˈsɔntsʲa]
dawn	світанок (m)	[swiˈtanok]
early morning	ранній ранок (m)	[ˈranij ˈranok]
sunset	захід (m)	[ˈzahid]

early in the morning	рано вранці	[ˈrano ˈwrantsi]
this morning	сьогодні вранці	[sɜˈɣodni ˈwrantsi]
tomorrow morning	завтра вранці	[ˈzawtra ˈwrantsi]

this afternoon	сьогодні вдень	[sɜˈɣodni wdɛɲ]
in the afternoon	після обіду	[ˈpisʎa oˈbidu]
tomorrow afternoon	завтра після обіду (m)	[ˈzawtra ˈpisʎa oˈbidu]

tonight (this evening)	сьогодні увечері	[sɜˈɣodni uˈwɛtʃɛri]
tomorrow night	завтра увечері	[ˈzawtra uˈwɛtʃɛri]

at 3 o'clock sharp	рівно о третій годині	[ˈriwno o ˈtrɛtij ɣoˈdɪnɪ]
about 4 o'clock	біля четвертої години	[ˈbiʎa tʃɛtˈwɛrtojɪ ɣoˈdɪnɪ]
by 12 o'clock	до дванадцятої години	[do dwaˈnadtsʲatojɪ ɣoˈdɪnɪ]

in 20 minutes	за двадцять хвилин	[za ˈdwadtsʲatʲ hwɪˈlɪn]
in an hour	за годину	[za ɣoˈdɪnu]
on time (adv)	вчасно	[ˈwtʃasno]

a quarter of ...	без чверті	[bɛz ˈtʃwɛrti]
within an hour	на протязі години	[na ˈprotʲazi ɣoˈdɪnɪ]
every 15 minutes	що п'ятнадцять хвилин	[ɕo pʲjatˈnadtsʲatʲ hwɪˈlɪn]
round the clock	цілодобово	[tsilodoˈbowo]

21. Months. Seasons

January	січень (m)	[ˈsitʃɛɲ]
February	лютий (m)	[ˈlytɪj]
March	березень (m)	[ˈbɛrɛzɛɲ]
April	квітень (m)	[ˈkwitɛɲ]

| May | травень (m) | ['trawɛɲ] |
| June | червень (m) | ['ʧɛrwɛɲ] |

July	липень (m)	['lɪpɛɲ]
August	серпень (m)	['sɛrpɛɲ]
September	вересень (m)	['wɛrɛsɛɲ]
October	жовтень (m)	['ʒɔwtɛɲ]
November	листопад (m)	[lɪsto'pad]
December	грудень (m)	['ɣrudɛɲ]

spring	весна (f)	[wɛs'na]
in spring	навесні	[nɑwɛs'ni]
spring (as adj)	весняний	[wɛs'nɑnɪj]

summer	літо (n)	['lito]
in summer	влітку	['wlitku]
summer (as adj)	літній	['litnij]

fall	осінь (f)	['ɔsiɲ]
in fall	восени	[wosɛ'nɪ]
fall (as adj)	осінній	[o'siɲij]

winter	зима (f)	[zɪ'ma]
in winter	взимку	['wzɪmku]
winter (as adj)	зимовий	[zɪ'mɔwɪj]

month	місяць (m)	['misʲats]
this month	в цьому місяці (m)	[w 'tsʒmu 'misʲatsi]
next month	в наступному місяці (m)	[w nas'tupnomu 'misʲatsi]
last month	в минулому місяці (m)	[w mɪ'nulomu 'misʲatsi]

a month ago	місяць (m) тому	['misʲats to'mu]
in a month	через місяць	['ʧɛrɛz 'misʲats]
in two months	через 2 місяці	['ʧɛrɛz dwa 'misʲatsi]
the whole month	весь місяць (m)	[wɛsʲ 'misʲats]
all month long	цілий місяць	['tsilɪj 'misʲats]

monthly (~ magazine)	щомісячний	[ɕo'misʲatʃnɪj]
monthly (adv)	щомісяця	[ɕo'misʲatsʲa]
every month	кожний місяць (m)	['kɔʒnɪj 'misʲats]
twice a month	два рази на місяць	[dwa 'razɪ na 'misʲats]

year	рік (m)	[rik]
this year	в цьому році	[w 'tsʒmu 'rɔtsi]
next year	в наступному році	[w nas'tupnomu 'rɔtsi]
last year	в минулому році	[w mɪ'nulomu 'rɔtsi]

a year ago	рік тому	[rik 'tomu]
in a year	через рік	['ʧɛrɛz rik]
in two years	через два роки	['ʧɛrɛz dwa 'rɔkɪ]
the whole year	увесь рік	[u'wɛsʲ ɾik]
all year long	цілий рік	['tsilɪj rik]

every year	кожен рік	['kɔʒɛn 'rik]
annual (adj)	щорічний	[ɕo'ritʃnɪj]
annually (adv)	щороку	[ɕo'rɔku]
4 times a year	чотири рази на рік	[tʃo'tɪrɪ 'razɪ na rik]

date (e.g., today's ~)	число (n)	[tʃɪs'lɔ]
date (e.g., ~ of birth)	дата (f)	['data]
calendar	календар (m)	[kalɛn'dar]

half a year	півроку	[piw'rɔku]
six months	піврічча (n)	[piw'ritʃa]
season (summer, etc.)	сезон (m)	[sɛ'zɔn]
century	вік (m)	[wik]

22. Time. Miscellaneous

time	час (n)	[tʃas]
instant (n)	мить (f)	[mɪtʲ]
moment	момент (m)	[mo'mɛnt]
instant (adj)	миттєвий	[mɪt'tɛwɪj]
lapse (of time)	відрізок (m)	[wid'rizok]
life	життя (n)	[ʒɪt'tʲa]
eternity	вічність (f)	['witʃnistʲ]

epoch	епоха (f)	[ɛ'pɔha]
era	ера (f)	['ɛra]
cycle	цикл (m)	[tsɪkl]
period	період (m)	[pɛ'riod]
term (short-~)	термін (m)	['tɛrmin]

the future	майбутнє (n)	[maj'butnɛ]
future (as adj)	майбутній	[maj'butnij]
next time	наступного разу (m)	[nas'tupnoɣo 'razu]
the past	минуле (n)	[mɪ'nulɛ]
past (recent)	минулий	[mɪ'nulɪj]
last time	минулого разу	[mɪ'nuloɣo 'razu]

later (adv)	пізніше	[piz'niʃɛ]
after (prep.)	після	['pisʎa]
nowadays (adv)	сьогодення	[sɔɣo'dɛnja]
now (adv)	зараз	['zaraz]
immediately (adv)	негайно	[nɛ'ɣajno]
soon (adv)	незабаром	[nɛza'barom]
in advance (beforehand)	завчасно	[zaw'tʃasno]

a long time ago	давно	[daw'nɔ]
recently (adv)	нещодавно	[nɛɕo'dawno]
destiny	доля (f)	['dɔʎa]
memories (childhood ~)	пам'ять (f)	['pamʲjatʲ]
archives	архів (m)	[ar'hiw]

during ...	під час	[pid 'ʧas]
long, a long time (adv)	довго	['dɔwɣo]
not long (adv)	недовго	[nɛ'dɔwɣo]
early (in the morning)	рано	['rano]
late (not early)	пізно	['pizno]

forever (for good)	назавжди	[na'zawʒdɪ]
to start (begin)	починати	[poʧɪ'natɪ]
to postpone (vt)	перенести	[pɛrɛ'nɛstɪ]

at the same time	одночасно	[odno'ʧasno]
permanently (adv)	постійно	[pos'tijno]
constant (noise, pain)	постійний	[pos'tijnɪj]
temporary (adj)	тимчасовий	[tɪmʧa'sɔwɪj]

sometimes (adv)	інколи	['iŋkolɪ]
rarely (adv)	рідко	['ridko]
often (adv)	часто	['ʧasto]

23. Opposites

| rich (adj) | багатий | [ba'ɣatɪj] |
| poor (adj) | бідний | ['bidnɪj] |

| ill, sick (adj) | хворий | ['hwɔrɪj] |
| healthy (adj) | здоровий | [zdo'rɔwɪj] |

| big (adj) | великий | [wɛ'lɪkɪj] |
| small (adj) | маленький | [ma'lɛɲkɪj] |

| quickly (adv) | швидко | ['ʃwɪdko] |
| slowly (adv) | повільно | [po'wiʎno] |

| fast (adj) | швидкий | [ʃwɪd'kɪj] |
| slow (adj) | повільний | [po'wiʎnɪj] |

| cheerful (adj) | веселий | [wɛ'sɛlɪj] |
| sad (adj) | сумний | [sum'nɪj] |

| together (adv) | разом | ['razom] |
| separately (adv) | окремо | [ok'rɛmo] |

| aloud (to read) | вголос | ['wɣɔlos] |
| silently (to oneself) | про себе | [pro 'sɛbɛ] |

| tall (adj) | високий | [wɪ'sɔkɪj] |
| low (adj) | низький | [nɪzɪ'kɪj] |

| deep (adj) | глибокий | [ɣlɪ'bɔkɪj] |
| shallow (adj) | мілкий | [mil'kɪj] |

| yes | так | [tɑk] |
| no | ні | [ni] |

| distant (in space) | далекий | [dɑˈlɛkɪj] |
| nearby (adj) | близький | [blɪziˈkɪj] |

| far (adv) | далеко | [dɑˈlɛko] |
| nearby (adv) | поруч | [ˈpɔrutʃ] |

| long (adj) | довгий | [ˈdɔwɣɪj] |
| short (adj) | короткий | [koˈrɔtkɪj] |

| good (kindhearted) | добрий | [ˈdɔbrɪj] |
| evil (adj) | злий | [ˈzlɪj] |

| married (adj) | одружений | [odˈruʒɛnɪj] |
| single (adj) | холостий | [holosˈtɪj] |

| to forbid (vt) | заборонити | [zaboroˈnɪtɪ] |
| to permit (vt) | дозволити | [dozˈwolɪtɪ] |

| end | кінець (m) | [kiˈnɛts] |
| beginning | початок (m) | [poˈtʃatok] |

| left (adj) | лівий | [ˈliwɪj] |
| right (adj) | правий | [ˈprawɪj] |

| first (adj) | перший | [ˈpɛrʃɪj] |
| last (adj) | останній | [osˈtɑɲɪj] |

| crime | злочин (m) | [ˈzlɔtʃɪn] |
| punishment | кара (f) | [ˈkɑrɑ] |

| to order (vt) | наказати | [nakaˈzɑtɪ] |
| to obey (vi, vt) | підкоритися | [pidkoˈrɪtɪsia] |

| straight (adj) | прямий | [priaˈmɪj] |
| curved (adj) | кривий | [krɪˈwɪj] |

| paradise | рай (m) | [rɑj] |
| hell | пекло (n) | [ˈpɛklo] |

| to be born | народитися | [nɑroˈdɪtɪsia] |
| to die (vi) | померти | [poˈmɛrtɪ] |

| strong (adj) | сильний | [ˈsɪʎnɪj] |
| weak (adj) | слабкий | [slɑbˈkɪj] |

old (adj)	старий	[stɑˈrɪj]
young (adj)	молодий	[moloˈdɪj]
old (adj)	старий	[stɑˈrɪj]
new (adj)	новий	[noˈwɪj]

| hard (adj) | твердий | [twɛr'dɪj] |
| soft (adj) | м'який | [mʰja'kɪj] |

| warm (adj) | теплий | ['tɛplɪj] |
| cold (adj) | холодний | [ho'lɔdnɪj] |

| fat (adj) | товстий | [tows'tɪj] |
| thin (adj) | худий | [hu'dɪj] |

| narrow (adj) | вузький | [wuzʲ'kɪj] |
| wide (adj) | широкий | [ʃɪ'rɔkɪj] |

| good (adj) | добрий | ['dɔbrɪj] |
| bad (adj) | поганий | [po'ɣanɪj] |

| brave (adj) | хоробрий | [ho'rɔbrɪj] |
| cowardly (adj) | боягузливий | [boja'ɣuzlɪwɪj] |

24. Lines and shapes

square	квадрат (m)	[kwad'rat]
square (as adj)	квадратний	[kwad'ratnɪj]
circle	коло (n)	['kɔlo]
round (adj)	круглий	['kruɣlɪj]
triangle	трикутник (m)	[trɪ'kutnɪk]
triangular (adj)	трикутний	[trɪ'kutnɪj]

oval	овал (m)	[o'wal]
oval (as adj)	овальний	[o'waʎnɪj]
rectangle	прямокутник (m)	[prʲamo'kutnɪk]
rectangular (adj)	прямокутний	[prʲamo'kutnɪj]

pyramid	піраміда (f)	[pira'mida]
rhombus	ромб (m)	[romb]
trapezoid	трапеція (f)	[tra'pɛtsija]
cube	куб (m)	[kub]
prism	призма (f)	['prɪzma]

circumference	коло (n)	['kɔlo]
sphere	сфера (f)	['sfɛra]
ball (solid sphere)	куля (f)	['kuʎa]
diameter	діаметр (m)	[di'amɛtr]
radius	радіус (m)	['radius]
perimeter (circle's ~)	периметр (m)	[pɛ'rɪmɛtr]
center	центр (m)	[tsɛntr]

horizontal (adj)	горизонтальний	[ɣorɪzon'taʎnɪj]
vertical (adj)	вертикальний	[wɛrtɪ'kaʎnɪj]
parallel (n)	паралель (f)	[para'lɛʎ]
parallel (as adj)	паралельний	[para'lɛʎnɪj]

line	лінія (f)	['linija]
stroke	риса (f)	['rɪsɑ]
straight line	пряма (f)	[prɑ'mɑ]
curve (curved line)	крива (f)	[krɪ'wɑ]
thin (line, etc.)	тонкий	[to'ŋkɪj]
contour (outline)	контур (m)	['kɔntur]
intersection	перетин (m)	[pɛ'rɛtɪn]
right angle	прямий кут (m)	[prɑ'mɪj kut]
segment	сегмент (m)	[sɛɣ'mɛnt]
sector	сектор (m)	['sɛktor]
side (of triangle)	бік (m)	[bik]
angle	кут (m)	[kut]

25. Units of measurement

weight	вага (f)	[wɑ'ɣɑ]
length	довжина (f)	[dowʒɪ'nɑ]
width	ширина (f)	[ʃɪrɪ'nɑ]
height	висота (f)	[wɪso'tɑ]
depth	глибина (f)	[ɣlɪbɪ'nɑ]
volume	об'єм (m)	[obʰ'ɛm]
area	площа (f)	['plɔɕɑ]
gram	грам (m)	[ɣrɑm]
milligram	міліграм (m)	[miliɣ'rɑm]
kilogram	кілограм (m)	[kiloɣ'rɑm]
ton	тонна (f)	['tɔŋɑ]
pound	фунт (m)	['funt]
ounce	унція (f)	['untsija]
meter	метр (m)	[mɛtr]
millimeter	міліметр (m)	[mili'mɛtr]
centimeter	сантиметр (m)	[sɑnti'mɛtr]
kilometer	кілометр (m)	[kilo'mɛtr]
mile	миля (f)	['mɪʎɑ]
inch	дюйм (m)	[dyjm]
foot	фут (m)	[fut]
yard	ярд (m)	[jɑrd]
square meter	квадратний метр (m)	[kwad'ratnɪj mɛtr]
hectare	гектар (m)	[ɣɛk'tar]
liter	літр (m)	[litr]
degree	градус (m)	['ɣradus]
volt	вольт (m)	[woʎt]
ampere	ампер (m)	[am'pɛr]
horsepower	кінська сила (f)	['kins'kɑ 'sɪlɑ]
quantity	кількість (f)	['kiʎkistʲ]

a little bit of …	небагато … (f)	[nɛbaˈɣato]
half	половина (f)	[poloˈwɪna]
dozen	дюжина (f)	[ˈdyʒɪna]
piece (item)	штука (f)	[ˈʃtuka]

| size | розмір (m) | [ˈrozmir] |
| scale (map ~) | масштаб (m) | [masʃˈtab] |

minimal (adj)	мінімальний	[miniˈmaʎnɪj]
the smallest (adj)	найменший	[najˈmɛnʃɪj]
medium (adj)	середній	[sɛˈrɛdnij]
maximal (adj)	максимальний	[maksɪˈmaʎnɪj]
the largest (adj)	найбільший	[najˈbiʎʃɪj]

26. Containers

jar (glass)	банка (f)	[ˈbaŋka]
can	банка (f)	[ˈbaŋka]
bucket	відро (n)	[widˈrɔ]
barrel	бочка (f)	[ˈbɔtʃka]

basin (for washing)	таз (m)	[taz]
tank (for liquid, gas)	бак (m)	[bak]
hip flask	фляжка (f)	[ˈfʎaʒka]
jerrycan	каністра (f)	[kaˈnistra]
cistern (tank)	цистерна (f)	[tsɪsˈtɛrna]

mug	кухоль (m)	[ˈkuhoʎ]
cup (of coffee, etc.)	чашка (f)	[ˈtʃaʃka]
saucer	блюдце (n)	[ˈblydtsɛ]
glass (tumbler)	склянка (f)	[ˈskʎaŋka]
wineglass	келих (m)	[ˈkɛlɪh]
saucepan	каструля (f)	[kastˈruʎa]

| bottle (~ of wine) | пляшка (f) | [ˈpʎaʃka] |
| neck (of the bottle) | шийка (f) | [ˈʃijka] |

carafe	карафа (f)	[kaˈrafa]
pitcher (earthenware)	глечик (m)	[ˈɣlɛtʃɪk]
vessel (container)	посудина (f)	[poˈsudɪna]
pot (crock)	горщик (m)	[ˈɣɔrɕɪk]
vase	ваза (f)	[ˈwaza]

bottle (~ of perfume)	флакон (m)	[flaˈkɔn]
vial, small bottle	пляшечка (f)	[ˈpʎaʃɛtʃka]
tube (of toothpaste)	тюбик (m)	[ˈtybɪk]

sack (bag)	мішок (m)	[miˈʃɔk]
bag (paper ~, plastic ~)	пакет (m)	[paˈkɛt]
pack (of cigarettes, etc.)	пачка (f)	[ˈpatʃka]

box (e.g., shoebox)	коробка (f)	[koʹrɔbka]
crate	ящик (m)	[ʹjaçɪk]
basket	кошик (m)	[ʹkɔʃɪk]

27. Materials

material	матеріал (m)	[matɛriʹal]
wood	дерево (n)	[ʹdɛrɛwo]
wooden (adj)	дерев'яний	[dɛrɛwʰʹjanɪj]

| glass (n) | скло (n) | [sklo] |
| glass (as adj) | скляний | [skʎaʹnɪj] |

| stone (n) | камінь (m) | [ʹkamiɲ] |
| stone (as adj) | кам'яний | [kamʰjaʹnɪj] |

| plastic (n) | пластмаса (f) | [plastʹmasa] |
| plastic (as adj) | пластмасовий | [plastʹmasowɪj] |

| rubber (n) | гума (f) | [ʹɣuma] |
| rubber (as adj) | гумовий | [ʹɣumowɪj] |

| cloth, fabric (n) | тканина (f) | [tkaʹnɪna] |
| fabric (as adj) | з тканини | [z tkaʹnɪnɪ] |

| paper (n) | папір (m) | [paʹpir] |
| paper (as adj) | паперовий | [papɛʹrɔwɪj] |

| cardboard (n) | картон (m) | [karʹtɔn] |
| cardboard (as adj) | картоновий | [karʹtɔnowɪj] |

polyethylene	поліетилен (m)	[poliɛtɪʹlɛn]
cellophane	целофан (m)	[ʦɛloʹfan]
plywood	фанера (f)	[faʹnɛra]

porcelain (n)	фарфор (m)	[ʹfarfor]
porcelain (as adj)	порцеляновий	[porʦɛʹʎanowɪj]
clay (n)	глина (f)	[ʹɣlɪna]
clay (as adj)	глиняний	[ʹɣlɪɲanɪj]
ceramics (n)	кераміка (f)	[kɛʹramika]
ceramic (as adj)	керамічний	[kɛraʹmiʧnɪj]

28. Metals

metal (n)	метал (m)	[mɛʹtal]
metal (as adj)	металевий	[mɛtaʹlɛwɪj]
alloy (n)	сплав (m)	[splaw]
gold (n)	золото (n)	[ʹzɔloto]

gold, golden (adj)	**золотий**	[zolo'tɪj]
silver (n)	**срібло** (n)	['sriblo]
silver (as adj)	**срібний**	['sribnɪj]
iron (n)	**залізо** (n)	[za'lizo]
iron (adj), made of iron	**залізний**	[za'liznɪj]
steel (n)	**сталь** (f)	[staʎ]
steel (as adj)	**сталевий**	[sta'lɛwɪj]
copper (n)	**мідь** (f)	[midʲ]
copper (as adj)	**мідний**	['midnɪj]
aluminum (n)	**алюміній** (m)	[aly'minij]
aluminum (as adj)	**алюмінієвий**	[aly'miniɛwɪj]
bronze (n)	**бронза** (f)	['brɔnza]
bronze (as adj)	**бронзовий**	['brɔnzowɪj]
brass	**латунь** (f)	[la'tuɲ]
nickel	**нікель** (m)	['nikɛʎ]
platinum	**платина** (f)	['platɪna]
mercury	**ртуть** (f)	[rtutʲ]
tin	**олово** (n)	['ɔlowo]
lead	**свинець** (m)	[swɪ'nɛts]
zinc	**цинк** (m)	[tsɪŋk]

HUMAN BEING

Human being. The body

29. Humans. Basic concepts

human being	людина (f)	[lyˈdɪnɑ]
man (adult male)	чоловік (m)	[tʃoloˈwik]
woman	жінка (f)	[ˈʒiŋkɑ]
child	дитина (f)	[dɪˈtɪnɑ]
girl	дівчинка (f)	[ˈdiwtʃɪŋkɑ]
boy	хлопчик (m)	[ˈhlɔptʃɪk]
teenager	підліток (m)	[ˈpidlitok]
old man	старий (m)	[stɑˈrɪj]
old woman	стара (f)	[stɑˈrɑ]

30. Human anatomy

organism	організм (m)	[orɣɑˈnizm]
heart	серце (n)	[ˈsɛrtsɛ]
blood	кров (f)	[krow]
artery	артерія (f)	[ɑrˈtɛrijɑ]
vein	вена (f)	[ˈwɛnɑ]
brain	мозок (m)	[ˈmɔzok]
nerve	нерв (m)	[nɛrw]
nerves	нерви (pl)	[ˈnɛrwɪ]
vertebra	хребець (m)	[hrɛˈbɛts]
spine	хребет (m)	[hrɛˈbɛt]
stomach (organ)	шлунок (m)	[ˈʃlunok]
intestines, bowel	кишечник (m)	[kɪˈʃɛtʃnɪk]
intestine (e.g., large ~)	кишка (f)	[ˈkɪʃkɑ]
liver	печінка (f)	[pɛˈtʃiŋkɑ]
kidney	нирка (f)	[ˈnɪrkɑ]
bone	кістка (f)	[ˈkistkɑ]
skeleton	скелет (m)	[skɛˈlɛt]
rib	ребро (n)	[rɛbˈrɔ]
skull	череп (m)	[ˈtʃɛrɛp]
muscle	м'яз (m)	[mʰjɑz]
biceps	біцепс (m)	[ˈbitsɛps]

triceps	трицепс (m)	['trɪʦɛps]
tendon	сухожилля (n)	[suho'ʒɪʎɑ]
joint	суглоб (m)	[suɣ'lɔb]
lungs	легені (pl)	[lɛ'ɣɛni]
genitals	статеві органи (pl)	[stɑ'tɛwi 'ɔrɣɑnɪ]
skin	шкіра (f)	['ʃkirɑ]

31. Head

head	голова (f)	[ɣolo'wɑ]
face	обличчя (n)	[ob'lɪʧɑ]
nose	ніс (m)	[nis]
mouth	рот (m)	[rot]

eye	око (n)	['ɔko]
eyes	очі (pl)	['ɔʧi]
pupil	зіниця (m)	[zi'nɪʦʲɑ]
eyebrow	брова (f)	[bro'wɑ]
eyelash	вія (f)	['wijɑ]
eyelid	повіка (f)	[po'wikɑ]

tongue	язик (m)	[jɑ'zɪk]
tooth	зуб (m)	[zub]
lips	губи (pl)	['ɣubɪ]
cheekbones	вилиці (pl)	['wɪlɪʦi]
gum	ясна (pl)	['jɑsnɑ]
palate	піднебіння (n)	[pidnɛ'binjɑ]

nostrils	ніздрі (pl)	['nizdri]
chin	підборіддя (n)	[pidbo'riddʲɑ]
jaw	щелепа (f)	[ɕɛ'lɛpɑ]
cheek	щока (f)	[ɕo'kɑ]

forehead	чоло (n)	[ʧo'lɔ]
temple	скроня (f)	['skrɔnɑ]
ear	вухо (n)	['wuho]
back of the head	потилиця (f)	[po'tɪlɪʦʲɑ]
neck	шия (f)	['ʃɪjɑ]
throat	горло (n)	['ɣɔrlo]

hair	волосся (n)	[wo'lɔssʲɑ]
hairstyle	зачіска (f)	['zɑʧiskɑ]
haircut	стрижка (f)	['strɪʒkɑ]
wig	парик (m)	[pɑ'rɪk]

mustache	вуса (pl)	['wusɑ]
beard	борода (f)	[boro'dɑ]
to have (a beard, etc.)	носити	[no'sɪtɪ]
braid	коса (f)	[ko'sɑ]
sideburns	бакенбарди (pl)	[bɑkɛn'bɑrdɪ]

red-haired (adj)	рудий	[ru'dıj]
gray (hair)	сивий	['sıwıj]
bald (adj)	лисий	['lısıj]
bald patch	лисина (f)	['lısına]

| ponytail | хвіст (m) | [hwist] |
| bangs | чубчик (m) | ['tʃubtʃık] |

32. Human body

| hand | кисть (f) | [kıstʲ] |
| arm | рука (f) | [ru'ka] |

finger	палець (m)	['palɛts]
thumb	великий палець (m)	[wɛ'lıkıj 'palɛts]
little finger	мізинець (m)	[mi'zınɛts]
nail	ніготь (m)	['niɣotʲ]

fist	кулак (m)	[ku'lak]
palm	долоня (f)	[do'lɔɲa]
wrist	зап'ясток (m)	[zapʰʲjastok]
forearm	передпліччя (n)	[pɛrɛdp'litʃʲa]
elbow	лікоть (m)	['likotʲ]
shoulder	плече (n)	[plɛ'tʃɛ]

leg	гомілка (f)	[ɣo'milka]
foot	ступня (f)	[stup'ɲa]
knee	коліно (n)	[ko'lino]
calf (part of leg)	литка (f)	['lıtka]
hip	стегно (n)	[stɛɣ'nɔ]
heel	п'ятка (f)	['pʰjatka]

body	тіло (n)	['tilo]
stomach	живіт (m)	[ʒı'wit]
chest	груди (pl)	['ɣrudı]
breast	груди (pl)	['ɣrudı]
flank	бік (m)	[bik]

back	спина (f)	['spına]
lower back	поперек (m)	[popɛ'rɛk]
waist	талія (f)	['talija]

navel	пупок (m)	[pu'pɔk]
buttocks	сідниці (pl)	[sid'nıtsi]
bottom	зад (m)	[zad]

beauty mark	родимка (f)	['rɔdımka]
birthmark	родима пляма (f)	[ro'dıma 'pʌama]
tattoo	татуювання (n)	[tatuju'waɲa]
scar	рубець (m)	[ru'bɛts]

Clothing & Accessories

33. Outerwear. Coats

clothes	одяг (m)	['ɔdʲaɣ]
outer clothes	верхній одяг (m)	['wɛrhnij 'ɔdʲaɣ]
winter clothes	зимовий одяг (m)	[zɪ'mɔwɪj 'ɔdʲaɣ]
overcoat	пальто (n)	[paʎ'tɔ]
fur coat	шуба (f)	['ʃuba]
fur jacket	кожушок (m)	[koʒu'ʃɔk]
down coat	пуховик (m)	[puho'wɪk]
jacket (e.g., leather ~)	куртка (f)	['kurtka]
raincoat	плащ (m)	[plaɕ]
waterproof (adj)	непромокальний	[nɛpromo'kaʎnɪj]

34. Men's & women's clothing

shirt	сорочка (f)	[so'rɔtʃka]
pants	штани (pl)	[ʃta'nɪ]
jeans	джинси (pl)	['dʒɪnsɪ]
jacket (of man's suit)	піджак (m)	[pi'dʒak]
suit	костюм (m)	[kos'tym]
dress (frock)	сукня (f)	['sukɲa]
skirt	спідниця (f)	[spid'nɪtsʲa]
blouse	блузка (f)	['bluzka]
knitted jacket	кофта (f)	['kɔfta]
jacket (of woman's suit)	жакет (m)	[ʒa'kɛt]
T-shirt	футболка (f)	[fut'bɔlka]
shorts (short trousers)	шорти (pl)	['ʃɔrtɪ]
tracksuit	спортивний костюм (m)	[spor'tɪwnɪj kos'tym]
bathrobe	халат (m)	[ha'lat]
pajamas	піжама (f)	[pi'ʒama]
sweater	светр (m)	[swɛtr]
pullover	пуловер (m)	[pulo'wɛr]
vest	жилет (m)	[ʒɪ'lɛt]
tailcoat	фрак (m)	[frak]
tuxedo	смокінг (m)	['smɔkiŋ]
uniform	форма (f)	['fɔrma]

workwear	робочий одяг (f)	[ro'bɔtʃıj 'ɔdʲaɣ]
overalls	комбінезон (m)	[kombinɛ'zɔn]
coat (e.g., doctor's smock)	халат (m)	[ha'lat]

35. Clothing. Underwear

underwear	білизна (f)	[bi'lızna]
undershirt (A-shirt)	майка (f)	['majka]
socks	шкарпетки (pl)	[ʃkar'pɛtkı]

nightgown	нічна сорочка (f)	[nitʃ'na so'rɔtʃka]
bra	бюстгальтер (m)	[byst'ɣaʎtɛr]
knee highs	гольфи (pl)	['ɣɔʎfı]
tights	колготки (pl)	[kol'ɣɔtkı]
stockings (thigh highs)	панчохи (pl)	[pan'tʃɔhı]
bathing suit	купальник (m)	[ku'paʎnık]

36. Headwear

hat	шапка (f)	['ʃapka]
fedora	капелюх (m)	[kapɛ'lyh]
baseball cap	бейсболка (f)	[bɛjs'bɔlka]
flatcap	кашкет (m)	[kaʃ'kɛt]

beret	берет (m)	[bɛ'rɛt]
hood	каптур (m)	[kap'tur]
panama hat	панамка (f)	[pa'namka]
knitted hat	в'язана шапочка (f)	['wʲjazana 'ʃapotʃka]

| headscarf | хустка (f) | ['hustka] |
| women's hat | капелюшок (m) | [kapɛ'lyʃok] |

hard hat	каска (f)	['kaska]
garrison cap	пілотка (f)	[pi'lɔtka]
helmet	шолом (m)	[ʃo'lɔm]

| derby | котелок (m) | [kotɛ'lɔk] |
| top hat | циліндр (m) | [ʦı'lindr] |

37. Footwear

footwear	взуття (n)	[wzut'tʲa]
ankle boots	черевики (pl)	[tʃɛrɛ'wıkı]
shoes (low-heeled ~)	туфлі (pl)	['tufli]
boots (cowboy ~)	чоботи (pl)	['tʃɔbotı]
slippers	капці (pl)	['kaptsi]

tennis shoes	кросівки (pl)	[kro'siwkı]
sneakers	кеди (pl)	['kɛdı]
sandals	сандалі (pl)	[san'dali]

cobbler	чоботар (m)	[ʧobo'tar]
heel	каблук (m)	[kab'luk]
pair (of shoes)	пара (f)	['para]

shoestring	шнурок (m)	[ʃnu'rok]
to lace (vt)	шнурувати	[ʃnuru'watı]
shoehorn	ложка (f)	['lɔʒka]
shoe polish	крем (m) для взуття	[krɛm dʎa wzut'tʲa]

38. Textile. Fabrics

cotton (n)	бавовна (f)	[ba'wɔwna]
cotton (as adj)	з бавовни	[z ba'wɔwnı]
flax (n)	льон (m)	['lɜn]
flax (as adj)	з льону	[z 'lɜnu]

silk (n)	шовк (m)	['ʃowk]
silk (as adj)	шовковий	[ʃow'kɔwıj]
wool (n)	вовна (f)	['wɔwna]
woolen (adj)	вовняний	['wɔwɲanıj]

velvet	оксамит (m)	[oksa'mıt]
suede	замша (f)	['zamʃa]
corduroy	вельвет (m)	[wɛʎ'wɛt]

nylon (n)	нейлон (m)	[nɛj'lɔn]
nylon (as adj)	з нейлону	[z nɛj'lɔnu]
polyester (n)	поліестр (m)	[poli'ɛstr]
polyester (as adj)	поліестровий	[poli'ɛstrowıj]

leather (n)	шкіра (f)	['ʃkira]
leather (as adj)	зі шкіри	[zi 'ʃkirı]
fur (n)	хутро (n)	['hutro]
fur (e.g., ~ coat)	хутряний	[hut'rʲanıj]

39. Personal accessories

gloves	рукавички (pl)	[ruka'wıʧkı]
mittens	рукавиці (pl)	[ruka'wıtsi]
scarf (muffler)	шарф (m)	[ʃarf]

glasses	окуляри (pl)	[oku'ʎarı]
frame (eyeglass ~)	оправа (f)	[op'rawa]
umbrella	парасолька (f)	[para'sɔʎka]

walking stick	ціпок (m)	[tsi'pɔk]
hairbrush	щітка (f) для волосся	['ɕitka dʎa wo'lɔssʲa]
fan	віяло (n)	['wijalo]

necktie	краватка (f)	[kra'watka]
bow tie	краватка-метелик (f)	[kra'watka mɛ'tɛlɪk]
suspenders	шлейки (pl)	['ʃlɛjkɪ]
handkerchief	носовичок (m)	[nosowɪ'tʃɔk]

comb	гребінець (m)	[ɣrɛbi'nɛts]
barrette	заколка (f)	[za'kɔlka]
hairpin	шпилька (f)	['ʃpɪʎka]
buckle	пряжка (f)	['prʲaʒka]

| belt | пасок (m) | ['pasok] |
| shoulder strap | ремінь (m) | ['rɛmiɲ] |

bag (handbag)	сумка (f)	['sumka]
purse	сумочка (f)	['sumotʃka]
backpack	рюкзак (m)	[ryk'zak]

40. Clothing. Miscellaneous

fashion	мода (f)	['mɔda]
in vogue (adj)	модний	['mɔdnɪj]
fashion designer	модельєр (m)	[modɛ'ʎjɛr]

collar	комір (m)	['kɔmir]
pocket	кишеня (f)	[kɪ'ʃɛɲa]
pocket (as adj)	кишеньковий	[kɪʃɛɲ'kowɪj]
sleeve	рукав (m)	[ru'kaw]
hanging loop	петелька (f)	[pɛ'tɛʎka]
fly (on trousers)	ширінка (f)	[ʃi'rinka]

zipper (fastener)	змійка (f)	['zmijka]
fastener	застібка (f)	['zastibka]
button	ґудзик (m)	['gudzɪk]
buttonhole	петля (f)	[pɛt'ʎa]
to come off (ab. button)	відірватися	[widir'watɪsʲa]

to sew (vi, vt)	шити	['ʃɪtɪ]
to embroider (vi, vt)	вишивати	[wɪʃɪ'watɪ]
embroidery	вишивка (f)	['wɪʃɪwka]
sewing needle	голка (f)	['ɣɔlka]
thread	нитка (f)	['nɪtka]
seam	шов (m)	[ʃow]

to get dirty (vi)	забруднитися	[zabrud'nɪtɪsʲa]
stain (mark, spot)	пляма (f)	['pʎama]
to crease, crumple (vi)	пом'ятися	[pomʲ'jatɪsʲa]

| to tear (vt) | порвати | [por'watɪ] |
| clothes moth | міль (f) | [miʎ] |

41. Personal care. Cosmetics

toothpaste	зубна паста (f)	[zub'na 'pasta]
toothbrush	зубна щітка (f)	[zub'na 'ɕitka]
to brush one's teeth	чистити зуби	['tʃɪstɪtɪ 'zubɪ]

razor	бритва (f)	['brɪtwa]
shaving cream	крем (m) для гоління	[krɛm dʎa ɣo'linja]
to shave (vi)	голитися	[ɣo'lɪtɪsʲa]

| soap | мило (n) | ['mɪlo] |
| shampoo | шампунь (m) | [ʃam'puɲ] |

scissors	ножиці (pl)	['nɔʒɪtsi]
nail file	пилочка (f) для нігтів	['pɪlotʃka dʎa 'niɣtiw]
nail clippers	щипчики (pl)	['ɕɪptʃɪkɪ]
tweezers	пінцет (m)	[pin'tsɛt]

cosmetics	косметика (f)	[kos'mɛtɪka]
face mask	маска (f)	['maska]
manicure	манікюр (m)	[mani'kyr]
to have a manicure	робити манікюр	[ro'bɪtɪ mani'kyr]
pedicure	педикюр (m)	[pɛdi'kyr]

make-up bag	косметичка (f)	[kosmɛ'tɪtʃka]
face powder	пудра (f)	['pudra]
powder compact	пудрениця (f)	['pudrɛnɪtsʲa]
blusher	рум'яна (pl)	[rumʰ'jana]

perfume (bottled)	парфуми (pl)	[par'fumɪ]
toilet water (perfume)	туалетна вода (f)	[tua'lɛtna wo'da]
lotion	лосьйон (m)	[lo'sjon]
cologne	одеколон (m)	[odɛko'lɔn]

eyeshadow	тіні (pl) для повік	['tini dʎa po'wik]
eyeliner	олівець (m) для очей	[oli'wɛts dʎa o'tʃɛj]
mascara	туш (f)	[tuʃ]

lipstick	губна помада (f)	[ɣub'na po'mada]
nail polish, enamel	лак (m) для нігтів	[lak dʎa 'niɣtiw]
hair spray	лак (m) для волосся	[lak dʎa wo'lɔssʲa]
deodorant	дезодорант (m)	[dɛzodo'rant]

cream	крем (m)	[krɛm]
face cream	крем (m) для обличчя	[krɛm dʎa ob'lɪtʃa]
hand cream	крем (m) для рук	[krɛm dʎa ruk]
anti-wrinkle cream	крем (m) проти зморшок	[krɛm 'protɪ 'zmɔrʃok]

| day (as adj) | денний | [ˈdɛnɪj] |
| night (as adj) | нічний | [nitʃˈnɪj] |

tampon	тампон (m)	[tamˈpɔn]
toilet paper	туалетний папір (m)	[tuaˈlɛtnɪj paˈpir]
hair dryer	фен (m)	[fɛn]

42. Jewelry

jewelry	коштовність (f)	[koʃˈtɔwnistʲ]
precious (e.g., ~ stone)	коштовний	[koʃˈtɔwnɪj]
hallmark	проба (f)	[ˈprɔba]
ring	каблучка (f)	[kabˈlutʃka]
wedding ring	обручка (f)	[obˈrutʃka]
bracelet	браслет (m)	[brasˈlɛt]

earrings	сережки (pl)	[sɛˈrɛʒkɪ]
necklace (~ of pearls)	намисто (n)	[naˈmɪsto]
crown	корона (f)	[koˈrɔna]
bead necklace	буси (pl)	[ˈbusɪ]

diamond	діамант (m)	[diaˈmant]
emerald	смарагд (m)	[smaˈraɣd]
ruby	рубін (m)	[ruˈbin]
sapphire	сапфір (m)	[sapˈfir]
pearl	перли (pl)	[ˈpɛrlɪ]
amber	бурштин (m)	[burʃˈtɪn]

43. Watches. Clocks

watch (wristwatch)	годинник (m)	[ɣoˈdɪnɪk]
dial	циферблат (m)	[tsɪfɛrbˈlat]
hand (of clock, watch)	стрілка (f)	[ˈstrilka]
metal watch band	браслет (m)	[brasˈlɛt]
watch strap	ремінець (m)	[rɛmiˈnɛts]

battery	батарейка (f)	[bataˈrɛjka]
to be dead (battery)	сісти	[ˈsistɪ]
to change a battery	поміняти батарейку	[pomiˈɲatɪ bataˈrɛjku]
to run fast	поспішати	[pospiˈʃatɪ]
to run slow	відставати	[widstaˈwatɪ]

wall clock	годинник (m)	[ɣoˈdɪnɪk]
hourglass	годинник (m) пісковий	[ɣoˈdɪnɪk pisˈkɔwɪj]
sundial	годинник (m) сонячний	[ɣoˈdɪnɪk ˈsɔɲatʃnɪj]
alarm clock	будильник (m)	[buˈdɪʌnɪk]
watchmaker	годинникар (m)	[ɣodɪɲɪˈkar]
to repair (vt)	ремонтувати	[rɛmontuˈwatɪ]

Food. Nutricion

44. Food

meat	м'ясо (n)	['mʰjaso]
chicken	курка (f)	['kurka]
young chicken	курча (n)	[kurˈʧa]
duck	качка (f)	['kaʧka]
goose	гусак (m)	[ɣuˈsak]
game	дичина (f)	[dıʧıˈna]
turkey	індичка (f)	[inˈdıʧka]
pork	свинина (f)	[swıˈnına]
veal	телятина (f)	[tɛˈʎatına]
lamb	баранина (f)	[baˈranına]
beef	яловичина (f)	['jalowıʧına]
rabbit	кріль (m)	[kriʎ]
sausage (salami, etc.)	ковбаса (f)	[kowbaˈsa]
vienna sausage	сосиска (f)	[soˈsıska]
bacon	бекон (m)	[bɛˈkɔn]
ham	шинка (f)	['ʃıŋka]
gammon (ham)	окіст (m)	['ɔkist]
pâté	паштет (m)	[paʃˈtɛt]
liver	печінка (f)	[pɛˈʧiŋka]
lard	сало (n)	['salo]
ground beef	фарш (m)	[farʃ]
tongue	язик (m)	[jaˈzık]
egg	яйце (n)	[jajˈʦɛ]
eggs	яйця (pl)	['jajʦʲa]
egg white	білок (m)	[biˈlɔk]
egg yolk	жовток (m)	[ʒowˈtɔk]
fish	риба (f)	['rıba]
seafood	морепродукти (pl)	[morɛproˈduktı]
caviar	ікра (f)	[ikˈra]
crab	краб (m)	[krab]
shrimp	креветка (f)	[krɛˈwɛtka]
oyster	устриця (f)	['ustrıʦʲa]
spiny lobster	лангуст (m)	[laˈŋust]
octopus	восьминіг (m)	[wosʲmıˈniɣ]
squid	кальмар (m)	[kaʎˈmar]

sturgeon	осетрина (f)	[osɛtˈrɪnɑ]
salmon	лосось (m)	[loˈsɔsʲ]
halibut	палтус (m)	[ˈpɑltus]
cod	тріска (f)	[trisˈkɑ]
mackerel	скумбрія (f)	[ˈskumbrijɑ]
tuna	тунець (m)	[tuˈnɛts]
eel	вугор (m)	[wuˈɣɔr]
trout	форель (f)	[foˈrɛʎ]
sardine	сардина (f)	[sɑrˈdɪnɑ]
pike	щука (f)	[ˈɕukɑ]
herring	оселедець (m)	[osɛˈlɛdɛts]
bread	хліб (m)	[hlib]
cheese	сир (m)	[sɪr]
sugar	цукор (m)	[ˈtsukor]
salt	сіль (f)	[siʎ]
rice	рис (m)	[rɪs]
pasta	макарони (pl)	[mɑkɑˈrɔnɪ]
noodles	локшина (f)	[lokʃɪˈnɑ]
butter	вершкове масло (n)	[wɛrʃˈkɔwɛ ˈmɑslo]
vegetable oil	олія (f) рослинна	[oˈlijɑ rosˈlɪnɑ]
sunflower oil	соняшникова олія (f)	[ˈsɔɲɑʃnɪkowɑ oˈlijɑ]
margarine	маргарин (m)	[mɑrɣɑˈrɪn]
olives	оливки (pl)	[oˈlɪwkɪ]
olive oil	олія (f) оливкова	[oˈlijɑ oˈlɪwkowɑ]
milk	молоко (n)	[moloˈkɔ]
condensed milk	згущене молоко (n)	[ˈzɣuɕɛnɛ moloˈkɔ]
yogurt	йогурт (m)	[ˈjɔɣurt]
sour cream	сметана (f)	[smɛˈtɑnɑ]
cream (of milk)	вершки (pl)	[wɛrʃˈkɪ]
mayonnaise	майонез (m)	[mɑjoˈnɛz]
buttercream	крем (m)	[krɛm]
cereal grain (wheat, etc.)	крупа (f)	[kruˈpɑ]
flour	борошно (n)	[ˈboroʃno]
canned food	консерви (pl)	[konˈsɛrwɪ]
cornflakes	кукурудзяні пластівці (pl)	[kukuˈrudzʲɑni plastiwˈtsi]
honey	мед (m)	[mɛd]
jam	джем (m)	[dʒɛm]
chewing gum	жувальна гумка (f)	[ʒuˈwɑʎnɑ ˈɣumkɑ]

45. Drinks

water	вода (f)	[wo'da]
drinking water	питна вода (f)	[pɪt'na wo'da]
mineral water	мінеральна вода (f)	[minɛ'raʎna wo'da]
still (adj)	без газу	[bɛz 'ɣazu]
carbonated (adj)	газований	[ɣa'zɔwanɪj]
sparkling (adj)	з газом	[z 'ɣazom]
ice	лід (m)	[lid]
with ice	з льодом	[z 'lɜdom]
non-alcoholic (adj)	безалкогольний	[bɛzalko'ɣoʎnɪj]
soft drink	безалкогольний напій (m)	[bɛzalko'ɣoʎnɪj na'pij]
cool soft drink	прохолодній напій (m)	[proho'lodnij na'pij]
lemonade	лимонад (m)	[lɪmo'nad]
liquor	алкогольні напої (pl)	[alko'ɣoʎni na'pojɪ]
wine	вино (n)	[wɪ'nɔ]
white wine	біле вино (n)	['bilɛ wɪ'nɔ]
red wine	червоне вино (n)	[tʃɛr'wonɛ wɪ'nɔ]
liqueur	лікер (m)	[li'kɛr]
champagne	шампанське (n)	[ʃam'pansʲkɛ]
vermouth	вермут (m)	['wɛrmut]
whisky	віскі (n)	['wiski]
vodka	горілка (f)	[ɣo'rilka]
gin	джин (m)	[dʒɪn]
cognac	коньяк (m)	[ko'njak]
rum	ром (m)	[rom]
coffee	кава (f)	['kawa]
black coffee	чорна кава (f)	['tʃorna 'kawa]
coffee with milk	кава (f) з молоком	['kawa z molo'kɔm]
cappuccino	кава (f) з вершками	['kawa z wɛrʃ'kamɪ]
instant coffee	розчинна кава (f)	[roz'tʃɪna 'kawa]
milk	молоко (n)	[molo'kɔ]
cocktail	коктейль (m)	[kok'tɛjʎ]
milk shake	молочний коктейль (m)	[mo'lotʃnɪj kok'tɛjʎ]
juice	сік (m)	[sik]
tomato juice	томатний сік (m)	[to'matnɪj sik]
orange juice	апельсиновий сік (m)	[apɛʎ'sɪnowɪj sik]
freshly squeezed juice	свіжовижатий сік (m)	[swiʒo'wɪʒatɪj sik]
beer	пиво (n)	['pɪwo]
light beer	світле пиво (n)	['switlɛ 'pɪwo]
dark beer	темне пиво (n)	['tɛmnɛ 'pɪwo]

tea	чай (m)	[tʃɑj]
black tea	чорний чай (m)	[ˈtʃɔrnɪj tʃɑj]
green tea	зелений чай (m)	[zɛˈlɛnɪj tʃɑj]

46. Vegetables

vegetables	овочі (pl)	[ˈɔwɔtʃi]
greens	зелень (f)	[ˈzɛlɛɲ]
tomato	помідор (m)	[pomiˈdɔr]
cucumber	огірок (m)	[oɣiˈrɔk]
carrot	морква (f)	[ˈmɔrkwɑ]
potato	картопля (f)	[karˈtɔpʎɑ]
onion	цибуля (f)	[tsɪˈbuʎɑ]
garlic	часник (m)	[tʃasˈnɪk]
cabbage	капуста (f)	[kaˈpusta]
cauliflower	кольорова капуста (f)	[kolʲˈrɔwa kaˈpusta]
Brussels sprouts	брюссельська капуста (f)	[brʲˈsɛʎ⁣ka kaˈpusta]
broccoli	капуста броколі (f)	[kaˈpusta ˈbrɔkoli]
beetroot	буряк (m)	[buˈrʲak]
eggplant	баклажан (m)	[baklaˈʒan]
zucchini	кабачок (m)	[kabaˈtʃɔk]
pumpkin	гарбуз (m)	[ɣarˈbuz]
turnip	ріпа (f)	[ˈripa]
parsley	петрушка (f)	[pɛtˈruʃka]
dill	кріп (m)	[krip]
lettuce	салат (m)	[saˈlat]
celery	селера (f)	[sɛˈlɛra]
asparagus	спаржа (f)	[ˈsparʒa]
spinach	шпинат (m)	[ʃpɪˈnat]
pea	горох (m)	[ɣoˈrɔh]
beans	боби (pl)	[boˈbɪ]
corn (maize)	кукурудза (f)	[kukuˈrudza]
kidney bean	квасоля (f)	[kwaˈsɔʎa]
pepper	перець (m)	[ˈpɛrɛts]
radish	редька (f)	[ˈrɛdʲka]
artichoke	артишок (m)	[artɪˈʃɔk]

47. Fruits. Nuts

| fruit | фрукт (m) | [frukt] |
| apple | яблуко (n) | [ˈjabluko] |

pear	груша (f)	[ˈɣruʃa]
lemon	лимон (m)	[lɪˈmɔn]
orange	апельсин (m)	[apɛʎˈsɪn]
strawberry	полуниця (f)	[poluˈnɪtsʲa]

mandarin	мандарин (m)	[mandaˈrɪn]
plum	слива (f)	[ˈslɪwa]
peach	персик (m)	[ˈpɛrsɪk]
apricot	абрикос (m)	[abrɪˈkɔs]
raspberry	малина (f)	[maˈlɪna]
pineapple	ананас (m)	[anaˈnas]

banana	банан (m)	[baˈnan]
watermelon	кавун (m)	[kaˈwun]
grape	виноград (m)	[wɪnoɣˈrad]
sour cherry	вишня (f)	[ˈwɪʃna]
sweet cherry	черешня (f)	[ʧɛˈrɛʃna]
melon	диня (f)	[ˈdɪna]

grapefruit	грейпфрут (m)	[ɣrɛjpfˈrut]
avocado	авокадо (n)	[awoˈkado]
papaya	папайя (f)	[paˈpaja]
mango	манго (n)	[ˈmaŋo]
pomegranate	гранат (m)	[ɣraˈnat]

redcurrant	порічки (pl)	[poˈriʧkɪ]
blackcurrant	чорна смородина (f)	[ˈʧorna smoˈrɔdɪna]
gooseberry	аґрус (m)	[ˈagrus]
bilberry	чорниця (f)	[ʧorˈnɪtsʲa]
blackberry	ожина (f)	[oˈʒɪna]

raisin	родзинки (pl)	[roˈdzɪŋkɪ]
fig	інжир (m)	[inˈʒɪr]
date	фінік (m)	[ˈfinik]

peanut	арахіс (m)	[aˈrahis]
almond	мигдаль (m)	[mɪɣˈdaʎ]
walnut	горіх (m) волоський	[ɣoˈrih woˈlɔsʲkɪj]
hazelnut	ліщина (f)	[liˈɕɪna]
coconut	горіх (m) кокосовий	[ɣoˈrih koˈkɔsowɪj]
pistachios	фісташки (pl)	[fisˈtaʃkɪ]

48. Bread. Candy

confectionery (pastry)	кондитерські вироби (pl)	[konˈdɪtɛrsʲki ˈwɪrobɪ]
bread	хліб (m)	[hlib]
cookies	печиво (n)	[ˈpɛʧɪwo]

| chocolate (n) | шоколад (m) | [ʃokoˈlad] |
| chocolate (as adj) | шоколадний | [ʃokoˈladnɪj] |

candy	цукерка (f)	[ʦu'kɛrkɑ]
cake (e.g., cupcake)	тістечко (n)	['tistɛʧko]
cake (e.g., birthday ~)	торт (m)	[tort]
pie (e.g., apple ~)	пиріг (m)	[pɪ'riɣ]
filling (for cake, pie)	начинка (f)	[nɑ'ʧɪŋkɑ]
whole fruit jam	варення (n)	[wɑ'rɛɲɑ]
marmalade	мармелад (m)	[mɑrmɛ'lɑd]
waffle	вафлі (pl)	['wɑfli]
ice-cream	морозиво (n)	[mo'rɔzɪwo]

49. Cooked dishes

course, dish	страва (f)	['strɑwɑ]
cuisine	кухня (f)	['kuhɲɑ]
recipe	рецепт (m)	[rɛ'ʦɛpt]
portion	порція (f)	['porʦijɑ]
salad	салат (m)	[sɑ'lɑt]
soup	юшка (f)	['juʃkɑ]
clear soup (broth)	бульйон (m)	[bu'ʎjon]
sandwich (bread)	канапка (f)	[kɑ'nɑpkɑ]
fried eggs	яєчня (f)	[jɑ'ɛʧɲɑ]
cutlet (croquette)	котлета (m)	[kot'lɛtɑ]
hamburger (beefburger)	гамбургер (m)	['ɣɑmburɣɛr]
beefsteak	біфштекс (m)	[bifʃ'tɛks]
stew	печеня (f)	[pɛ'ʧɛɲɑ]
side dish	гарнір (m)	[ɣɑr'nir]
spaghetti	спагеті (pl)	[spɑ'ɣɛti]
mashed potatoes	картопляне пюре (n)	[kɑrtop'ʎɑnɛ py'rɛ]
pizza	піца (f)	['pitsɑ]
porridge (oatmeal, etc.)	каша (f)	['kɑʃɑ]
omelet	омлет (m)	[om'lɛt]
boiled (e.g., ~ beef)	варений	[wɑ'rɛnɪj]
smoked (adj)	копчений	[kop'ʧɛnɪj]
fried (adj)	смажений	['smɑʒɛnɪj]
dried (adj)	сушений	['suʃɛnɪj]
frozen (adj)	заморожений	[zɑmo'rɔʒɛnɪj]
pickled (adj)	маринований	[mɑrɪ'nɔwɑnɪj]
sweet (sugary)	солодкий	[so'lɔdkɪj]
salty (adj)	солоний	[so'lɔnɪj]
cold (adj)	холодний	[ho'lɔdnɪj]
hot (adj)	гарячий	[ɣɑ'rʲɑʧɪj]
bitter (adj)	гіркий	[ɣir'kɪj]

tasty (adj)	смачний	[smatʃ'nıj]
to cook in boiling water	варити	[wa'rıtı]
to cook (dinner)	готувати	[ɣotu'watı]
to fry (vt)	смажити	['smaʒıtı]
to heat up (food)	розігрівати	[roziɣri'watı]

to salt (vt)	солити	[so'lıtı]
to pepper (vt)	перчити	[pɛr'tʃıtı]
to grate (vt)	терти	['tɛrtı]
peel (n)	шкірка (f)	['ʃkirka]
to peel (vt)	чистити	['tʃıstıtı]

50. Spices

salt	сіль (f)	[siʎ]
salty (adj)	солоний	[so'lɔnıj]
to salt (vt)	солити	[so'lıtı]

black pepper	чорний перець (m)	['tʃɔrnıj 'pɛrɛts]
red pepper	червоний перець (m)	[tʃɛr'wonıj 'pɛrɛts]
mustard	гірчиця (f)	[ɣir'tʃıtsʲa]
horseradish	хрін (m)	[hrin]

condiment	приправа (f)	[prıp'rawa]
spice	прянощі (pl)	[prʲa'nɔɕi]
sauce	соус (m)	['sɔus]
vinegar	оцет (m)	['ɔtsɛt]

anise	аніс (m)	['anis]
basil	базилік (m)	[bazı'lik]
cloves	гвоздика (f)	[ɣwoz'dıka]
ginger	імбир (m)	[im'bır]
coriander	коріандр (m)	[kori'andr]
cinnamon	кориця (f)	[ko'rıtsʲa]

sesame	кунжут (m)	[kun'ʒut]
bay leaf	лавровий лист (m)	[law'rɔwıj lıst]
paprika	паприка (f)	['paprıka]
caraway	кмин (m)	[kmın]
saffron	шафран (m)	[ʃaf'ran]

51. Meals

| food | їжа (f) | ['jıʒa] |
| to eat (vi, vt) | їсти | ['jıstı] |

| breakfast | сніданок (m) | [sni'danok] |
| to have breakfast | снідати | ['snidatı] |

lunch	обід (m)	[oʹbid]
to have lunch	обідати	[oʹbidɑtɪ]
dinner	вечеря (f)	[wɛʹʧɛrʲɑ]
to have dinner	вечеряти	[wɛʹʧɛrʲɑtɪ]
appetite	апетит (m)	[ɑpɛʹtɪt]
Enjoy your meal!	Смачного!	[smɑʧʹnɔɣo]
to open (~ a bottle)	відкривати	[widkrɪʹwɑtɪ]
to spill (liquid)	пролити	[proʹlɪtɪ]
to spill out (vi)	пролитись	[proʹlɪtɪsʲ]
to boil (vi)	кипіти	[kɪʹpiti]
to boil (vt)	кип'ятити	[kɪpʰjɑʹtɪtɪ]
boiled (~ water)	кип'ячений	[kɪpʰjɑʹʧɛnɪj]
to chill, cool down (vt)	охолодити	[oholoʹdɪtɪ]
to chill (vi)	охолоджуватись	[ohoʹlɔʤuwɑtɪsʲ]
taste, flavor	смак (m)	[smɑk]
aftertaste	присмак (m)	[ʹprɪsmɑk]
to be on a diet	худнути	[ʹhudnutɪ]
diet	дієта (f)	[diʹɛtɑ]
vitamin	вітамін (m)	[witɑʹmin]
calorie	калорія (f)	[kɑʹlɔrijɑ]
vegetarian (n)	вегетаріанець (m)	[wɛɣɛtɑriʹɑnɛʦ]
vegetarian (adj)	вегетаріанський	[wɛɣɛtɑriʹɑnsʲkɪj]
fats (nutrient)	жири (pl)	[ʒɪʹrɪ]
proteins	білки (pl)	[bilʹkɪ]
carbohydrates	вуглеводи (m)	[wuɣlɛʹwɔdɪ]
slice (of lemon, ham)	скибка (f)	[ʹskɪbkɑ]
piece (of cake, pie)	шматок (m)	[ʃmɑʹtɔk]
crumb (of bread)	крихта (f)	[ʹkrɪhtɑ]

52. Table setting

spoon	ложка (f)	[ʹlɔʒkɑ]
knife	ніж (m)	[niʒ]
fork	виделка (f)	[wɪʹdɛlkɑ]
cup (of coffee)	чашка (f)	[ʹʧɑʃkɑ]
plate (dinner ~)	тарілка (f)	[tɑʹrilkɑ]
saucer	блюдце (n)	[ʹblydʦɛ]
napkin (on table)	серветка (f)	[sɛrʹwɛtkɑ]
toothpick	зубочистка (f)	[zuboʹʧɪstkɑ]

53. Restaurant

restaurant	ресторан (m)	[rɛstoˈran]
coffee house	кав'ярня (f)	[kawʰˈjarɲa]
pub, bar	бар (m)	[bar]
tearoom	чайна (f)	[ˈʧajna]
waiter	офіціант (m)	[ofitsiˈant]
waitress	офіціантка (f)	[ofitsiˈantka]
bartender	бармен (m)	[barˈmɛn]
menu	меню (n)	[mɛˈny]
wine list	карта (f) вин	[ˈkarta wɪn]
to book a table	забронювати столик	[zabronyˈwatɪ ˈstɔlɪk]
course, dish	страва (f)	[ˈstrawa]
to order (meal)	замовити	[zaˈmɔwɪtɪ]
to make an order	зробити замовлення	[zroˈbɪtɪ zaˈmɔwlɛɲa]
aperitif	аперитив (m)	[apɛrɪˈtɪw]
appetizer	закуска (f)	[zaˈkuska]
dessert	десерт (m)	[dɛˈsɛrt]
check	рахунок (m)	[raˈhunok]
to pay the check	оплатити рахунок	[oplaˈtɪtɪ raˈhunok]
to give change	дати решту	[ˈdatɪ ˈrɛʃtu]
tip	чайові (pl)	[ʧaɜˈwi]

Family, relatives and friends

54. Personal information. Forms

name, first name	ім'я (n)	[im^h'ja]
family name	прізвище (n)	['prizwɪɕɛ]
date of birth	дата (f) народження	['data na'rɔdʒɛnja]
place of birth	місце (n) народження	['mistsɛ na'rɔdʒɛnja]
nationality	національність (f)	[natsio'naʎnistʲ]
place of residence	місце (n) проживання	['mistsɛ proʒɪ'wanja]
country	країна (f)	[kra'jɪna]
profession (occupation)	професія (f)	[pro'fɛsija]
gender, sex	стать (f)	[statʲ]
height	зріст (m)	[zrist]
weight	вага (f)	[wa'ɣa]

55. Family members. Relatives

mother	мати (f)	['matɪ]
father	батько (m)	['batʲko]
son	син (m)	[sɪn]
daughter	дочка (f)	[dotʃ'ka]
younger daughter	молодша дочка (f)	[mo'lɔdʃa dotʃ'ka]
younger son	молодший син (m)	[mo'lɔdʃij sɪn]
eldest daughter	старша дочка (f)	['starʃa dotʃ'ka]
eldest son	старший син (m)	['starʃij sɪn]
brother	брат (m)	[brat]
sister	сестра (f)	[sɛst'ra]
cousin (masc.)	двоюрідний брат (m)	[dwoju'ridnɪj brat]
cousin (fem.)	двоюрідна сестра (f)	[dwoju'ridna sɛst'ra]
mom	мати (f)	['matɪ]
dad, daddy	тато (m)	['tato]
parents	батьки (pl)	[batʲ'kɪ]
child	дитина (f)	[dɪ'tɪna]
children	діти (pl)	['ditɪ]
grandmother	бабуся (f)	[ba'busʲa]
grandfather	дід (m)	['did]
grandson	онук (m)	[o'nuk]

| granddaughter | онука (f) | [oˈnuka] |
| grandchildren | онуки (pl) | [oˈnukɪ] |

uncle	дядько (m)	[ˈdʲadʲko]
aunt	тітка (f)	[ˈtitka]
nephew	племінник (m)	[plɛˈminŋk]
niece	племінниця (f)	[plɛˈminɪtsʲa]

mother-in-law (wife's mother)	теща (f)	[ˈtɛɕa]
father-in-law (husband's father)	свекор (m)	[ˈswɛkor]
son-in-law (daughter's husband)	зять (m)	[zʲatʲ]
stepmother	мачуха (f)	[ˈmatʃuha]
stepfather	вітчим (m)	[ˈwitʃɪm]

infant	немовля (n)	[nɛmowˈʎa]
baby (infant)	немовля (n)	[nɛmowˈʎa]
little boy, kid	малюк (m)	[maˈlyk]

wife	дружина (f)	[druˈʒɪna]
husband	чоловік (m)	[tʃoloˈwik]
spouse (husband)	чоловік (m)	[tʃoloˈwik]
spouse (wife)	дружина (f)	[druˈʒɪna]

married (masc.)	одружений	[odˈruʒɛnɪj]
married (fem.)	заміжня	[zaˈmiʒɲa]
single (unmarried)	холостий	[holosˈtɪj]
bachelor	холостяк (m)	[holosˈtʲak]
divorced (masc.)	розведений	[rozˈwɛdɛnɪj]
widow	вдова (f)	[wdoˈwa]
widower	вдівець (m)	[wdiˈwɛts]

relative	родич (m)	[ˈrɔdɪtʃ]
close relative	близький родич (m)	[blɪzʲˈkɪj ˈrɔdɪtʃ]
distant relative	далекий родич (m)	[daˈlɛkɪj ˈrɔdɪtʃ]
relatives	рідні (pl)	[ˈridni]

orphan (boy or girl)	сирота (m)	[sɪroˈta]
guardian (of minor)	опікун (m)	[opiˈkun]
to adopt (a boy)	усиновити	[usɪnoˈwɪtɪ]
to adopt (a girl)	удочерити	[udotʃɛˈrɪtɪ]

56. Friends. Coworkers

friend (masc.)	товариш (m)	[toˈwarɪʃ]
friend (fem.)	подруга (f)	[ˈpɔdruɣa]
friendship	дружба (f)	[ˈdruʒba]
to be friends	дружити	[druˈʒɪtɪ]

buddy (masc.)	приятель (m)	[ˈprijatɛʎ]
buddy (fem.)	приятелька (f)	[ˈprijatɛʎka]
partner	партнер (m)	[partˈnɛr]

chief (boss)	шеф (m)	[ʃɛf]
superior	начальник (m)	[naˈtʃaʎnɪk]
subordinate	підлеглий (m)	[pidˈlɛɣlɪj]
colleague	колега (m)	[koˈlɛɣa]

acquaintance (person)	знайомий (m)	[znaˈjɔmɪj]
fellow traveler	попутник (m)	[poˈputnɪk]
classmate	однокласник (m)	[odnokˈlasnɪk]

neighbor (masc.)	сусід (m)	[suˈsid]
neighbor (fem.)	сусідка (f)	[suˈsidka]
neighbors	сусіди (pl)	[suˈsidɪ]

57. Man. Woman

woman	жінка (f)	[ˈʒiŋka]
girl (young woman)	дівчина (f)	[ˈdiwtʃɪna]
bride	наречена (f)	[narɛˈtʃɛna]

beautiful (adj)	гарна	[ˈɣarna]
tall (adj)	висока	[wɪˈsɔka]
slender (adj)	струнка	[struˈŋka]
short (adj)	невисокого зросту	[nɛwɪˈsɔkoɣo ˈzrɔstu]

blonde (n)	блондинка (f)	[blonˈdɪŋka]
brunette (n)	брюнетка (f)	[bryˈnɛtka]
ladies' (adj)	дамський	[ˈdamsʲkɪj]
virgin (girl)	незаймана дівчина (f)	[nɛˈzajmana ˈdiwtʃɪna]
pregnant (adj)	вагітна	[waˈɣitna]

man (adult male)	чоловік (m)	[tʃoloˈwik]
blond (n)	блондин (m)	[blonˈdɪn]
brunet (n)	брюнет (m)	[bryˈnɛt]
tall (adj)	високий	[wɪˈsɔkɪj]
short (adj)	невисокого зросту	[nɛwɪˈsɔkoɣo ˈzrɔstu]

rude (rough)	брутальний	[bruˈtaʎnɪj]
stocky (adj)	кремезний	[krɛˈmɛznɪj]
robust (adj)	міцний	[mitsˈnɪj]
strong (adj)	сильний	[ˈsɪʎnɪj]
strength	сила (f)	[ˈsɪla]

stout, fat (adj)	повний	[ˈpɔwnɪj]
swarthy (adj)	смаглявий	[smaɣˈʎawɪj]
well-built (adj)	стрункий	[struˈŋkɪj]
elegant (adj)	елегантний	[ɛlɛˈɣantnɪj]

58. Age

age	вік (m)	[wik]
youth (young age)	юність (f)	[ˈjunistʲ]
young (adj)	молодий	[moloˈdɪj]
younger (adj)	молодший	[moˈlɔdʃɪj]
older (adj)	старший	[ˈstarʃɪj]
young man	юнак (m)	[juˈnak]
teenager	підліток (m)	[ˈpidlitok]
guy, fellow	хлопець (m)	[ˈhlɔpɛts]
old man	старий (m)	[staˈrɪj]
old woman	стара (f)	[staˈra]
adult	дорослий	[doˈrɔslɪj]
middle-aged (adj)	середніх років	[sɛˈrɛdnih roˈkiw]
elderly (adj)	похилий	[poˈhɪlɪj]
old (adj)	старий	[staˈrɪj]
retirement	пенсія (f)	[ˈpɛnsija]
to retire (from job)	вийти на пенсію	[ˈwɪjtɪ na ˈpɛnsiju]
retiree	пенсіонер (m)	[pɛnsioˈnɛr]

59. Children

child	дитина (f)	[dɪˈtɪna]
children	діти (pl)	[ˈditɪ]
twins	близнюки (pl)	[blɪznyˈkɪ]
cradle	колиска (f)	[koˈlɪska]
rattle	брязкальце (n)	[ˈbrʲazkaʎtsɛ]
diaper	підгузок (m)	[pidˈɣuzok]
pacifier	соска (f)	[ˈsɔska]
baby carriage	коляска (f)	[koˈʎaska]
kindergarten	дитячий садок (m)	[dɪˈtʲatʃɪj saˈdɔk]
babysitter	няня (f)	[ˈɲaɲa]
childhood	дитинство (n)	[dɪˈtɪnstwo]
doll	лялька (f)	[ˈʎaʎka]
toy	іграшка (f)	[ˈiɣraʃka]
construction set	конструктор (m)	[konstˈruktor]
well-bred (adj)	вихований	[ˈwɪhowanɪj]
ill-bred (adj)	невихований	[nɛˈwɪhowanɪj]
spoiled (adj)	розбещений	[rozˈbɛɕɛnɪj]
to be naughty	бешкетувати	[bɛʃkɛtuˈwatɪ]

mischievous (adj)	пустотливий	[pustot'lıwıj]
mischievousness	витівка (f)	['wıtiwka]
mischievous child	пустун (m)	[pus'tun]
obedient (adj)	слухняний	[sluh'ɲanıj]
disobedient (adj)	неслухняний	[nɛsluh'ɲanıj]
docile (adj)	розумний	[ro'zumnıj]
clever (smart)	розумний	[ro'zumnıj]
child prodigy	вундеркінд (m)	[wundɛr'kind]

60. Married couples. Family life

to kiss (vt)	цілувати	[tsilu'watı]
to kiss (vi)	цілуватися	[tsilu'watısʲa]
family (n)	сім'я (f)	[simʰ'ja]
family (as adj)	сімейний	[si'mɛjnıj]
couple	пара (f)	['para]
marriage (state)	шлюб (m)	[ʃlyb]
hearth (home)	домашнє вогнище (n)	[do'maʃnɛ 'woɣnıɕɛ]
dynasty	династія (f)	[dı'nastija]
date	побачення (n)	[po'batʃɛnja]
kiss	поцілунок (m)	[potsi'lunok]
love (for sb)	кохання (n)	[ko'haɲa]
to love (sb)	кохати	[ko'hatı]
beloved	кохана людина (f)	[ko'hana ly'dına]
tenderness	ніжність (f)	['niʒnistʲ]
tender (affectionate)	ніжний	['niʒnıj]
faithfulness	незрадливість (f)	[nɛzrad'lıwistʲ]
faithful (adj)	незрадливий	[nɛzrad'lıwıj]
care (attention)	турбота (f)	[tur'bota]
caring (~ father)	турботливий	[tur'botlıwıj]
newlyweds	молодята (pl)	[molo'dʲata]
honeymoon	медовий місяць (m)	[mɛ'dowıj 'misʲatsʲ]
to get married (ab. woman)	вийти заміж	['wıjtı 'zamiʒ]
to get married (ab. man)	одружуватися	[od'ruʒuwatısʲa]
wedding	весілля (n)	[wɛ'siʎa]
golden wedding	золоте весілля (n)	[zolo'tɛ wɛ'siʎa]
anniversary	річниця (f)	[ritʃ'nıtsʲa]
lover (masc.)	коханець (m)	[ko'hanɛts]
mistress	коханка (f)	[ko'haŋka]
adultery	зрада (f)	['zrada]
to cheat on ... (commit adultery)	зрадити	['zradıtı]

jealous (adj)	ревнивий	[rɛw'nɪwɪj]
to be jealous	ревнувати	[rɛwnu'watɪ]
divorce	розлучення (n)	[roz'luʧɛnja]
to divorce (vi)	розлучитися	[rozlu'ʧitɪsʲa]

to quarrel (vi)	сваритися	[swa'rɪtɪsʲa]
to be reconciled	миритися	[mɪ'rɪtɪsʲa]
together (adv)	разом	['razom]
sex	секс (m)	[sɛks]

happiness	щастя (n)	['ɕastʲa]
happy (adj)	щасливий	[ɕas'lɪwɪj]
misfortune (accident)	нещастя (n)	[nɛ'ɕastʲa]
unhappy (adj)	нещасний	[nɛ'ɕasnɪj]

Character. Feelings. Emotions

61. Feelings. Emotions

feeling (emotion)	почуття (n)	[poˈʃutʲtʲa]
feelings	почуття (pl)	[poˈʃutʲtʲa]
hunger	голод (m)	[ˈɣɔlod]
to be hungry	хотіти їсти	[hoˈtitɪ ˈjɪstɪ]
thirst	спрага (f)	[ˈspraɣa]
to be thirsty	хотіти пити	[hoˈtitɪ ˈpɪtɪ]
sleepiness	сонливість (f)	[sonˈlɪwistʲ]
to feel sleepy	хотіти спати	[hoˈtitɪ ˈspatɪ]
tiredness	втома (f)	[ˈwtɔma]
tired (adj)	втомлений	[ˈwtɔmlɛnɪj]
to get tired	втомитися	[wtoˈmɪtɪsʲa]
mood (humor)	настрій (m)	[ˈnastrij]
boredom	нудьга (f)	[nudʲˈɣa]
to be bored	нудьгувати	[nudʲɣuˈwatɪ]
seclusion	самота (f)	[samoˈta]
to seclude oneself	усамітнюватися	[usaˈmitnywatɪsʲa]
to worry (make anxious)	хвилювати	[hwɪlʲuˈwatɪ]
to be worried	хвилюватися	[hwɪlʲuˈwatɪsʲa]
worrying (n)	хвилювання (n)	[hwɪlʲuˈwanʲa]
anxiety	занепокоєння (n)	[zanɛpoˈkɔɛnja]
preoccupied (adj)	занепокоєний	[zanɛpoˈkɔɛnɪj]
to be nervous	нервуватися	[nɛrwuˈwatɪsʲa]
to panic (vi)	панікувати	[panikuˈwatɪ]
hope	надія (f)	[naˈdija]
to hope (vi, vt)	сподіватися	[spodiˈwatɪsʲa]
certainty	упевненість (f)	[uˈpɛwnɛnistʲ]
certain, sure (adj)	упевнений	[uˈpɛwnɛnɪj]
uncertainty	непевність (f)	[nɛˈpɛwnistʲ]
uncertain (adj)	невпевнений	[nɛwˈpɛwnɛnɪj]
drunk (adj)	п'яний	[ˈpʰjanɪj]
sober (adj)	тверезий	[twɛˈrɛzɪj]
weak (adj)	слабкий	[slabˈkɪj]
happy (adj)	щасливий	[ɕasˈlɪwɪj]
to scare (vt)	налякати	[naʎaˈkatɪ]
fury (madness)	шаленство (n)	[ʃaˈlɛnstwo]

rage (fury)	лють (f)	[lytʲ]
depression	депресія (f)	[dɛpˈrɛsija]
discomfort	дискомфорт (m)	[dɪskomˈfɔrt]
comfort	комфорт (m)	[komˈfɔrt]
to regret (be sorry)	жалкувати	[ʒalkuˈwatɪ]
regret	жаль (m)	[ʒaʎ]
bad luck	невезіння (n)	[nɛwɛˈzinja]
sadness	прикрість (f)	[ˈprɪkristʲ]
shame (remorse)	сором (m)	[ˈsɔrom]
gladness	веселість (f)	[wɛˈsɛlistʲ]
enthusiasm, zeal	ентузіазм (m)	[ɛntuziˈazm]
enthusiast	ентузіаст (m)	[ɛntuziˈast]
to show enthusiasm	проявити ентузіазм	[projaˈwɪtɪ ɛntuziˈazm]

62. Character. Personality

character	характер (m)	[haˈraktɛr]
character flaw	вада (f)	[ˈwada]
mind	ум (m)	[um]
reason	розум (m)	[ˈrɔzum]
conscience	совість (f)	[ˈsɔwistʲ]
habit (custom)	звичка (f)	[ˈzwɪʧka]
ability	здібність (f)	[ˈzdibnistʲ]
can (e.g., ~ swim)	уміти	[uˈmitɪ]
patient (adj)	терплячий	[tɛrpˈʎaʧɪj]
impatient (adj)	нетерплячий	[nɛtɛrpˈʎaʧɪj]
curious (inquisitive)	допитливий	[doˈpɪtlɪwɪj]
curiosity	цікавість (f)	[ʦiˈkawistʲ]
modesty	скромність (f)	[ˈskrɔmnistʲ]
modest (adj)	скромний	[ˈskrɔmnɪj]
immodest (adj)	нескромний	[nɛskˈrɔmnɪj]
laziness	лінь (f)	[liɲ]
lazy (adj)	ледачий	[lɛˈdaʧɪj]
lazy person (masc.)	ледар (m)	[ˈlɛdar]
cunning (n)	хитрість (f)	[ˈhɪtristʲ]
cunning (as adj)	хитрий	[ˈhɪtrɪj]
distrust	недовіра (f)	[nɛdoˈwira]
distrustful (adj)	недовірливий	[nɛdoˈwirlɪwɪj]
generosity	щедрість (f)	[ˈʤɛdristʲ]
generous (adj)	щедрий	[ˈʤɛdrɪj]
talented (adj)	талановитий	[talanoˈwɪtɪj]
talent	талант (m)	[taˈlant]
courageous (adj)	сміливий	[smiˈlɪwɪj]

courage	сміливість (f)	[smi'lıwistʲ]
honest (adj)	чесний	['tʃɛsnıj]
honesty	чесність (f)	['tʃɛsnistʲ]

careful (cautious)	обережний	[obɛ'rɛʒnıj]
brave (courageous)	відважний	[wid'waʒnıj]
serious (adj)	серйозний	[sɛ'rʒznıj]
strict (severe, stern)	суворий	[su'wɔrıj]

decisive (adj)	рішучий	[ri'ʃutʃıj]
indecisive (adj)	нерішучий	[nɛri'ʃutʃıj]
shy, timid (adj)	сором'язливий	[soromʰ'jazlıwıj]
shyness, timidity	сором'язливість (f)	[soromʰ'jazlıwistʲ]

confidence (trust)	довіра (f)	[do'wira]
to believe (trust)	вірити	['wirıtı]
trusting (naïve)	довірливий	[do'wirlıwıj]

sincerely (adv)	щиро	['ɕıro]
sincere (adj)	щирий	['ɕırıj]
sincerity	щирість (f)	['ɕıristʲ]
open (person)	відкритий	[widk'rıtıj]

calm (adj)	тихий	['tıhıj]
frank (sincere)	відвертий	[wid'wɛrtıj]
naïve (adj)	наївний	[na'jıwnıj]
absent-minded (adj)	неуважний	[nɛu'waʒnıj]
funny (odd)	кумедний	[ku'mɛdnıj]

greed	жадібність (f)	['ʒadibnistʲ]
greedy (adj)	жадібний	['ʒadibnıj]
stingy (adj)	скупий	[sku'pıj]
evil (adj)	злий	['zlıj]
stubborn (adj)	впертий	['wpɛrtıj]
unpleasant (adj)	неприємний	[nɛprı'ɛmnıj]

selfish person (masc.)	егоїст (m)	[ɛɣo'jıst]
selfish (adj)	егоїстичний	[ɛɣojıs'tıtʃnıj]
coward	боягуз (m)	[boja'ɣuz]
cowardly (adj)	боягузливий	[boja'ɣuzlıwıj]

63. Sleep. Dreams

to sleep (vi)	спати	['spatı]
sleep, sleeping	сон (m)	[son]
dream	сон (m)	[son]
to dream (in sleep)	бачити сни	['batʃıtı snı]
sleepy (adj)	сонний	['sɔŋıj]
bed	ліжко (n)	['liʒko]
mattress	матрац (m)	[mat'rats]

blanket (comforter)	**ковдра** (f)	['kɔwdrɑ]
pillow	**подушка** (f)	[pɔ'duʃkɑ]
sheet	**простирадло** (n)	[prostɪ'rɑdlo]
insomnia	**безсоння** (n)	[bɛz'sɔnjɑ]
sleepless (adj)	**безсонний**	[bɛz'sɔnɪj]
sleeping pill	**снодійне** (n)	[sno'dijnɛ]
to take a sleeping pill	**прийняти снодійне**	[prɪj'nɑtɪ sno'dijnɛ]
to feel sleepy	**хотіти спати**	[ho'titɪ 'spɑtɪ]
to yawn (vi)	**позіхати**	[pozi'hɑtɪ]
to go to bed	**йти спати**	[jtɪ 'spɑtɪ]
to make up the bed	**стелити ліжко**	[stɛ'lɪtɪ 'liʒko]
to fall asleep	**заснути**	[zɑs'nutɪ]
nightmare	**страхіття** (n)	[strɑ'hitʲɑ]
snoring	**хропіння** (n)	[hro'pinjɑ]
to snore (vi)	**хропіти**	[hro'pitɪ]
alarm clock	**будильник** (m)	[bu'dɪʎnɪk]
to wake (vt)	**розбудити**	[rozbu'dɪtɪ]
to wake up	**прокидатися**	[prokɪ'dɑtɪsʲɑ]
to get up (vi)	**вставати**	[wstɑ'wɑtɪ]
to wash up (vi)	**умитися**	[u'mɪtɪsʲɑ]

64. Humour. Laughter. Gladness

humor (wit, fun)	**гумор** (m)	['ɣumor]
sense of humor	**почуття** (n)	[potʃut'tʲɑ]
to have fun	**веселитися**	[wɛsɛ'lɪtɪsʲɑ]
cheerful (adj)	**веселий**	[wɛ'sɛlɪj]
merriment, fun	**веселощі** (pl)	[wɛ'sɛloɕi]
smile	**посмішка** (f)	['posmiʃkɑ]
to smile (vi)	**посміхатися**	[posmi'hɑtɪsʲɑ]
to start laughing	**засміятися**	[zɑsmi'jɑtɪsʲɑ]
to laugh (vi)	**сміятися**	[smi'jɑtɪsʲɑ]
laugh, laughter	**сміх** (m)	[smih]
anecdote	**анекдот** (m)	[anɛk'dɔt]
funny (anecdote, etc.)	**смішний**	[smiʃ'nɪj]
funny (odd)	**кумедний**	[ku'mɛdnɪj]
to joke (vi)	**жартувати**	[ʒartu'wɑtɪ]
joke (verbal)	**жарт** (m)	[ʒart]
joy (emotion)	**радість** (f)	['rɑdistʲ]
to rejoice (vi)	**радіти**	[rɑ'ditɪ]
glad, cheerful (adj)	**радісний**	['rɑdisnɪj]

65. Discussion, conversation. Part 1

communication	спілкування (n)	[spilku'wanja]
to communicate	спілкуватися	[spilku'watısʲa]
conversation	розмова (f)	[roz'mowa]
dialog	діалог (m)	[dia'loɣ]
discussion (discourse)	дискусія (f)	[dıs'kusija]
debate	суперечка (m)	[supe'rɛtʃka]
to debate (vi)	сперечатися	[spɛrɛ'tʃatısʲa]
interlocutor	співрозмовник (m)	[spiwroz'mownık]
topic (theme)	тема (f)	['tɛma]
point of view	точка (f) зору	['tɔtʃka 'zɔru]
opinion (viewpoint)	погляд (m)	['pɔɣʎad]
speech (talk)	промова (f)	[pro'mɔwa]
discussion (of report, etc.)	обговорення (n)	[obɣo'wɔrɛnja]
to discuss (vt)	обговорювати	[obɣo'wɔrywatı]
talk (conversation)	бесіда (f)	['bɛsida]
to talk (vi)	розмовляти	[rozmow'ʎatı]
meeting	зустріч (f)	['zustritʃ]
to meet (vi, vt)	зустрічатися	[zustri'tʃatısʲa]
proverb	прислів'я (n)	[prıs'liwʰja]
saying	приказка (f)	['prıkazka]
riddle (poser)	загадка (f)	['zaɣadka]
to ask a riddle	загадувати загадку	[za'ɣaduwatı 'zaɣadku]
password	пароль (m)	[pa'rɔʎ]
secret	секрет (m)	[sɛk'rɛt]
oath (vow)	клятва (f)	['kʎatwa]
to swear (an oath)	клястися	['kʎastısʲa]
promise	обіцянка (f)	[obi'tsʲanka]
to promise (vt)	обіцяти	[obi'tsʲatı]
advice (counsel)	порада (f)	[po'rada]
to advise (vt)	радити	['radıtı]
to listen to … (obey)	слухатись	['sluhatısʲ]
news	новина (f)	[nowı'na]
sensation (news)	сенсація (f)	[sɛn'satsija]
information (data)	відомості (pl)	[wi'dɔmosti]
conclusion (decision)	висновок (m)	['wısnowok]
voice	голос (m)	['ɣɔlos]
compliment	комплімент (m)	[kompli'mɛnt]
kind (nice)	люб'язний	[lybʰ'jaznıj]
word	слово (n)	['slɔwo]
phrase	фраза (f)	['fraza]
answer	відповідь (f)	['widpowidʲ]

| truth | правда (f) | ['prawda] |
| lie | брехня (f) | [brɛh'ɲa] |

thought	думка (f)	['dumka]
idea (inspiration)	думка (f)	['dumka]
fantasy	вигадка (f)	['wɪɣadka]

66. Discussion, conversation. Part 2

respected (adj)	шановний	[ʃa'nɔwnɪj]
to respect (vt)	поважати	[powa'ʒatɪ]
respect	повага (f)	[po'waɣa]
Dear ... (letter)	Шановний ...	[ʃa'nɔwnɪj]

to introduce (present)	познайомити	[pozna'jɔmɪtɪ]
intention	намір (m)	['namir]
to intend (have in mind)	мати наміри	['matɪ 'namɪrɪ]
wish	побажання (n)	[poba'ʒaɲja]
to wish (~ good luck)	побажати	[poba'ʒatɪ]

surprise (astonishment)	здивування (n)	[zdɪwu'waɲja]
to surprise (amaze)	дивувати	[dɪwu'watɪ]
to be surprised	дивуватись	[dɪwu'watɪsʲ]

to give (vt)	дати	['datɪ]
to take (get hold of)	взяти	['wzʲatɪ]
to give back	повернути	[powɛr'nutɪ]
to return (give back)	віддати	[wid'datɪ]

to apologize (vi)	вибачатися	[wɪba'tʃatɪsʲa]
apology	вибачення (n)	['wɪbatʃɛɲja]
to forgive (vt)	прощати	[pro'ɕatɪ]

to talk (speak)	розмовляти	[rozmow'ʎatɪ]
to listen (vi)	слухати	['sluhatɪ]
to hear out	вислухати	['wɪsluhatɪ]
to understand (vt)	зрозуміти	[zrozu'mitɪ]

to show (display)	показати	[poka'zatɪ]
to look at ...	дивитися	[dɪ'wɪtɪsʲa]
to call (with one's voice)	покликати	[pok'lɪkatɪ]
to disturb (vt)	заважати	[zawa'ʒatɪ]
to pass (to hand sth)	передати	[pɛrɛ'datɪ]

demand (request)	прохання (n)	[pro'haɲja]
to request (ask)	просити	[pro'sɪtɪ]
demand (firm request)	вимога (f)	[wɪ'mɔɣa]
to demand (request firmly)	вимагати	[wɪma'ɣatɪ]
to tease (nickname)	дражнити	[draʒ'nɪtɪ]
to mock (make fun of)	насміхатися	[nasmi'hatɪsʲa]

| mockery, derision | насмішка (f) | [nasˈmiʃka] |
| nickname | прізвисько (n) | [ˈprizwɪsʲko] |

allusion	натяк (m)	[ˈnatʲak]
to allude (vi)	натякати	[natʲaˈkatɪ]
to imply (vt)	мати на увазі	[ˈmatɪ na uˈwazi]

description	опис (m)	[ˈɔpɪs]
to describe (vt)	описати	[opɪˈsatɪ]
praise (compliments)	похвала (f)	[pohwaˈla]
to praise (vt)	похвалити	[pohwaˈlɪtɪ]

disappointment	розчарування (n)	[roztʃaruˈwanja]
to disappoint (vt)	розчарувати	[roztʃaruˈwatɪ]
to be disappointed	розчаруватися	[roztʃaruˈwatɪsʲa]

supposition	припущення (n)	[prɪˈpuɕɛnja]
to suppose (assume)	припускати	[prɪpusˈkatɪ]
warning (caution)	застереження (n)	[zastɛˈrɛʒɛnja]
to warn (vt)	застерегти	[zastɛrɛɣˈtɪ]

67. Discussion, conversation. Part 3

| to talk into (convince) | умовити | [uˈmɔwɪtɪ] |
| to calm down (vt) | заспокоювати | [zaspoˈkɔjuwatɪ] |

silence (~ is golden)	мовчання (n)	[mowˈtʃanja]
to keep silent	мовчати	[mowˈtʃatɪ]
to whisper (vi, vt)	шепнути	[ʃɛpˈnutɪ]
whisper	шепіт (m)	[ˈʃɛpit]

| frankly, sincerely (adv) | відверто | [widˈwɛrto] |
| in my opinion … | на мою думку … | [na moˈju ˈdumku] |

detail (of the story)	подробиця (f)	[podˈrɔbɪtsʲa]
detailed (adj)	докладний	[dokˈladnɪj]
in detail (adv)	докладно	[dokˈladno]

| hint, clue | підказка (f) | [pidˈkazka] |
| to give a hint | підказувати | [pidˈkazuwatɪ] |

look (glance)	погляд (m)	[ˈpɔɣlad]
to have a look	поглянути	[poɣˈlʲanutɪ]
fixed (look)	нерухомий	[nɛruˈhɔmɪj]
to blink (vi)	кліпати	[ˈklipatɪ]
to wink (vi)	підморгнути	[pidmorɣˈnutɪ]
to nod (in assent)	кивнути	[kɪwˈnutɪ]

| sigh | зітхання (n) | [zitˈhanja] |
| to sigh (vi) | зітхнути | [zithˈnutɪ] |

to shudder (vi)	здригатися	[zdrɪ'ɣatɪsʲa]
gesture	жест (m)	[ʒɛst]
to touch (one's arm, etc.)	доторкнутися	[dotork'nutɪsʲa]
to seize (by the arm)	хапати	[ha'patɪ]
to tap (on the shoulder)	плескати	[plɛs'katɪ]

Look out!	Обережно!	[obɛ'rɛʒno]
Really?	Невже?	[nɛw'ʒɛ]
Are you sure?	Ти впевнений?	[tɪ 'wpɛwnɛnɪj]
Good luck!	Хай щастить!	[haj ɕas'tɪtʲ]
I see!	Зрозуміло!	[zrozu'milo]
It's a pity!	Шкода!	['ʃkɔda]

68. Agreement. Refusal

consent (agreement)	згода (f)	['zɣɔda]
to agree (say yes)	погоджуватися	[po'ɣɔdʒuwatɪsʲa]
approval	схвалення (n)	['shwalɛnja]
to approve (vt)	схвалити	[shwa'lɪtɪ]

| refusal | відмова (f) | [wid'mɔwa] |
| to refuse (vi, vt) | відмовлятися | [widmow'ʎatɪsʲa] |

Great!	Чудово!	[tʃu'dɔwo]
All right!	Добре!	['dɔbrɛ]
Okay! (I agree)	Згода!	['zɣɔda]

| forbidden (adj) | заборонений | [zabo'rɔnɛnɪj] |
| it's forbidden | не можна | [nɛ 'mɔʒna] |

| it's impossible | неможливо | [nɛmoʒ'lɪwo] |
| incorrect (adj) | помилковий | [pomɪl'kɔwɪj] |

to reject (~ a demand)	відхилити	[widhɪ'lɪtɪ]
to support (cause, idea)	підтримати	[pidt'rɪmatɪ]
to accept (~ an apology)	прийняти	[prɪj'ɲatɪ]

to confirm (vt)	підтвердити	[pidt'wɛrdɪtɪ]
confirmation	підтвердження (n)	[pidt'wɛrdʒɛnja]
permission	дозвіл (m)	['dɔzwil]
to permit (vt)	дозволити	[doz'wɔlɪtɪ]

| decision | рішення (n) | ['riʃɛnja] |
| to say nothing | промовчати | [promow'tʃatɪ] |

| condition (term) | умова (f) | [u'mɔwa] |
| excuse (pretext) | відмовка (f) | [wid'mɔwka] |

| praise (compliments) | похвала (f) | [pohwa'la] |
| to praise (vt) | хвалити | [hwa'lɪtɪ] |

69. Success. Good luck. Failure

success	успіх (m)	['uspih]
successfully (adv)	успішно	[us'piʃno]
successful (adj)	успішний	[us'piʃnɪj]
good luck	везіння (n)	[wɛ'zinja]
Good luck!	Хай щастить!	[haj ɕas'tɪtʲ]
lucky (e.g., ~ day)	вдалий	['wdalɪj]
lucky (fortunate)	щасливий	[ɕas'lɪwɪj]
failure	невдача (f)	[nɛw'datʃa]
misfortune	невдача (f)	[nɛw'datʃa]
bad luck	невезіння (n)	[nɛwɛ'zinja]
unsuccessful (adj)	невдалий	[nɛw'dalɪj]
catastrophe	катастрофа (f)	[katast'rofa]
pride	гордість (f)	['ɣordistʲ]
proud (adj)	гордовитий	[ɣordo'wɪtɪj]
to be proud	пишатися	[pɪ'ʃatɪsʲa]
winner	переможець (m)	[pɛrɛ'moʒɛts]
to win (vi)	перемогти	[pɛrɛmoɣ'tɪ]
to lose (not win)	програти	[proɣ'ratɪ]
try	спроба (f)	['sproba]
to try (vi)	намагатися	[nama'ɣatɪsʲa]
chance (opportunity)	шанс (m)	[ʃans]

70. Quarrels. Negative emotions

shout (scream)	крик (m)	[krɪk]
to shout (vi)	кричати	[krɪ'tʃatɪ]
to start to cry out	закричати	[zakrɪ'tʃatɪ]
quarrel	сварка (f)	['swarka]
to quarrel (vi)	сваритися	[swa'rɪtɪsʲa]
fight (scandal)	скандал (m)	[skan'dal]
to have a fight	сваритися	[swa'rɪtɪsʲa]
conflict	конфлікт (m)	[konf'likt]
misunderstanding	непорозуміння (n)	[nɛporozu'minja]
insult	образа (f)	[ob'raza]
to insult (vt)	ображати	[obra'ʒatɪ]
insulted (adj)	ображений	[ob'raʒɛnɪj]
resentment	образа (f)	[ob'raza]
to offend (vt)	образити	[ob'razɪtɪ]
to take offense	образитись	[ob'razɪtɪsʲ]
indignation	обурення (n)	[o'burɛɲja]
to be indignant	обурюватися	[o'burywatɪsʲa]

complaint	**скарга** (f)	['skarɣa]
to complain (vi, vt)	**скаржитися**	['skarʒɪtɪsʲa]
apology	**вибачення** (n)	['wɪbatʃɛnja]
to apologize (vi)	**вибачатися**	[wɪba'tʃatɪsʲa]
to beg pardon	**просити вибачення**	[pro'sɪtɪ 'wɪbatʃɛnja]
criticism	**критика** (f)	['krɪtɪka]
to criticize (vt)	**критикувати**	[krɪtɪku'watɪ]
accusation	**обвинувачення** (n)	[obwɪnu'watʃɛnja]
to accuse (vt)	**звинувачувати**	[zwɪnu'watʃuwatɪ]
revenge	**помста** (f)	['pɔmsta]
to revenge (vt)	**мстити**	['mstɪtɪ]
to pay back	**помститися**	[poms'tɪtɪsʲa]
disdain	**зневага** (f)	[znɛ'waɣa]
to despise (vt)	**зневажати**	[znɛwa'ʒatɪ]
hatred, hate	**ненависть** (f)	[nɛ'nawɪstʲ]
to hate (vt)	**ненавидіти**	[nɛna'wɪditɪ]
nervous (adj)	**нервовий**	[nɛr'wɔwɪj]
to be nervous	**нервувати**	[nɛrwu'watɪ]
angry (mad)	**сердитий**	[sɛr'dɪtɪj]
to make angry	**розсердити**	[roz'sɛrdɪtɪ]
humiliation	**приниження** (n)	[prɪ'nɪʒɛnja]
to humiliate (vt)	**принижувати**	[prɪ'nɪʒuwatɪ]
to humiliate oneself	**принижуватись**	[prɪ'nɪʒuwatɪsʲ]
shock	**шок** (m)	[ʃok]
to shock (vt)	**шокувати**	[ʃoku'watɪ]
trouble (annoyance)	**неприємність** (f)	[nɛprɪ'ɛmnistʲ]
unpleasant (adj)	**неприємний**	[nɛprɪ'ɛmnɪj]
fear (dread)	**страх** (m)	[strah]
terrible (storm, heat)	**страшний**	['straʃnɪj]
scary (e.g., ~ story)	**страшний**	['straʃnɪj]
horror	**жах** (m)	[ʒah]
awful (crime, news)	**жахливий**	[ʒah'lɪwɪj]
to cry (weep)	**плакати**	['plakatɪ]
to start crying	**заплакати**	[zap'lakatɪ]
tear	**сльоза** (f)	[slɜ'za]
fault	**вина** (f)	[wɪ'na]
guilt (feeling)	**провина** (f)	[pro'wɪna]
dishonor (disgrace)	**ганьба** (f)	[ɣanʲ'ba]
protest	**протест** (m)	[pro'tɛst]
stress	**стрес** (m)	[strɛs]
to disturb (vt)	**заважати**	[zawa'ʒatɪ]

to be furious	лютувати	[lytu'watɪ]
mad, angry (adj)	злий	['zlɪj]
to end (~ a relationship)	припиняти	[prɪpɪ'ɲatɪ]
to swear (at sb)	лаятися	['lajatɪsʲa]

to be scared	лякатися	[ʎa'katɪsʲa]
to hit (strike with hand)	ударити	[u'darɪtɪ]
to fight (vi)	битися	['bɪtɪsʲa]

to settle (a conflict)	урегулювати	[urɛɣuly'watɪ]
discontented (adj)	незадоволений	[nɛzado'wɔlɛnɪj]
furious (adj)	розлючений	[roz'lytʃɛnɪj]

| It's not good! | Це недобре! | [ʦɛ nɛ'dɔbrɛ] |
| It's bad! | Це погано! | [ʦɛ po'ɣano] |

Medicine

71. Diseases

sickness	хвороба (f)	[hwo'rɔbɑ]
to be sick	хворіти	[hwo'ritɪ]
health	здоров'я (n)	[zdo'rɔwʰjɑ]
runny nose (coryza)	нежить (m)	['nɛʒɪtʲ]
angina	ангіна (f)	[ɑ'ɲinɑ]
cold (illness)	застуда (f)	[zɑs'tudɑ]
to catch a cold	застудитися	[zɑstu'dɪtɪsʲɑ]
bronchitis	бронхіт (m)	[bron'hit]
pneumonia	запалення (n) легенів	[zɑ'pɑlɛɲɑ lɛ'ɣɛniw]
flu, influenza	грип (m)	[ɣrɪp]
near-sighted (adj)	короткозорий	[korotko'zɔrɪj]
far-sighted (adj)	далекозорий	[dɑlɛko'zɔrɪj]
strabismus (crossed eyes)	косоокість (f)	[koso'ɔkistʲ]
cross-eyed (adj)	косоокий	[koso'ɔkɪj]
cataract	катаракта (f)	[kɑtɑ'rɑktɑ]
glaucoma	глаукома (f)	[ɣlɑu'kɔmɑ]
stroke	інсульт (m)	[in'suʎt]
heart attack	інфаркт (m)	[in'fɑrkt]
myocardial infarction	інфаркт (m) міокарду	[in'fɑrkt mio'kɑrdu]
paralysis	параліч (m)	[pɑrɑ'litʃ]
to paralyze (vt)	паралізувати	[pɑrɑlizu'wɑtɪ]
allergy	алергія (f)	[ɑlɛr'ɣijɑ]
asthma	астма (f)	['ɑstmɑ]
diabetes	діабет (m)	[diɑ'bɛt]
toothache	зубний біль (m)	[zub'nɪj biʎ]
caries	карієс (m)	['kɑriɛs]
diarrhea	діарея (f)	[diɑ'rɛjɑ]
constipation	запор (m)	[zɑ'pɔr]
stomach upset	розлад (m) шлунку	['rɔzlɑd 'ʃluŋku]
food poisoning	отруєння (n)	[ot'ruɛɲɑ]
to have a food poisoning	отруїтись	[otru'jitɪsʲ]
arthritis	артрит (m)	[ɑrt'rɪt]
rickets	рахіт (m)	[rɑ'hit]
rheumatism	ревматизм (m)	[rɛwmɑ'tɪzm]

atherosclerosis	атеросклероз (m)	[atɛroskle'rɔz]
gastritis	гастрит (m)	[ɣast'rɪt]
appendicitis	апендицит (m)	[apɛndɪ'ʦɪt]
cholecystitis	холецистит (m)	[holɛʦɪs'tɪt]
ulcer	виразка (f)	['wɪrazka]
measles	кір (m)	[kir]
German measles	краснуха (f)	[kras'nuha]
jaundice	жовтуха (f)	[ʒow'tuha]
hepatitis	гепатит (m)	[ɣɛpa'tɪt]
schizophrenia	шизофренія (f)	[ʃɪzofrɛ'nija]
rabies (hydrophobia)	сказ (m)	[skaz]
neurosis	невроз (m)	[nɛw'rɔz]
concussion	струс (m) мозку	[strus 'mɔzku]
cancer	рак (m)	[rak]
sclerosis	склероз (m)	[skle'rɔz]
multiple sclerosis	розсіяний склероз (m)	[roz'sijanɪj skle'rɔz]
alcoholism	алкоголізм (m)	[alkoɣo'lizm]
alcoholic (n)	алкоголік (m)	[alko'ɣolik]
syphilis	сифіліс (m)	['sɪfilis]
AIDS	СНІД (m)	[snid]
tumor	пухлина (f)	[puh'lɪna]
malignant (adj)	злоякісна	[zlo'jakisna]
benign (adj)	доброякісний	[dobro'jakisnɪj]
fever	гарячка (f)	[ɣa'rʲaʧka]
malaria	малярія (f)	[maʎa'rija]
gangrene	гангрена (f)	[ɣaŋ'rɛna]
seasickness	морська хвороба (f)	[morsʲ'ka hwo'rɔba]
epilepsy	епілепсія (f)	[ɛpi'lɛpsija]
epidemic	епідемія (f)	[ɛpi'dɛmija]
typhus	тиф (m)	[tɪf]
tuberculosis	туберкульоз (m)	[tubɛrku'lʲɔz]
cholera	холера (f)	[ho'lɛra]
plague (bubonic ~)	чума (f)	[ʧu'ma]

72. Symptoms. Treatments. Part 1

symptom	симптом (m)	[sɪmp'tɔm]
temperature	температура (f)	[tɛmpɛra'tura]
high temperature	висока температура (f)	[wɪ'sɔka tɛmpɛra'tura]
pulse	пульс (m)	[puʎs]
giddiness	запаморочення (n)	[za'pamoroʧɛŋja]
hot (adj)	гарячий	[ɣa'rʲaʧɪj]

| shivering | озноб (m) | [oz'nɔb] |
| pale (e.g., ~ face) | блідий | [bli'dɪj] |

cough	кашель (m)	['kaʃɛʎ]
to cough (vi)	кашляти	['kaʃʎatɪ]
to sneeze (vi)	чхати	['ʧhatɪ]
faint	непритомність (f)	[nɛprɪ'tɔmnistʲ]
to faint (vi)	знепритомніти	[znɛprɪ'tɔmnitɪ]

bruise (hématome)	синець (m)	[sɪ'nɛts]
bump (lump)	гуля (f)	['ɣuʎa]
to bruise oneself	ударитись	[u'darɪtɪsʲ]
bruise (contusion)	забите місце (n)	[za'bɪtɛ 'mistsɛ]
to get bruised	забитися	[za'bɪtɪsʲa]

to limp (vi)	кульгати	[kuʎ'ɣatɪ]
dislocation	вивих (m)	['wɪwɪh]
to dislocate (vt)	вивихнути	['wɪwɪhnutɪ]
fracture	перелом (m)	[pɛrɛ'lɔm]
to have a fracture	дістати перелом	[dis'tatɪ pɛrɛ'lɔm]

cut (e.g., paper ~)	поріз (m)	[po'riz]
to cut oneself	порізатися	[po'rizatɪsʲa]
bleeding	кровотеча (f)	[krowo'tɛʧa]

| burn (injury) | опік (m) | ['ɔpik] |
| to scald oneself | обпектися | [obpɛk'tɪsʲa] |

to prick (vt)	уколоти	[uko'lɔtɪ]
to prick oneself	уколотися	[uko'lɔtɪsʲa]
to injure (vt)	пошкодити	[poʃ'kɔdɪtɪ]
injury	ушкодження (n)	[uʃ'kɔdʒɛnja]
wound	рана (f)	['rana]
trauma	травма (f)	['trawma]

to be delirious	марити	['marɪtɪ]
to stutter (vi)	заїкатися	[zajɪ'katɪsʲa]
sunstroke	сонячний удар (m)	['sɔnaʧnɪj u'dar]

73. Symptoms. Treatments. Part 2

| pain | біль (m) | [biʎ] |
| splinter (in foot, etc.) | скалка (f) | ['skalka] |

sweat (perspiration)	піт (m)	[pit]
to sweat (perspire)	спітніти	[spit'nitɪ]
vomiting	блювота (f)	[bly'wɔta]
convulsions	судома (f)	[su'dɔma]
pregnant (adj)	вагітна	[wa'ɣitna]
to be born	народитися	[naro'dɪtɪsʲa]

delivery, labor	пологи (pl)	[po'lɔɣɪ]
to deliver (~ a baby)	народжувати	[naˈrɔdʒuwatɪ]
abortion	аборт (m)	[a'bɔrt]
breathing, respiration	дихання (n)	['dɪhaɲa]
inhalation	вдих (m)	[wdɪh]
exhalation	видих (m)	['wɪdɪh]
to exhale (vi)	видихнути	['wɪdɪhnutɪ]
to inhale (vi)	зробити вдих	[zrɔ'bɪtɪ wdɪh]
disabled person	інвалід (m)	[inwa'lid]
cripple	каліка (m)	[ka'lika]
drug addict	наркоман (m)	[narkɔ'man]
deaf (adj)	глухий (m)	[ɣlu'hɪj]
dumb, mute	німий (m)	[ni'mɪj]
deaf-and-dumb (adj)	глухонімий (m)	[ɣluhoni'mɪj]
mad, insane (adj)	божевільний	[bɔʒɛ'wiʎnɪj]
madman	божевільний (m)	[bɔʒɛ'wiʎnɪj]
madwoman	божевільна (f)	[bɔʒɛ'wiʎna]
to go insane	збожеволіти	[zbɔʒɛ'wɔlitɪ]
gene	ген (m)	[ɣɛn]
immunity	імунітет (m)	[imuni'tɛt]
hereditary (adj)	спадковий	[spad'kɔwɪj]
congenital (adj)	вроджений	['wrɔdʒɛnɪj]
virus	вірус (m)	['wirus]
microbe	мікроб (m)	[mik'rɔb]
bacterium	бактерія (f)	[bak'tɛrija]
infection	інфекція (f)	[in'fɛktsija]

74. Symptoms. Treatments. Part 3

hospital	лікарня (f)	[li'karɲa]
patient	пацієнт (m)	[patsi'ɛnt]
diagnosis	діагноз (m)	[di'aɣnoz]
cure	лікування (n)	[liku'waɲa]
medical treatment	лікування (n)	[liku'waɲa]
to get treatment	лікуватися	[liku'watɪsʲa]
to treat (vt)	лікувати	[liku'watɪ]
to nurse (look after)	доглядати	[dɔɣʎa'datɪ]
care (nursing ~)	догляд (m)	['dɔɣʎad]
operation, surgery	операція (f)	[opɛ'ratsija]
to bandage (head, limb)	перев'язати	[pɛrɛwʲja'zatɪ]
bandaging	перев'язка (f)	[pɛrɛwʰ'jazka]
vaccination	щеплення (n)	['ɕɛplɛɲa]

to vaccinate (vt)	робити щеплення	[ro'bɪtɪ 'ɕɛplɛnja]
injection, shot	ін'єкція (f)	[inʰ'ɛktsija]
to give an injection	робити укол	[ro'bɪtɪ u'kɔl]

amputation	ампутація (f)	[ampu'tatsija]
to amputate (vt)	ампутувати	[amputu'watɪ]
coma	кома (f)	['kɔma]
to be in a coma	бути в комі	['bʊtɪ w 'kɔmi]
intensive care	реанімація (f)	[rɛani'matsija]

to recover (~ from flu)	видужувати	[wɪ'duʒuwatɪ]
state (patient's ~)	стан (m)	[stan]
consciousness	свідомість (f)	[swi'dɔmistʲ]
memory (faculty)	пам'ять (f)	['pamʰjatʲ]

to extract (tooth)	видалити	['wɪdalɪtɪ]
filling	пломба (f)	['plɔmba]
to fill (a tooth)	пломбувати	[plombu'watɪ]

| hypnosis | гіпноз (m) | [ɣip'nɔz] |
| to hypnotize (vt) | гіпнотизувати | [ɣipnotɪzu'watɪ] |

75. Doctors

doctor	лікар (m)	['likar]
nurse	медсестра (f)	[mɛdsɛst'ra]
private physician	особистий лікар (m)	[oso'bɪstɪj 'likar]

dentist	дантист (m)	[dan'tɪst]
ophthalmologist	окуліст (m)	[oku'list]
internist	терапевт (m)	[tɛra'pɛwt]
surgeon	хірург (m)	[hi'rurɣ]

psychiatrist	психіатр (m)	[psɪhi'atr]
pediatrician	педіатр (m)	[pɛdi'atr]
psychologist	психолог (m)	[psɪ'hɔloɣ]
gynecologist	гінеколог (m)	[ɣinɛ'kɔloɣ]
cardiologist	кардіолог (m)	[kardi'ɔloɣ]

76. Medicine. Drugs. Accessories

medicine, drug	ліки (pl)	['likɪ]
remedy	засіб (m)	['zasib]
to prescribe (vt)	прописати	[propɪ'satɪ]
prescription	рецепт (m)	[rɛ'tsɛpt]

| tablet, pill | пігулка (f) | [pi'ɣulka] |
| ointment | мазь (f) | [mazʲ] |

ampule	ампула (f)	['ampula]
mixture	мікстура (f)	[miks'tura]
syrup	сироп (m)	[sɪ'rɔp]
pill	пілюля (f)	[pi'lyʎa]
powder	порошок (m)	[poro'ʃɔk]

bandage	бинт (m)	[bɪnt]
cotton wool	вата (f)	['wata]
iodine	йод (m)	[jod]

Band-Aid	лейкопластир (m)	[lɛjkop'lastɪr]
eyedropper	піпетка (f)	[pi'pɛtka]
thermometer	градусник (m)	['ɣradusnɪk]
syringe	шприц (m)	[ʃprɪts]

| wheelchair | коляска (f) | [ko'ʎaska] |
| crutches | милиці (pl) | ['mɪlɪtsi] |

painkiller	знеболювальне (n)	[znɛ'bɔlywaʎnɛ]
laxative	проносне (n)	[pronos'nɛ]
spirit (ethanol)	спирт (m)	[spɪrt]
medicinal herbs	трава (f)	[tra'wa]
herbal (~ tea)	трав'яний	[trawʰja'nɪj]

77. Smoking. Tobacco products

tobacco	тютюн (m)	[ty'tyn]
cigarette	цигарка (f)	[tsɪ'ɣarka]
cigar	сигара (f)	[sɪ'ɣara]
pipe	люлька (f)	['lyʎka]
pack (of cigarettes)	пачка (f)	['patʃka]

matches	сірники (pl)	[sirnɪ'kɪ]
matchbox	сірникова коробка (f)	[sirnɪ'kɔwa ko'rɔbka]
lighter	запальничка (f)	[zapaʎ'nɪtʃka]
ashtray	попільниця (f)	[popiʎ'nɪtsʲa]
cigarette case	портсигар (m)	[portsɪ'ɣar]

| cigarette holder | мундштук (m) | [mundʃ'tuk] |
| filter (cigarette tip) | фільтр (m) | ['fiʎtr] |

| to smoke (vi, vt) | палити | [pa'lɪtɪ] |
| to light a cigarette | запалити | [zapa'lɪtɪ] |

| smoking | паління (n) | [pa'linja] |
| smoker | курець (m) | [ku'rɛts] |

stub, butt (of cigarette)	недопалок (m)	[nɛdo'palok]
smoke, fumes	дим (m)	[dɪm]
ash	попіл (m)	['pɔpil]

HUMAN HABITAT

City

78. City. Life in the city

city, town	місто (n)	['misto]
capital city	столиця (f)	[stoˈlɪtsʲa]
village	село (n)	[sɛˈlɔ]
city map	план (m) міста	[plan ˈmista]
downtown	центр (m) міста	[tsɛntr ˈmista]
suburb	передмістя (n)	[pɛrɛdˈmistʲa]
suburban (adj)	приміський	[prɪmisʲˈkɪj]
outskirts	околиця (f)	[oˈkɔlɪtsʲa]
environs (suburbs)	околиці (pl)	[oˈkɔlɪtsi]
city block	квартал (m)	[kwarˈtal]
residential block	житловий квартал (m)	[ʒɪtloˈwɪj kwarˈtal]
traffic	рух (m)	[ruh]
traffic lights	світлофор (m)	[switloˈfɔr]
public transportation	міський транспорт (m)	[misʲˈkɪj ˈtransport]
intersection	перехрестя (n)	[pɛrɛhˈrɛstʲa]
crosswalk	перехід (m)	[pɛrɛˈhid]
pedestrian underpass	підземний перехід (m)	[piˈdzɛmnɪj pɛrɛˈhid]
to cross (vt)	переходити	[pɛrɛˈhɔdɪtɪ]
pedestrian	пішохід (m)	[piʃoˈhid]
sidewalk	тротуар (m)	[trotuˈar]
bridge	міст (m)	[mist]
bank (riverbank)	набережна (f)	[ˈnabɛrɛʒna]
fountain	фонтан (m)	[fonˈtan]
allée	алея (f)	[aˈlɛja]
park	парк (m)	[park]
boulevard	бульвар (m)	[buʎˈwar]
square	площа (f)	[ˈplɔɕa]
avenue (wide street)	проспект (m)	[prosˈpɛkt]
street	вулиця (f)	[ˈwulɪtsʲa]
side street	провулок (m)	[proˈwulok]
dead end	глухий кут (m)	[ɣluˈhɪj kut]
house	будинок (m)	[buˈdɪnok]
building	споруда (f)	[spoˈruda]

skyscraper	хмарочос (m)	[hmaro'tʃɔs]
facade	фасад (m)	[fa'sad]
roof	дах (m)	[dɑh]
window	вікно (n)	[wik'nɔ]
arch	арка (f)	['ɑrkɑ]
column	колона (f)	[ko'lɔnɑ]
corner	ріг (m)	[riɣ]

store window	вітрина (f)	[wit'rɪnɑ]
store sign	вивіска (f)	['wɪwiskɑ]
poster	афіша (f)	[a'fiʃa]
advertising poster	рекламний плакат (m)	[rɛk'lamnɪj pla'kat]
billboard	рекламний щит (m)	[rɛk'lamnɪj ɕit]

garbage, trash	сміття (n)	[smit'tʲa]
garbage can	урна (f)	['urnɑ]
to litter (vi)	смітити	[smi'tɪtɪ]
garbage dump	смітник (m)	[smit'nɪk]

phone booth	телефонна будка (f)	[tɛlɛ'fɔnɑ 'budkɑ]
lamppost	ліхтарний стовп (m)	[lih'tarnɪj stowp]
bench (park ~)	лавка (f)	['lawkɑ]

police officer	поліцейський (m)	[poli'tsɛjsʲkɪj]
police	поліція (f)	[po'litsija]
beggar	жебрак (m)	[ʒɛb'rak]
homeless, bum	безпритульний (m)	[bɛzprɪ'tuʎnɪj]

79. Urban institutions

store	магазин (m)	[maɣa'zɪn]
drugstore, pharmacy	аптека (f)	[ap'tɛkɑ]
optical store	оптика (f)	['ɔptɪkɑ]
shopping mall	торгівельний центр (m)	[torɣi'wɛʎnɪj 'tsɛntr]
supermarket	супермаркет (m)	[supɛr'markɛt]

bakery	булочна (f)	['bulotʃnɑ]
baker	пекар (m)	['pɛkar]
candy store	кондитерська (f)	[kon'dɪtɛrsʲka]
grocery store	бакалія (f)	[baka'lija]
butcher shop	м'ясний магазин (m)	[mʰjas'nɪj maɣa'zɪn]

| produce store | овочевий магазин (m) | [owo'tʃɛwɪj maɣa'zɪn] |
| market | ринок (m) | ['rɪnok] |

coffee house	кав'ярня (f)	[kawʰ'jarɲa]
restaurant	ресторан (m)	[rɛsto'ran]
pub	пивна (f)	[pɪw'na]
pizzeria	піцерія (f)	[pitsɛ'rija]
hair salon	перукарня (f)	[pɛru'karɲa]

post office	**пошта** (f)	[ˈpɔʃta]
dry cleaners	**хімчистка** (f)	[himˈtʃistka]
photo studio	**фотоательє** (n)	[fotoatɛˈʎjɛ]
shoe store	**взуттєвий магазин** (m)	[wzutˈtɛwij maɣaˈzin]
bookstore	**книгарня** (f)	[knɪˈɣarɲa]
sporting goods store	**спортивний магазин** (m)	[sporˈtɪwnij maɣaˈzin]
clothes repair	**ремонт** (m) **одягу**	[rɛˈmɔnt ˈɔdʲaɣu]
formal wear rental	**прокат** (m) **одягу**	[proˈkat ˈɔdʲaɣu]
movie rental store	**прокат** (m) **фільмів**	[proˈkat ˈfiʎmiw]
circus	**цирк** (m)	[ʦirk]
zoo	**зоопарк** (m)	[zoːˈpark]
movie theater	**кінотеатр** (m)	[kinotɛˈatr]
museum	**музей** (m)	[muˈzɛj]
library	**бібліотека** (f)	[biblioˈtɛka]
theater	**театр** (m)	[tɛˈatr]
opera	**опера** (f)	[ˈɔpɛra]
nightclub	**нічний клуб** (m)	[nitʃˈnij klub]
casino	**казино** (n)	[kazɪˈnɔ]
mosque	**мечеть** (f)	[mɛˈtʃɛtʲ]
synagogue	**синагога** (f)	[sɪnaˈɣɔɣa]
cathedral	**собор** (m)	[soˈbɔr]
temple	**храм** (m)	[hram]
church	**церква** (f)	[ˈʦɛrkwa]
college	**інститут** (m)	[instɪˈtut]
university	**університет** (m)	[uniwɛrsɪˈtɛt]
school	**школа** (f)	[ˈʃkɔla]
prefecture	**префектура** (f)	[prɛfɛkˈtura]
city hall	**мерія** (f)	[ˈmɛrija]
hotel	**готель** (m)	[ɣoˈtɛʎ]
bank	**банк** (m)	[baŋk]
embassy	**посольство** (n)	[poˈsɔʎstwo]
travel agency	**турагентство** (n)	[turaˈɣɛntstwo]
information office	**довідкове бюро** (n)	[dowidˈkɔwɛ byˈrɔ]
money exchange	**обмінний пункт** (m)	[obˈminij puŋkt]
subway	**метро** (n)	[mɛtˈrɔ]
hospital	**лікарня** (f)	[liˈkarɲa]
gas station	**бензоколонка** (f)	[bɛnzokoˈlɔŋka]
parking lot	**стоянка** (f)	[stoˈjaŋka]

80. Signs

store sign	вивіска (f)	['wiwiska]
notice (written text)	напис (m)	['napis]
poster	плакат (m)	[pla'kat]
direction sign	дороговказ (m)	[doroɣow'kaz]
arrow (sign)	стрілка (f)	['strilka]
caution	застереження (n)	[zastɛ'rɛʒɛnja]
warning sign	попередження (n)	[popɛ'rɛdʒɛnja]
to warn (vt)	попереджувати	[popɛ'rɛdʒuwati]
day off	вихідний день (m)	[wihid'nij dɛn]
timetable (schedule)	розклад (m)	['rozklad]
opening hours	години (pl) роботи	[ɣo'dini ro'boti]
WELCOME!	ЛАСКАВО ПРОСИМО!	[las'kawo 'prosimo]
ENTRANCE	ВХІД	[whid]
EXIT	ВИХІД	['wihid]
PUSH	ВІД СЕБЕ	[wid 'sɛbɛ]
PULL	ДО СЕБЕ	[do 'sɛbɛ]
OPEN	ВІДЧИНЕНО	[wid'tʃinɛno]
CLOSED	ЗАЧИНЕНО	[za'tʃinɛno]
WOMEN	ДЛЯ ЖІНОК	[dʎa ʒi'nok]
MEN	ДЛЯ ЧОЛОВІКІВ	[dʎa tʃolowi'kiw]
DISCOUNTS	ЗНИЖКИ	['zniʒki]
SALE	РОЗПРОДАЖ	[rozp'rodaʒ]
NEW!	НОВИНКА!	[no'winka]
FREE	БЕЗКОШТОВНО	[bɛzkoʃ'towno]
ATTENTION!	УВАГА!	[u'waɣa]
NO VACANCIES	МІСЦЬ НЕМАЄ	[mists nɛ'maɛ]
RESERVED	ЗАРЕЗЕРВОВАНО	[zarɛzɛr'wowano]
ADMINISTRATION	АДМІНІСТРАЦІЯ	[administ'ratsija]
STAFF ONLY	ТІЛЬКИ	['tiʎki
	ДЛЯ ПЕРСОНАЛУ	dʎa pɛrso'nalu]
BEWARE OF THE DOG!	ОБЕРЕЖНО! ЗЛИЙ ПЕС	[obɛrɛʒno zlij pɛs]
NO SMOKING	ПАЛИТИ ЗАБОРОНЕНО	[pa'liti zabo'ronɛno]
DO NOT TOUCH!	НЕ ТОРКАТИСЯ!	[nɛ tor'katisʲa]
DANGEROUS	НЕБЕЗПЕЧНО	[nɛbɛz'pɛtʃno]
DANGER	НЕБЕЗПЕКА	[nɛbɛz'pɛka]
HIGH TENSION	ВИСОКА НАПРУГА	[wi'soka nap'ruɣa]
NO SWIMMING!	КУПАТИСЯ	[ku'patisʲa
	ЗАБОРОНЕНО	zabo'ronɛno]
OUT OF ORDER	НЕ ПРАЦЮЄ	[nɛ pra'tsyɛ]

FLAMMABLE	ВОГНЕНЕБЕЗПЕЧНО	[woɣnɛnɛbɛz'pɛʧno]
FORBIDDEN	ЗАБОРОНЕНО	[zabo'rɔnɛno]
NO TRESPASSING!	ПРОХІД ЗАБОРОНЕНО	[pro'hid zabo'rɔnɛno]
WET PAINT	ПОФАРБОВАНО	[pofar'bɔwano]

81. Urban transportation

bus	автобус (m)	[aw'tɔbus]
streetcar	трамвай (m)	[tram'waj]
trolley	тролейбус (m)	[tro'lɛjbus]
route (of bus)	маршрут (m)	[marʃ'rut]
number (e.g., bus ~)	номер (m)	['nɔmɛr]

to go by ...	їхати на ...	['jihatı na]
to get on (~ the bus)	сісти	['sistı]
to get off ...	зійти	[zij'tı]

stop (e.g., bus ~)	зупинка (f)	[zu'pınka]
next stop	наступна зупинка (f)	[nas'tupna zu'pınka]
terminus	кінцева зупинка (f)	[kin'tsɛwa zu'pınka]
schedule	розклад (m)	['rɔzklad]
to wait (vt)	чекати	[ʧɛ'katı]

| ticket | квиток (m) | [kwı'tɔk] |
| fare | вартість (f) квитка | ['wartistʲ kwıt'ka] |

cashier (ticket seller)	касир (m)	[ka'sır]
ticket inspection	контроль (m)	[kont'rɔʎ]
conductor	контролер (m)	[kontro'lɛr]

to be late (for ...)	запізнюватися	[za'piznywatısʲa]
to miss (~ the train, etc.)	спізнитися	[spiz'nıtısʲa]
to be in a hurry	поспішати	[pospi'ʃatı]

taxi, cab	таксі (n)	[tak'si]
taxi driver	таксист (m)	[tak'sıst]
by taxi	на таксі	[na tak'si]
taxi stand	стоянка (n) таксі	[sto'janka tak'si]
to call a taxi	викликати таксі	['wıklıkatı tak'si]
to take a taxi	взяти таксі	['wzʲatı tak'si]

traffic	вуличний рух (m)	['wulıʧnıj ruh]
traffic jam	пробка (f)	['prɔbka]
rush hour	години (pl) пік	[ɣo'dını pik]
to park (vi)	паркуватися	[parku'watısʲa]
to park (vt)	паркувати	[parku'watı]
parking lot	стоянка (f)	[sto'janka]

| subway | метро (n) | [mɛt'rɔ] |
| station | станція (f) | ['stantsija] |

to take the subway	їхати в метро	['jihatı w mɛt'rɔ]
train	поїзд (m)	['pɔjızd]
train station	вокзал (m)	[wok'zal]

82. Sightseeing

monument	пам'ятник (m)	['pamʰjatnık]
fortress	фортеця (f)	[for'tɛtsʲa]
palace	палац (m)	[pa'lats]
castle	замок (m)	['zamok]
tower	вежа (f)	['wɛʒa]
mausoleum	мавзолей (m)	[mawzo'lɛj]

architecture	архітектура (f)	[arhitɛk'tura]
medieval (adj)	середньовічний	[sɛrɛdnɔ'witʃnıj]
ancient (adj)	старовинний	[staro'wınıj]
national (adj)	національний	[natsio'naʎnıj]
well-known (adj)	відомий	[wi'dɔmıj]

tourist	турист (m)	[tu'rıst]
guide (person)	гід (m)	[ɣid]
excursion, guided tour	екскурсія (f)	[ɛks'kursija]
to show (vt)	показувати	[po'kazuwatı]
to tell (vt)	розповідати	[rozpowi'datı]

to find (vt)	знайти	[znaj'tı]
to get lost (lose one's way)	загубитися	[zaɣu'bıtısʲa]
map (e.g., subway ~)	схема (f)	['shɛma]
map (e.g., city ~)	план (m)	[plan]

souvenir, gift	сувенір (m)	[suwɛ'nir]
gift shop	магазин (m) сувенірів	[maɣa'zın suwɛ'niriw]
to take pictures	фотографувати	[fotoɣrafu'watı]
to be photographed	фотографуватися	[fotoɣrafu'watısʲa]

83. Shopping

to buy (purchase)	купляти	[kup'ʎatı]
purchase	покупка (f)	[po'kupka]
to go shopping	робити покупки	[ro'bıtı po'kupkı]
shopping	шопінг (m)	['ʃopiŋ]

| to be open (ab. store) | працювати | [pratsy'watı] |
| to be closed | зачинитися | [zatʃı'nıtısʲa] |

footwear	взуття (n)	[wzut'tʲa]
clothes, clothing	одяг (m)	['ɔdʲaɣ]
cosmetics	косметика (f)	[kos'mɛtıka]

food products	продукти (pl)	[pro'duktɪ]
gift, present	подарунок (m)	[poda'runok]
salesman	продавець (m)	[proda'wɛts]
saleswoman	продавщиця (f)	[prodaw'çɪtsʲa]
check out, cash desk	каса (f)	['kasa]
mirror	дзеркало (n)	['dzɛrkalo]
counter (in shop)	прилавок (m)	[prɪ'lawok]
fitting room	примірочна (f)	[prɪ'mirotʃna]
to try on	приміряти	[prɪ'mirʲatɪ]
to fit (ab. dress, etc.)	пасувати	[pasu'watɪ]
to like (I like ...)	подобатися	[po'dobatɪsʲa]
price	ціна (f)	[tsi'na]
price tag	цінник (m)	['tsinɪk]
to cost (vt)	коштувати	['koʃtuwatɪ]
How much?	Скільки?	['skiʎkɪ]
discount	знижка (f)	['znɪʒka]
inexpensive (adj)	недорогий	[nɛdoro'ɣɪj]
cheap (adj)	дешевий	[dɛ'ʃɛwɪj]
expensive (adj)	дорогий	[doro'ɣɪj]
It's expensive	Це дорого.	[tsɛ 'dɔroɣo]
rental (n)	прокат (m)	[pro'kat]
to rent (~ a tuxedo)	взяти напрокат	['wzʲatɪ napro'kat]
credit	кредит (m)	[krɛ'dɪt]
on credit (adv)	в кредит (m)	[w krɛ'dɪt]

84. Money

money	гроші (pl)	['ɣrɔʃi]
currency exchange	обмін (m)	['ɔbmin]
exchange rate	курс (m)	[kurs]
ATM	банкомат (m)	[baŋko'mat]
coin	монета (f)	[mo'nɛta]
dollar	долар (m)	['dɔlar]
euro	євро (m)	['ɛwro]
lira	ліра (f)	['lira]
Deutschmark	марка (f)	['marka]
franc	франк (m)	['fraŋk]
pound sterling	фунт (m)	['funt]
yen	ієна (f)	[i'ɛna]
debt	борг (m)	['bɔrɣ]
debtor	боржник (m)	[borʒ'nɪk]

| to lend (money) | позичити | [po'zitʃıtı] |
| to borrow (vi, vt) | взяти в борг | ['wzʲatı w borɣ] |

bank	банк (m)	[baŋk]
account	рахунок (m)	[ra'hunok]
to deposit into the account	покласти на рахунок	[pok'lastı na ra'hunok]
to withdraw (vt)	зняти з рахунку	['zɲatı z ra'huŋku]

credit card	кредитна картка (f)	[krɛ'dıtna 'kartka]
cash	готівка (f)	[ɣo'tiwka]
check	чек (m)	[tʃɛk]
to write a check	виписати чек	['wıpısatı tʃɛk]
checkbook	чекова книжка (f)	['tʃɛkowa 'knıʒka]

wallet	гаманець (m)	[ɣama'nɛts]
change purse	гаманець (m)	[ɣama'nɛts]
billfold	портмоне (n)	[portmo'nɛ]
safe	сейф (m)	[sɛjf]

heir	спадкоємець (m)	[spadko'ɛmɛts]
inheritance	спадщина (n)	['spadɕına]
fortune (wealth)	статок (m)	['statok]

lease, rent	оренда (f)	[o'rɛnda]
rent money	квартирна плата (f)	[kwar'tırna 'plata]
to rent (sth from sb)	наймати	[naj'matı]

price	ціна (f)	[tsi'na]
cost	вартість (f)	['wartistʲ]
sum	сума (f)	['suma]

to spend (vt)	витрачати	[wıtra'tʃatı]
expenses	витрати (pl)	['wıtratı]
to economize (vi, vt)	економити	[ɛko'nɔmıtı]
economical	економний	[ɛko'nɔmnıj]

to pay (vi, vt)	платити	[pla'tıtı]
payment	оплата (f)	[op'lata]
change (give the ~)	решта (f)	['rɛʃta]

tax	податок (m)	[po'datok]
fine	штраф (m)	[ʃtraf]
to fine (vt)	штрафувати	[ʃtrafu'watı]

85. Post. Postal service

post office	пошта (f)	['pɔʃta]
mail (letters, etc.)	пошта (f)	['pɔʃta]
mailman	листоноша (m)	[lısto'nɔʃa]
opening hours	години (pl) роботи	[ɣo'dını ro'bɔtı]

letter	лист (m)	[lıst]
registered letter	рекомендований лист (m)	[rɛkomɛnʹdɔwanıj list]
postcard	листівка (f)	[lısʹtiwka]
telegram	телеграма (f)	[tɛlɛɣʹrama]
parcel	посилка (f)	[poʹsılka]
money transfer	грошовий переказ (m)	[ɣroʃoʹwıj pɛʹrɛkaz]
to receive (vt)	отримати	[otʹrımatı]
to send (vt)	відправити	[widpʹrawıtı]
sending	відправлення (n)	[widpʹrawlɛnja]
address	адреса (f)	[adʹrɛsa]
ZIP code	індекс (m)	[ʹindɛks]
sender	відправник (m)	[widpʹrawnık]
receiver, addressee	одержувач (m)	[oʹdɛrʒuwatʃ]
name	ім'я (n)	[imʰʹja]
family name	прізвище (n)	[ʹprizwıɕɛ]
rate (of postage)	тариф (m)	[taʹrıf]
standard (adj)	звичайний	[zwıʹtʃajnıj]
economical (adj)	економічний	[ɛkonoʹmitʃnıj]
weight	вага (f)	[waʹɣa]
to weigh up (vt)	важити	[ʹwaʒıtı]
envelope	конверт (m)	[konʹwɛrt]
postage stamp	марка (f)	[ʹmarka]

Dwelling. House. Home

86. House. Dwelling

house	**будинок** (m)	[bu'dınok]
at home (adv)	**вдома**	['wdɔma]
courtyard	**двір** (m)	[dwir]
fence	**грати** (pl)	['ɣratı]
brick (n)	**цегла** (f)	['ʦɛɣla]
brick (as adj)	**цегляний**	[ʦɛɣʎa'nıj]
stone (n)	**камінь** (m)	['kamıɲ]
stone (as adj)	**кам'яний**	[kam'ja'nıj]
concrete (n)	**бетон** (m)	[bɛ'tɔn]
concrete (as adj)	**бетонний**	[bɛ'tɔɲıj]
new (new-built)	**новий**	[no'wıj]
old (adj)	**старий**	[sta'rıj]
decrepit (house)	**старий, ветхий**	[sta'rıj], ['wɛthıj]
modern (adj)	**сучасний**	[su'ʧasnıj]
multistory (adj)	**багатоповерховий**	[baɣatopowɛr'hɔwıj]
high (adj)	**високий**	[wı'sɔkıj]
floor, story	**поверх** (m)	['pɔwɛrh]
single-story (adj)	**одноповерховий**	[odnopowɛr'hɔwıj]
ground floor	**нижній поверх** (m)	['nıʒnij 'pɔwɛrh]
top floor	**верхній поверх** (m)	['wɛrhnij 'pɔwɛrh]
roof	**дах** (m)	[dɑh]
chimney (stack)	**труба** (f)	[tru'ba]
roof tiles	**черепиця** (f)	[ʧɛrɛ'pıtsʲa]
tiled (adj)	**черепичний**	[ʧɛrɛ'pıʧnıj]
loft (attic)	**горище** (n)	[ɣo'rıɕɛ]
window	**вікно** (n)	[wik'nɔ]
glass	**скло** (n)	[sklo]
window ledge	**підвіконня** (n)	[pidwi'kɔnja]
shutters	**віконниці** (pl)	[wi'kɔnıtsi]
wall	**стіна** (f)	[sti'na]
balcony	**балкон** (m)	[bal'kɔn]
downspout	**ринва** (f)	['rınwa]
upstairs (to be ~)	**нагорі**	[naɣo'ri]
to go upstairs	**підніматися**	[pidni'matısʲa]
to come down	**спускатися**	[spus'katısʲa]
to move (to new premises)	**переїздити**	[pɛrɛjız'dıtı]

87. House. Entrance. Lift

entrance	під'їзд (m)	[pidʰ'jɪzd]
stairs (stairway)	сходи (pl)	['shɔdɪ]
steps	сходинки (pl)	['shɔdɪŋkɪ]
banisters	поруччя (pl)	[po'ruʧʲa]
lobby (hotel ~)	хол (m)	[hol]
mailbox	поштова скринька (f)	[poʃ'towa 'skrɪŋka]
trash container	бак (m) для сміття	[bak dʎa smit'tʲa]
trash chute	сміттєпровід (m)	[smittɛp'rɔwid]
elevator	ліфт (m)	[lift]
freight elevator	вантажний ліфт (m)	[wan'taʒnɪj lift]
elevator cage	кабіна (f)	[ka'bina]
to take the elevator	їхати в ліфті	['jihatɪ w 'lifti]
apartment	квартира (f)	[kwar'tɪra]
residents, inhabitants	мешканці (pl)	['mɛʃkanʦi]
neighbor (masc.)	сусід (m)	[su'sid]
neighbor (fem.)	сусідка (f)	[su'sidka]
neighbors	сусіди (pl)	[su'sidɪ]

88. House. Electricity

electricity	електрика (f)	[ɛ'lɛktrɪka]
light bulb	лампочка (f)	['lampoʧka]
switch	вимикач (m)	[wɪmɪ'kaʧ]
fuse	пробка (f)	['prɔbka]
cable, wire (electric ~)	провід (m)	['prɔwid]
wiring	проводка (f)	[pro'wodka]
electricity meter	лічильник (m)	[li'ʧiʎnɪk]
readings	показання (n)	[poka'zanja]

89. House. Doors. Locks

door	двері (pl)	['dwɛri]
vehicle gate	брама (f)	['brama]
handle, doorknob	ручка (f)	['ruʧka]
to unlock (unbolt)	відкрити	[widk'rɪtɪ]
to open (vt)	відкривати	[widkrɪ'watɪ]
to close (vt)	закривати	[zakrɪ'watɪ]
key	ключ (m)	[klyʧ]
bunch (of keys)	в'язка (f)	['wʰjazka]
to creak (door hinge)	скрипіти	[skrɪ'pitɪ]

creak	скрипіння (n)	[skrɪˈpinja]
hinge (of door)	петля (f)	[pɛtˈʎa]
doormat	килимок (m)	[kɪlɪˈmɔk]

door lock	замок (m)	[zaˈmɔk]
keyhole	замкова щілина (f)	[zamˈkɔwa ɕiˈlɪna]
bolt (sliding bar)	засув (m)	[ˈzasuw]
door latch	засувка (f)	[ˈzasuwka]
padlock	навісний замок (m)	[nawisˈnɪj zaˈmɔk]

to ring (~ the door bell)	дзвонити	[dʒwoˈnɪtɪ]
ringing (sound)	дзвінок (m)	[dʒwiˈnɔk]
doorbell	дзвінок (m)	[dʒwiˈnɔk]
doorbell button	кнопка (f)	[ˈknɔpka]
knock (at the door)	стукіт (m)	[ˈstukit]
to knock (vi)	стукати	[ˈstukatɪ]

code	код (m)	[kod]
code lock	кодовий замок (m)	[ˈkɔdowɪj zaˈmɔk]
door phone	домофон (m)	[domoˈfɔn]
number (on the door)	номер (m)	[ˈnɔmɛr]
doorplate	табличка (f)	[tabˈlɪʧka]
peephole	вічко (n)	[ˈwiʧko]

90. Country house

village	село (n)	[sɛˈlɔ]
vegetable garden	город (m)	[ɣoˈrɔd]
fence	паркан (m)	[parˈkan]

| picket fence | тин (m) | [tɪn] |
| wicket gate | хвіртка (f) | [ˈhwirtka] |

| granary | комора (f) | [koˈmɔra] |
| cellar | льох (m) | [ˈlɔh] |

| shed (in garden) | сарай (m) | [saˈraj] |
| well (water) | криниця (f) | [krɪˈnɪtsʲa] |

| stove (wood-fired ~) | піч (f) | [piʧ] |
| to stoke the stove | палити | [paˈlɪtɪ] |

| firewood | дрова (pl) | [ˈdrɔwa] |
| log (firewood) | поліно (n) | [poˈlino] |

| veranda, stoop | веранда (f) | [wɛˈranda] |
| terrace (patio) | тераса (f) | [tɛˈrasa] |

| front steps | ганок (m) | [ˈɣanok] |
| swing (hanging seat) | гойдалка (f) | [ˈɣɔjdalka] |

91. Villa. Mansion

country house	будинок (m) за містом	[bu'dınok za 'mistom]
villa (by sea)	вілла (f)	['willa]
wing (of building)	крило (n)	[krı'lɔ]

garden	сад (m)	[sad]
park	парк (m)	[park]
tropical greenhouse	оранжерея (f)	[oranʒɛ'rɛja]
to look after (garden, etc.)	доглядати	[doɣʎa'datı]

swimming pool	басейн (m)	[ba'sɛjn]
gym	спортивний зал (m)	[spor'tıwnıj 'zal]
tennis court	тенісний корт (m)	['tɛnisnıj 'kort]
home theater room	кінотеатр (m)	[kinotɛ'atr]
garage	гараж (m)	[ɣa'raʒ]

| private property | приватна власність (f) | [prı'watna 'wlasnistʲ] |
| private land | приватні володіння (pl) | [prı'watni wolo'dinʲja] |

| warning (caution) | попередження (n) | [popɛ'rɛdʒɛnʲja] |
| warning sign | попереджувальний напис (m) | [popɛ'rɛdʒuwaʎnıj 'napıs] |

security	охорона (f)	[oho'rɔna]
security guard	охоронник (m)	[oho'rɔnık]
burglar alarm	сигналізація (f)	[sıɣnali'zatsija]

92. Castle. Palace

castle	замок (m)	['zamok]
palace	палац (m)	[pa'lats]
fortress	фортеця (f)	[for'tɛtsʲa]

wall (round castle)	стіна (f)	[sti'na]
tower	вежа (f)	['wɛʒa]
keep, donjon	головна вежа (f)	[ɣolow'na 'wɛʒa]

portcullis	підйомна брама (f)	[pid'jomna 'brama]
underground passage	підземний хід (m)	[pi'dzɛmnıj hid]
moat	рів (m)	[riw]

| chain | ланцюг (m) | [lan'tsyɣ] |
| arrow loop | бійниця (f) | [bij'nıtsʲa] |

magnificent (adj)	пишний	['pıʃnıj]
majestic (adj)	величний	[wɛ'lıtʃnıj]
impregnable (adj)	неприступний	[nɛprıs'tupnıj]
medieval (adj)	середньовічний	[sɛrɛdnʲ'witʃnıj]

93. Apartment

apartment	квартира (f)	[kwar'tɪra]
room	кімната (f)	[kim'nata]
bedroom	спальня (f)	['spaʎɲa]
dining room	їдальня (f)	['jidaʎɲa]
living room	вітальня (f)	[wi'taʎɲa]
study (home office)	кабінет (m)	[kabi'nɛt]
entry room	передпокій (m)	[pɛrɛd'pokij]
bathroom	ванна кімната (f)	['waɲa kim'nata]
half bath	туалет (m)	[tua'lɛt]
ceiling	стеля (f)	['stɛʎa]
floor	підлога (f)	[pid'loɣa]
corner	куток (m)	[ku'tɔk]

94. Apartment. Cleaning

to clean (vi, vt)	прибирати	[prɪbɪ'ratɪ]
to put away (to stow)	прибирати	[prɪbɪ'ratɪ]
dust	пил (m)	[pɪl]
dusty (adj)	курний	[kur'nɪj]
to dust (vt)	витирати пил	[wɪtɪ'ratɪ pɪl]
vacuum cleaner	пилосос (m)	[pɪlo'sɔs]
to vacuum (vt)	пилососити	[pɪlo'sɔsɪtɪ]
to sweep (vi, vt)	підмітати	[pidmi'tatɪ]
sweepings	сміття (n)	[smit'tʲa]
order	лад (m)	[lad]
disorder, mess	безлад (m)	['bɛzlad]
mop	швабра (f)	['ʃwabra]
dust cloth	ганчірка (f)	[ɣan'tʃirka]
broom	віник (m)	['winɪk]
dustpan	совок (m) для сміття	[so'wɔk dʎa smit'tʲa]

95. Furniture. Interior

furniture	меблі (pl)	['mɛbli]
table	стіл (m)	[stil]
chair	стілець (m)	[sti'lɛts]
bed	ліжко (n)	['liʒko]
couch, sofa	диван (m)	[dɪ'wan]
armchair	крісло (n)	['krislo]
bookcase	шафа (f)	['ʃafa]
shelf	полиця (f)	[po'lɪtsʲa]

set of shelves	етажерка (f)	[ɛtɑ'ʒɛrkɑ]
wardrobe	шафа (f)	['ʃɑfɑ]
coat rack	вішалка (f)	['wiʃɑlkɑ]
coat stand	вішак (m)	[wi'ʃɑk]

| dresser | комод (m) | [ko'mɔd] |
| coffee table | журнальний столик (m) | [ʒur'nɑʎnij 'stɔlɪk] |

mirror	дзеркало (n)	['dzɛrkɑlo]
carpet	килим (m)	['kɪlɪm]
rug, small carpet	килимок (m)	[kɪlɪ'mɔk]

fireplace	камін (m)	[kɑ'min]
candle	свічка (f)	['switʃkɑ]
candlestick	свічник (m)	[switʃ'nɪk]

drapes	штори (pl)	['ʃtɔrɪ]
wallpaper	шпалери (pl)	[ʃpɑ'lɛrɪ]
blinds (jalousie)	жалюзі (pl)	['ʒɑlyzi]

table lamp	настільна лампа (f)	[nɑs'tiʎnɑ 'lɑmpɑ]
wall lamp (sconce)	світильник (m)	[swi'tɪʎnɪk]
floor lamp	торшер (m)	[tor'ʃɛr]
chandelier	люстра (f)	['lystrɑ]

leg (of chair, table)	ніжка (f)	['niʒkɑ]
armrest	підлокітник (m)	[pidlo'kitnɪk]
back (backrest)	спинка (f)	['spɪŋkɑ]
drawer	шухляда (f)	[ʃuh'ʎɑdɑ]

96. Bedding

bedclothes	білизна (f)	[bi'lɪznɑ]
pillow	подушка (f)	[po'duʃkɑ]
pillowcase	наволочка (f)	['nɑwolotʃkɑ]
blanket (comforter)	ковдра (f)	['kɔwdrɑ]
sheet	простирадло (n)	[prostɪ'rɑdlo]
bedspread	покривало (n)	[pokrɪ'wɑlo]

97. Kitchen

kitchen	кухня (f)	['kuhɲɑ]
gas	газ (m)	[ɣɑz]
gas cooker	плита (f) газова	[plɪ'tɑ 'ɣɑzowɑ]
electric cooker	плита (f) електрична	[plɪ'tɑ ɛlɛkt'rɪtʃnɑ]
oven	духовка (f)	[du'hɔwkɑ]
microwave oven	мікрохвильова піч (f)	[mikrohwɪlɜ'wɑ pitʃ]
refrigerator	холодильник (m)	[holo'dɪʎnɪk]

freezer	морозильник (m)	[moro'ziʎnɪk]
dishwasher	посудомийна машина (f)	[posudo'mɪjna maˈʃɪna]
meat grinder	м'ясорубка (f)	[mʰjaso'rubka]
juicer	соковижималка (f)	[sokowɪʒɪ'malka]
toaster	тостер (m)	['tɔstɛr]
mixer	міксер (m)	['miksɛr]
coffee maker	кавоварка (f)	[kawo'warka]
coffee pot	кавник (m)	[kaw'nɪk]
coffee grinder	кавомолка (f)	[kawo'mɔlka]
kettle	чайник (m)	['ʧajnɪk]
teapot	заварник (m)	[za'warnɪk]
lid	кришка (f)	['krɪʃka]
tea strainer	ситечко (n)	['sɪtɛʧko]
spoon	ложка (f)	['lɔʒka]
teaspoon	чайна ложка (f)	['ʧajna 'lɔʒka]
tablespoon	столова ложка (f)	[sto'lɔwa 'lɔʒka]
fork	виделка (f)	[wɪ'dɛlka]
knife	ніж (m)	[niʒ]
tableware (dishes)	посуд (m)	['pɔsud]
plate (dinner ~)	тарілка (f)	[ta'rilka]
saucer	блюдце (n)	['blydtsɛ]
shot glass	чарка (f)	['ʧarka]
glass (~ of water)	склянка (f)	['skʎaŋka]
cup	чашка (f)	['ʧaʃka]
sugar bowl	цукорниця (f)	['tsukornɪtsʲa]
salt shaker	сільничка (f)	[siʎ'nɪʧka]
pepper shaker	перечниця (f)	['pɛrɛʧnɪtsʲa]
butter dish	маслянка (f)	['masʎaŋka]
saucepan	каструля (f)	[kast'ruʎa]
frying pan	сковорідка (f)	[skowo'ridka]
ladle	черпак (m)	[ʧɛr'pak]
colander	друшляк (m)	[druʃ'ʎak]
tray	піднос (m)	[pid'nɔs]
bottle	пляшка (f)	['pʎaʃka]
jar (glass)	банка (f)	['baŋka]
can	банка (f)	['baŋka]
bottle opener	відкривачка (f)	[widkrɪ'waʧka]
can opener	відкривачка (f)	[widkrɪ'waʧka]
corkscrew	штопор (m)	['ʃtɔpor]
filter	фільтр (m)	['fiʎtr]
to filter (vt)	фільтрувати	[fiʎtru'watɪ]
trash	сміття (n)	[smit'tʲa]
trash can	відро (n) для сміття	[widro dʎa smit'tʲa]

98. Bathroom

bathroom	ванна кімната (f)	['waŋa kim'nata]
water	вода (f)	[wo'da]
tap, faucet	кран (m)	[kran]
hot water	гаряча вода (f)	[ɣa'rʲatʃa wo'da]
cold water	холодна вода (f)	[ho'lɔdna wo'da]
toothpaste	зубна паста (f)	[zub'na 'pasta]
to brush one's teeth	чистити зуби	['tʃistiti 'zubi]
to shave (vi)	голитися	[ɣo'litisʲa]
shaving foam	піна (f) для гоління	['pina dʲʌa ɣo'linʲa]
razor	бритва (f)	['britwa]
to wash (one's hands, etc.)	мити	['miti]
to take a bath	митися	['mitisʲa]
shower	душ (m)	[duʃ]
to take a shower	приймати душ	[prij'mati duʃ]
bathtub	ванна (f)	['waŋa]
toilet (toilet bowl)	унітаз (m)	[uni'taz]
sink (washbasin)	раковина (f)	['rakowina]
soap	мило (n)	['milo]
soap dish	мильниця (f)	['miʌnitsʲa]
sponge	губка (f)	['ɣubka]
shampoo	шампунь (m)	[ʃam'puɲ]
towel	рушник (m)	[ruʃ'nik]
bathrobe	халат (m)	[ha'lat]
laundry (process)	прання (n)	[pra'ɲʲa]
washing machine	пральна машина (f)	['praʌna ma'ʃina]
to do the laundry	прати білизну	['prati bi'liznu]
laundry detergent	пральний порошок (m)	['praʌnij poro'ʃok]

99. Household appliances

TV set	телевізор (m)	[tɛlɛ'wizor]
tape recorder	магнітофон (m)	[maɣnito'fon]
video, VCR	відеомагнітофон (m)	['widɛomaɣnito'fon]
radio	приймач (m)	[prij'matʃ]
player (CD, MP3, etc.)	плеєр (m)	['plɛ:r]
video projector	відеопроектор (m)	[widɛopro'ɛktor]
home movie theater	домашній кінотеатр (m)	[do'maʃnij kinotɛ'atr]
DVD player	програвач (m) DVD	[proɣra'watʃ diwi'di]
amplifier	підсилювач (m)	[pid'silywatʃ]

video game console	гральна приставка (f)	['ɣraʎna prɪs'tawka]
video camera	відеокамера (f)	[wideo'kamɛra]
camera (photo)	фотоапарат (m)	[fotoapa'rat]
digital camera	цифровий фотоапарат (m)	[tsɪfro'wɪj fotoapa'rat]

vacuum cleaner	пилосос (m)	[pɪlo'sɔs]
iron (e.g., steam ~)	праска (f)	['praska]
ironing board	дошка (f) для прасування	['dɔʃka dʎa prasu'wanja]

telephone	телефон (m)	[tɛlɛ'fɔn]
mobile phone	мобільний телефон (m)	[mo'biʎnɪj tɛlɛ'fɔn]
typewriter	машинка (f)	[ma'ʃɪnka]
sewing machine	швейна машинка (f)	['ʃwɛjna ma'ʃɪnka]

microphone	мікрофон (m)	[mikro'fɔn]
headphones	навушники (pl)	[na'wuʃnɪkɪ]
remote control (TV)	пульт (m)	[puʎt]

CD, compact disc	CD-диск (m)	[si'di dɪsk]
cassette	касета (f)	[ka'sɛta]
vinyl record	платівка (f)	[pla'tiwka]

100. Repairs. Renovation

renovations	ремонт (m)	[rɛ'mɔnt]
to renovate (vt)	робити ремонт	[ro'bɪtɪ rɛ'mɔnt]
to repair (vt)	ремонтувати	[rɛmontu'watɪ]
to put in order	привести до ладу	[prɪ'wɛstɪ do 'ladu]
to redo (do again)	переробляти	[pɛrɛrob'ʎatɪ]

paint	фарба (f)	['farba]
to paint (~ a wall)	фарбувати	[farbu'watɪ]
house painter	маляр (f)	['maʎar]
paintbrush	щітка (f)	['ɕitka]
whitewash	побілка (f)	[po'bilka]
to whitewash (vt)	білити	[bi'lɪtɪ]

wallpaper	шпалери (pl)	[ʃpa'lɛrɪ]
to wallpaper (vt)	поклеїти шпалерами	[pok'lɛjɪtɪ ʃpa'lɛramɪ]
varnish	лак (m)	[lak]
to varnish (vt)	покривати лаком	[pokrɪ'watɪ 'lakom]

101. Plumbing

| water | вода (f) | [wo'da] |
| hot water | гаряча вода (f) | [ɣa'rʲatʃa wo'da] |

cold water	холодна вода (f)	[hoˈlɔdna woˈda]
tap, faucet	кран (m)	[kran]
drop (of water)	крапля (f)	[ˈkrapʎa]
to drip (vi)	крапати	[ˈkrapatı]
to leak (ab. pipe)	текти	[tɛkˈtı]
leak (pipe ~)	теча (f)	[ˈtɛtʃa]
puddle	калюжа (f)	[kaˈlyʒa]
pipe	труба (f)	[truˈba]
stop valve	вентиль (m)	[ˈwɛntıʎ]
to be clogged up	забитись	[zaˈbıtısʲ]
tools	інструменти (pl)	[instruˈmɛntı]
adjustable wrench	розвідний ключ (m)	[rozˈwidnıj klytʃ]
to unscrew, untwist (vt)	відкрутити	[widkruˈtıtı]
to screw (tighten)	закручувати	[zakˈrutʃuwatı]
to unclog (vt)	прочищати	[protʃıˈɕatı]
plumber	сантехнік (m)	[sanˈtɛhnik]
basement	підвал (m)	[pidˈwal]
sewerage (system)	каналізація (f)	[kanaliˈzatsija]

102. Fire. Conflagration

fire (to catch ~)	вогонь (m)	[woˈɣɔɲ]
flame	полум'я (n)	[ˈpolumʲja]
spark	іскра (f)	[ˈiskra]
smoke (from fire)	дим (m)	[dım]
torch (flaming stick)	смолоскип (m)	[smolosˈkıp]
campfire	багаття (n)	[baˈɣattʲa]
gas, gasoline	бензин (m)	[bɛnˈzın]
kerosene (for aircraft)	керосин (m)	[kɛroˈsın]
flammable (adj)	горючий	[ɣoˈrytʃıj]
explosive (adj)	вибухонебезпечний	[wıbuhonɛbɛzˈpɛtʃnıj]
NO SMOKING	ПАЛИТИ ЗАБОРОНЕНО	[paˈlıtı zaboˈrɔnɛno]
safety	безпека (f)	[bɛzˈpɛka]
danger	небезпека (f)	[nɛbɛzˈpɛka]
dangerous (adj)	небезпечний	[nɛbɛzˈpɛtʃnıj]
to catch fire	загорітися	[zaɣoˈritısʲa]
explosion	вибух (m)	[ˈwıbuh]
to set fire	підпалити	[pidpaˈlıtı]
incendiary (arsonist)	підпалювач (m)	[pidˈpalywatʃ]
arson	підпал (m)	[ˈpidpal]
to blaze (vi)	палати	[paˈlatı]
to burn (be on fire)	горіти	[ɣoˈritı]

to burn down	**згоріти**	[zɣoˈritɪ]
fireman	**пожежник** (m)	[poˈʒɛʒnɪk]
fire truck	**пожежна машина** (f)	[poˈʒɛʒna maˈʃɪna]
fire department	**пожежна команда** (f)	[poˈʒɛʒna koˈmanda]
fire truck ladder	**драбина** (f)	[draˈbɪna]
fire hose	**шланг** (m)	[ʃlaŋ]
fire extinguisher	**вогнегасник** (m)	[woɣnɛˈɣasnɪk]
helmet	**каска** (f)	[ˈkaska]
siren	**сирена** (f)	[sɪˈrɛna]
to call out	**кричати**	[krɪˈtʃatɪ]
to call for help	**кликати на допомогу**	[ˈklɪkatɪ na dopoˈmoɣu]
rescuer	**рятувальник** (m)	[rʲatuˈwaʎnɪk]
to rescue (vt)	**рятувати**	[rʲatuˈwatɪ]
to arrive (vi)	**приїхати**	[prɪˈjihatɪ]
to extinguish (vt)	**тушити**	[tuˈʃɪtɪ]
water	**вода** (f)	[woˈda]
sand	**пісок** (m)	[piˈsɔk]
ruins (destruction)	**руїни** (pl)	[ruˈjɪnɪ]
to collapse (building, etc.)	**повалитися**	[powaˈlɪtɪsʲa]
to fall down (vi)	**обвалитися**	[obwaˈlɪtɪsʲa]
to cave in (ceiling, floor)	**завалитися**	[zawaˈlɪtɪsʲa]
piece of wreckage	**уламок** (m)	[uˈlamok]
ash	**попіл** (m)	[ˈpɔpil]
to suffocate (die)	**задихнутися**	[zadɪhˈnutɪsʲa]
to be killed (perish)	**загинути**	[zaˈɣɪnutɪ]

HUMAN ACTIVITIES

Job. Business. Part 1

103. Office. Working in the office

office (of firm)	офіс (m)	['ɔfis]
office (of director, etc.)	кабінет (m)	[kabi'nɛt]
front desk	ресепшн (m)	[rɛ'sɛpʃn]
secretary	секретар (m)	[sɛkrɛ'tar]
secretary (fem.)	секретарка (f)	[sɛkrɛ'tarka]
director	директор (m)	[dɪ'rɛktor]
manager	менеджер (m)	['mɛnɛdʒɛr]
accountant	бухгалтер (m)	[buh'ɣaltɛr]
employee	робітник (m)	[ro'bitnɪk]
furniture	меблі (pl)	['mɛbli]
desk	стіл (m)	[stil]
desk chair	крісло (n)	['krislo]
chest of drawers	тумбочка (m)	['tumbotʃka]
coat stand	вішак (m)	[wi'ʃak]
computer	комп'ютер (m)	[kompʰ'jutɛr]
printer	принтер (m)	['prɪntɛr]
fax machine	факс (m)	[faks]
photocopier	копіювальний апарат (m)	[kopiju'waʎnɪj apa'rat]
paper	папір (m)	[pa'pir]
office supplies	канцелярське приладдя (n)	[kantsɛ'ʎarsʲkɛ prɪ'laddʲa]
mouse pad	килимок (m)	[kɪlɪ'mɔk]
sheet (of paper)	аркуш (m)	['arkuʃ]
folder, binder	папка (f)	['papka]
catalog	каталог (m)	[kata'lɔɣ]
phone book (directory)	довідник (m)	[do'widnɪk]
documentation	документація (f)	[dokumɛn'tatsija]
brochure (e.g., 12 pages ~)	брошура (f)	[bro'ʃura]
leaflet	листівка (f)	[lɪs'tiwka]
sample	зразок (m)	[zra'zɔk]
training meeting	тренінг (m)	['trɛniŋ]
meeting (of managers)	нарада (f)	[na'rada]

lunch time	перерва (f) на обід	[pɛ'rɛrwa na o'bid]
to make a copy	робити копію	[ro'bıtı 'kɔpiju]
to make copies	розмножити	[rozm'nɔʒıtı]
to receive a fax	отримувати факс	[ot'rımuwatı faks]
to send a fax	відправити факс	[widp'rawıtı faks]
to call (by phone)	подзвонити	[podzwo'nıtı]
to answer (vt)	відповісти	[widpo'wistı]
to put through	з'єднати	[zʰɛd'natı]
to arrange, to set up	призначити	[prız'natʃıtı]
to demonstrate (vt)	демонструвати	[dɛmonstru'watı]
to be absent	бути відсутнім	['butı wid'sutnim]
absence	пропуск (m)	['prɔpusk]

104. Business processes. Part 1

occupation	справа (f)	['sprawa]
firm	фірма (f)	['firma]
company	компанія (f)	[kom'panija]
corporation	корпорація (f)	[korpo'ratsija]
enterprise	підприємство (n)	[pidprı'ɛmstwo]
agency	агентство (n)	[a'ɣɛntstwo]
agreement (contract)	договір (m)	['dɔɣowir]
contract	контракт (m)	[kont'rakt]
deal	угода (f)	[u'ɣɔda]
order (to place an ~)	замовлення (n)	[za'mɔwlɛnja]
term (of contract)	умова (f)	[u'mɔwa]
wholesale (adv)	оптом	['ɔptom]
wholesale (adj)	оптовий	[op'tɔwıj]
wholesale (n)	оптова торгівля (f)	[op'tɔwa tor'ɣiwʌa]
retail (adj)	роздрібний	[rozd'ribnıj]
retail (n)	продаж (m) в роздріб	['prɔdaʒ w 'rozdrib]
competitor	конкурент (m)	[koŋku'rɛnt]
competition	конкуренція (f)	[koŋku'rɛntsija]
to compete (vi)	конкурувати	[koŋkuru'watı]
partner (associate)	партнер (m)	[part'nɛr]
partnership	партнерство (n)	[part'nɛrstwo]
crisis	криза (f)	['krıza]
bankruptcy	банкрутство (n)	[baŋk'rutstwo]
to go bankrupt	збанкрутувати	[zbaŋkrutu'watı]
difficulty	складність (f)	['skladnistʲ]
problem	проблема (f)	[prob'lɛma]
catastrophe	катастрофа (f)	[katast'rɔfa]
economy	економіка (f)	[ɛko'nɔmika]

| economic (~ growth) | економічний | [ɛkono'mitʃnij] |
| economic recession | економічний спад (m) | [ɛkono'mitʃnij spad] |

| goal (aim) | мета (f) | [mɛ'ta] |
| task | завдання (n) | [zaw'danja] |

to trade (vi)	торгувати	[torɣu'watı]
network (distribution ~)	мережа (f)	[mɛ'rɛʒa]
inventory (stock)	склад (m)	[sklad]
assortment	асортимент (m)	[asortı'mɛnt]

leader (leading company)	лідер (m)	['lidɛr]
large (~ company)	великий	[wɛ'lıkıj]
monopoly	монополія (f)	[mono'polija]

theory	теорія (f)	[tɛ'orija]
practice	практика (f)	['praktıka]
experience (in my ~)	досвід (m)	['doswid]
trend (tendency)	тенденція (f)	[tɛn'dɛntsija]
development	розвиток (m)	['rozwıtok]

105. Business processes. Part 2

| benefit, profit | вигода (f) | ['wıɣoda] |
| profitable (adj) | вигідний | ['wıɣidnıj] |

delegation (group)	делегація (f)	[dɛlɛ'ɣatsija]
salary	заробітна платня (f)	[zaro'bitna plat'ɲa]
to correct (an error)	виправляти	[wıpraw'ʎatı]
business trip	відрядження (n)	[wid'rʲadʒɛnja]
commission	комісія (f)	[ko'misija]

to control (vt)	контролювати	[kontroly'watı]
conference	конференція (f)	[konfɛ'rɛntsija]
license	ліцензія (f)	[li'tsɛnzija]
reliable (~ partner)	надійний	[na'dijnıj]

initiative (undertaking)	починання (n)	[potʃı'nanja]
norm (standard)	норма (f)	['norma]
circumstance	обставина (f)	[obs'tawına]
duty (of employee)	обов'язок (m)	[o'bowʰjazok]

organization (company)	організація (f)	[orɣani'zatsija]
organization (process)	організація (f)	[orɣani'zatsija]
organized (adj)	організований	[orɣani'zowanıj]
cancellation	скасування (n)	[skasu'wanja]
to cancel (call off)	скасувати	[skasu'watı]
report (official ~)	звіт (m)	[zwit]
patent	патент (m)	[pa'tɛnt]
to patent (obtain patent)	патентувати	[patɛntu'watı]

to plan (vt)	**планувати**	[planu'watɪ]
bonus (money)	**премія** (f)	['prɛmija]
professional (adj)	**професійний**	[profɛ'sijnɪj]
procedure	**процедура** (f)	[protsɛ'dura]
to examine (contract, etc.)	**розглянути**	[rozɣ'ʎanutɪ]
calculation	**розрахунок** (m)	[rozra'hunok]
reputation	**репутація** (f)	[rɛpu'tatsija]
risk	**ризик** (m)	['rɪzɪk]
to manage, to run	**керувати**	[kɛru'watɪ]
information	**відомості** (pl)	[wi'dɔmosti]
property	**власність** (f)	['wlasnistʲ]
union	**союз** (m)	[so'juz]
life insurance	**страхування** (n) **життя**	[strahu'wanja ʒɪt'tʲa]
to insure (vt)	**страхувати**	[strahu'watɪ]
insurance	**страхування** (n)	[strahu'wanja]
auction (~ sale)	**торги** (pl)	[tor'ɣɪ]
to notify (inform)	**повідомити**	[powi'dɔmɪtɪ]
management (process)	**управління** (n)	[upraw'linja]
service (~ industry)	**послуга** (f)	['pɔsluɣa]
forum	**форум** (m)	['fɔrum]
to function (vi)	**функціонувати**	[funktsionu'watɪ]
stage (phase)	**етап** (m)	[ɛ'tap]
legal (~ services)	**юридичний**	[jurɪ'dɪtʃnɪj]
lawyer (legal expert)	**юрист** (m)	[ju'rɪst]

106. Production. Works

plant	**завод** (m)	[za'wɔd]
factory	**фабрика** (f)	['fabrɪka]
workshop	**цех** (m)	[tsɛh]
works, production site	**виробництво** (n)	[wɪrob'nɪtstwo]
industry	**промисловість** (f)	[promɪs'lɔwistʲ]
industrial (adj)	**промисловий**	[promɪs'lɔwɪj]
heavy industry	**важка промисловість** (f)	[waʒ'ka promɪs'lɔwistʲ]
light industry	**легка промисловість** (f)	[lɛɣ'ka promɪs'lɔwistʲ]
products	**продукція** (f)	[pro'duktsija]
to produce (vt)	**виробляти**	[wɪrob'ʎatɪ]
raw materials	**сировина** (f)	[sɪrowɪ'na]
foreman	**бригадир** (m)	[brɪɣa'dɪr]
workers team	**бригада** (f)	[brɪ'ɣada]
worker	**робочий** (m)	[ro'bɔtʃɪj]
working day	**робочий день** (m)	[ro'bɔtʃɪj dɛɲ]

pause	**перерва** (f)	[pɛ'rɛrwa]
meeting	**збори** (pl)	['zbɔrɪ]
to discuss (vt)	**обговорювати**	[obɣo'wɔrywatɪ]
plan	**план** (m)	[plan]
to fulfill the plan	**виконати план**	['wɪkonatɪ plan]
rate of output	**норма** (f)	['nɔrma]
quality	**якість** (f)	['jakistʲ]
checking (control)	**контроль** (m)	[kont'rɔʎ]
quality control	**контроль** (m) **якості**	[kont'rɔʎ 'jakosti]
work safety	**безпека** (f) **праці**	[bɛz'pɛka 'pratsi]
discipline	**дисципліна** (f)	[dɪstsɪp'lina]
violation	**порушення** (n)	[po'ruʃɛnja]
(of safety rules, etc.)		
to violate (rules)	**порушувати**	[po'ruʃuwatɪ]
strike	**страйк** (m)	['strajk]
striker	**страйкар** (m)	[straj'kar]
to be on strike	**страйкувати**	[strajku'watɪ]
labor union	**профспілка** (f)	[profs'pilka]
to invent (machine, etc.)	**винайти**	['wɪnajtɪ]
invention	**винахід** (m)	['wɪnahid]
research	**дослідження** (n)	[dos'lidʒɛnja]
to improve (make better)	**покращувати**	[pok'raɕuwatɪ]
technology	**технологія** (f)	[tɛhno'lɔɣija]
technical drawing	**креслення** (n)	['krɛslɛnja]
load, cargo	**вантаж** (m)	[wan'taʒ]
loader (person)	**вантажник** (m)	[wan'taʒnɪk]
to load (vehicle, etc.)	**вантажити**	[wan'taʒɪtɪ]
loading (process)	**завантаження** (n)	[zawan'taʒɛnja]
to unload (vi, vt)	**розвантажувати**	[rozwan'taʒuwatɪ]
unloading	**розвантаження** (n)	[rozwan'taʒɛnja]
transportation	**транспорт** (m)	['transport]
transportation company	**транспортна компанія** (f)	['transportna kom'panija]
to transport (vt)	**транспортувати**	[transportu'watɪ]
freight car	**товарний вагон** (m)	[to'warnɪj wa'ɣɔn]
cistern	**цистерна** (f)	[tsɪs'tɛrna]
truck	**вантажівка** (f)	[wanta'ʒiwka]
machine tool	**станок** (m)	[sta'nɔk]
mechanism	**механізм** (m)	[mɛha'nizm]
industrial waste	**відходи** (pl)	[wid'hɔdɪ]
packing (process)	**пакування** (n)	[paku'wanja]
to pack (vt)	**упакувати**	[upaku'watɪ]

107. Contract. Agreement

contract	контракт (m)	[kont′rakt]
agreement	угода (f)	[u′ɣɔda]
addendum	додаток (m)	[do′datok]

to sign a contract	укласти контракт	[uk′lastɪ kont′rakt]
signature	підпис (m)	[′pidpɪs]
to sign (vt)	підписати	[pidpɪ′satɪ]
stamp (seal)	печатка (f)	[pɛ′tʃatka]

subject of contract	предмет (m) договору	[prɛd′mɛt ′dɔɣoworu]
clause	пункт (m)	[puŋkt]
parties (in contract)	сторони (pl)	[′stɔronɪ]
legal address	юридична адреса (f)	[jurɪ′dɪtʃna ad′rɛsa]

to break the contract	порушити контракт	[po′ruʃɪtɪ kont′rakt]
commitment	зобов'язання (n)	[zobowʰ′jazaŋja]
responsibility	відповідальність (f)	[widpowi′daʎnistʲ]
force majeure	форс-мажор (m)	[fors ma′ʒor]
dispute	суперечка (f)	[supɛ′rɛtʃka]
penalties	штрафні санкції (pl)	[ʃtraf′ni ′saŋktsijɪ]

108. Import & Export

import	імпорт (m)	[′import]
importer	імпортер (m)	[impor′tɛr]
to import (vt)	імпортувати	[importu′watɪ]
import (e.g., ~ goods)	імпортний	[′importnɪj]

| exporter | експортер (m) | [ɛkspor′tɛr] |
| to export (vi, vt) | експортувати | [ɛksportu′watɪ] |

goods	товар (m)	[to′war]
consignment, lot	партія (f)	[′partija]
weight	вага (f)	[wa′ɣa]
volume	об'єм (m)	[obʰ′ɛm]
cubic meter	кубічний метр (m)	[ku′bitʃnɪj mɛtr]

manufacturer	виробник (m)	[wɪrob′nɪk]
transportation company	транспортна компанія (f)	[′transportna kom′panija]
container	контейнер (m)	[kon′tɛjnɛr]

border	кордон (m)	[kor′dɔn]
customs	митниця (f)	[′mɪtnɪtsʲa]
customs duty	митний збір (m)	[′mɪtnɪj zbir]
customs officer	митник (m)	[′mɪtnɪk]
smuggling	контрабанда (f)	[kontra′banda]
contraband (goods)	контрабанда (f)	[kontra′banda]

109. Finances

stock (share)	акція (f)	[ˈaktsija]
bond (certificate)	облігація (f)	[obliˈɣatsija]
bill of exchange	вексель (m)	[ˈwɛksɛʎ]
stock exchange	біржа (f)	[ˈbirʒa]
stock price	курс (m) акцій	[kurs ˈaktsij]
to go down	подешевшати	[podɛˈʃɛwʃatɪ]
to go up	подорожчати	[podoˈrɔʒtʃatɪ]
controlling interest	контрольний пакет (m)	[kontˈrɔʎnɪj paˈkɛt]
investment	інвестиції (pl)	[inwɛsˈtɪtsijɪ]
to invest (vt)	інвестувати	[inwɛstuˈwatɪ]
percent	відсоток (m)	[widˈsɔtok]
interest (on investment)	відсотки (pl)	[widˈsɔtkɪ]
profit	прибуток (m)	[prɪˈbutok]
profitable (adj)	прибутковий	[prɪbutˈkɔwɪj]
tax	податок (m)	[poˈdatok]
currency (foreign ~)	валюта (f)	[waˈlyta]
national (adj)	національний	[natsioˈnaʎnɪj]
exchange (currency ~)	обмін (m)	[ˈɔbmin]
accountant	бухгалтер (m)	[buhˈɣaltɛr]
accounting	бухгалтерія (f)	[buhɣalˈtɛrija]
bankruptcy	банкрутство (n)	[baŋkˈrutstwo]
collapse, crash	крах (m)	[krah]
ruin	розорення (n)	[roˈzɔrɛnja]
to be ruined	розоритися	[rozoˈrɪtɪsʲa]
inflation	інфляція (f)	[infˈʎatsija]
devaluation	девальвація (f)	[dɛwaʎˈwatsija]
capital	капітал (m)	[kapiˈtal]
income	прибуток (m)	[prɪˈbutok]
turnover	обіг (m)	[ˈɔbiɣ]
resources	ресурси (pl)	[rɛˈsursɪ]
monetary resources	кошти (pl)	[ˈkɔʃtɪ]
to reduce (expenses)	скоротити	[skoroˈtɪtɪ]

110. Marketing

marketing	маркетинг (m)	[marˈkɛtɪŋ]
market	ринок (m)	[ˈrɪnok]
market segment	сегмент (m) ринку	[sɛɣˈmɛnt ˈrɪŋku]
product	продукт (m)	[proˈdukt]

goods	товар (m)	[to'war]
brand	марка (f), бренд (m)	['marka], [brɛnd]
trademark	торгова марка (f)	[tor'ɣowa 'marka]
logotype	фірмовий знак (m)	['firmowɪj znak]
logo	логотип (m)	[loɣo'tɪp]
demand	попит (m)	['pɔpɪt]
supply	пропозиція (f)	[propo'zɪtsija]
need	потреба (f)	[pot'rɛba]
consumer	споживач (m)	[spoʒɪ'watʃ]
analysis	аналіз (m)	[a'naliz]
to analyze (vt)	аналізувати	[analizu'watɪ]
positioning	позиціонування (n)	[pozɪtsionu'wanja]
to position (vt)	позиціонувати	[pozɪtsionu'watɪ]
price	ціна (f)	[tsi'na]
pricing policy	цінова політика (f)	[tsino'wa po'litɪka]
formation of price	ціноутворення (n)	[tsinout'worɛnja]

111. Advertising

advertising	реклама (f)	[rɛk'lama]
to advertise (vt)	рекламувати	[rɛklamu'watɪ]
budget	бюджет (m)	[by'dʒɛt]
ad, advertisement	реклама (f)	[rɛk'lama]
TV advertising	телереклама (f)	[tɛlɛrɛk'lama]
radio advertising	реклама (f) на радіо	[rɛk'lama na 'radio]
outdoor advertising	зовнішня реклама (f)	['zɔwniʃna rɛklama]
mass media	засоби (pl) масової інформації	['zasobɪ 'masowoji infor'matsijɪ]
periodical (n)	періодичне видання (n)	[pɛrio'dɪtʃnɛ wɪda'ɲʲa]
image (public appearance)	імідж (m)	['imidʒ]
slogan	гасло (n)	['ɣaslo]
motto (maxim)	девіз (m)	[dɛ'wiz]
campaign	кампанія (f)	[kam'panija]
advertising campaign	рекламна кампанія (f)	[rɛk'lamna kam'panija]
target group	цільова аудиторія (f)	[tsilʲɔ'wa audɪ'torija]
business card	візитка (f)	[wi'zɪtka]
leaflet	листівка (f)	[lɪs'tiwka]
brochure (e.g., 12 pages ~)	брошура (f)	[bro'ʃura]
pamphlet	буклет (m)	[buk'lɛt]
newsletter	бюлетень (m)	[bylɛ'tɛɲ]
store sign	вивіска (f)	['wɪwiska]

| poster | плакат (m) | [pla'kat] |
| billboard | щит (m) | [ɕıt] |

112. Banking

| bank | банк (m) | [baŋk] |
| branch (of bank, etc.) | відділення (n) | [wid'dilɛnja] |

| bank clerk, consultant | консультант (m) | [konsuʎ'tant] |
| manager (director) | управляючий (m) | [upraw'ʎajutʃij] |

banking account	рахунок (m)	[ra'hunok]
account number	номер (m) рахунка	['nɔmɛr ra'huŋka]
checking account	поточний рахунок (m)	[po'totʃnij ra'hunok]
savings account	накопичувальний рахунок (m)	[nako'pitʃuwaʎnij ra'hunok]

to open an account	відкрити рахунок	[widk'rıtı ra'hunok]
to close the account	закрити рахунок	[zak'rıtı ra'hunok]
to deposit into the account	покласти на рахунок	[pok'lastı na ra'hunok]
to withdraw (vt)	зняти з рахунку	['zɲatı z ra'huŋku]

deposit	внесок (m)	['wnɛsok]
to make a deposit	зробити внесок	[zro'bıtı 'wnɛsok]
wire transfer	переказ (m)	[pɛ'rɛkaz]
to wire, to transfer	зробити переказ	[zro'bıtı pɛ'rɛkaz]

| sum | сума (f) | ['suma] |
| How much? | Скільки? | ['skiʎkı] |

| signature | підпис (m) | ['pidpıs] |
| to sign (vt) | підписати | [pidpı'satı] |

| credit card | кредитна картка (f) | [krɛ'dıtna 'kartka] |
| code | код (m) | [kod] |

| credit card number | номер (m) кредитної картки | ['nɔmɛr krɛ'dıtnojı 'kartkı] |

| ATM | банкомат (m) | [baŋko'mat] |

check	чек (m)	[tʃɛk]
to write a check	виписати чек	['wıpısatı tʃɛk]
checkbook	чекова книжка (f)	['tʃɛkowa 'knıʒka]

loan (bank ~)	кредит (m)	[krɛ'dıt]
to apply for a loan	звертатися за кредитом	[zwɛr'tatısja za krɛ'dıtom]
to get a loan	брати кредит	['bratı krɛ'dıt]
to give a loan	надавати кредит	[nada'watı krɛ'dıt]
guarantee	застава (f)	[zas'tawa]

113. Telephone. Phone conversation

telephone	**телефон** (m)	[tɛlɛ'fɔn]
mobile phone	**мобільний телефон** (m)	[mo'biʎnıj tɛlɛ'fɔn]
answering machine	**автовідповідач** (m)	[awtowidpowi'datʃ]
to call (telephone)	**телефонувати**	[tɛlɛfonu'watı]
phone call	**дзвінок** (m)	[dzwi'nɔk]
to dial a number	**набрати номер**	[nab'ratı 'nɔmɛr]
Hello!	**Алло!**	[a'lɔ]
to ask (vt)	**запитати**	[zapı'tatı]
to answer (vi, vt)	**відповісти**	[widpo'wistı]
to hear (vt)	**чути**	['tʃutı]
well (adv)	**добре**	['dɔbrɛ]
not well (adv)	**погано**	[po'ɣano]
noises (interference)	**перешкоди** (pl)	[pɛrɛʃ'kɔdı]
receiver	**трубка** (f)	['trubka]
to pick up (~ the phone)	**зняти трубку**	['zɲatı 'trubku]
to hang up (~ the phone)	**покласти трубку**	[pok'lastı 'trubku]
busy (adj)	**зайнятий**	['zajɲatıj]
to ring (ab. phone)	**дзвонити**	[dzwo'nıtı]
telephone book	**телефонна книга** (f)	[tɛlɛ'fɔɲa 'knıɣa]
local (adj)	**місцевий**	[mis'tsɛwıj]
local call	**місцевий зв'язок** (m)	[mis'tsɛwıj 'zwʲazok]
long distance (~ call)	**міжміський**	[miʒmisʲ'kıj]
long-distance call	**міжміський зв'язок** (m)	[miʒmisʲ'kıj 'zwʲazok]
international (adj)	**міжнародний**	[miʒna'rɔdnıj]
international call	**міжнародний зв'язок** (m)	[miʒna'rɔdnıj 'zwʲazok]

114. Mobile telephone

mobile phone	**мобільний телефон** (m)	[mo'biʎnıj tɛlɛ'fɔn]
display	**дисплей** (m)	[dıs'lɛj]
button	**кнопка** (f)	['knɔpka]
SIM card	**SIM-карта** (f)	[sim 'karta]
battery	**батарея** (f)	[bata'rɛja]
to be dead (battery)	**розрядитися**	[rozrʲa'dıtısʲa]
charger	**зарядний пристрій** (m)	[za'rʲadnıj 'prıstrij]
menu	**меню** (n)	[mɛ'ny]
settings	**настройки** (pl)	[nast'rɔjki]
tune (melody)	**мелодія** (f)	[mɛ'lɔdija]
to select (vt)	**вибрати**	['wıbratı]

calculator	калькулятор (m)	[kaʎkuˈʎɑtor]
voice mail	автовідповідач (m)	[awtowidpowiˈdɑtʃ]
alarm clock	будильник (m)	[buˈdiʎnɪk]
contacts	телефонна книга (f)	[tɛlɛˈfɔnɑ ˈkniɣɑ]
SMS (text message)	SMS-повідомлення (n)	[ɛsɛˈmɛs powiˈdɔmlɛnjɑ]
subscriber	абонент (m)	[aboˈnɛnt]

115. Stationery

ballpoint pen	авторучка (f)	[awtoˈrutʃkɑ]
fountain pen	ручка-перо (n)	[ˈrutʃkɑ pɛˈrɔ]
pencil	олівець (m)	[oliˈwɛts]
highlighter	маркер (m)	[ˈmɑrkɛr]
felt-tip pen	фломастер (m)	[floˈmɑstɛr]
notepad	блокнот (m)	[blokˈnɔt]
agenda (diary)	щоденник (m)	[ɕoˈdɛnɪk]
ruler	лінійка (f)	[liˈnijkɑ]
calculator	калькулятор (m)	[kaʎkuˈʎɑtor]
eraser	гумка (f)	[ˈɣumkɑ]
thumbtack	кнопка (f)	[ˈknɔpkɑ]
paper clip	скріпка (f)	[ˈskripkɑ]
glue	клей (m)	[klɛj]
stapler	степлер (m)	[ˈstɛplɛr]
hole punch	діркопробивач (m)	[dirkoprobɪˈwɑtʃ]
pencil sharpener	стругачка (f)	[struˈɣɑtʃkɑ]

116. Various kinds of documents

account (report)	звіт (m)	[zwit]
agreement	угода (f)	[uˈɣɔdɑ]
application form	заявка (f)	[zaˈjawkɑ]
authentic (adj)	оригінальний	[orɪɣiˈnɑʎnɪj]
badge (identity tag)	бедж (m)	[bɛdʒ]
business card	візитка (f)	[wiˈzɪtkɑ]
certificate (~ of quality)	сертифікат (m)	[sɛrtɪfiˈkɑt]
check (e.g., draw a ~)	чек (m)	[tʃɛk]
check (in restaurant)	рахунок (m)	[raˈhunok]
constitution	конституція (f)	[konstɪˈtutsijɑ]
contract	договір (m)	[ˈdɔɣowir]
copy	копія (f)	[ˈkɔpijɑ]
copy (of contract, etc.)	примірник (m)	[prɪˈmirnɪk]

customs declaration	декларація (f)	[dɛklɑˈrɑtsija]
document	документ (m)	[dokuˈmɛnt]
driver's license	посвідчення (n) водія	[posˈwidtʃɛɲɑ wodiˈjɑ]
addendum	додаток (m)	[doˈdɑtok]
form	анкета (f)	[ɑˈɲkɛtɑ]
identity card, ID	посвідчення (n)	[posˈwidtʃɛɲɑ]
inquiry (request)	запит (m)	[ˈzɑpɪt]
invitation card	запрошення (n)	[zɑpˈrɔʃɛɲɑ]
invoice	рахунок (m)	[rɑˈhunok]
law	закон (m)	[zɑˈkɔn]
letter (mail)	лист (m)	[lɪst]
letterhead	бланк (m)	[blɑŋk]
list (of names, etc.)	список (m)	[ˈspɪsok]
manuscript	рукопис (m)	[ruˈkɔpɪs]
newsletter	бюлетень (m)	[bylɛˈtɛɲ]
note (short message)	записка (f)	[zɑˈpɪskɑ]
pass (for worker, visitor)	перепустка (f)	[pɛˈrɛpustkɑ]
passport	паспорт (m)	[ˈpɑsport]
permit	дозвіл (m)	[ˈdɔzwil]
résumé	резюме (n)	[rɛzyˈmɛ]
debt note, IOU	розписка (f)	[rozˈpɪskɑ]
receipt (for purchase)	квитанція (f)	[kwɪˈtɑntsija]
sales slip, receipt	чек (m)	[tʃɛk]
report	рапорт (m)	[ˈrɑport]
to show (ID, etc.)	пред'являти	[prɛdʰjɑwˈʎɑtɪ]
to sign (vt)	підписати	[pidpɪˈsɑtɪ]
signature	підпис (m)	[ˈpidpɪs]
stamp (seal)	печатка (f)	[pɛˈtʃɑtkɑ]
text	текст (m)	[tɛkst]
ticket (for entry)	квиток (m)	[kwɪˈtɔk]
to cross out	закреслити	[zɑkˈrɛslɪtɪ]
to fill out (~ a form)	заповнити	[zɑˈpownɪtɪ]
waybill	накладна (f)	[nɑklɑdˈnɑ]
will (testament)	заповіт (m)	[zɑpoˈwit]

117. Kinds of business

accounting services	бухгалтерські послуги (pl)	[buhˈɣɑltɛrsʲki ˈpɔsluɣɪ]
advertising	реклама (f)	[rɛkˈlɑmɑ]
advertising agency	рекламне агентство (n)	[rɛkˈlɑmnɛ ɑˈɣɛntstwo]
air-conditioners	кондиціонери (pl)	[kondɪtsiˈɔnɛrɪ]
airline	авіакомпанія (f)	[ɑwiɑkomˈpɑnija]
alcoholic drinks	спиртні напої (pl)	[spɪrtˈni nɑˈpɔjɪ]

antiquities	антикваріат (m)	[antıkwari'at]
art gallery	галерея (f)	[ɣalɛ'rɛja]
audit services	аудиторські послуги (pl)	[auˈdɪtorsʲki ˈpɔsluɣɪ]

banks	банківський бізнес (m)	[ˈbaŋkiwsʲkɪj ˈbiznɛs]
bar	бар (m)	[bar]
beauty parlor	салон (m) краси	[saˈlɔn kraˈsɪ]
bookstore	книгарня (f)	[knɪˈɣarɲa]
brewery	броварня (f)	[broˈwarɲa]
business center	бізнес-центр (m)	[ˈbiznɛs tsɛntr]
business school	бізнес-школа (f)	[ˈbiznɛs ˈʃkɔla]

casino	казино (n)	[kazɪˈnɔ]
construction	будівництво (n)	[budiwˈnɪtstwo]
consulting	консалтинг (m)	[kɔnˈsaltɪŋ]

dental clinic	стоматологія (f)	[stomatoˈlɔɣija]
design	дизайн (m)	[dɪˈzajn]
drugstore, pharmacy	аптека (f)	[apˈtɛka]
dry cleaners	хімчистка (f)	[himˈtʃɪstka]
employment agency	кадрове агентство (n)	[ˈkadrowɛ aˈɣɛntstwo]

financial services	фінансові послуги (pl)	[fiˈnansowi ˈpɔsluɣɪ]
food products	продукти (pl) харчування	[proˈduktɪ hartʃuˈwaɲa]
funeral home	похоронне бюро (n)	[pohoˈrɔɲɛ byro]
furniture (e.g., house ~)	меблі (pl)	[ˈmɛbli]
garment	одяг (m)	[ˈɔdʲaɣ]
hotel	готель (m)	[ɣoˈtɛʎ]

ice-cream	морозиво (n)	[moˈrɔzɪwo]
industry	промисловість (f)	[promɪsˈlɔwistʲ]
insurance	страхування (n)	[strahuˈwaɲa]
Internet	інтернет (m)	[intɛrˈnɛt]
investment	інвестиції (pl)	[inwɛsˈtɪtsiji]

jeweler	ювелір (m)	[juwɛˈlir]
jewelry	ювелірні вироби (pl)	[juwɛˈlirni ˈwɪrobɪ]
laundry (shop)	пральня (f)	[ˈpraʎɲa]
legal advisor	юридичні послуги (pl)	[jurɪˈdɪtʃni ˈpɔsluɣɪ]
light industry	легка промисловість (f)	[lɛɣˈka promɪsˈlɔwistʲ]

magazine	журнал (m)	[ʒurˈnal]
mail-order selling	торгівля (f) за каталогом	[torˈɣiwʎa za kataˈlɔɣom]
medicine	медицина (f)	[mɛdɪˈtsɪna]
movie theater	кінотеатр (m)	[kinotɛˈatr]
museum	музей (m)	[muˈzɛj]

news agency	інформаційне агентство (n)	[informaˈtsijnɛ aˈɣɛntstwo]
newspaper	газета (f)	[ɣaˈzɛta]
nightclub	нічний клуб (m)	[nitʃˈnɪj klub]

oil (petroleum)	нафта (f)	['nafta]
parcels service	кур'єрська служба (f)	[kurʰ'ɛrsʲka 'sluʒba]
pharmaceuticals	фармацевтика (f)	[farma'ʦɛwtika]
printing (industry)	поліграфія (f)	[poliɣra'fija]
publishing house	видавництво (n)	[wɪdaw'nɪʦtwo]

radio (~ station)	радіо (n)	['radio]
real estate	нерухомість (f)	[nɛru'homistʲ]
restaurant	ресторан (m)	[rɛsto'ran]

security agency	охоронне агентство (n)	[oho'roɳɛ a'ɣɛnʦtwo]
sports	спорт (m)	[sport]
stock exchange	біржа (f)	['birʒa]
store	магазин (m)	[maɣa'zin]
supermarket	супермаркет (m)	[supɛr'markɛt]
swimming pool	басейн (m)	[ba'sɛjn]

tailors	ательє (n)	[atɛ'ʎɛ]
television	телебачення (n)	[tɛlɛ'batʃɛnja]
theater	театр (m)	[tɛ'atr]
trade	торгівля (f)	[tor'ɣiwʎa]
transportation	перевезення (n)	[pɛrɛ'wɛzɛnja]
travel	туризм (m)	[tu'rɪzm]

veterinarian	ветеринар (m)	[wɛtɛrɪ'nar]
warehouse	склад (m)	[sklad]
waste collection	вивіз (m) сміття	['wɪwiz smit'tʲa]

Job. Business. Part 2

118. Show. Exhibition

exhibition, show	виставка (f)	['wıstawka]
trade show	торгівельна виставка (f)	[torɣi'wɛʌna 'wıstawka]
participation	участь (f)	['utʃastʲ]
to participate (vi)	брати участь	['bratı 'utʃastʲ]
participant (exhibitor)	учасник (m)	[u'tʃasnık]
director	директор (m)	[dı'rɛktor]
organizer's office	дирекція (f)	[dı'rɛktsija]
organizer	організатор (m)	[orɣani'zator]
to organize (vt)	організовувати	[orɣani'zɔwuwatı]
participation form	заявка (f) на участь	[za'jawka na 'utʃastʲ]
to fill out (vt)	заповнити	[za'pownıtı]
details	деталі (pl)	[dɛ'tali]
information	інформація (f)	[infor'matsija]
price	ціна (f)	[tsi'na]
including	включно	['wklytʃno]
to include (vt)	включати	[wkly'tʃatı]
to pay (vi, vt)	платити	[pla'tıtı]
registration fee	реєстраційний внесок (m)	[rɛ:stra'tsijnıj w'nɛsok]
entrance	вхід (m)	[whid]
pavilion, hall	павільйон (m)	[pawiʎ'jon]
to register (vt)	реєструвати	[rɛ:stru'watı]
badge (identity tag)	бедж (m)	[bɛdʒ]
booth, stand	стенд (m)	[stɛnd]
to reserve, to book	резервувати	[rɛzɛrwu'watı]
display case	вітрина (f)	[wit'rına]
spotlight	світильник (m)	[swi'tıʎnık]
design	дизайн (m)	[dı'zajn]
to place (put, set)	розташовувати	[rozta'ʃowuwatı]
distributor	дистриб'ютор (m)	[dıstrıbʰ'jutor]
supplier	постачальник (m)	[posta'tʃaʎnık]
country	країна (f)	[kra'jına]
foreign (adj)	іноземний	[ino'zɛmnıj]

product	продукт (m)	[pro'dukt]
association	асоціація (f)	[asotsi'atsija]
conference hall	конференц-зал (m)	[konfε'rεnts zal]
congress	конгрес (m)	[koŋ'rεs]
contest (competition)	конкурс (m)	['koŋkurs]
visitor	відвідувач (m)	[wid'widuwatʃ]
to visit (attend)	відвідувати	[wid'widuwatı]
customer	замовник (m)	[za'mɔwnık]

119. Mass Media

newspaper	газета (f)	[ɣa'zεta]
magazine	журнал (m)	[ʒur'nal]
press (printed media)	преса (f)	['prεsa]
radio	радіо (n)	['radio]
radio station	радіостанція (f)	[radios'tantsija]
television	телебачення (n)	[tεlε'batʃεnja]
presenter, host	ведучий (m)	[wε'dutʃıj]
newscaster	диктор (m)	['dıktor]
commentator	коментатор (m)	[komεn'tator]
journalist	журналіст (m)	[ʒurna'list]
correspondent (reporter)	кореспондент (m)	[korεspon'dεnt]
press photographer	фотокореспондент (m)	[fotokorεspon'dεnt]
reporter	репортер (m)	[rεpor'tεr]
editor	редактор (m)	[rε'daktor]
editor-in-chief	головний редактор (m)	[ɣolow'nıj rε'daktor]
to subscribe (to …)	передплатити	[pεrεdpla'tıtı]
subscription	передплата (f)	[pεrεdp'lata]
subscriber	передплатник (m)	[pεrεdp'latnık]
to read (vi, vt)	читати	[tʃı'tatı]
reader	читач (m)	[tʃı'tatʃ]
circulation (of newspaper)	наклад (m)	['naklad]
monthly (adj)	щомісячний	[ɕo'misiatʃnıj]
weekly (adj)	щотижневий	[ɕotıʒ'nεwıj]
issue (edition)	номер (m)	['nɔmεr]
new (~ issue)	свіжий	['swiʒıj]
headline	заголовок (m)	[zaɣo'lɔwok]
short article	замітка (f)	[za'mitka]
column (regular article)	рубрика (f)	['rubrıka]
article	стаття (f)	[stat't'a]
page	сторінка (f)	[sto'riŋka]
reportage, report	репортаж (m)	[rεpor'taʒ]
event (happening)	подія (f)	[po'dija]

sensation (news)	сенсація (f)	[sɛn'satsija]
scandal	скандал (m)	[skan'dal]
scandalous (adj)	скандальний	[skan'daʌnij]
great (~ scandal)	гучний	[ɣutʃ'nij]

program	передача (f)	[pɛrɛ'datʃa]
interview	інтерв'ю (n)	[intɛrwʰ'ju]
live broadcast	пряма трансляція (f)	[prʲa'ma trans'ʌatsija]
channel	канал (m)	[ka'nal]

120. Agriculture

agriculture	сільське господарство (n)	[siʌsʲ'kɛ ɣospo'darstwo]
peasant (masc.)	селянин (m)	[sɛʌa'nın]
peasant (fem.)	селянка (f)	[sɛ'ʌaŋka]
farmer	фермер (m)	['fɛrmɛr]

tractor	трактор (m)	['traktor]
combine, harvester	комбайн (m)	[kom'bajn]

plow	плуг (m)	[pluɣ]
to plow (vi, vt)	орати	[o'ratı]
plowland	рілля (f)	[ri'ʌa]
furrow (in field)	борозна (f)	[boroz'na]

to sow (vi, vt)	сіяти	['sijatı]
seeder	сівалка (f)	[si'walka]
sowing (process)	посів (m)	[po'siw]

scythe	коса (f)	[ko'sa]
to mow, to scythe	косити	[ko'sıtı]

spade (tool)	лопата (f)	[lo'pata]
to dig (to till)	копати	[ko'patı]

hoe	сапка (f)	['sapka]
to hoe, to weed	полоти	[po'lotı]
weed (plant)	бур'ян (m)	[burʰ'jan]

watering can	лійка (f)	['lijka]
to water (plants)	поливати	[polı'watı]
watering (act)	поливання (n)	[polı'waŋja]

pitchfork	вила (pl)	['wıla]
rake	граблі (pl)	[ɣrab'li]

fertilizer	добриво (n)	['dɔbrıwo]
to fertilize (vt)	удобрювати	[u'dɔbrywatı]
manure (fertilizer)	гній (m)	[ɣnij]

field	поле (n)	['pɔlɛ]
meadow	лука (f)	['luka]
vegetable garden	город (m)	[ɣo'rɔd]
orchard (e.g., apple ~)	сад (m)	[sad]

to pasture (vt)	пасти	['pastɪ]
herdsman	пастух (m)	[pas'tuh]
pastureland	пасовище (n)	[paso'wiɕɛ]

cattle breeding	тваринництво (n)	[twa'rɪŋɪtstwo]
sheep farming	вівчарство (n)	[wiw'tʃarstwo]

plantation	плантація (f)	[plan'tatsija]
row (garden bed ~s)	грядка (f)	['ɣrʲadka]
hothouse	парник (m)	[par'nɪk]

drought (lack of rain)	посуха (f)	['pɔsuha]
dry (~ summer)	посушливий	[po'suʃlɪwɪj]

cereal crops	зернові (pl)	[zɛrno'wi]
to harvest, to gather	збирати	[zbɪ'ratɪ]

miller (person)	мірошник (m)	[mi'rɔʃnɪk]
mill (e.g., gristmill)	млин (m)	[mlɪn]
to grind (grain)	молотити зерно	[molo'tɪtɪ zɛr'nɔ]
flour	борошно (n)	['bɔroʃno]
straw	солома (f)	[so'lɔma]

121. Building. Building process

construction site	будівництво (n)	[budiw'nɪtstwo]
to build (vt)	будувати	[budu'watɪ]
construction worker	будівельник (m)	[budi'wɛʌnɪk]

project	проект (m)	[pro'ɛkt]
architect	архітектор (m)	[arhi'tɛktor]
worker	робочий (m)	[ro'bɔtʃɪj]

foundation (of building)	фундамент (m)	[fun'damɛnt]
roof	дах (m)	[dah]
foundation pile	паля (f)	['paʌa]
wall	стіна (f)	[sti'na]

reinforcing bars	арматура (f)	[arma'tura]
scaffolding	риштування (pl)	[rɪʃtu'wanja]

concrete	бетон (m)	[bɛ'tɔn]
granite	граніт (m)	[ɣra'nit]
stone	камінь (m)	['kamiɲ]
brick	цегла (f)	['tsɛɣla]

sand	пісок (m)	[pi'sɔk]
cement	цемент (m)	[ʦɛ'mɛnt]
plaster (for walls)	штукатурка (f)	[ʃtuka'turka]
to plaster (vt)	штукатурити	[ʃtuka'turɪtɪ]
paint	фарба (f)	['farba]
to paint (~ a wall)	фарбувати	[farbu'watɪ]
barrel	бочка (f)	['bɔʧka]

crane	кран (m)	[kran]
to lift (vt)	піднімати	[pidni'matɪ]
to lower (vt)	опускати	[opus'katɪ]

bulldozer	бульдозер (m)	[buʎ'dɔzɛr]
excavator	екскаватор (m)	[ɛkska'wator]
scoop, bucket	ківш (m)	[kiwʃ]
to dig (excavate)	копати	[ko'patɪ]
hard hat	каска (f)	['kaska]

122. Science. Research. Scientists

science	наука (f)	[na'uka]
scientific (adj)	науковий	[nau'kɔwɪj]
scientist	вчений (m)	['wʧɛnɪj]
theory	теорія (f)	[tɛ'ɔrija]

axiom	аксіома (f)	[aksi'ɔma]
analysis	аналіз (m)	[a'naliz]
to analyze (vt)	аналізувати	[analizu'watɪ]
argument (strong ~)	аргумент (m)	[arɣu'mɛnt]
substance (matter)	речовина (f)	[rɛʧɔwɪ'na]

hypothesis	гіпофіз (m)	[ɣi'pɔfiz]
dilemma	дилема (f)	[dɪ'lɛma]
dissertation	дисертація (f)	[dɪsɛr'taʦija]
dogma	догма (f)	['dɔɣma]

doctrine	доктрина (f)	[dokt'rɪna]
research	дослідження (n)	[dos'liʤɛnja]
to do research	досліджувати	[dos'liʤuwatɪ]
testing	контроль (m)	[kont'rɔʎ]
laboratory	лабораторія (f)	[labora'tɔrija]

method	метод (m)	['mɛtod]
molecule	молекула (f)	[mo'lɛkula]
monitoring	моніторинг (m)	[moni'tɔrɪŋ]
discovery (act, event)	відкриття (n)	[widkrɪt'tʲa]

postulate	постулат (m)	[postu'lat]
principle	принцип (m)	['prɪnʦɪp]
forecast	прогноз (m)	[proɣ'nɔz]

prognosticate (vt)	прогнозувати	[proɣnozu'watɪ]
synthesis	синтез (m)	['sɪntɛz]
trend (tendency)	тенденція (f)	[tɛn'dɛntsija]
theorem	теорема (f)	[tɛo'rɛma]
teachings	вчення (n)	['wtʃɛnja]
fact	факт (m)	[fakt]
expedition	експедиція (f)	[ɛkspɛ'dɪtsija]
experiment	експеримент (m)	[ɛkspɛrɪ'mɛnt]
academician	академік (m)	[aka'dɛmik]
bachelor (e.g., ~ of Arts)	бакалавр (m)	[baka'lawr]
doctor (PhD)	доктор (m)	['dɔktor]
Associate Professor	доцент (m)	[do'tsɛnt]
Master (e.g., ~ of Arts)	магістр (m)	[ma'ɣistr]
professor	професор (m)	[pro'fɛsor]

Professions and occupations

123. Job search. Dismissal

job	робота (f)	[ro'bota]
staff (work force)	колектив, штат (m)	[kolɛk'tiw], [ʃtat]
personnel	персонал (m)	[pɛrso'nal]
career	кар'єра (f)	[karʰ'ɛra]
prospects	перспектива (f)	[pɛrspɛk'tɪwa]
skills (mastery)	майстерність (f)	[majs'tɛrnistʲ]
selection (screening)	підбір (m)	[pid'bir]
employment agency	кадрове агентство (n)	['kadrowɛ a'ɣɛntstwo]
résumé	резюме (n)	[rɛzy'mɛ]
interview (for job)	співбесіда (f)	[spiw'bɛsida]
vacancy, opening	вакансія (f)	[wa'kansija]
salary, pay	зарплатня (f)	[zarplat'ɲa]
fixed salary	оклад (m)	[ok'lad]
pay, compensation	оплата (f)	[op'lata]
position (job)	посада (f)	[po'sada]
duty (of employee)	обов'язок (m)	[o'bowʲazok]
range of duties	коло (n)	['kolo]
busy (I'm ~)	зайнятий	['zajɲatɪj]
to fire (dismiss)	звільнити	[zwilʲ'nɪtɪ]
dismissal	звільнення (n)	['zwilʲnɛɲa]
unemployment	безробіття (n)	[bɛzro'bittʲa]
unemployed (n)	безробітний (m)	[bɛzro'bitnɪj]
retirement	пенсія (f)	['pɛnsija]
to retire (from job)	вийти на пенсію	['wɪjtɪ na 'pɛnsiju]

124. Business people

director	директор (m)	[dɪ'rɛktor]
manager (director)	управляючий (m)	[upraw'ʎajutʃɪj]
boss	керівник (m)	[kɛriw'nɪk]
superior	начальник (m)	[na'tʃaʎnɪk]
superiors	керівництво (n)	[kɛriw'nɪtstwo]
president	президент (m)	[prɛzɪ'dɛnt]

chairman	голова (m)	[ɣolo'wa]
deputy (substitute)	заступник (m)	[zas'tupnɪk]
assistant	помічник (m)	[pomitʃ'nɪk]
secretary	секретар (m)	[sɛkrɛ'tar]
personal assistant	особистий секретар (m)	[oso'bɪstɪj sɛkrɛ'tar]

businessman	бізнесмен (m)	[biznɛs'mɛn]
entrepreneur	підприємець (m)	[pidprɪ'ɛmɛʦ]
founder	засновник (m)	[zas'nɔwnɪk]
to found (vt)	заснувати	[zasnu'watɪ]

incorporator	фундатор (m)	[fun'dator]
partner	партнер (m)	[part'nɛr]
stockholder	акціонер (m)	[akʦio'nɛr]

millionaire	мільйонер (m)	[miʎjo'nɛr]
billionaire	мільярдер (m)	[miʎjar'dɛr]
owner, proprietor	власник (m)	['wlasnɪk]
landowner	землевласник (m)	[zɛmlɛw'lasnɪk]

client	клієнт (m)	[kli'ɛnt]
regular client	постійний клієнт (m)	[pos'tijnɪj kli'ɛnt]
buyer (customer)	покупець (m)	[poku'pɛʦ]
visitor	відвідувач (m)	[wid'widuwatʃ]

professional (n)	професіонал (m)	[profɛsio'nal]
expert	експерт (m)	[ɛks'pɛrt]
specialist	фахівець (m)	[fahi'wɛʦ]

| banker | банкір (m) | [ba'ŋkir] |
| broker | брокер (m) | ['brɔkɛr] |

cashier, teller	касир (m)	[ka'sɪr]
accountant	бухгалтер (m)	[buh'ɣaltɛr]
security guard	охоронник (m)	[oho'rɔŋɪk]

investor	інвестор (m)	[in'wɛstor]
debtor	боржник (m)	[borʒ'nɪk]
creditor	кредитор (m)	[krɛdɪ'tor]
borrower	боржник (m)	[borʒ'nɪk]

| importer | імпортер (m) | [impor'tɛr] |
| exporter | експортер (m) | [ɛkspor'tɛr] |

manufacturer	виробник (m)	[wɪrob'nɪk]
distributor	дистриб'ютор (m)	[dɪstrɪbʰ'jutor]
middleman	посередник (m)	[posɛ'rɛdnɪk]

consultant	консультант (m)	[konsuʎ'tant]
sales representative	представник (m)	[prɛdstaw'nɪk]
agent	агент (m)	[a'ɣɛnt]
insurance agent	страховий агент (m)	[straho'wɪj a'ɣɛnt]

125. Service professions

cook	кухар (m)	['kuhɑr]
chef (kitchen chef)	шеф-кухар (m)	[ʃɛf 'kuhɑr]
baker	пекар (m)	['pɛkɑr]
bartender	бармен (m)	[bɑr'mɛn]
waiter	офіціант (m)	[ofitsi'ɑnt]
waitress	офіціантка (f)	[ofitsi'ɑntkɑ]
lawyer, attorney	адвокат (m)	[ɑdwo'kɑt]
lawyer (legal expert)	юрист (m)	[ju'rɪst]
notary	нотаріус (m)	[no'tɑrius]
electrician	електрик (m)	[ɛ'lɛktrɪk]
plumber	сантехнік (m)	[sɑn'tɛhnik]
carpenter	тесля (m)	['tɛsʎɑ]
masseur	масажист (m)	[mɑsɑ'ʒɪst]
masseuse	масажистка (f)	[mɑsɑ'ʒɪstkɑ]
doctor	лікар (m)	['likɑr]
taxi driver	таксист (m)	[tɑk'sɪst]
driver	шофер (m)	[ʃo'fɛr]
delivery man	кур'єр (m)	[kurʰ'ɛr]
chambermaid	покоївка (f)	[poko'jɪwkɑ]
security guard	охоронник (m)	[oho'rɔŋɪk]
flight attendant	стюардеса (f)	[styar'dɛsɑ]
teacher (in primary school)	вчитель (m)	['wtʃitɛʎ]
librarian	бібліотекар (m)	[biblio'tɛkɑr]
translator	перекладач (m)	[pɛrɛklɑ'dɑtʃ]
interpreter	перекладач (m)	[pɛrɛklɑ'dɑtʃ]
guide	гід (m)	[ɣid]
hairdresser	перукар (m)	[pɛru'kɑr]
mailman	листоноша (m)	[lɪsto'nɔʃɑ]
salesman (store staff)	продавець (m)	[prodɑ'wɛts]
gardener	садівник (m)	[sɑdiw'nɪk]
domestic servant	слуга (m)	[slu'ɣɑ]
maid	служниця (f)	[sluʒ'nɪtsʲɑ]
cleaner (cleaning lady)	прибиральниця (f)	[prɪbɪ'rɑʎnɪtsʲɑ]

126. Military professions and ranks

private	рядовий (m)	[rʲɑdo'wɪj]
sergeant	сержант (m)	[sɛr'ʒɑnt]

| lieutenant | лейтенант (m) | [lɛjtɛ'nant] |
| captain | капітан (m) | [kapi'tan] |

major	майор (m)	[ma'jɔr]
colonel	полковник (m)	[pol'kɔwnɪk]
general	генерал (m)	[ɣɛnɛ'ral]
marshal	маршал (m)	['marʃal]
admiral	адмірал (m)	[admi'ral]

military man	військовий (m)	[wijsʲ'kɔwɪj]
soldier	солдат (m)	[sol'dat]
officer	офіцер (m)	[ofi'ʦɛr]
commander	командир (m)	[koman'dɪr]

border guard	прикордонник (m)	[prɪkor'dɔnɪk]
radio operator	радист (m)	[ra'dɪst]
scout (searcher)	розвідник (m)	[roz'widnɪk]
pioneer (sapper)	сапер (m)	[sa'pɛr]
marksman	стрілок (m)	[stri'lɔk]
navigator	штурман (m)	['ʃturman]

127. Officials. Priests

| king | король (m) | [ko'rɔʎ] |
| queen | королева (f) | [koro'lɛwa] |

| prince | принц (m) | [prɪnʦ] |
| princess | принцеса (f) | [prɪn'ʦɛsa] |

| tsar, czar | цар (m) | [ʦar] |
| czarina | цариця (f) | [ʦa'rɪtsʲa] |

president	президент (m)	[prɛzɪ'dɛnt]
Secretary (~ of State)	міністр (m)	[mi'nistr]
prime minister	прем'єр-міністр (m)	[prɛmʲ'ɛr mi'nistr]
senator	сенатор (m)	[sɛ'nator]

diplomat	дипломат (m)	[dɪplo'mat]
consul	консул (m)	['kɔnsul]
ambassador	посол (m)	[po'sɔl]
advisor (military ~)	радник (m)	['radnɪk]

official (civil servant)	чиновник (m)	[ʧɪ'nɔwnɪk]
prefect	префект (m)	[prɛ'fɛkt]
mayor	мер (m)	[mɛr]

judge	суддя (m)	[sud'dʲa]
district attorney (prosecutor)	прокурор (m)	[proku'rɔr]
missionary	місіонер (m)	[misio'nɛr]

monk	чернець (m)	[ʧɛrˈnɛʦ]
abbot	абат (m)	[aˈbat]
rabbi	рабин (m)	[raˈbɪn]

vizier	візир (m)	[wiˈzɪr]
shah	шах (m)	[ʃah]
sheikh	шейх (m)	[ʃɛjh]

128. Agricultural professions

beekeeper	пасічник (m)	[ˈpasiʧnɪk]
herder, shepherd	пастух (m)	[pasˈtuh]
agronomist	агроном (m)	[aɣroˈnɔm]
cattle breeder	тваринник (m)	[twaˈrɪnɪk]
veterinarian	ветеринар (m)	[wɛtɛrɪˈnar]

farmer	фермер (m)	[ˈfɛrmɛr]
winemaker	винороб (m)	[wɪnoˈrɔb]
zoologist	зоолог (m)	[zoˈɔloɣ]
cowboy	ковбой (m)	[kowˈbɔj]

129. Art professions

| actor | актор (m) | [akˈtor] |
| actress | акторка (f) | [akˈtorka] |

| singer (masc.) | співак (m) | [spiˈwak] |
| singer (fem.) | співачка (f) | [spiˈwaʧka] |

| dancer (masc.) | танцюрист (m) | [tanʦyˈrɪst] |
| dancer (fem.) | танцюристка (f) | [tanʦyˈrɪstka] |

| performing artist (masc.) | артист (m) | [arˈtɪst] |
| performing artist (fem.) | артистка (f) | [arˈtɪstka] |

musician	музикант (m)	[muzɪˈkant]
pianist	піаніст (m)	[piaˈnist]
guitar player	гітарист (m)	[ɣitaˈrɪst]

conductor (orchestra ~)	диригент (m)	[dɪrɪˈɣɛnt]
composer	композитор (m)	[kompoˈzɪtor]
impresario	імпресаріо (m)	[imprɛˈsario]

movie director	режисер (m)	[rɛʒɪˈsɛr]
producer	продюсер (m)	[proˈdysɛr]
scriptwriter	сценарист (m)	[sʦɛnaˈrɪst]
critic	критик (m)	[ˈkrɪtɪk]
writer	письменник (m)	[pɪsʲˈmɛnɪk]

poet	**поет** (m)	[po'ɛt]
sculptor	**скульптор** (m)	['skuʎptor]
artist (painter)	**художник** (m)	[hu'dɔʒnik]

juggler	**жонглер** (m)	[ʒoŋ'lɛr]
clown	**клоун** (m)	['klɔun]
acrobat	**акробат** (m)	[akro'bat]
magician	**фокусник** (m)	['fɔkusnik]

130. Various professions

doctor	**лікар** (m)	['likar]
nurse	**медсестра** (f)	[mɛdsɛst'ra]
psychiatrist	**психіатр** (m)	[psihi'atr]
dentist	**стоматолог** (m)	[stoma'tɔloɣ]
surgeon	**хірург** (m)	[hi'rurɣ]

| astronaut | **астронавт** (m) | [astro'nawt] |
| astronomer | **астроном** (m) | [astro'nɔm] |

driver (of taxi, etc.)	**водій** (m)	[wo'dij]
engineer (train driver)	**машиніст** (m)	[maʃi'nist]
mechanic	**механік** (m)	[mɛ'hanik]

miner	**шахтар** (m)	[ʃah'tar]
worker	**робочий** (m)	[ro'bɔtʃij]
metalworker	**слюсар** (m)	['slysar]
joiner (carpenter)	**столяр** (m)	['stɔʎar]
turner	**токар** (m)	['tɔkar]
construction worker	**будівельник** (m)	[budi'wɛʎnik]
welder	**зварник** (m)	['zwarnik]

professor (title)	**професор** (m)	[pro'fɛsor]
architect	**архітектор** (m)	[arhi'tɛktor]
historian	**історик** (m)	[is'tɔrik]
scientist	**вчений** (m)	['wtʃɛnij]
physicist	**фізик** (m)	['fizik]
chemist (scientist)	**хімік** (m)	['himik]

archeologist	**археолог** (m)	[arhɛ'ɔloɣ]
geologist	**геолог** (m)	[ɣɛ'ɔloɣ]
researcher	**дослідник** (m)	[dos'lidnik]

| babysitter | **няня** (f) | ['ɲaɲa] |
| teacher, educator | **педагог** (m) | [pɛda'ɣɔɣ] |

editor	**редактор** (m)	[rɛ'daktor]
editor-in-chief	**головний редактор** (m)	[ɣolow'nij rɛ'daktor]
correspondent	**кореспондент** (m)	[korɛspon'dɛnt]
typist (fem.)	**машиністка** (f)	[maʃi'nistka]

designer	**дизайнер** (m)	[dɪ'zajnɛr]
computer expert	**комп'ютерник** (m)	[kompʰ'jutɛrnɪk]
programmer	**програміст** (m)	[proɣ'ramist]
engineer (designer)	**інженер** (m)	[inʒɛ'nɛr]

sailor	**моряк** (m)	[mo'rʲak]
seaman	**матрос** (m)	[mat'ros]
rescuer	**рятувальник** (m)	[rʲatu'waʎnɪk]

fireman	**пожежник** (m)	[po'ʒɛʒnɪk]
policeman	**поліцейський** (m)	[poli'tsɛjsʲkɪj]
watchman	**сторож** (m)	['storoʒ]
detective	**сищик** (m)	['sɪɕɪk]

customs officer	**митник** (m)	['mɪtnɪk]
bodyguard	**охоронець** (m)	[oho'ronɛts]
prison guard	**доглядач** (m)	[doɣlʲa'datʃ]
inspector	**інспектор** (m)	[ins'pɛktor]

sportsman	**спортсмен** (m)	[sports'mɛn]
trainer, coach	**тренер** (m)	['trɛnɛr]
butcher	**м'ясник** (m)	[mʰjas'nɪk]
cobbler	**чоботар** (m)	[tʃobo'tar]
merchant	**комерсант** (m)	[komɛr'sant]
loader (person)	**вантажник** (m)	[wan'taʒnɪk]

| fashion designer | **модельєр** (m) | [modɛ'ʎjɛr] |
| model (fem.) | **модель** (f) | [modɛʎ] |

131. Occupations. Social status

| schoolboy | **школяр** (m) | [ʃko'ʎar] |
| student (college ~) | **студент** (m) | [stu'dɛnt] |

philosopher	**філософ** (m)	[fi'lɔsof]
economist	**економіст** (m)	[ɛkono'mist]
inventor	**винахідник** (m)	[wɪna'hidnɪk]

unemployed (n)	**безробітний** (m)	[bɛzro'bitnɪj]
retiree	**пенсіонер** (m)	[pɛnsio'nɛr]
spy, secret agent	**шпигун** (m)	[ʃpi'ɣun]

prisoner	**в'язень** (m)	['wʰjazɛɲ]
striker	**страйкар** (m)	[straj'kar]
bureaucrat	**бюрократ** (m)	[byrok'rat]
traveler	**мандрівник** (m)	[mandriw'nɪk]

homosexual	**гомосексуаліст** (m)	[ɣomosɛksua'list]
hacker	**хакер** (m)	['hakɛr]
bandit	**бандит** (m)	[ban'dɪt]

hit man, killer	**найманий вбивця** (m)	[ˈnajmanɪj ˈwbɪwt͡sʲa]
drug addict	**наркоман** (m)	[narkoˈman]
drug dealer	**наркоторгівець** (m)	[narkotorˈɣiwɛt͡s]
prostitute (fem.)	**проститутка** (f)	[prostɪˈtutka]
pimp	**сутенер** (m)	[sutɛˈnɛr]
sorcerer	**чаклун** (m)	[t͡ʃakˈlun]
sorceress	**чаклунка** (f)	[t͡ʃakˈluŋka]
pirate	**пірат** (m)	[piˈrat]
slave	**раб** (m)	[rab]
samurai	**самурай** (m)	[samuˈraj]
savage (primitive)	**дикун** (m)	[dɪˈkun]

Sports

132. Kinds of sports. Sportspersons

sportsman	спортсмен (m)	[sports'mɛn]
kind of sports	вид спорту (m)	[wɪd 'sportu]
basketball	баскетбол (m)	[baskɛt'bɔl]
basketball player	баскетболіст (m)	[baskɛtbo'list]
baseball	бейсбол (m)	[bɛjs'bɔl]
baseball player	бейсболіст (m)	[bɛjsbo'list]
soccer	футбол (m)	[fut'bɔl]
soccer player	футболіст (m)	[futbo'list]
goalkeeper	воротар (m)	[woro'tar]
hockey	хокей (m)	[ho'kɛj]
hockey player	хокеїст (m)	[hokɛ'jɪst]
volleyball	волейбол (m)	[wolɛj'bɔl]
volleyball player	волейболіст (m)	[wolɛjbo'list]
boxing	бокс (m)	[boks]
boxer	боксер (m)	[bok'sɛr]
wrestling	боротьба (f)	[borotʲ'ba]
wrestler	борець (m)	[bo'rɛʦ]
karate	карате (n)	[kara'tɛ]
karate fighter	каратист (m)	[kara'tɪst]
judo	дзюдо (n)	[ʤy'dɔ]
judo athlete	дзюдоїст (m)	[ʤydo'jɪst]
tennis	теніс (m)	['tɛnis]
tennis player	тенісист (m)	[tɛni'sɪst]
swimming	плавання (n)	['plawanja]
swimmer	плавець (m)	[pla'wɛʦ]
fencing	фехтування (n)	[fɛhtu'wanja]
fencer	фехтувальник (m)	[fɛhtu'waʎnɪk]
chess	шахи (pl)	['ʃahɪ]
chess player	шахіст (m)	[ʃa'hist]

| alpinism | **альпінізм** (m) | [aʎpi'nizm] |
| alpinist | **альпініст** (m) | [aʎpi'nist] |

running	**біг** (m)	[biɣ]
runner	**бігун** (m)	[bi'ɣun]
athletics	**легка атлетика** (f)	[lɛɣ'ka at'lɛtɪka]
athlete	**атлет** (m)	[at'lɛt]

| horseback riding | **кінний спорт** (m) | ['kiɲɪj 'sport] |
| horse rider | **наїзник** (m) | [na'jɪznɪk] |

figure skating	**фігурне катання** (n)	[fi'ɣurnɛ ka'taɲa]
figure skater (masc.)	**фігурист** (m)	[fiɣu'rist]
figure skater (fem.)	**фігуристка** (f)	[fiɣu'rɪstka]

weightlifting	**важка атлетика** (f)	[waʒ'ka at'lɛtɪka]
car racing	**автогонки** (pl)	[awto'ɣɔŋki]
racing driver	**гонщик** (m)	['ɣɔnɕɪk]

| cycling | **велоспорт** (m) | [wɛlos'port] |
| cyclist | **велосипедист** (m) | [wɛlosɪpɛ'dɪst] |

broad jump	**стрибки** (pl) **в довжину**	[strɪb'kɪ w dowʒɪ'nu]
pole vault	**стрибки** (pl) **з жердиною**	[strɪb'kɪ z ʒɛr'dɪnoju]
jumper	**стрибун** (m)	[strɪ'bun]

133. Kinds of sports. Miscellaneous

football	**американський футбол** (m)	[amɛrɪ'kansʲkɪj fut'bɔl]
badminton	**бадмінтон** (m)	[badmin'tɔn]
biathlon	**біатлон** (m)	[biat'lɔn]
billiards	**більярд** (m)	[bi'ʎjard]

bobsled	**бобслей** (m)	[bobs'lɛj]
bodybuilding	**бодібілдинг** (m)	[bodi'bildɪŋ]
water polo	**водне поло** (n)	['wodnɛ 'polo]
handball	**гандбол** (m)	[ɣand'bɔl]
golf	**гольф** (m)	[ɣoʎf]

rowing	**гребля** (m)	['ɣrɛbʎa]
scuba diving	**дайвінг** (m)	['dajwiŋ]
cross-country skiing	**лижні гонки** (pl)	['lɪʒni 'ɣɔŋkɪ]
ping-pong	**настільний теніс** (m)	[nas'tiʎnɪj 'tɛnis]

sailing	**парусний спорт** (m)	['parusnɪj sport]
rally racing	**ралі** (n)	['rali]
rugby	**регбі** (n)	['rɛɣbi]
snowboarding	**сноуборд** (m)	[snou'bord]
archery	**стрільба** (f) **з луку**	[striʎ'ba z 'luku]

134. Gym

barbell	штанга (f)	['ʃtaŋa]
dumbbells	гантелі (pl)	[ɣan'tɛlɪ]
training machine	тренажер (m)	[trɛna'ʒɛr]
bicycle trainer	велотренажер (m)	[wɛlotrɛna'ʒɛr]
treadmill	бігова доріжка (f)	[biɣo'wa do'riʒka]
horizontal bar	перекладина (f)	[pɛrɛk'ladɪna]
parallel bars	бруси (pl)	['brusɪ]
vaulting horse	кінь (m)	[kiɲ]
mat (in gym)	мат (m)	[mat]
aerobics	аеробіка (f)	[aɛ'rɔbika]
yoga	йога (f)	['jɔɣa]

135. Hockey

hockey	хокей (m)	[ho'kɛj]
hockey player	хокеїст (m)	[hokɛ'jɪst]
to play hockey	грати в хокей	['ɣratɪ w ho'kɛj]
ice	лід (m)	[lid]
puck	шайба (f)	['ʃajba]
hockey stick	ключка (f)	['klyʧka]
ice skates	ковзани (pl)	[kowza'nɪ]
board	борт (m)	[bort]
shot	кидок (m)	[kɪ'dɔk]
goaltender	воротар (m)	[woro'tar]
goal (score)	гол (m)	[ɣol]
to score a goal	забити гол	[za'bɪtɪ ɣol]
period	період (m)	[pɛ'riod]
substitutes bench	лава (f) запасних	['lawa zapas'nɪh]

136. Football

soccer	футбол (m)	[fut'bɔl]
soccer player	футболіст (m)	[futbo'list]
to play soccer	грати в футбол	['ɣratɪ w fut'bɔl]
major league	вища ліга (f)	['wɪɕa 'liɣa]
soccer club	футбольний клуб (m)	[fut'bɔʎnɪj klub]
coach	тренер (m)	['trɛnɛr]

owner, proprietor	власник (m)	['wlasnık]
team	команда (f)	[ko'manda]
team captain	капітан (m) команди	[kapi'tan ko'mandı]
player	гравець (m)	[ɣra'wɛts]
substitute	запасний гравець (m)	[zapas'nıj ɣra'wɛts]
forward	нападаючий (m)	[napa'dajuʧıj]
center forward	центральний нападаючий	[ʦɛnt'raʎnıj napa'dajuʧıj]
striker, scorer	бомбардир (m)	[bombar'dır]
defender, back	захисник (m)	[zahıs'nık]
halfback	півзахисник (m)	[piwzahıs'nık]
match	матч (m)	[maʧ]
to meet (vi, vt)	зустрічатися	[zustri'ʧatısʲa]
final	фінал (m)	[fi'nal]
semi-final	напівфінал (m)	[napiwfi'nal]
championship	чемпіонат (m)	[ʧɛmpio'nat]
period, half	тайм (m)	[tajm]
first period	перший тайм (m)	['pɛrʃıj tajm]
half-time	перерва (f)	[pɛ'rɛrwa]
goal	ворота (pl)	[wo'rɔta]
goalkeeper	воротар (m)	[woro'tar]
goalpost	штанга (f)	['ʃtaŋa]
crossbar	перекладина (f)	[pɛrɛk'ladına]
net	сітка (f)	['sitka]
to concede a goal	пропустити гол	[propus'tıtı ɣol]
ball	м'яч (m)	[mʰjaʧ]
pass	пас (m)	[pas]
kick	удар (m)	[u'dar]
to kick (~ the ball)	нанести удар	[na'nɛstı u'dar]
free kick	штрафний удар (m)	[ʃtraf'nıj u'dar]
corner kick	кутовий удар (m)	[ku'towıj u'dar]
attack	атака (f)	[a'taka]
counterattack	контратака (f)	[kontra'taka]
combination	комбінація (f)	[kombi'natsija]
referee	арбітр (m)	[ar'bitr]
to whistle (vi)	свистіти	[swıs'titı]
whistle (sound)	свисток (m)	[swıs'tɔk]
foul, misconduct	порушення (n)	[po'ruʃɛnja]
to commit a foul	порушувати	[po'ruʃuwatı]
to send off	видалити з поля	['wıdalıtı z 'pɔʎa]
yellow card	жовта картка (f)	['ʒɔwta 'kartka]
red card	червона картка (f)	[ʧɛr'wɔna 'kartka]
disqualification	дискваліфікація (f)	[dıskwalifi'katsija]
to disqualify (vt)	дискваліфікувати	[dıskwalifiku'watı]

penalty kick	пенальті (n)	[pɛ'naʎti]
wall	стінка (f)	['stiŋka]
to score (vi, vt)	забити	[za'bɪtɪ]
goal (score)	гол (m)	[ɣol]
to score a goal	забити гол	[za'bɪtɪ ɣol]

substitution	заміна (f)	[za'mina]
to replace (vt)	замінити	[zami'nɪtɪ]
rules	правила (pl)	['prawɪla]
tactics	тактика (f)	['taktɪka]

stadium	стадіон (m)	[stadi'ɔn]
stand (bleachers)	трибуна (f)	[trɪ'buna]
fan, supporter	болільник (m)	[bo'liʎnɪk]
to shout (vi)	кричати	[krɪ'ʧatɪ]
scoreboard	табло (n)	[tab'lɔ]
score	рахунок (m)	[ra'hunok]

defeat	поразка (f)	[po'razka]
to lose (not win)	програти	[proɣ'ratɪ]
draw	нічия (f)	[niʧɪ'ja]
to draw (vi)	зіграти внічию	[ziɣ'ratɪ wniʧɪ'ju]

victory	перемога (f)	[pɛrɛ'mɔɣa]
to win (vi, vt)	перемогти	[pɛrɛmoɣ'tɪ]
champion	чемпіон (m)	[ʧɛmpi'ɔn]
best (adj)	кращий	['kraɕɪj]
to congratulate (vt)	вітати	[wi'tatɪ]

commentator	коментатор (m)	[komɛn'tator]
to commentate (vt)	коментувати	[komɛntu'watɪ]
broadcast	трансляція (f)	[trans'ʎatsija]

137. Alpine skiing

skis	лижі (pl)	['lɪʒi]
to ski (vi)	кататися на лижах	[ka'tatɪsʲa na 'lɪʒah]
mountain-ski resort	гірськолижній курорт (m)	[ɣirsʲko'lɪʒnij ku'rort]
ski lift	підйомник (m)	[pid'jɔmnɪk]
ski poles	палиці (pl)	['palɪtsi]
slope	схил (m)	[shɪl]
slalom	слалом (m)	['slalom]

138. Tennis. Golf

| golf | гольф (m) | [ɣoʎf] |
| golf club | гольф-клуб (m) | [ɣoʎf klub] |

golfer	гравець (m) в гольф	[ɣra'wɛts w ɣoʎf]
hole	лунка (f)	['luŋka]
club	ключка (f)	['klytʃka]
golf trolley	візок (m) для ключок	[wi'zɔk dʎa 'klytʃok]

tennis	теніс (m)	['tɛnis]
tennis court	корт (m)	[kort]
serve	подача (f)	[po'datʃa]
to serve (vt)	подавати	[poda'watı]
racket	ракетка (f)	[ra'kɛtka]
net	сітка (f)	['sitka]
ball	м'яч (m)	[mʰjatʃ]

139. Chess

chess	шахи (pl)	['ʃahı]
chessmen	шахи (pl)	['ʃahı]
chess player	шахіст (m)	[ʃa'hist]
chessboard	шахова дошка (f)	['ʃahowa 'doʃka]
chessman	фігура (f)	[fi'ɣura]

White (white pieces)	білі (pl)	['bili]
Black (black pieces)	чорні (pl)	['tʃorni]
pawn	пішак (m)	[pi'ʃak]
bishop	слон (m)	[slon]
knight	кінь (m)	[kiɲ]
rook (castle)	тура (f)	[tu'ra]
queen	ферзь (m)	[fɛrzʲ]
king	король (m)	[ko'rɔʎ]

move	хід (m)	[hid]
to move (vi, vt)	ходити	[ho'dıtı]
to sacrifice (vt)	пожертвувати	[po'ʒɛrtwuwatı]
castling	рокірування (n)	[rokiru'waŋja]
check	шах (m)	[ʃah]
checkmate	мат (m)	[mat]

chess tournament	шаховий турнір (m)	['ʃahowıj tur'nir]
Grand Master	гросмейстер (m)	[ɣros'mɛjstɛr]
combination	комбінація (f)	[kombi'natsija]
game (in chess)	партія (f)	['partija]
checkers	шашки (pl)	['ʃaʃkı]

140. Boxing

boxing	бокс (m)	[boks]
fight (bout)	бій (m)	[bij]
boxing match	двобій (m)	[dwo'bij]

round (in boxing)	**раунд** (m)	['raund]
ring	**ринг** (m)	[rɪŋ]
gong	**гонг** (m)	[ɣoŋ]
punch	**удар** (m)	[u'daɾ]
knock-down	**нокдаун** (m)	[nok'daun]
knockout	**нокаут** (m)	[no'kaut]
to knock out	**нокаутувати**	[nokautu'watɪ]
boxing glove	**боксерська рукавичка** (f)	[bok'sɛrsʲka ruka'wɪtʃka]
referee	**реферí** (m)	['rɛfɛri]
lightweight	**легка вага** (f)	['lɛɣka wa'ɣa]
middleweight	**середня вага** (f)	[sɛ'rɛdɲa wa'ɣa]
heavyweight	**важка вага** (f)	[waʒ'ka wa'ɣa]

141. Sports. Miscellaneous

Olympic Games	**Олімпíйські ігри** (pl)	[olim'pijsʲki 'iɣrɪ]
winner	**переможець** (m)	[pɛrɛ'mɔʒɛts]
to be winning	**перемагати**	[pɛrɛma'ɣatɪ]
to win (vi)	**виграти**	['wɪɣratɪ]
leader	**лíдер** (m)	['lidɛr]
to lead (vi)	**лідирувати**	[li'dɪruwatɪ]
first place	**перше місце** (n)	['pɛrʃɛ 'mistsɛ]
second place	**друге місце** (n)	['druɣɛ 'mistsɛ]
third place	**третє місце** (n)	['trɛtɛ 'mistsɛ]
medal	**медаль** (f)	[mɛ'daʎ]
trophy	**трофей** (m)	[tro'fɛj]
prize cup (trophy)	**кубок** (m)	['kubok]
prize (in game)	**приз** (m)	[prɪz]
main prize	**головний приз** (m)	[ɣolow'nɪj prɪz]
record	**рекорд** (m)	[rɛ'kɔrd]
to set a record	**встановлювати рекорд**	[wsta'nowlywatɪ rɛ'kɔrd]
final	**фінал** (m)	[fi'nal]
final (adj)	**фінальний**	[fi'naʎnɪj]
champion	**чемпіон** (m)	[tʃɛmpi'ɔn]
championship	**чемпіонат** (m)	[tʃɛmpio'nat]
stadium	**стадіон** (m)	[stadi'ɔn]
stand (bleachers)	**трибуна** (f)	[trɪ'buna]
fan, supporter	**уболівальник** (m)	[uboli'waʎnɪk]
opponent, rival	**супротивник** (m)	[supro'tɪwnɪk]

start	старт (m)	[stɑrt]
finish line	фініш (m)	[ˈfiniʃ]
defeat	поразка (f)	[poˈrazka]
to lose (not win)	програти	[proɣˈratɪ]
referee	суддя (m)	[sudˈdʲɑ]
jury	журі (n)	[ʒuˈri]
score	рахунок (m)	[raˈhunok]
draw	нічия (f)	[nitʃɪˈja]
to draw (vi)	зіграти внічию	[ziɣˈratɪ wnitʃɪˈju]
point	очко (n)	[otʃˈkɔ]
result (final score)	результат (m)	[rɛzuʎˈtat]
half-time	перерва (f)	[pɛˈrɛrwa]
doping	допінг (m)	[ˈdɔpiŋ]
to penalize (vt)	штрафувати	[ʃtrafuˈwatɪ]
to disqualify (vt)	дискваліфікувати	[dɪskwalifikuˈwatɪ]
apparatus	снаряд (m)	[snaˈrʲad]
javelin	спис (m)	[spɪs]
shot put ball	ядро (n)	[jadˈrɔ]
ball (snooker, etc.)	куля (f)	[ˈkuʎa]
aim (target)	ціль (f)	[tsiʎ]
target	мішень (f)	[miˈʃɛɲ]
to shoot (vi)	стріляти	[striˈ ʎatɪ]
precise (~ shot)	влучний	[ˈwlutʃnɪj]
trainer, coach	тренер (m)	[ˈtrɛnɛr]
to train (sb)	тренувати	[trɛnuˈwatɪ]
to train (vi)	тренуватися	[trɛnuˈwatɪsʲa]
training	тренування (n)	[trɛnuˈwaɲa]
gym	спортзал (m)	[sportˈzal]
exercise (physical)	вправа (f)	[ˈwprawa]
warm-up (of athlete)	розминка (f)	[rozˈmɪŋka]

Education

142. School

school	**школа** (f)	[ˈʃkɔla]
headmaster	**директор** (m) **школи**	[dɪˈrɛktor ˈʃkɔlɪ]
pupil (boy)	**учень** (m)	[ˈutʃɛɲ]
pupil (girl)	**учениця** (f)	[utʃɛˈnɪtsʲa]
schoolboy	**школяр** (m)	[ʃkoˈʎar]
schoolgirl	**школярка** (f)	[ʃkoˈʎarka]
to teach (sb)	**вчити**	[ˈwtʃɪtɪ]
to learn (language, etc.)	**вчити**	[ˈwtʃɪtɪ]
to learn by heart	**вчити напам'ять**	[ˈwtʃɪtɪ naˈpamʰjatʲ]
to study (work to learn)	**вчитися**	[ˈwtʃɪtɪsʲa]
to be in school	**вчитися**	[ˈwtʃɪtɪsʲa]
to go to school	**йти до школи**	[jtɪ do ʃkɔlɪ]
alphabet	**алфавіт** (m)	[alfaˈwit]
subject (at school)	**предмет** (m)	[prɛdˈmɛt]
classroom	**клас** (m)	[klas]
lesson	**урок** (m)	[uˈrɔk]
recess	**перерва** (f)	[pɛˈrɛrwa]
school bell	**дзвінок** (m)	[dzwiˈnɔk]
school desk	**парта** (f)	[ˈparta]
chalkboard	**дошка** (f)	[ˈdɔʃka]
grade	**відмітка** (f)	[widˈmitka]
good grade	**добра оцінка** (f)	[ˈdɔbra oˈtsiŋka]
bad grade	**погана оцінка** (f)	[poˈɣana oˈtsiŋka]
to give a grade	**ставити оцінку**	[ˈstawɪtɪ oˈtsiŋku]
mistake, error	**помилка** (f)	[poˈmɪlka]
to make mistakes	**робити помилки**	[roˈbɪtɪ ˈpomɪlkɪ]
to correct (an error)	**виправляти**	[wɪprawˈʎatɪ]
cheat sheet	**шпаргалка** (f)	[ʃparˈɣalka]
homework	**домашнє завдання** (n)	[doˈmaʃnɛ zawˈdanja]
exercise (in education)	**вправа** (f)	[ˈwprawa]
to be present	**бути присутнім**	[ˈbutɪ prɪˈsutnim]
to be absent	**бути відсутнім**	[ˈbutɪ widˈsutnim]
to punish (vt)	**покарати**	[pokaˈratɪ]

punishment	покарання (n)	[poka'ranja]
conduct (behavior)	поведінка (f)	[powɛ'diŋka]
report card	щоденник (m)	[ɕo'dɛŋık]
pencil	олівець (m)	[oli'wɛts]
eraser	гумка (f)	['ɣumka]
chalk	крейда (f)	['krɛjda]
pencil case	пенал (m)	[pɛ'nal]
schoolbag	портфель (m)	[port'fɛʎ]
pen	ручка (f)	['rutʃka]
school notebook	зошит (m)	['zɔʃıt]
textbook	підручник (m)	[pid'rutʃnık]
compasses	циркуль (m)	['tsırkuʎ]
to draw (a blueprint, etc.)	креслити	['krɛslıtı]
technical drawing	креслення (n)	['krɛslɛnja]
poem	вірш (m)	[wirʃ]
by heart (adv)	напам'ять	[na'pamʰjatʲ]
to learn by heart	вчити напам'ять	['wtʃıtı na'pamʰjatʲ]
school vacation	канікули (pl)	[ka'nikulı]
to be on vacation	бути на канікулах	['butı na ka'nikulah]
test (written math ~)	контрольна робота (f)	[kont'rɔʎna ro'bota]
essay (composition)	твір (m)	[twir]
dictation	диктант (m)	[dık'tant]
exam	іспит (m)	['ispıt]
to take an exam	складати іспити	[skla'datı 'ispıtı]
experiment (chemical ~)	досвід (m)	['dɔswid]

143. College. University

academy	академія (f)	[aka'dɛmija]
university	університет (m)	[uniwɛrsı'tɛt]
faculty (section)	факультет (m)	[fakuʎ'tɛt]
student (masc.)	студент (m)	[stu'dɛnt]
student (fem.)	студентка (f)	[stu'dɛntka]
lecturer (teacher)	викладач (m)	[wıkla'datʃ]
lecture hall, room	аудиторія (f)	[audı'torija]
graduate	випускник (m)	[wıpusk'nık]
diploma	диплом (m)	[dıp'lom]
dissertation	дисертація (f)	[dısɛr'tatsija]
study (report)	дослідження (n)	[dos'lidʒɛnja]
laboratory	лабораторія (f)	[labora'torija]
lecture	лекція (f)	['lɛktsija]

course mate	однокурсник (m)	[odno'kursnık]
scholarship	стипендія (f)	[stɪ'pɛndija]
academic degree	вчений ступінь (m)	['wtʃɛnɪj 'stupiɲ]

144. Sciences. Disciplines

mathematics	математика (f)	[matɛ'matɪka]
algebra	алгебра (f)	['alɣɛbra]
geometry	геометрія (f)	[ɣɛo'mɛtrija]

astronomy	астрономія (f)	[astro'nɔmija]
biology	біологія (f)	[bio'lɔyija]
geography	географія (f)	[ɣɛoɣ'rafija]
geology	геологія (f)	[ɣɛo'lɔyija]
history	історія (f)	[is'torija]

medicine	медицина (f)	[mɛdɪ'ʦɪna]
pedagogy	педагогіка (f)	[pɛda'ɣɔyika]
law	право (n)	['prawo]

physics	фізика (f)	['fizɪka]
chemistry	хімія (f)	['himija]
philosophy	філософія (f)	[filo'sofija]
psychology	психологія (f)	[psɪho'lɔyija]

145. Writing system. Orthography

grammar	граматика (f)	[ɣra'matɪka]
vocabulary	лексика (f)	['lɛksɪka]
phonetics	фонетика (f)	[fo'nɛtɪka]

noun	іменник (m)	[i'mɛɲɪk]
adjective	прикметник (m)	[prɪk'mɛtnɪk]
verb	дієслово (n)	[diɛs'lɔwo]
adverb	прислівник (m)	[prɪs'liwnɪk]

pronoun	займенник (m)	[zaj'mɛɲɪk]
interjection	вигук (m)	['wɪyuk]
preposition	прийменник (m)	[prɪj'mɛɲɪk]

root	корінь (m) слова	['koriɲ 'slɔwa]
ending	закінчення (n)	[za'kintʃɛɲa]
prefix	префікс (m)	['prɛfiks]

syllable	склад (m)	[sklad]
suffix	суфікс (m)	['sufiks]
stress mark	наголос (m)	['naɣolos]
apostrophe	апостроф (m)	[a'postrof]

period, dot	**крапка** (f)	['krɑpkɑ]
comma	**кома** (f)	['kɔmɑ]
semicolon	**крапка** (f) **з комою**	['krɑpkɑ z 'kɔmoju]

| colon | **двокрапка** (f) | [dwok'rɑpkɑ] |
| ellipsis | **крапки** (pl) | [krɑp'kɪ] |

| question mark | **знак** (m) **питання** | [znɑk pɪ'tɑnjɑ] |
| exclamation point | **знак** (m) **оклику** | [znɑk 'ɔklɪku] |

| quotation marks | **лапки** (pl) | [lɑp'kɪ] |
| in quotation marks | **в лапках** | [w lɑp'kɑh] |

| parenthesis | **дужки** (pl) | [duʒ'kɪ] |
| in parenthesis | **в дужках** | [w duʒ'kɑh] |

hyphen	**дефіс** (m)	[dɛ'fis]
dash	**тире** (n)	[tɪ'rɛ]
space (between words)	**пробіл** (m)	[pro'bil]

| letter | **літера** (f) | ['litɛrɑ] |
| capital letter | **велика літера** (f) | [wɛ'lɪkɑ 'litɛrɑ] |

| vowel (n) | **голосний звук** (m) | [ɣolos'nɪj zwuk] |
| consonant (n) | **приголосний** (m) | ['prɪɣolosnɪj] |

sentence	**речення** (n)	['rɛtʃɛnjɑ]
subject	**підмет** (m)	['pidmɛt]
predicate	**присудок** (m)	['prɪsudok]

line	**рядок** (m)	[rʲɑ'dɔk]
on a new line	**с нової стрічки** (f)	[s no'wojɪ 'stritʃkɪ]
paragraph	**абзац** (m)	[ɑb'zɑts]

word	**слово** (n)	['slɔwo]
group of words	**словосполучення** (n)	[slowospo'lutʃɛnjɑ]
expression	**вислів** (m)	['wɪsliw]

| synonym | **синонім** (m) | [sɪ'nɔnim] |
| antonym | **антонім** (m) | [ɑn'tɔnim] |

rule	**правило** (n)	['prɑwɪlo]
exception	**виняток** (m)	['wɪɲɑtok]
correct (adj)	**вірний**	['wirnɪj]

conjugation	**дієвідміна** (f)	[diɛwid'minɑ]
declension	**відміна** (f)	[wid'minɑ]
nominal case	**відмінок** (m)	[wid'minok]
question	**питання** (n)	[pɪ'tɑnjɑ]
to underline (vt)	**підкреслити**	[pidk'rɛslɪtɪ]
dotted line	**пунктир** (m)	[puŋk'tɪr]

146. Foreign languages

language	мова (f)	['mɔwɑ]
foreign language	іноземна мова (f)	[ino'zɛmnɑ 'mɔwɑ]
to study (vt)	вивчати	[wɪw'tʃɑtɪ]
to learn (language, etc.)	вчити	['wtʃɪtɪ]
to read (vi, vt)	читати	[tʃɪ'tɑtɪ]
to speak (vi, vt)	розмовляти	[rozmow'ʎɑtɪ]
to understand (vt)	розуміти	[rozu'mitɪ]
to write (vt)	писати	[pɪ'sɑtɪ]
fast (adv)	швидко	['ʃwɪdko]
slowly (adv)	повільно	[po'wiʎno]
fluently (adv)	вільно	['wiʎno]
rules	правила (pl)	['prɑwɪlɑ]
grammar	граматика (f)	[ɣrɑ'mɑtɪkɑ]
vocabulary	лексика (f)	['lɛksɪkɑ]
phonetics	фонетика (f)	[fo'nɛtɪkɑ]
textbook	підручник (m)	[pid'rutʃnɪk]
dictionary	словник (m)	[slow'nɪk]
teach-yourself book	самовчитель (m)	[samow'tʃɪtɛʎ]
phrasebook	розмовник (m)	[roz'mɔwnɪk]
cassette	касета (f)	[kɑ'sɛtɑ]
videotape	відеокасета (f)	[widɛokɑ'sɛtɑ]
CD, compact disc	CD-диск (m)	[si'di dɪsk]
DVD	DVD (m)	[dɪwi'di]
alphabet	алфавіт (m)	[ɑlfɑ'wit]
to spell (vt)	говорити по буквах	[ɣowo'rɪtɪ po 'bukwɑh]
pronunciation	вимова (f)	[wɪ'mɔwɑ]
accent	акцент (m)	[ɑk'tsɛnt]
with an accent	з акцентом	[z ɑk'tsɛntom]
without an accent	без акценту (m)	[bɛz ɑk'tsɛntu]
word	слово (n)	['slɔwo]
meaning	сенс (m)	[sɛns]
course (e.g., a French ~)	курси (pl)	['kursɪ]
to sign up	записатися	[zɑpɪ'sɑtɪsʲɑ]
teacher	викладач (m)	[wɪklɑ'dɑtʃ]
translation (process)	переклад (m)	[pɛ'rɛklɑd]
translation (text, etc.)	переклад (m)	[pɛ'rɛklɑd]
translator	перекладач (m)	[pɛrɛklɑ'dɑtʃ]
interpreter	перекладач (m)	[pɛrɛklɑ'dɑtʃ]
polyglot	поліглот (m)	[poliɣ'lɔt]
memory	пам'ять (f)	['pamʰjɑtʲ]

147. Fairy tale characters

Santa Claus	Санта Клаус (m)	['sɑntɑ 'klɑus]
mermaid	русалка (f)	[ru'sɑlkɑ]
magician, wizard	чарівник (m)	[ʧɑriw'nɪk]
fairy	чарівниця (f)	[ʧɑriw'nɪʦʲɑ]
magic (adj)	чарівний	[ʧɑriw'nɪj]
magic wand	чарівна паличка (f)	[ʧɑ'riwnɑ 'pɑlɪʧkɑ]
fairy tale	казка (f)	['kɑzkɑ]
miracle	диво (n)	['dɪʋo]
dwarf	гном (m)	[ɣnom]
to turn into ...	перетворитися на	[pɛrɛtwo'rɪtɪsʲɑ nɑ]
ghost	привид (m)	['prɪwɪd]
phantom	примара (f)	[prɪ'mɑrɑ]
monster	чудовисько (n)	[ʧu'dowɪsko]
dragon	дракон (m)	[drɑ'kɔn]
giant	велетень (m)	['wɛlɛtɛɲ]

148. Zodiac Signs

Aries	Овен (m)	['ɔwɛn]
Taurus	Тілець (m)	[ti'lɛʦ]
Gemini	Близнюки (pl)	[blɪzny'kɪ]
Cancer	Рак (m)	[rɑk]
Leo	Лев (m)	[lɛw]
Virgo	Діва (f)	['diwɑ]
Libra	Терези (pl)	[tɛrɛ'zɪ]
Scorpio	Скорпіон (m)	[skorpi'ɔn]
Sagittarius	Стрілець (m)	[stri'lɛʦ]
Capricorn	Козерог (m)	[kozɛ'rɔɣ]
Aquarius	Водолій (m)	[wodo'lij]
Pisces	Риби (pl)	['rɪbɪ]
character	характер (m)	[hɑ'rɑktɛr]
features of character	риси (pl) характеру	['rɪsɪ hɑ'rɑktɛru]
behavior	поведінка (f)	[powɛ'diŋkɑ]
to tell fortunes	ворожити	[woro'ʒɪtɪ]
fortune-teller	гадалка (f)	[ɣɑ'dɑlkɑ]
horoscope	гороскоп (m)	[ɣoros'kɔp]

Arts

149. Theater

theater	театр (m)	[tɛ'atr]
opera	опера (f)	['ɔpɛra]
operetta	оперета (f)	[opɛ'rɛta]
ballet	балет (m)	[ba'lɛt]

theater poster	афіша (f)	[a'fiʃa]
theatrical company	трупа (f)	['trupa]
tour	гастролі (pl)	[ɣast'rɔli]
to be on tour	гастролювати	[ɣastroly'watɪ]
to rehearse (vi, vt)	репетирувати	[rɛpɛ'tɪruwatɪ]
rehearsal	репетиція (f)	[rɛpɛ'tɪtsija]
repertoire	репертуар (m)	[rɛpɛrtu'ar]

performance	вистава (f)	[wɪs'tawa]
theatrical show	спектакль (m)	[spɛk'takʎ]
play	п'єса (f)	['pʲɛsa]

ticket	квиток (m)	[kwɪ'tɔk]
Box office	квиткова каса (f)	[kwɪt'kɔwa 'kasa]
lobby, foyer	хол (m)	[hol]
coat check	гардероб (f)	[ɣardɛ'rɔb]
coat check tag	номерок (m)	[nomɛ'rɔk]
binoculars	бінокль (m)	[bi'nɔkʎ]
usher	контролер (m)	[kontro'lɛr]

orchestra seats	партер (m)	[par'tɛr]
balcony	балкон (m)	[bal'kɔn]
dress circle	бельетаж (m)	[bɛʎʲɛ'taʒ]
box	ложа (f)	['lɔʒa]
row	ряд (m)	[rʲad]
seat	місце (n)	['mistsɛ]

audience	публіка (f)	['publika]
spectator	глядач (m)	[ɣʎa'datʃ]
to clap (vi, vt)	плескати	[plɛs'katɪ]
applause	аплодисменти (pl)	[aplodɪs'mɛntɪ]
ovation	овації (pl)	[o'watsijɪ]

stage	сцена (f)	['stsɛna]
curtain	завіса (f)	[za'wisa]
scenery	декорація (f)	[dɛko'ratsija]
backstage	куліси (pl)	[ku'lisɪ]

scene (e.g., the last ~)	дія (f)	['dija]
act	акт (m)	[akt]
intermission	антракт (m)	[ant'rakt]

150. Cinema

actor	актор (m)	[ak'tɔr]
actress	акторка (f)	[ak'tɔrka]
movie	кіно (n)	[ki'nɔ]
episode	серія (f)	['sɛrija]
detective	детектив (m)	[dɛtɛk'tıw]
action movie	бойовик (m)	[bojo'wık]
adventure movie	пригодницький фільм (m)	[prı'ɣɔdnıtskıj fiʎm]
science fiction movie	фантастичний фільм (m)	[fantas'tıtʃnıj fiʎm]
horror movie	фільм (m) жахів	[fiʎm 'ʒahiw]
comedy movie	кінокомедія (f)	[kinoko'mɛdija]
melodrama	мелодрама (f)	[mɛlod'rama]
drama	драма (f)	['drama]
fictional movie	художній фільм (m)	[hu'dɔʒnij fiʎm]
documentary	документальний фільм (m)	[dokumɛn'taʎnıj fiʎm]
cartoon	мультфільм (m)	[muʎt'fiʎm]
silent movies	німе кіно (n)	[ni'mɛ ki'nɔ]
role (part)	роль (f)	[rɔʎ]
leading role	головна роль (f)	[ɣolow'na rɔʎ]
to play (vi, vt)	грати	['ɣratı]
movie star	кінозірка (f)	[kino'zirka]
well-known (adj)	відомий	[wi'dɔmıj]
famous (adj)	відомий	[wi'dɔmıj]
popular (adj)	популярний	[popu'ʎarnıj]
script (screenplay)	сценарій (m)	[stsɛ'narij]
scriptwriter	сценарист (m)	[stsɛna'rıst]
movie director	режисер (m)	[rɛʒı'sɛr]
producer	продюсер (m)	[pro'dysɛr]
assistant	асистент (m)	[asıs'tɛnt]
cameraman	оператор (m)	[opɛ'rator]
stuntman	каскадер (m)	[kaska'dɛr]
to shoot a movie	знімати фільм	[zni'matı fiʎm]
audition, screen test	проби (pl)	['prɔbı]
shooting	зйомки (pl)	[zʰɔmkı]
movie crew	знімальна група (f)	[zni'maʎna 'ɣrupa]

movie set	знімальний майданчик (m)	[zni'maʎnıj maj'dantʃık]
camera	кінокамера (f)	[kino'kamɛra]
movie theater	кінотеатр (m)	[kinotɛ'atr]
screen (e.g., big ~)	екран (m)	[ɛk'ran]
to show a movie	показувати фільм	[po'kazuwatı fiʎm]
soundtrack	звукова доріжка (f)	[zwuko'wa do'riʒka]
special effects	спеціальні ефекти (pl)	[spɛtsi'aʎni ɛ'fɛktı]
subtitles	субтитри (pl)	[sub'tıtrı]
credits	титри (pl)	['tıtrı]
translation	переклад (m)	[pɛ'rɛklad]

151. Painting

art	мистецтво (n)	[mıs'tɛtstwo]
fine arts	образотворчі мистецтва (pl)	[obrazot'worʧi mıs'tɛtstwa]
art gallery	галерея (f)	[ɣalɛ'rɛja]
art exhibition	виставка (f) картин	['wıstawka kar'tın]
painting (art)	живопис (m)	[ʒı'wɔpıs]
graphic art	графіка (f)	['ɣrafika]
abstract art	абстракціонізм (m)	[abstraktsio'nizm]
impressionism	імпресіонізм (m)	[imprɛsio'nizm]
picture (painting)	картина (f)	[kar'tına]
drawing	малюнок (m)	[ma'lynok]
poster	плакат (m)	[pla'kat]
illustration (picture)	ілюстрація (f)	[ilyst'ratsija]
miniature	мініатюра (f)	[minia'tyra]
copy (of painting, etc.)	копія (f)	['kɔpija]
reproduction	репродукція (f)	[rɛpro'duktsija]
mosaic	мозаїка (f)	[mo'zajıka]
stained glass	вітраж (m)	[wit'raʒ]
fresco	фреска (f)	['frɛska]
engraving	гравюра (f)	[ɣra'wyra]
bust (sculpture)	бюст (m)	[byst]
sculpture	скульптура (f)	[skuʎp'tura]
statue	статуя (f)	['statuja]
plaster of Paris	гіпс (m)	[ɣips]
plaster (as adj)	з гіпсу	[z 'ɣipsu]
portrait	портрет (m)	[port'rɛt]
self-portrait	автопортрет (m)	[awtoport'rɛt]
landscape painting	пейзаж (m)	[pɛj'zaʒ]

still life	натюрморт (m)	[natyr'mɔrt]
caricature	карикатура (f)	[karıka'tura]
sketch	нарис (m)	['narıs]

paint	фарба (f)	['farba]
watercolor	акварель (f)	[akwa'rɛʎ]
oil (paint)	масло (n)	['maslo]
pencil	олівець (m)	[oli'wɛts]
Indian ink	туш (f)	[tuʃ]
charcoal	вугілля (n)	[wu'ɣiʎa]

to draw (vi, vt)	малювати	[maly'watı]
to paint (vi, vt)	малювати	[maly'watı]
to pose (vi)	позувати	[pozu'watı]
artist's model (masc.)	натурник (m)	[na'turnık]
artist's model (fem.)	натурниця (f)	[na'turnıtsʲa]

artist (painter)	художник (m)	[hu'dɔʒnık]
work of art	витвір (m)	['wıtwir]
masterpiece	шедевр (m)	[ʃɛ'dɛwr]
artist's workshop	майстерня (f)	[majs'tɛrɲa]

canvas (cloth)	полотно (n)	[polot'nɔ]
easel	мольберт (m)	[moʎ'bɛrt]
palette	палітра (f)	[pa'litra]

frame (of picture, etc.)	рама (f)	['rama]
restoration	реставрація (f)	[rɛstaw'ratsija]
to restore (vt)	реставрувати	[rɛstawru'watı]

152. Literature & Poetry

literature	література (f)	[litɛra'tura]
author (writer)	автор (m)	['awtor]
pseudonym	псевдонім (m)	[psɛwdo'nim]

book	книга (f)	['knıɣa]
volume	видання (n)	[wıda'ɲʲa]
table of contents	зміст (m)	[zmist]
page	сторінка (f)	[sto'rinka]
main character	головний герой (m)	[ɣolow'nıj ɣɛ'rɔj]
autograph	автограф (m)	[aw'toɣraf]

short story	оповідання (n)	[opowi'daɲa]
story (novella)	повість (f)	['pɔwistʲ]
novel	роман (m)	[ro'man]
work (writing)	твір (m)	[twir]
fable	байка (f)	['bajka]
detective novel	детектив (m)	[dɛtɛk'tıw]
poem (verse)	вірш (m)	[wirʃ]

poetry	поезія (f)	[po'ɛzija]
poem (epic, ballad)	поема (f)	[po'ɛma]
poet	поет (m)	[po'ɛt]

fiction	белетристика (f)	[bɛlɛt'rıstıka]
science fiction	наукова фантастика (f)	[nau'kɔwa fan'tastıka]
adventures	пригоди (pl)	[prı'ɣɔdı]
educational literature	учбова література (f)	[uʧ'bɔwa litɛra'tura]
children's literature	дитяча література (f)	[dı'tʲatʃa litɛra'tura]

153. Circus

circus	цирк (m)	[tsırk]
chapiteau circus	цирк-шапіто (m)	[tsırk ʃapi'tɔ]
program	програма (f)	[proɣ'rama]
performance	вистава (f)	[wıs'tawa]

| act (circus ~) | номер (m) | ['nɔmɛr] |
| circus ring | арена (f) | [a'rɛna] |

| pantomime (act) | пантоміма (f) | [panto'mima] |
| clown | клоун (m) | ['klɔun] |

acrobat	акробат (m)	[akro'bat]
acrobatics	акробатика (f)	[akro'batıka]
gymnast	гімнаст (m)	[ɣim'nast]
gymnastics	гімнастика (f)	[ɣim'nastıka]
somersault	сальто (n)	['saʎto]

athlete (strongman)	атлет (m)	[at'lɛt]
animal-tamer	приборкувач (m)	[prı'bɔrkuwaʧ]
equestrian	наїзник (m)	[na'jıznık]
assistant	асистент (m)	[asıs'tɛnt]

stunt	трюк (m)	[tryk]
magic trick	фокус (m)	['fɔkus]
conjurer, magician	фокусник (m)	['fɔkusnık]

juggler	жонглер (m)	[ʒoŋ'lɛr]
to juggle (vi, vt)	жонглювати	[ʒoŋly'watı]
animal trainer	дресирувальник (m)	[drɛsıru'waʎnık]
animal training	дресура (f)	[drɛ'sura]
to train (animals)	дресирувати	[drɛsıru'watı]

154. Music. Pop music

| music | музика (f) | ['muzıka] |
| musician | музикант (m) | [muzı'kant] |

musical instrument	**музичний інструмент** (m)	[muˈzɪʧnɪj instruˈmɛnt]
to play ...	**грати на ...**	[ˈɣratɪ na]
guitar	**гітара** (f)	[ɣiˈtara]
violin	**скрипка** (f)	[ˈskrɪpka]
cello	**віолончель** (f)	[wiolonˈʧɛʎ]
double bass	**контрабас** (m)	[kontraˈbas]
harp	**арфа** (f)	[ˈarfa]
piano	**піаніно** (n)	[piaˈnino]
grand piano	**рояль** (m)	[roˈjaʎ]
organ	**орган** (m)	[orˈɣan]
wind instruments	**духові інструменти** (pl)	[duhoˈwi instruˈmɛntɪ]
oboe	**гобой** (m)	[ɣoˈbɔj]
saxophone	**саксофон** (m)	[saksoˈfɔn]
clarinet	**кларнет** (m)	[klarˈnɛt]
flute	**флейта** (f)	[ˈflɛjta]
trumpet	**труба** (f)	[truˈba]
accordion	**акордеон** (m)	[akordɛˈɔn]
drum	**барабан** (m)	[baraˈban]
duo	**дует** (m)	[duˈɛt]
trio	**тріо** (n)	[ˈtrio]
quartet	**квартет** (m)	[kwarˈtɛt]
choir	**хор** (m)	[hor]
orchestra	**оркестр** (m)	[orˈkɛstr]
pop music	**поп-музика** (f)	[pop ˈmuzɪka]
rock music	**рок-музика** (f)	[rok ˈmuzɪka]
rock group	**рок-група** (f)	[rok ˈɣrupa]
jazz	**джаз** (m)	[ʤaz]
idol	**кумир** (m)	[kuˈmɪr]
admirer, fan	**шанувальник** (m)	[ʃanuˈwaʎnɪk]
concert	**концерт** (m)	[konˈʦɛrt]
symphony	**симфонія** (f)	[sɪmˈfɔnija]
composition	**твір** (m)	[twir]
to compose (write)	**створити**	[stwoˈrɪtɪ]
singing	**спів** (m)	[spiw]
song	**пісня** (f)	[ˈpisɲa]
tune (melody)	**мелодія** (f)	[mɛˈlɔdija]
rhythm	**ритм** (m)	[rɪtm]
blues	**блюз** (m)	[blyz]
sheet music	**ноти** (pl)	[ˈnɔtɪ]
baton	**паличка** (f)	[ˈpalɪʧka]
bow	**смичок** (m)	[smɪˈʧɔk]
string	**струна** (f)	[struˈna]
case (e.g., guitar ~)	**футляр** (m)	[futˈʎar]

Rest. Entertainment. Travel

155. Trip. Travel

tourism	туризм (m)	[tu'rızm]
tourist	турист (m)	[tu'rıst]
trip, voyage	мандрівка (f)	[mand'riwka]
adventure	пригода (f)	[prı'ɣɔda]
trip, journey	поїздка (f)	[po'jızdka]
vacation	відпустка (f)	[wid'pustka]
to be on vacation	бути у відпустці	['butı u wid'pusttsi]
rest	відпочинок (m)	[widpo'tʃınok]
train	поїзд (m)	['pojızd]
by train	поїздом	['pojızdom]
airplane	літак (m)	[li'tak]
by airplane	літаком	[lita'kɔm]
by car	автомобілем	[awtomo'bilɛm]
by ship	кораблем	[korab'lɛm]
luggage	багаж (m)	[ba'ɣaʒ]
suitcase, luggage	валіза (f)	[wa'liza]
luggage cart	візок (m) для багажу	[wi'zɔk dʌa baɣa'ʒu]
passport	паспорт (m)	['pasport]
visa	віза (f)	['wiza]
ticket	квиток (m)	[kwı'tɔk]
air ticket	авіаквиток (m)	[awiakwı'tɔk]
guidebook	путівник (m)	[putiw'nık]
map	карта (f)	['karta]
area (rural ~)	місцевість (f)	[mis'tsɛwistʲ]
place, site	місце (n)	['mistsɛ]
exotic (n)	екзотика (f)	[ɛk'zɔtıka]
exotic (adj)	екзотичний	[ɛkzo'tıtʃnıj]
amazing (adj)	дивовижний	['dıwowıʒnıj]
group	група (f)	['ɣrupa]
excursion	екскурсія (f)	[ɛks'kursija]
guide (person)	екскурсовод (m)	[ɛkskurso'wɔd]

156. Hotel

hotel	готель (m)	[ɣo'tɛʎ]
motel	мотель (m)	[mo'tɛʎ]
three-star	три зірки	[trɪ 'zirkɪ]
five-star	п'ять зірок	[pʰjatʲ zi'rɔk]
to stay (in hotel, etc.)	зупинитися	[zupɪ'nɪtɪsʲa]
room	номер (m)	['nɔmɛr]
single room	одномісний номер (m)	[odno'misnɪj nomɛr]
double room	двомісний номер (m)	[dwo'misnɪj 'nɔmɛr]
to book a room	резервувати номер	[rɛzɛrwu'watɪ 'nɔmɛr]
half board	напівпансіон (m)	[napiwpansi'ɔn]
full board	повний пансіон (m)	['pɔwnɪj pansi'ɔn]
with bath	з ванною	[z 'waɲoju]
with shower	з душем	[z 'duʃɛm]
satellite television	супутникове телебачення (n)	[su'putnɪkowɛ tɛlɛ'batʃɛɲja]
air-conditioner	кондиціонер (m)	[kondɪtsio'nɛr]
towel	рушник (m)	[ruʃ'nɪk]
key	ключ (m)	[klytʃ]
administrator	адміністратор (m)	[administ'rator]
chambermaid	покоївка (f)	[poko'jɪwka]
porter, bellboy	носильник (m)	[no'sɪʎnɪk]
doorman	портьє (m)	[por'tʲɛ]
restaurant	ресторан (m)	[rɛsto'ran]
pub, bar	бар (m)	[bar]
breakfast	сніданок (m)	[sni'danok]
dinner	вечеря (f)	[wɛ'tʃɛrʲa]
buffet	шведський стіл (m)	['ʃwɛdsʲkɪj stil]
lobby	вестибюль (m)	[wɛstɪ'byʎ]
elevator	ліфт (m)	[lift]
DO NOT DISTURB	НЕ ТУРБУВАТИ	[nɛ turbu'watɪ]
NO SMOKING	ПАЛИТИ ЗАБОРОНЕНО	[pa'lɪtɪ zabo'rɔnɛno]

157. Books. Reading

book	книга (f)	['knɪɣa]
author	автор (m)	['awtor]
writer	письменник (m)	[pɪsʲ'mɛŋɪk]
to write (~ a book)	написати	[napɪ'satɪ]
reader	читач (m)	[tʃɪ'tatʃ]

| to read (vi, vt) | читати | [t͡ʃɪˈtatɪ] |
| reading (activity) | читання (n) | [t͡ʃɪˈtaɲa] |

| silently (to oneself) | про себе | [pro ˈsɛbɛ] |
| aloud (adv) | вголос | [ˈwɣɔlɔs] |

to publish (vt)	видавати	[wɪdaˈwatɪ]
publishing (process)	примірник (m)	[prɪˈmirnɪk]
publisher	видавець (m)	[wɪdaˈwɛt͡s]
publishing house	видавництво (n)	[wɪdawˈnɪt͡stwo]

to come out (be released)	вийти	[ˈwɪjtɪ]
release (of a book)	вихід (m)	[ˈwɪhid]
print run	наклад (m)	[ˈnaklad]

| bookstore | книгарня (f) | [knɪˈɣarɲa] |
| library | бібліотека (f) | [biblioˈtɛka] |

story (novella)	повість (f)	[ˈpɔwistʲ]
short story	оповідання (n)	[opowiˈdaɲa]
novel	роман (m)	[roˈman]
detective novel	детектив (m)	[dɛtɛkˈtɪw]

memoirs	мемуари (pl)	[mɛmuˈarɪ]
legend	легенда (f)	[lɛˈɣɛnda]
myth	міф (m)	[mif]

poetry, poems	вірші (pl)	[ˈwirʃɪ]
autobiography	автобіографія (f)	[awtobioɣˈrafija]
selected works	вибране (n)	[ˈwɪbranɛ]
science fiction	фантастика (f)	[fanˈtastɪka]

title	назва (f)	[ˈnazwa]
introduction	вступ (m)	[wstup]
title page	титульна сторінка (f)	[ˈtɪtuʎna stoˈriŋka]

chapter	розділ (m)	[ˈrɔzdil]
extract	уривок (m)	[uˈrɪwok]
episode	епізод (m)	[ɛpiˈzɔd]

plot (storyline)	сюжет (m)	[syˈʒɛt]
contents	зміст (m)	[zmist]
table of contents	зміст (m)	[zmist]
main character	головний герой (m)	[ɣolowˈnɪj ɣɛˈrɔj]

volume	том (m)	[tom]
cover	обкладинка (f)	[obkˈladɪŋka]
binding	палітура (f)	[paliˈtura]
bookmark	закладка (f)	[zakˈladka]

| page | сторінка (f) | [stoˈriŋka] |
| to flick through | гортати | [ɣorˈtatɪ] |

margins	поля (pl)	[po'ʎa]
annotation	позначка (f)	['pɔznatʃka]
footnote	примітка (f)	[prɪ'mitka]

text	текст (m)	[tɛkst]
type, font	шрифт (m)	[ʃrɪft]
misprint, typo	помилка (f)	[po'mɪlka]

translation	переклад (m)	[pɛ'rɛklad]
to translate (vt)	перекладати	[pɛrɛkla'datɪ]
original (n)	оригінал (m)	[orɪɣi'nal]

famous (adj)	відомий	[wi'dɔmɪj]
unknown (adj)	невідомий	[nɛwi'dɔmɪj]
interesting (adj)	цікавий	[tsi'kawɪj]
bestseller	бестселер (m)	[bɛs'tsɛlɛr]

dictionary	словник (m)	[slow'nɪk]
textbook	підручник (m)	[pid'rutʃnɪk]
encyclopedia	енциклопедія (f)	[ɛntsɪklo'pɛdija]

158. Hunting. Fishing

hunting	полювання (n)	[poly'waŋja]
to hunt (vi, vt)	полювати	[poly'watɪ]
hunter	мисливець (m)	[mɪs'lɪwɛts]

to shoot (vi)	стріляти	[stri'ʎatɪ]
rifle	рушниця (f)	[ruʃ'nɪtsʲa]
bullet (shell)	патрон (m)	[pat'rɔn]
shot (lead balls)	шріт (m)	[ʃrit]

trap (e.g., bear ~)	капкан (m)	[kap'kan]
snare (for birds, etc.)	пастка (f)	['pastka]
to lay a trap	ставити пастку	['stawɪtɪ 'pastku]

poacher	браконьєр (m)	[brako'njɛr]
game (in hunting)	дичина (f)	[dɪtʃɪ'na]
hound dog	мисливський пес (m)	[mɪs'lɪwsʲkɪj pɛs]
safari	сафарі (n)	[sa'fari]
mounted animal	опудало (n)	[o'pudalo]

fisherman	рибалка (m)	[rɪ'balka]
fishing	риболовля (f)	[rɪbo'lowʎa]
to fish (vi)	ловити рибу	[lo'wɪtɪ 'rɪbu]

fishing rod	вудочка (f)	['wudotʃka]
fishing line	волосінь (f)	[wolo'siɲ]
hook	гачок (m)	[ɣa'tʃɔk]
float	поплавець (m)	[popla'wɛts]

bait	наживка (f)	[naˈʒɪwka]
to cast a line	закинути вудочку	[zaˈkɪnutɪ ˈwudotʃku]
to bite (ab. fish)	клювати	[klyˈwatɪ]
catch (of fish)	улов (m)	[uˈlɔw]
ice-hole	ополонка (f)	[opoˈlɔŋka]

fishing net	сітка (f)	[ˈsitka]
boat	човен (m)	[ˈtʃɔwɛn]
to net (catch with net)	ловити	[loˈwɪtɪ]
to cast the net	закидати сіті	[zakɪˈdatɪ ˈsiti]
to haul in the net	витягати сіті	[wɪtʲaˈɣatɪ ˈsiti]

whaler (person)	китобій (m)	[kɪtoˈbij]
whaleboat	китобійне судно (n)	[kɪtoˈbijnɛ ˈsudno]
harpoon	гарпун (m)	[ɣarˈpun]

159. Games. Billiards

billiards	більярд (m)	[biˈʎjard]
billiard room, hall	більярдна (f)	[biˈʎjardna]
ball	більярдна куля (f)	[biˈʎjardna ˈkuʎa]

to pocket a ball	загнати кулю	[zaɣˈnatɪ ˈkuly]
cue	кий (m)	[kɪj]
pocket	луза (f)	[ˈluza]

160. Games. Playing cards

diamonds	бубни (pl)	[ˈbubnɪ]
spades	піки (pl)	[ˈpikɪ]
hearts	черви (pl)	[ˈtʃɛrwɪ]
clubs	трефи (pl)	[ˈtrɛfɪ]

ace	туз (m)	[tuz]
king	король (m)	[koˈrɔʎ]
queen	дама (f)	[ˈdama]
jack, knave	валет (m)	[waˈlɛt]

| playing card | карта (f) | [ˈkarta] |
| cards | карти (pl) | [ˈkartɪ] |

| trump | козир (m) | [ˈkɔzɪr] |
| deck of cards | колода (f) | [koˈlɔda] |

to deal (vi, vt)	здавати	[zdaˈwatɪ]
to shuffle (cards)	тасувати	[tasuˈwatɪ]
lead, turn (n)	хід (m)	[hid]
cardsharp	шулер (m)	[ˈʃulɛr]

161. Casino. Roulette

casino	казино (n)	[kɑzɪ'nɔ]
roulette (game)	рулетка (f)	[ru'lɛtkɑ]
bet, stake	ставка (f)	['stɑwkɑ]
to place bets	робити ставки	[ro'bɪtɪ 'stɑwkɪ]
red	червоне (n)	[ʧɛr'wɔnɛ]
black	чорне (n)	['ʧɔrnɛ]
to bet on red	ставити на червоне	['stɑwɪtɪ nɑ ʧɛr'wɔnɛ]
to bet on black	ставити на чорне	['stɑwɪtɪ nɑ 'ʧɔrnɛ]
croupier (dealer)	круп'є (m)	[kruphɛ]
to turn the wheel	крутити барабан	[kru'tɪtɪ bɑrɑ'bɑn]
rules (of game)	правила (pl) гри	['prɑwɪlɑ ɣrɪ]
chip	фішка (f)	['fiʃkɑ]
to win (vi, vt)	виграти	['wɪɣrɑtɪ]
winnings	виграш (m)	['wɪɣrɑʃ]
to lose (~ 100 dollars)	програти	[proɣ'rɑtɪ]
loss	програш (m)	['prɔɣrɑʃ]
player	гравець (m)	[ɣrɑ'wɛʧs]
blackjack (card game)	блек джек (m)	[blɛk ʤɛk]
craps (dice game)	гра (f) в кості	[ɣrɑ w 'kɔsti]
slot machine	гральний автомат (m)	['ɣrɑʎnɪj ɑwto'mɑt]

162. Rest. Games. Miscellaneous

to walk, to stroll (vi)	прогулюватися	[pro'ɣulywɑtɪsʲɑ]
walk, stroll	прогулянка (f)	[pro'ɣuʎɑŋkɑ]
road trip	поїздка (f)	[po'jɪzdkɑ]
adventure	пригода (f)	[prɪ'ɣɔdɑ]
picnic	пікнік (m)	[pik'nik]
game (chess, etc.)	гра (f)	[ɣrɑ]
player	гравець (m)	[ɣrɑ'wɛʧs]
game (one ~ of chess)	партія (f)	['pɑrtijɑ]
collector (e.g., philatelist)	колекціонер (m)	[kolɛkʦio'nɛr]
to collect (vt)	колекціонувати	[kolɛkʦionu'wɑtɪ]
collection	колекція (f)	[ko'lɛkʦijɑ]
crossword puzzle	кросворд (m)	[kros'wɔrd]
racetrack (hippodrome)	іподром (m)	[ipod'rɔm]
discotheque	дискотека (f)	[dɪsko'tɛkɑ]
sauna	сауна (f)	['sɑunɑ]
lottery	лотерея (f)	[lotɛ'rɛjɑ]

camping trip	**похід** (m)	[po'hid]
camp	**табір** (m)	['tabir]
tent (for camping)	**намет** (m)	[na'mɛt]
compass	**компас** (m)	['kɔmpas]
camper	**турист** (m)	[tu'rɪst]

to watch (movie, etc.)	**дивитися**	[dɪ'wɪtɪsʲa]
viewer	**телеглядач** (m)	[tɛlɛɣʎa'datʃ]
TV show	**телепередача** (f)	[tɛlɛpɛrɛ'datʃa]

163. Photography

| camera (photo) | **фотоапарат** (m) | [fotoapa'rat] |
| photo, picture | **фото** (n) | ['foto] |

photographer	**фотограф** (m)	[fo'toɣraf]
photo studio	**фотостудія** (f)	[fotos'tudija]
photo album	**фотоальбом** (m)	[fotoaʎ'bɔm]

camera lens	**об'єктив** (m)	[obʰɛk'tɪw]
telephoto lens	**телеоб'єктив** (m)	[tɛlɛobʰɛk'tɪw]
filter	**фільтр** (m)	['fiʎtr]
lens	**лінза** (f)	['linza]

optics (high-quality ~)	**оптика** (f)	['ɔptɪka]
diaphragm (aperture)	**діафрагма** (f)	[diaf'raɣma]
exposure time	**витримка** (f)	['wɪtrɪmka]
viewfinder	**видошукач** (m)	[wɪdoʃu'katʃ]

digital camera	**цифрова камера** (f)	[tsɪfro'wa 'kamɛra]
tripod	**штатив** (m)	[ʃta'tɪw]
flash	**спалах** (m)	['spalah]

to photograph (vt)	**фотографувати**	[fotoɣrafu'watɪ]
to take pictures	**знімати**	[zni'matɪ]
to be photographed	**фотографуватися**	[fotoɣrafu'watɪsʲa]

focus	**різкість** (f)	['rizkistʲ]
to adjust the focus	**наводити різкість**	[na'wɔdɪtɪ 'rizkistʲ]
sharp, in focus (adj)	**різкий**	[riz'kɪj]
sharpness	**різкість** (f)	['rizkistʲ]

| contrast | **контраст** (m) | [kont'rast] |
| contrasty (adj) | **контрастний** | [kont'rastnɪj] |

picture (photo)	**знімок** (m)	['znimok]
negative (n)	**негатив** (m)	[nɛɣa'tɪw]
film (a roll of ~)	**фотоплівка** (f)	[fotop'liwka]
frame (still)	**кадр** (m)	[kadr]
to print (photos)	**друкувати**	[druku'watɪ]

164. Beach. Swimming

beach	пляж (m)	[pʎaʒ]
sand	пісок (m)	[pi'sɔk]
deserted (beach)	пустельний	[pus'tɛʎnij]
suntan	засмага (f)	[zas'maɣa]
to get a tan	засмагати	[zasma'ɣatı]
tan (adj)	засмаглий	[zas'maɣlij]
sunscreen	крем (m) для засмаги	[krɛm dʎa zas'maɣı]
bikini	бікіні (pl)	[bi'kini]
bathing suit	купальник (m)	[ku'paʎnık]
swim briefs	плавки (pl)	['plawkı]
swimming pool	басейн (m)	[ba'sɛjn]
to swim (vi)	плавати	['plawatı]
shower	душ (m)	[duʃ]
to change (one's clothes)	перевдягатися	[pɛrɛwdʲa'ɣatısʲa]
towel	рушник (m)	[ruʃ'nık]
boat	човен (m)	['tʃɔwɛn]
motorboat	катер (m)	['katɛr]
water ski	водяні лижі (pl)	[wodʲa'ni 'lıʒi]
paddle boat	водяний велосипед (m)	[wodʲa'nij wɛlosı'pɛd]
surfing	серфінг (m)	['sɛrfiŋ]
surfer	серфінгіст (m)	[sɛrfi'ŋist]
scuba set	акваланг (m)	[akwa'laŋ]
flippers (swimfins)	ласти (pl)	['lastı]
mask	маска (f)	['maska]
diver	нирець (m)	[nı'rɛts]
to dive (vi)	пірнати	[pir'natı]
underwater (adv)	під водою	[pid wo'dɔju]
beach umbrella	парасолька (f)	[para'sɔʎka]
beach chair	шезлонг (m)	[ʃɛz'lɔn]
sunglasses	окуляри (pl)	[oku'ʎarı]
air mattress	плавальний матрац (m)	['plawaʎnij mat'rats]
to play (amuse oneself)	грати	['ɣratı]
to go for a swim	купатися	[ku'patısʲa]
beach ball	м'яч (m)	[mʰjatʃ]
to inflate (vt)	надувати	[nadu'watı]
inflatable, air- (adj)	надувний	[naduw'nij]
wave	хвиля (f)	['hwıʎa]
buoy	буй (m)	[buj]
to drown (ab. person)	тонути	[to'nutı]

to save, to rescue	**рятувати**	[rʲɑtuˈwɑtɪ]
life vest	**рятувальний жилет** (m)	[rʲɑtuˈwɑʎnɪj ʒɪˈlɛt]
to observe, to watch	**спостерігати**	[spostɛriˈɣɑtɪ]
lifeguard	**рятувальник** (m)	[rʲɑtuˈwɑʎnɪk]

TECHNICAL EQUIPMENT. TRANSPORTATION

Technical equipment

165. Computer

computer	комп'ютер (m)	[kompʰʲjutɛr]
notebook, laptop	ноутбук (m)	[nout'buk]
to turn on	увімкнути	[uwimk'nutɪ]
to turn off	вимкнути	['wɪmknutɪ]
keyboard	клавіатура (f)	[klawia'tura]
key	клавіша (f)	['klawiʃa]
mouse	миша (f)	['mɪʃa]
mouse pad	килимок (m)	[kɪlɪ'mɔk]
button	кнопка (f)	['knɔpka]
cursor	курсор (m)	[kur'sɔr]
monitor	монітор (m)	[moni'tɔr]
screen	екран (m)	[ɛk'ran]
hard disk	жорсткий диск (m)	[ʒorst'kɪj dɪsk]
hard disk volume	об'єм (m)	[obʰ'ɛm]
memory	пам'ять (f)	['pamʰjatʲ]
random access memory	оперативна пам'ять (f)	[opɛra'tɪwna 'pamʰjatʲ]
file	файл (m)	[fajl]
folder	папка (f)	['papka]
to open (vt)	відкрити файл	[widk'rɪtɪ 'fajl]
to close (vt)	закрити файл	[zak'rɪtɪ 'fajl]
to save (vt)	зберегти	[zbɛrɛɣ'tɪ]
to delete (vt)	видалити	['wɪdalɪtɪ]
to copy (vt)	скопіювати	[skopiju'watɪ]
to sort (vt)	сортувати	[sortu'watɪ]
to transfer (copy)	переписати	[pɛrɛpɪ'satɪ]
program	програма (f)	[proɣ'rama]
software	програмне забезпечення (n)	[proɣ'ramnɛ zabɛz'pɛʧɛnja]
programmer	програміст (m)	[proɣ'ramist]
to program (vt)	програмувати	[proɣramu'watɪ]
hacker	хакер (m)	['hakɛr]

password	пароль (m)	[pɑ'rɔʎ]
virus	вірус (m)	['wirus]
to find, to detect	виявити	['wɪjɑwɪtɪ]
byte	байт (m)	[bɑjt]
megabyte	мегабайт (m)	[mɛɣɑ'bɑjt]
data	дані (pl)	['dɑni]
database	база (f) даних	['bɑzɑ 'dɑnɪh]
cable (USB, etc.)	кабель (m)	['kɑbɛʎ]
to disconnect (vt)	від'єднати	[widʰɛd'nɑtɪ]
to connect (sth to sth)	під'єднати	[pidʰɛd'nɑtɪ]

166. Internet. E-mail

Internet	інтернет (m)	[intɛr'nɛt]
browser	браузер (m)	['brauzɛr]
search engine	пошуковий ресурс (m)	[poʃu'kowɪj rɛ'surs]
provider	провайдер (m)	[pro'wajdɛr]
web master	веб-майстер (m)	[wɛb 'majstɛr]
website	веб-сайт (m)	[wɛb 'sajt]
web page	веб-сторінка (f)	[wɛb sto'riŋkɑ]
address	адреса (f)	[ad'rɛsɑ]
address book	адресна книга (f)	['adrɛsnɑ 'knɪɣɑ]
mailbox	поштова скринька (f)	[poʃ'towɑ 'skrɪŋkɑ]
mail	пошта (f)	['poʃtɑ]
message	повідомлення (n)	[powi'dɔmlɛŋjɑ]
sender	відправник (m)	[widp'rawnɪk]
to send (vt)	відправити	[widp'rawɪtɪ]
sending (of mail)	відправлення (n)	[widp'rawlɛŋjɑ]
receiver	одержувач (m)	[o'dɛrʒuwɑtʃ]
to receive (vt)	отримати	[ot'rɪmɑtɪ]
correspondence	листування (n)	[lɪstu'wɑŋjɑ]
to correspond (vi)	листуватися	[lɪstu'wɑtɪsʲɑ]
file	файл (m)	[fɑjl]
to download (vt)	скачати	[skɑ'tʃɑtɪ]
to create (vt)	створити	[stwo'rɪtɪ]
to delete (vt)	видалити	['wɪdɑlɪtɪ]
deleted (adj)	видалений	['wɪdɑlɛnɪj]
connection (ADSL, etc.)	зв'язок (m)	[zwʰjɑ'zɔk]
speed	швидкість (f)	['ʃwɪdkistʲ]

modem	модем (m)	[mo'dɛm]
access	доступ (m)	['dɔstup]
port (e.g., input ~)	порт (m)	[port]
connection (make a ~)	підключення (n)	[pidk'lytʃɛŋja]
to connect to … (vi)	підключитися	[pidkly'tʃıtısʲa]
to select (vt)	вибрати	['wıbratı]
to search (for …)	шукати	[ʃu'katı]

167. Electricity

electricity	електрика (f)	[ɛ'lɛktrıka]
electrical (adj)	електричний	[ɛlɛkt'rıtʃnıj]
electric power station	електростанція (f)	[ɛlɛktros'tantsija]
energy	енергія (f)	[ɛ'nɛrɣija]
electric power	електроенергія (f)	[ɛlɛktroɛ'nɛrɣija]
light bulb	лампочка (f)	['lampotʃka]
flashlight	ліхтар (m)	[lih'tar]
street light	ліхтар (m)	[lih'tar]
light	світло (n)	['switlo]
to turn on	вмикати	[wmı'katı]
to turn off	вимикати	[wımı'katı]
to turn off the light	погасити світло	[poɣa'sıtı 'switlo]
to burn out (vi)	перегоріти	[pɛrɛɣo'ritı]
short circuit	коротке замикання (n)	[ko'rotkɛ zamı'kaŋja]
broken wire	обрив (m)	[ob'rıw]
contact	контакт (m)	[kon'takt]
light switch	вимикач (m)	[wımı'katʃ]
wall socket	розетка (f)	[ro'zɛtka]
plug	штепсель (m)	['ʃtɛpsɛʎ]
extension cord	подовжувач (m)	[po'dɔwʒuwatʃ]
fuse	запобіжник (m)	[zapo'biʒnık]
cable, wire	провід (m)	['prɔwid]
wiring	проводка (f)	[pro'wɔdka]
ampere	ампер (m)	[am'pɛr]
amperage	сила (f) струму	['sıla 'strumu]
volt	вольт (m)	[woʎt]
voltage	напруга (f)	[nap'ruɣa]
electrical device	електроприлад (m)	[ɛlɛktrop'rılad]
indicator	індикатор (m)	[indı'kator]
electrician	електрик (m)	[ɛ'lɛktrık]
to solder (vt)	паяти	[pa'jatı]

| soldering iron | **паяльник** (m) | [pɑ'jɑʎnɪk] |
| electric current | **струм** (m) | [strum] |

168. Tools

tool, instrument	**інструмент** (m)	[instru'mɛnt]
tools	**інструменти** (pl)	[instru'mɛntɪ]
equipment (factory ~)	**обладнання** (n)	[ob'lɑdnɑnjɑ]

hammer	**молоток** (m)	[molo'tɔk]
screwdriver	**викрутка** (f)	['wɪkrutkɑ]
ax	**сокира** (f)	[so'kɪrɑ]

saw	**пила** (f)	['pɪlɑ]
to saw (vt)	**пиляти**	[pɪ'ʎɑtɪ]
plane (tool)	**рубанок** (m)	[ru'bɑnok]
to plane (vt)	**стругати**	[stru'ɣɑtɪ]
soldering iron	**паяльник** (m)	[pɑ'jɑʎnɪk]
to solder (vt)	**паяти**	[pɑ'jɑtɪ]

file (for metal)	**терпуг** (m)	[tɛr'puɣ]
carpenter pincers	**обценьки** (pl)	[ob'ʦɛɲkɪ]
lineman's pliers	**плоскогубці** (pl)	[plosko'ɣubʦi]
chisel	**стамеска** (f)	[stɑ'mɛskɑ]

drill bit	**свердло** (n)	[swɛr'lɔ]
electric drill	**дриль** (m)	[drɪʎ]
to drill (vi, vt)	**свердлити**	[swɛr'lɪtɪ]

knife	**ніж** (m)	[niʒ]
pocket knife	**кишеньковий ніж** (m)	[kɪʃɛɲ'kowɪj niʒ]
folding (~ knife)	**складний**	[sklɑd'nɪj]
blade	**лезо** (n)	['lɛzo]

sharp (blade, etc.)	**гострий**	['ɣostrɪj]
blunt (adj)	**тупий**	[tu'pɪj]
to become blunt	**затупитися**	[zɑtu'pɪtisʲɑ]
to sharpen (vt)	**точити**	[to'ʧɪtɪ]

bolt	**болт** (m)	[bolt]
nut	**гайка** (f)	['ɣɑjkɑ]
thread (of a screw)	**різьба** (f)	[rizʲ'bɑ]
wood screw	**шуруп** (m)	[ʃu'rup]

| nail | **цвях** (m) | [ʦwʲɑh] |
| nailhead | **головка** (f) | [ɣo'lɔwkɑ] |

ruler (for measuring)	**лінійка** (f)	[li'nijkɑ]
tape measure	**рулетка** (f)	[ru'lɛtkɑ]
spirit level	**рівень** (m)	['riwɛɲ]

magnifying glass	**лупа** (f)	[ˈlupɑ]
measuring instrument	**вимірювальний прилад** (m)	[wɪˈmirywɑʎnij pˈrɪlɑd]
to measure (vt)	**вимірювати**	[wɪˈmirywɑtɪ]
scale (of thermometer, etc.)	**шкала** (f)	[ʃkɑˈlɑ]
readings	**показання** (n)	[pokɑˈzɑɲjɑ]
compressor	**компресор** (m)	[kompˈrɛsor]
microscope	**мікроскоп** (m)	[mikrosˈkɔp]
pump (e.g., water ~)	**помпа** (f)	[ˈpɔmpɑ]
robot	**робот** (m)	[ˈrɔbot]
laser	**лазер** (m)	[ˈlɑzɛr]
wrench	**гайковий ключ** (m)	[ˈɣɑjkowɪj klytʃ]
adhesive tape	**стрічка-скотч** (m)	[ˈstritʃkɑ skotʃ]
glue	**клей** (m)	[klɛj]
emery paper	**наждачний папір** (m)	[nɑʒˈdɑtʃnɪj pɑˈpir]
spring	**пружина** (f)	[pruˈʒɪnɑ]
magnet	**магніт** (m)	[mɑˈɣˈnit]
gloves	**рукавички** (pl)	[rukɑˈwɪtʃkɪ]
rope	**мотузка** (f)	[moˈtuzkɑ]
cord	**шнур** (m)	[ʃnur]
wire (e.g., telephone ~)	**провід** (m)	[ˈprɔwid]
cable	**кабель** (m)	[ˈkɑbɛʎ]
sledgehammer	**кувалда** (f)	[kuˈwɑldɑ]
crowbar	**лом** (m)	[lom]
ladder	**драбина** (f)	[drɑˈbɪnɑ]
stepladder	**стрем'янка** (f)	[strɛmʰˈjɑŋkɑ]
to screw (tighten)	**закручувати**	[zɑkˈrutʃuwɑtɪ]
to unscrew, untwist (vt)	**відкручувати**	[widkˈrutʃuwɑtɪ]
to tighten (vt)	**затискати**	[zɑtɪsˈkɑtɪ]
to glue, to stick	**приклеїти**	[prɪkˈlɛjɪtɪ]
to cut (vt)	**різати**	[ˈrizɑtɪ]
malfunction (fault)	**несправність** (f)	[nɛspˈrɑwnistʲ]
repair (mending)	**ремонт** (m)	[rɛˈmont]
to repair, to mend (vt)	**ремонтувати**	[rɛmontuˈwɑtɪ]
to adjust (machine, etc.)	**регулювати**	[rɛɣulyˈwɑtɪ]
to check (to examine)	**перевіряти**	[pɛrɛwiˈrʲɑtɪ]
checking	**перевірка** (f)	[pɛrɛˈwirkɑ]
readings	**показання** (n)	[pokɑˈzɑɲjɑ]
reliable (machine)	**надійний**	[nɑˈdijnɪj]
complicated (adj)	**складний**	[sklɑdˈnɪj]
to rust (get rusted)	**іржавіти**	[irʒɑˈwitɪ]

| rusty, rusted (adj) | **іржавий** | [irˈʒawɪj] |
| rust | **іржа** (f) | [irˈʒɑ] |

Transportation

169. Airplane

airplane	літак (m)	[li'tak]
air ticket	авіаквиток (m)	[awiakwɪ'tɔk]
airline	авіакомпанія (f)	[awiakom'panija]
airport	аеропорт (m)	[aɛro'pɔrt]
supersonic (adj)	надзвуковий	[nadzwuko'wɪj]
captain	командир (m) корабля	[koman'dɪr korab'ʎa]
crew	екіпаж (m)	[ɛki'paʒ]
pilot	пілот (m)	[pi'lɔt]
flight attendant	стюардеса (f)	[styar'dɛsa]
navigator	штурман (m)	['ʃturman]
wings	крила (pl)	['krɪla]
tail	хвіст (m)	[hwist]
cockpit	кабіна (f)	[ka'bina]
engine	двигун (m)	[dwɪ'ɣun]
undercarriage	шасі (n)	[ʃa'si]
turbine	турбіна (f)	[tur'bina]
propeller	пропелер (m)	[pro'pɛlɛr]
black box	чорна скринька (f)	['ʧɔrna 'skrɪnka]
control column	штурвал (m)	[ʃtur'wal]
fuel	пальне (n)	[paʎ'nɛ]
safety card	інструкція (f)	[inst'rukʦija]
oxygen mask	киснева маска (f)	['kɪsnɛwa 'maska]
uniform	уніформа (f)	[uni'fɔrma]
life vest	рятувальний жилет (m)	[rʲatu'waʎnɪj ʒɪ'lɛt]
parachute	парашут (m)	[para'ʃut]
takeoff	зліт (m)	[zlit]
to take off (vi)	злітати	[zli'tatɪ]
runway	злітна смуга (f)	['zlitna 'smuɣa]
visibility	видимість (f)	['wɪdɪmistʲ]
flight (act of flying)	політ (m)	[po'lit]
altitude	висота (f)	[wɪso'ta]
air pocket	повітряна яма (f)	[po'witrʲana 'jama]
seat	місце (n)	['mistsɛ]
headphones	навушники (pl)	[na'wuʃnɪkɪ]
folding tray	відкидний столик (m)	[widkɪd'nɪj 'stɔlɪk]

| airplane window | ілюмінатор (m) | [ilymi'nator] |
| aisle | прохід (m) | [pro'hid] |

170. Train

train	поїзд (m)	['pojızd]
suburban train	електропоїзд (m)	[ɛlɛktro'pojızd]
express train	швидкий поїзд (m)	[ʃwıd'kıj 'pojızd]
diesel locomotive	тепловоз (m)	[tɛplo'wɔz]
steam engine	паровоз (m)	[paro'wɔz]

| passenger car | вагон (m) | [wa'ɣɔn] |
| dining car | вагон-ресторан (m) | [wa'ɣɔn rɛsto'ran] |

rails	рейки (pl)	['rɛjkı]
railroad	залізниця (f)	[zaliz'nıtsʲa]
railway tie	шпала (f)	['ʃpala]

platform (railway ~)	платформа (f)	[plat'fɔrma]
track (~ 1, 2, etc.)	колія (f)	['kɔlija]
semaphore	семафор (m)	[sɛma'fɔr]
station	станція (f)	['stantsija]

engineer	машиніст (m)	[maʃı'nist]
porter (of luggage)	носильник (m)	[no'sıʎnık]
train steward	провідник (m)	[prowid'nık]
passenger	пасажир (m)	[pasa'ʒır]
conductor	контролер (m)	[kontro'lɛr]

| corridor (in train) | коридор (m) | [korı'dɔr] |
| emergency break | стоп-кран (m) | [stop kran] |

compartment	купе (n)	[ku'pɛ]
berth	полиця (f)	[po'lıtsʲa]
upper berth	полиця (f) верхня	[po'lıtsʲa 'wɛrhɲa]
lower berth	полиця (f) нижня	[po'lıtsʲa 'nıʒɲa]
bed linen	білизна (f)	[bi'lızna]

ticket	квиток (m)	[kwı'tɔk]
schedule	розклад (m)	['rɔzklad]
information display	табло (n)	[tab'lɔ]

to leave, to depart	відходити	[wid'hɔdıtı]
departure (of train)	відправлення (n)	[widp'rawlɛɲa]
to arrive (ab. train)	прибувати	[prıbu'watı]
arrival	прибуття (n)	[prıbut'tʲa]

to arrive by train	приїхати поїздом	[prı'jıhatı 'pojızdom]
to get on the train	сісти на поїзд	['sisti na 'pojızd]
to get off the train	зійти з поїзду	[zij'tı z 'pojızdu]

train wreck	катастрофа (f)	[katast'rɔfa]
steam engine	паровоз (m)	[paro'wɔz]
stoker, fireman	кочегар (m)	[koʧɛ'ɣar]
firebox	топка (f)	['tɔpka]
coal	вугілля (n)	[wu'ɣiʎa]

171. Ship

| ship | корабель (m) | [kora'bɛʎ] |
| vessel | судно (n) | ['sudnɔ] |

steamship	пароплав (m)	[parop'law]
riverboat	теплохід (m)	[tɛplo'hid]
ocean liner	лайнер (m)	['lajnɛr]
cruiser	крейсер (m)	['krɛjsɛr]

yacht	яхта (f)	['jahta]
tugboat	буксир (m)	[buk'sɪr]
barge	баржа (f)	['barʒa]
ferry	паром (m)	[pa'rɔm]

| sailing ship | вітрильник (m) | [wit'rɪʎnɪk] |
| brigantine | бригантина (f) | [brɪɣan'tɪna] |

| ice breaker | криголам (m) | [krɪɣo'lam] |
| submarine | човен (m) підводний | ['ʧɔwɛn pid'wɔdnɪj] |

boat (flat-bottomed ~)	човен (m)	['ʧɔwɛn]
dinghy	шлюпка (f)	['ʃlypka]
lifeboat	шлюпка (f) рятувальна	['ʃlypka rʲatu'waʎna]
motorboat	катер (m)	['katɛr]

captain	капітан (m)	[kapi'tan]
seaman	матрос (m)	[mat'rɔs]
sailor	моряк (m)	[mo'rʲak]
crew	екіпаж (m)	[ɛki'paʒ]

boatswain	боцман (m)	['bɔʦman]
ship's boy	юнга (f)	['juŋa]
cook	кок (m)	[kok]
ship's doctor	судновий лікар (m)	['sudnowɪj 'likar]

deck	палуба (f)	['paluba]
mast	щогла (f)	['ɕɔɣla]
sail	вітрило (n)	[wit'rɪlo]

hold	трюм (m)	[trym]
bow (prow)	ніс (m)	[nis]
stern	корма (f)	[kor'ma]
oar	весло (n)	[wɛs'lɔ]

screw propeller	гвинт (m)	[ɣwɪnt]
cabin	каюта (f)	[kaˈjuta]
wardroom	кают-компанія (f)	[kaˈjut komˈpanija]
engine room	машинне відділення (n)	[maˈʃɪnɛ widˈdilɛɲa]
bridge	капітанський місток (m)	[kapiˈtansʲkɪj misˈtɔk]
radio room	радіорубка (f)	[radioˈrubka]
wave (radio)	хвиля (f)	[ˈhwɪʎa]
logbook	судновий журнал (m)	[ˈsudnowɪj ʒurˈnal]

spyglass	підзорна труба (f)	[piˈdzɔrna truˈba]
bell	дзвін (m)	[dzwin]
flag	прапор (m)	[ˈprapɔr]

| rope (mooring ~) | канат (m) | [kaˈnat] |
| knot (bowline, etc.) | вузол (m) | [ˈwuzɔl] |

| deckrail | поручень (m) | [ˈpɔrutʃɛɲ] |
| gangway | трап (m) | [trap] |

anchor	якір (m)	[ˈjakir]
to weigh anchor	підняти якір	[pidˈɲatɪ ˈjakir]
to drop anchor	кинути якір	[ˈkɪnutɪ ˈjakir]
anchor chain	якірний ланцюг (m)	[ˈjakirnɪj lanˈtsyɣ]

port (harbor)	порт (m)	[pɔrt]
berth, wharf	причал (m)	[prɪˈtʃal]
to berth (moor)	причалювати	[prɪˈtʃalywatɪ]
to cast off	відчалювати	[widˈtʃalywatɪ]

trip, voyage	подорож (f)	[ˈpɔdorɔʒ]
cruise (sea trip)	круїз (m)	[kruˈjɪz]
course (route)	курс (m)	[kurs]
route (itinerary)	маршрут (m)	[marˈʃrut]

fairway	фарватер (m)	[farˈwatɛr]
shallows (shoal)	мілина (f)	[milɪˈna]
to run aground	сісти на мілину	[ˈsistɪ na milɪˈnu]

storm	буря (f)	[ˈburʲa]
signal	сигнал (m)	[sɪɣˈnal]
to sink (vi)	тонути	[toˈnutɪ]
SOS	SOS	[sos]
ring buoy	рятувальний круг (m)	[rʲatuˈwaʎnɪj kruɣ]

172. Airport

airport	аеропорт (m)	[aɛroˈpɔrt]
airplane	літак (m)	[liˈtak]
airline	авіакомпанія (f)	[awiakomˈpanija]
air-traffic controller	диспетчер (m)	[dɪsˈpɛtʃɛr]

departure	виліт (m)	['wɪlit]
arrival	приліт (m)	[prɪ'lit]
to arrive (by plane)	прилетіти	[prɪ'lɛtitɪ]

| departure time | час (m) вильоту | [tʃas wɪ'lɜtu] |
| arrival time | час (m) прильоту | [tʃas prɪ'lɜtu] |

| to be delayed | затримуватися | [zat'rɪmuwatɪsʲa] |
| flight delay | затримка (f) вильоту | [zat'rɪmka 'wɪlɜtu] |

information board	інформаційне табло (n)	[informa'tsijnɛ tab'lɔ]
information	інформація (f)	[infor'matsija]
to announce (vt)	оголошувати	[oɣo'lɔʃuwatɪ]
flight (e.g., next ~)	рейс (m)	[rɛjs]

| customs | митниця (f) | ['mɪtnɪtsʲa] |
| customs officer | митник (m) | ['mɪtnɪk] |

customs declaration	декларація (f)	[dɛkla'ratsija]
to fill out (vt)	заповнити	[za'pownɪtɪ]
to fill out the declaration	заповнити декларацію	[za'pownɪtɪ dɛkla'ratsiju]
passport control	паспортний контроль (m)	['pasportnɪj kont'rɔʎ]

luggage	багаж (m)	[ba'ɣaʒ]
hand luggage	ручний вантаж (f)	[rutʃ'nɪj wan'taʒ]
Lost Luggage Desk	пошук (m) багажу	['pɔʃuk baɣa'ʒu]
luggage cart	візок (m) для багажу	[wi'zɔk dʎa baɣa'ʒu]

landing	посадка (f)	[po'sadka]
landing strip	посадкова смуга (f)	[po'sadkowa 'smuɣa]
to land (vi)	сідати	[si'datɪ]
airstairs	трап (m)	[trap]

check-in	реєстрація (f)	[rɛ:st'ratsija]
check-in desk	реєстрація (f)	[rɛ:st'ratsija]
to check-in (vi)	зареєструватися	[zarɛ:stru'watɪsʲa]
boarding pass	посадковий талон (m)	[po'sadkowɪj ta'lɔn]
departure gate	вихід (m)	['wɪhid]

transit	транзит (m)	[tran'zɪt]
to wait (vt)	чекати	[tʃɛ'katɪ]
departure lounge	зал (m) очікування	['zal o'tʃikuwaɲja]
to see off	проводжати	[prowo'dʒatɪ]
to say goodbye	прощатися	[prɔ'ɕatɪsʲa]

173. Bicycle. Motorcycle

| bicycle | велосипед (m) | [wɛlosɪ'pɛd] |
| scooter | моторолер (m) | [moto'rɔlɛr] |

motorcycle, bike	**мотоцикл** (m)	[moto'tsɪkl]
to go by bicycle	**їхати на велосипеді**	['jɪhɑtɪ nɑ wɛlosɪ'pɛdi]
handlebars	**кермо** (n)	[kɛr'mɔ]
pedal	**педаль** (f)	[pɛ'dɑʎ]
brakes	**гальма** (pl)	[ˈɣɑʎmɑ]
bicycle seat	**сідло** (n)	[sid'lɔ]

pump	**помпа** (f)	['pɔmpɑ]
luggage rack	**багажник** (m)	[bɑ'ɣaʒnɪk]
front lamp	**ліхтар** (m)	[lih'tɑr]
helmet	**шолом** (m)	[ʃo'lɔm]

wheel	**колесо** (n)	['kɔlɛso]
fender	**крило** (n)	[krɪ'lɔ]
rim	**обвід** (m)	['ɔbwid]
spoke	**спиця** (f)	['spɪtsʲɑ]

Cars

174. Types of cars

automobile, car	автомобіль (m)	[awtomo'biʎ]
sports car	спортивний автомобіль (m)	[spor'tıwnıj awtomo'biʎ]
limousine	лімузин (m)	[limu'zın]
off-road vehicle	позадорожник (m)	[pozado'rɔʒnık]
convertible	кабріолет (m)	[kabrio'lɛt]
minibus	мікроавтобус (m)	[mikroaw'tɔbus]
ambulance	швидка допомога (f)	[ʃwıd'ka dopo'mɔɣa]
snowplow	снігоприбиральна машина (f)	[sniɣoprıbı'raʎna ma'ʃına]
truck	вантажівка (f)	[wanta'ʒiwka]
tank truck	бензовоз (m)	[bɛnzo'wɔz]
van (small truck)	фургон (m)	[fur'ɣon]
tractor (big rig)	тягач (m)	[tʲa'ɣatʃ]
trailer	причіп (m)	[prı'tʃip]
comfortable (adj)	комфортабельний	[komfor'tabɛʎnıj]
second hand (adj)	вживаний	['wʒıwanıj]

175. Cars. Bodywork

hood	капот (m)	[ka'pɔt]
fender	крило (n)	[krı'lɔ]
roof	дах (m)	[dah]
windshield	вітрове скло (n)	[witro'wɛ sklo]
rear-view mirror	дзеркало (n) заднього виду	['dzɛrkalo 'zadnɔɣo 'wıdu]
windshield washer	омивач (m)	[omı'watʃ]
windshield wipers	склоочисники (pl)	[sklo:'tʃısnıkı]
side window	бічне скло (n)	['bitʃnɛ sklo]
window lift	склопідіймач (m)	[sklopidij'matʃ]
antenna	антена (f)	[an'tɛna]
sun roof	люк (m)	[lyk]
bumper	бампер (m)	['bampɛr]

trunk	багажник (m)	[ba'ɣaʒnɪk]
door	дверцята (pl)	[dwɛr'ts^jata]
door handle	ручка (f)	['rutʃka]
door lock	замок (m)	[za'mɔk]

license plate	номер (m)	['nɔmɛr]
muffler	глушник (m)	[ɣluʃ'nɪk]
gas tank	бензобак (m)	[bɛnzo'bak]
tail pipe	вихлопна труба (f)	[wɪhlop'na tru'ba]

gas, accelerator	газ (m)	[ɣaz]
pedal	педаль (f)	[pɛ'daʎ]
gas pedal	педаль (f) газу	[pɛ'daʎ 'ɣazu]

brake	гальмо (n)	[ɣaʎ'mɔ]
brake pedal	педаль (f) гальма	[pɛ'daʎ ɣaʎ'ma]
to slow down (to brake)	гальмувати	[ɣaʎmu'watɪ]
parking brake	стоянкове гальмо (n)	[sto'jaŋkowɛ ɣaʎ'mɔ]

clutch	зчеплення (n)	['ztʃɛplɛŋja]
clutch pedal	педаль (f) зчеплення	[pɛ'daʎ 'ztʃɛplɛŋja]
clutch plate	диск (m) зчеплення	['dɪsk 'ztʃɛplɛŋja]
shock absorber	амортизатор (m)	[amortɪ'zator]

wheel	колесо (n)	['kɔlɛso]
spare tire	запасне колесо (n)	[zapas'nɛ 'kɔlɛso]
hubcap	ковпак (m)	[kow'pak]

driving wheels	ведучі колеса (pl)	[wɛ'dutʃi ko'lɛsa]
front-wheel drive (as adj)	передньопривідний	[pɛrɛdnɔr'ɪwidnɪj]
rear-wheel drive (as adj)	задньопривідний	[zadnɔprɪwid'nɪj]
all-wheel drive (as adj)	повнопривідний	[pownɔr'ɪwidnɪj]

gearbox	коробка (f) передач	[ko'rɔbka pɛrɛ'datʃ]
automatic (adj)	автоматичний	[awtoma'tɪtʃnɪj]
mechanical (adj)	механічний	[mɛha'nitʃnɪj]
gear shift	важіль (m) коробки передач	['waʒiʎ ko'rɔbkɪ pɛrɛ'datʃ]

| headlight | фара (f) | ['fara] |
| headlights | фари (pl) | ['farɪ] |

low beam	ближнє світло (n)	['blɪʒnɛ 'switlo]
high beam	дальнє світло (n)	['daʎnɛ 'switlo]
brake light	стоп-сигнал (m)	[stop sɪɣ'nal]

parking lights	габаритні вогні (pl)	[ɣaba'rɪtni woɣ'ni]
hazard lights	аварійні вогні (pl)	[awa'rijni woɣ'ni]
fog lights	протитуманні фари (pl)	[protitu'maŋi 'farɪ]

| turn signal | поворотник (m) | [powo'rɔtnɪk] |
| back-up light | задній хід (m) | ['zadnij hid] |

176. Cars. Passenger compartment

car inside	салон (m)	[sɑ'lɔn]
leather (as adj)	шкіряний	[ʃkirⁱɑ'nij]
velour (as adj)	велюровий	[wɛ'lyrowij]
upholstery	оббивка (f)	[ob'bıwkɑ]
instrument (gage)	прилад (m)	['prılɑd]
dashboard	приладовий щиток (m)	['prılɑdowıj ɕı'tɔk]
speedometer	спідометр (m)	[spi'dɔmɛtr]
needle (pointer)	стрілка (f)	['strilkɑ]
odometer	лічильник (m)	[li'ʧıʌnık]
indicator (sensor)	датчик (m)	['dɑʧık]
level	рівень (m)	['riwɛɲ]
warning light	лампочка (f)	['lɑmpoʧkɑ]
steering wheel	кермо (n)	[kɛr'mɔ]
horn	сигнал (m)	[sıɣ'nɑl]
button	кнопка (f)	['knɔpkɑ]
switch	перемикач (m)	[pɛrɛmı'kɑʧ]
seat	сидіння (n)	[sı'diɲjɑ]
backrest	спинка (f)	['spıŋkɑ]
headrest	підголівник (m)	[pidɣo'liwnık]
seat belt	ремінь (m) безпеки	['rɛmiɲ bɛz'pɛkı]
to fasten the belt	пристебнути ремінь	[prısteb'nutı 'rɛmiɲ]
adjustment (of seats)	регулювання (n)	[rɛɣuly'wɑɲjɑ]
airbag	повітряна подушка (f)	[po'witrⁱɑnɑ po'duʃkɑ]
air-conditioner	кондиціонер (m)	[kondıtsio'nɛr]
radio	радіо (n)	['rɑdio]
CD player	CD-програвач (m)	[si'di proɣrɑ'wɑʧ]
to turn on	увімкнути	[uwimk'nutı]
antenna	антена (f)	[ɑn'tɛnɑ]
glove box	бардачок (m)	[bɑrdɑ'ʧɔk]
ashtray	попільниця (f)	[popiʌ'nıtsⁱɑ]

177. Cars. Engine

engine	двигун (m)	[dwı'ɣun]
motor	мотор (m)	[mo'tɔr]
diesel (as adj)	дизельний	['dızɛʌnij]
gasoline (as adj)	бензиновий	[bɛn'zınowij]
engine volume	об'єм (m) двигуна	[obʰ'ɛm dwıɣu'nɑ]
power	потужність (f)	[po'tuʒnistⁱ]
horsepower	кінська сила (f)	['kinsⁱkɑ 'sılɑ]

piston	поршень (m)	['pɔrʃɛɲ]
cylinder	циліндр (m)	[tsı'lindr]
valve	клапан (m)	['klɑpɑn]

injector	інжектор (m)	[in'ʒɛktɔr]
generator	генератор (m)	[ɣɛnɛ'rɑtɔr]
carburetor	карбюратор (m)	[kɑrby'rɑtɔr]
engine oil	масло (n) моторне	['mɑslɔ mɔ'tɔrnɛ]

radiator	радіатор (m)	[rɑdi'ɑtɔr]
coolant	охолоджувальна рідина (f)	[ɔhɔ'lɔdʒuwɑʎnɑ ridı'nɑ]
cooling fan	вентилятор (m)	[wɛntı'ʎɑtɔr]

battery (accumulator)	акумулятор (m)	[ɑkumu'ʎɑtɔr]
starter	стартер (m)	['stɑrtɛr]
ignition	запалювання (n)	[zɑ'pɑlywɑɲjɑ]
spark plug	свічка (f) запалювання	['switʃkɑ zɑ'pɑlywɑɲjɑ]

terminal (of battery)	клема (f)	['klɛmɑ]
positive terminal	плюс (m)	[plys]
negative terminal	мінус (m)	['minus]
fuse	запобіжник (m)	[zɑpɔ'biʒnık]

air filter	повітряний фільтр (m)	[pɔ'witrʲɑnıj 'fiʎtr]
oil filter	масляний фільтр (m)	['mɑsʎɑnıj 'fiʎtr]
fuel filter	паливний фільтр (m)	['pɑlıwnıj 'fiʎtr]

178. Cars. Crash. Repair

car accident	аварія (f)	[ɑ'wɑrijɑ]
road accident	дорожня пригода (f)	[dɔ'rɔʒɲɑ prı'ɣɔdɑ]
to run into ...	врізатися	['wrizɑtısʲɑ]
to have an accident	розбитися	[rɔz'bıtısʲɑ]
damage	пошкодження (n)	[pɔʃ'kɔdʒɛɲjɑ]
intact (adj)	цілий	[tsi'lıj]

| to break down (vi) | зламатися | [zlɑ'mɑtısʲɑ] |
| towrope | буксирний трос (m) | [buk'sırnıj tros] |

puncture	прокол (m)	[prɔ'kɔl]
to be flat	спустити	[spus'tıtı]
to pump up	накачати	[nɑkɑ'tʃɑtı]
pressure	тиск (m)	[tısk]
to check (to examine)	перевірити	[pɛrɛ'wirıtı]

repair	ремонт (m)	[rɛ'mɔnt]
auto repair shop	ремонтна майстерня (f)	[rɛ'mɔntnɑ mɑjs'tɛrɲɑ]
spare part	запчастина (f)	[zɑptʃɑs'tınɑ]
part	деталь (f)	[dɛ'tɑʎ]

bolt (with nut)	**болт** (m)	[bolt]
screw bolt (without nut)	**гвинт** (m)	[ɣwɪnt]
nut	**гайка** (f)	[ˈɣɑjkɑ]
washer	**шайба** (f)	[ˈʃɑjbɑ]
bearing	**підшипник** (m)	[pidˈʃɪpnɪk]
tube	**трубка** (f)	[ˈtrubkɑ]
gasket (head ~)	**прокладка** (f)	[prokˈlɑdkɑ]
cable, wire	**провід** (m)	[ˈprowid]
jack	**домкрат** (m)	[domkˈrɑt]
wrench	**ключ** (m)	[klytʃ]
hammer	**молоток** (m)	[moloˈtɔk]
pump	**помпа** (f)	[ˈpɔmpɑ]
screwdriver	**викрутка** (f)	[ˈwɪkrutkɑ]
fire extinguisher	**вогнегасник** (m)	[woɣneˈɣɑsnɪk]
warning triangle	**аварійний трикутник** (m)	[ɑwɑˈrijnɪj trɪˈkutnɪk]
to stall (vi)	**глохнути**	[ˈɣlɔhnutɪ]
stalling	**зупинка** (f)	[zuˈpɪŋkɑ]
to be broken	**бути зламаним**	[ˈbutɪ ˈzlɑmɑnɪm]
to overheat (vi)	**перегрітися**	[pɛrɛɣˈritɪsʲɑ]
to freeze up (pipes, etc.)	**замерзнути**	[zɑˈmɛrznutɪ]
to burst (vi, ab. tube)	**лопнути**	[ˈlɔpnutɪ]
pressure	**тиск** (m)	[tɪsk]
level	**рівень** (m)	[ˈriwɛɲ]
slack (~ belt)	**слабкий**	[slɑbˈkɪj]
dent	**вм'ятина** (f)	[ˈwmʲɑtɪnɑ]
abnormal noise (motor)	**стукіт** (m)	[ˈstukit]
crack	**тріщина** (f)	[ˈtriɕɪnɑ]
scratch	**подряпина** (f)	[podˈrʲɑpɪnɑ]

179. Cars. Road

road	**дорога** (f)	[doˈrɔɣɑ]
highway	**автомагістраль** (f)	[ɑwtomɑɣistˈrɑʎ]
freeway	**шосе** (n)	[ʃoˈsɛ]
direction (way)	**напрямок** (m)	[ˈnɑprʲɑmok]
distance	**відстань** (f)	[ˈwidstɑɲ]
bridge	**міст** (m)	[mist]
parking lot	**паркінг** (m)	[ˈpɑrkiŋ]
square	**площа** (f)	[ˈplɔɕɑ]
interchange	**розв'язка** (f)	[rozwˈʲjazkɑ]
tunnel	**тунель** (m)	[tuˈnɛʎ]
gas station	**автозаправка** (f)	[ɑwtozɑpˈrɑwkɑ]

parking lot	автостоянка (f)	[awtosto'jaŋka]
gas pump	бензоколонка (f)	[bɛnzoko'lɔŋka]
auto repair shop	гараж (m)	[ɣa'raʒ]
to get gas	заправити	[zap'rawıtı]
fuel	паливо (n)	['palıwo]
jerrycan	каністра (f)	[ka'nistra]

asphalt	асфальт (m)	[as'faʎt]
road markings	розмітка (f)	[roz'mitka]
curb	бордюр (m)	[bor'dyr]
guardrail	огорожа (f)	[oɣo'rɔʒa]
ditch	кювет (m)	[ky'wɛt]
roadside (shoulder)	узбіччя (n)	[uz'bitʃʲa]
lamppost	стовп (m)	[stowp]

to drive (a car)	вести	['wɛstı]
to turn (~ to the left)	повертати	[powɛr'tatı]
to make a U-turn	розвертатися	[rozwɛr'tatısʲa]
reverse (~ gear)	задній хід (m)	['zadnij hid]

to honk (vi)	сигналити	[sıɣ'nalıtı]
honk (sound)	звуковий сигнал (m)	[zwuko'wıj sıɣ'nal]
to get stuck	застрягти	[zast'rʲaɣtı]
to spin (in mud)	буксувати	[buksu'watı]
to cut, to turn off	глушити	[ɣlu'ʃıtı]

speed	швидкість (f)	['ʃwıdkistʲ]
to exceed the speed limit	перевищити швидкість	[pɛrɛ'wıɕıtı 'ʃwıdkistʲ]
to give a ticket	штрафувати	[ʃtrafu'watı]
traffic lights	світлофор (m)	[switlo'fɔr]
driver's license	посвідчення (n) водія	[pos'widtʃɛnja wodi'ja]

grade crossing	переїзд (m)	[pɛrɛ'jizd]
intersection	перехрестя (n)	[pɛrɛh'rɛstʲa]
crosswalk	пішохідний перехід (m)	[piʃo'hidnıj pɛrɛ'hid]
bend, curve	поворот (m)	[powo'rɔt]
pedestrian zone	пішохідна зона (f)	[piʃo'hidna 'zɔna]

180. Traffic signs

rules of the road	правила (pl) дорожнього руху	['prawıla dorɔʒnʲɣo 'ruhu]
traffic sign	знак (m)	[znak]
passing (overtaking)	обгін (m)	[ob'ɣin]
curve	поворот (m)	[powo'rɔt]
U-turn	розворот (m)	[rozwo'rɔt]
traffic circle	круговий рух (m)	[kruɣo'wıj ruh]

| No entry | в'їзд заборонено | [wʰjızd zabo'rɔnɛno] |
| No vehicles allowed | рух (m) заборонено | [ruh zabo'rɔnɛno] |

No passing	**обгін заборонено**	[ob'ɣin zabo'rɔnɛno]
No parking	**стоянку заборонено**	[sto'jaŋku zabo'rɔnɛno]
No stopping	**зупинку заборонено**	[zu'pɪŋku zabo'rɔnɛno]

dangerous turn	**небезпечний поворот** (m)	[nɛbɛz'pɛʧnɪj powo'rɔt]
steep descent	**крутий спуск** (m)	[kru'tɪj spusk]
one-way traffic	**односторонній рух** (m)	[odnosto'rɔnij ruh]
crosswalk	**пішохідний перехід** (m)	[piʃo'hidnɪj pɛrɛ'hid]
slippery road	**слизька дорога** (f)	[slɪz'ka do'rɔɣa]
YIELD	**дати дорогу**	['datɪ do'rɔɣu]

PEOPLE. LIFE EVENTS

Life events

181. Holidays. Event

celebration, holiday	**свято** (n)	[ˈswʲɑto]
national day	**національне свято** (n)	[nɑtsioˈnɑʌnɛ ˈswʲɑto]
public holiday	**святковий день** (m)	[swʲɑtˈkɔwɪj dɛɲ]
to commemorate (vt)	**святкувати**	[swʲɑtkuˈwɑtɪ]
event (happening)	**подія** (f)	[poˈdijɑ]
event (organized activity)	**захід** (m)	[ˈzɑhid]
banquet (party)	**бенкет** (m)	[bɛˈŋkɛt]
reception (formal party)	**прийом** (m)	[prɪˈjom]
feast	**бенкет** (m)	[bɛˈŋkɛt]
anniversary	**річниця** (f)	[ritʃˈnɪtsʲɑ]
jubilee	**ювілей** (m)	[juwiˈlɛj]
to celebrate (vt)	**відмітити**	[widˈmitɪtɪ]
New Year	**Новий рік** (m)	[noˈwɪj rik]
Happy New Year!	**З Новим Роком!**	[z noˈwɪm ˈrɔkom]
Christmas	**Різдво** (n)	[rizdˈwɔ]
Merry Christmas!	**Щасливого Різдва!**	[ɕɑsˈlɪwoɣo rizdˈwɑ]
Christmas tree	**Новорічна ялинка** (f)	[nowoˈritʃnɑ jaˈlɪŋkɑ]
fireworks	**салют** (m)	[sɑˈlyt]
wedding	**весілля** (n)	[wɛˈsiʌɑ]
groom	**наречений** (m)	[nɑrɛˈtʃɛnɪj]
bride	**наречена** (f)	[nɑrɛˈtʃɛnɑ]
to invite (vt)	**запрошувати**	[zɑpˈrɔʃuwɑtɪ]
invitation card	**запрошення** (n)	[zɑpˈrɔʃɛɲɑ]
guest	**гість** (m)	[ɣistʲ]
to visit	**йти в гості**	[jtɪ w ˈɣosti]
(~ your parents, etc.)		
to greet the guests	**зустрічати гостей**	[zustriˈtʃɑtɪ ɣosˈtɛj]
gift, present	**подарунок** (m)	[podɑˈrunok]
to give (sth as present)	**дарувати**	[dɑruˈwɑtɪ]
to receive gifts	**отримувати подарунки**	[otˈrɪmuwɑtɪ podɑˈruŋkɪ]
bouquet (of flowers)	**букет** (m)	[buˈkɛt]

| congratulations | привітання (n) | [prɪwiˈtanja] |
| to congratulate (vt) | вітати | [wiˈtatɪ] |

greeting card	вітальна листівка (f)	[wiˈtaʎna lɪsˈtiwka]
to send a postcard	надіслати листівку	[nadisˈlatɪ lɪsˈtiwku]
to get a postcard	отримати листівку	[otˈrɪmatɪ lɪsˈtiwku]

toast	тост (m)	[tost]
to offer (a drink, etc.)	пригощати	[prɪɣoˈɕatɪ]
champagne	шампанське (n)	[ʃamˈpansʲkɛ]

to have fun	веселитися	[wɛsɛˈlitɪsʲa]
fun, merriment	веселощі (pl)	[wɛˈsɛloɕi]
joy (emotion)	радість (f)	[ˈradistʲ]

| dance | танець (m) | [ˈtanɛts] |
| to dance (vi, vt) | танцювати | [tantsyˈwatɪ] |

| waltz | вальс (m) | [waʎs] |
| tango | танго (n) | [ˈtaŋo] |

182. Funerals. Burial

cemetery	цвинтар (m)	[ˈtswɪntar]
grave, tomb	могила (f)	[moˈɣɪla]
cross	хрест (m)	[hrɛst]
gravestone	нагробок (m)	[naɣˈrɔbok]
fence	огорожа (f)	[oɣoˈrɔʒa]
chapel	каплиця (f)	[kapˈlitsʲa]

death	смерть (f)	[smɛrtʲ]
to die (vi)	померти	[poˈmɛrtɪ]
the deceased	покійник (m)	[poˈkijnɪk]
mourning	траур (m)	[ˈtraur]

to bury (vt)	ховати	[hoˈwatɪ]
funeral home	похоронне бюро (n)	[pohoˈrɔnɛ byro]
funeral	похорон (m)	[ˈpɔhoron]

wreath	вінок (m)	[wiˈnɔk]
casket	труна (f)	[truˈna]
hearse	катафалк (m)	[kataˈfalk]
shroud	саван (m)	[sɑˈwan]

| cremation urn | урна (f) | [ˈurna] |
| crematory | крематорій (m) | [krɛmaˈtorij] |

obituary	некролог (m)	[nɛkroˈlɔɣ]
to cry (weep)	плакати	[ˈplakatɪ]
to sob (vi)	ридати	[rɪˈdatɪ]

183. War. Soldiers

platoon	взвод (m)	[wzwod]
company	рота (f)	[ˈrɔta]
regiment	полк (m)	[polk]
army	армія (f)	[ˈarmija]
division	дивізія (f)	[dɪˈwizija]
section, squad	загін (m)	[zaˈɣin]
host (army)	військо (n)	[ˈwijsʲko]
soldier	солдат (m)	[solˈdat]
officer	офіцер (m)	[ofiˈtsɛr]
private	рядовий (m)	[rʲadoˈwij]
sergeant	сержант (m)	[sɛrˈʒant]
lieutenant	лейтенант (m)	[lɛjtɛˈnant]
captain	капітан (m)	[kapiˈtan]
major	майор (m)	[maˈjor]
colonel	полковник (m)	[polˈkownɪk]
general	генерал (m)	[ɣɛnɛˈral]
sailor	моряк (m)	[moˈrʲak]
captain	капітан (m)	[kapiˈtan]
boatswain	боцман (m)	[ˈbɔtsman]
artilleryman	артилерист (m)	[artɪlɛˈrɪst]
paratrooper	десантник (m)	[dɛˈsantnɪk]
pilot	льотчик (m)	[ˈlʲɔtʃɪk]
navigator	штурман (m)	[ˈʃturman]
mechanic	механік (m)	[mɛˈhanik]
pioneer (sapper)	сапер (m)	[saˈpɛr]
parachutist	парашутист (m)	[paraʃuˈtist]
reconnaissance scout	розвідник (m)	[rozˈwidnɪk]
sniper	снайпер (m)	[ˈsnajpɛr]
patrol (group)	патруль (m)	[patˈruʎ]
to patrol (vt)	патрулювати	[patrulyˈwatɪ]
sentry, guard	вартовий (m)	[wartoˈwij]
warrior	воїн (m)	[ˈwɔjɪn]
hero	герой (m)	[ɣɛˈrɔj]
heroine	героїня (f)	[ɣɛroˈjɪɲa]
patriot	патріот (m)	[patriˈɔt]
traitor	зрадник (m)	[ˈzradnɪk]
deserter	дезертир (m)	[dɛzɛrˈtɪr]
to desert (vi)	дезертирувати	[dɛzɛrˈtɪruwatɪ]
mercenary	найманець (m)	[ˈnajmanɛts]
recruit	новобранець (m)	[nowobˈranɛts]

volunteer	доброволець (m)	[dobro'wɔlɛts]
dead (n)	убитий (m)	[u'bɪtɪj]
wounded (n)	поранений (m)	[po'ranɛnɪj]
prisoner of war	полонений (m)	[polo'nɛnɪj]

184. War. Military actions. Part 1

war	війна (f)	[wij'na]
to be at war	воювати	[woju'watɪ]
civil war	громадянська війна (f)	[ɣroma'dʲansʲka wij'na]

treacherously (adv)	віроломно	[wiro'lɔmno]
declaration of war	оголошення (n)	[oɣo'lɔʃɛnja]
to declare (~ war)	оголосити	[oɣolo'sɪtɪ]
aggression	агресія (f)	[aɣ'rɛsija]
to attack (invade)	нападати	[napa'datɪ]

to invade (vt)	захоплювати	[za'hoplywatɪ]
invader	загарбник (m)	[za'ɣarbnɪk]
conqueror	завойовник (m)	[zawo'jɔwnɪk]

defense	оборона (f)	[obo'rɔna]
to defend (a country, etc.)	обороняти	[oboro'ɲatɪ]
to defend oneself	оборонятися	[oboro'ɲatɪsʲa]

enemy	ворог (m)	['wɔroɣ]
foe, adversary	супротивник (m)	[supro'tɪwnɪk]
enemy (as adj)	ворожий	[wo'rɔʒɪj]

| strategy | стратегія (f) | [stra'tɛɣija] |
| tactics | тактика (f) | ['taktɪka] |

order	наказ (m)	[na'kaz]
command (order)	команда (f)	[ko'manda]
to order (vt)	наказувати	[na'kazuwatɪ]
mission	завдання (n)	[zaw'daɲa]
secret (adj)	таємний	[ta'ɛmnɪj]

| battle | битва (f) | ['bɪtwa] |
| combat | бій (m) | [bij] |

attack	атака (f)	[a'taka]
storming (assault)	штурм (m)	[ʃturm]
to storm (vt)	штурмувати	[ʃturmu'watɪ]
siege (to be under ~)	облога (f)	[ob'lɔɣa]

offensive (n)	наступ (m)	['nastup]
to go on the offensive	наступати	[nastu'patɪ]
retreat	відступ (m)	['widstup]
to retreat (vi)	відступати	[widstu'patɪ]

| encirclement | оточення (n) | [oˈtɔtʃɛnja] |
| to encircle (vt) | оточувати | [oˈtɔtʃuwatɪ] |

bombing (by aircraft)	бомбардування (n)	[bombarduˈwanja]
to drop a bomb	скинути бомбу	[ˈskɪnutɪ ˈbɔmbu]
to bomb (vt)	бомбардувати	[bombarduˈwatɪ]
explosion	вибух (m)	[ˈwɪbuh]

shot	постріл (m)	[ˈpɔstril]
to fire a shot	вистрілити	[ˈwɪstrilɪtɪ]
firing (burst of ~)	стрілянина (f)	[striʎaˈnɪna]

to take aim (at ...)	цілитися	[ˈtsilɪtɪsʲa]
to point (a gun)	навести	[naˈwɛstɪ]
to hit (the target)	влучити	[ˈwlutʃɪtɪ]

to sink (~ a ship)	потопити	[potoˈpɪtɪ]
hole (in a ship)	пробоїна (f)	[proˈbɔjɪna]
to founder, to sink (vi)	йти на дно	[jtɪ na dno]

front (war ~)	фронт (m)	[front]
rear (homefront)	тил (m)	[tɪl]
evacuation	евакуація (f)	[ɛwakuˈatsija]
to evacuate (vt)	евакуювати	[ɛwakujuˈwatɪ]

barbwire	колючий дріт (m)	[koˈlytʃɪj drit]
barrier (anti tank ~)	загородження (n)	[zaɣoˈrɔdʒɛnja]
watchtower	вишка (f)	[ˈwɪʃka]

hospital	госпіталь (m)	[ˈɣɔspitaʎ]
to wound (vt)	поранити	[poˈranɪtɪ]
wound	рана (f)	[ˈrana]
wounded (n)	поранений (m)	[poˈranɛnɪj]
to be wounded	одержати поранення	[oˈdɛrʒatɪ poˈranɛnja]
serious (wound)	важкий	[waʒˈkɪj]

185. War. Military actions. Part 2

captivity	полон (m)	[poˈlɔn]
to take captive	взяти в полон	[ˈwzʲatɪ w poˈlɔn]
to be in captivity	бути в полоні	[ˈbutɪ w poˈlɔni]
to be taken prisoner	потрапити в полон	[potˈrapɪtɪ w poˈlɔn]

concentration camp	концтабір (m)	[kontsˈtabir]
prisoner of war	полонений (m)	[poloˈnɛnɪj]
to escape (vi)	тікати	[tiˈkatɪ]

to betray (vt)	зрадити	[ˈzradɪtɪ]
betrayer	зрадник (m)	[ˈzradnɪk]
betrayal	зрада (f)	[ˈzrada]

to execute (shoot)	**розстріляти**	[rozstriˈʎatɪ]
execution (by firing squad)	**розстріл** (m)	[ˈrɔzstril]
equipment (military gear)	**обмундирування** (n)	[obmundɪruˈwaɲja]
shoulder board	**погон** (m)	[poˈɣɔn]
gas mask	**протигаз** (m)	[protɪˈɣaz]
radio transmitter	**рація** (f)	[ˈratsija]
cipher, code	**шифр** (m)	[ʃifr]
secrecy	**конспірація** (f)	[konspiˈratsija]
password	**пароль** (m)	[paˈrɔʎ]
land mine	**міна** (f)	[ˈmina]
to mine (road, etc.)	**мінувати**	[minuˈwatɪ]
minefield	**мінне поле** (n)	[ˈmiɲɛ ˈpɔlɛ]
air-raid warning	**повітряна тривога** (f)	[poˈwitrʲana trɪˈwɔɣa]
alarm (warning)	**тривога** (f)	[trɪˈwɔɣa]
signal	**сигнал** (m)	[sɪɣˈnal]
signal flare	**сигнальна ракета** (f)	[sɪɣˈnaʎna raˈkɛta]
headquarters	**штаб** (m)	[ʃtab]
reconnaissance	**розвідка** (f)	[ˈrɔzwidka]
situation	**обстановка** (f)	[obstaˈnɔwka]
report	**рапорт** (m)	[ˈrapɔrt]
ambush	**засідка** (f)	[ˈzasidka]
reinforcement (of army)	**підкріплення** (n)	[pidkˈriplɛɲja]
target	**мішень** (f)	[miˈʃɛɲ]
proving ground	**полігон** (m)	[poliˈɣɔn]
military exercise	**маневри** (pl)	[maˈnɛwrɪ]
panic	**паніка** (f)	[ˈpanika]
devastation	**розруха** (f)	[rozˈruha]
destruction, ruins	**руйнування** (pl)	[rujnuˈwaɲja]
to destroy (vt)	**зруйнувати**	[zrujnuˈwatɪ]
to survive (vi, vt)	**вижити**	[ˈwɪʒɪtɪ]
to disarm (vt)	**обеззброїти**	[obɛzzbˈrɔjitɪ]
to handle (~ a gun)	**поводитися**	[poˈwɔdɪtɪsʲa]
Attention!	**Струнко!**	[ˈstruŋko]
At ease!	**Вільно!**	[ˈwiʎno]
feat (of courage)	**подвиг** (m)	[ˈpɔdwɪɣ]
oath (vow)	**клятва** (f)	[ˈkʎatwa]
to swear (an oath)	**клястися**	[ˈkʎastɪsʲa]
decoration (medal, etc.)	**нагорода** (f)	[naɣoˈrɔda]
to award (give medal to)	**нагороджувати**	[naɣoˈrɔdʒuwatɪ]
medal	**медаль** (f)	[mɛˈdaʎ]
order (e.g., ~ of Merit)	**орден** (m)	[ˈɔrdɛn]

victory	перемога (f)	[pɛrɛ'mɔɣa]
defeat	поразка (f)	[po'razka]
armistice	перемир'я (n)	[pɛrɛ'mɪrʲja]

banner (standard)	прапор (m)	['prapor]
glory (honor, fame)	слава (f)	['slawa]
parade	парад (m)	[pa'rad]
to march (on parade)	марширувати	[marʃiru'watɪ]

186. Weapons

weapons	зброя (f)	['zbrɔja]
firearm	вогнепальна зброя	[woɣnɛ'paʎna 'zbrɔja]
cold weapons (knives, etc.)	холодна зброя (f)	[ho'lɔdna 'zbrɔja]

chemical weapons	хімічна зброя (f)	[hi'miʧna 'zbrɔja]
nuclear (adj)	ядерний	['jadɛrnɪj]
nuclear weapons	ядерна зброя (f)	['jadɛrna 'zbrɔja]

| bomb | бомба (f) | ['bɔmba] |
| atomic bomb | атомна бомба (f) | ['atomna 'bɔmba] |

pistol (gun)	пістолет (m)	[pisto'lɛt]
rifle	рушниця (f)	[ruʃ'nɪtsʲa]
submachine gun	автомат (m)	[awto'mat]
machine gun	кулемет (m)	[kulɛ'mɛt]

muzzle	дуло (n)	['dulo]
barrel	ствол (m)	[stwol]
caliber	калібр (m)	[ka'libr]

trigger	курок (m)	[ku'rɔk]
sight (aiming device)	приціл (m)	[prɪ'ʦil]
magazine	магазин (m)	[maɣa'zɪn]
butt (of rifle)	приклад (m)	[prɪk'lad]

| hand grenade | граната (f) | [ɣra'nata] |
| explosive | вибухівка (f) | [wɪbu'hiwka] |

bullet	куля (f)	['kuʎa]
cartridge	патрон (m)	[pat'rɔn]
charge	заряд (m)	[za'rʲad]
ammunition	боєприпаси (pl)	[boɛprɪ'pasɪ]

bomber (aircraft)	бомбардувальник (m)	[bombardu'waʎnɪk]
fighter	винищувач (m)	[wɪ'nɪɕuwaʧ]
helicopter	вертоліт (m)	[wɛrto'lit]
anti-aircraft gun	зенітка (f)	[zɛ'nitka]
tank	танк (m)	[taŋk]

tank gun	гармата (f)	[ɣarˈmata]
artillery	артилерія (f)	[artıˈlɛrija]
cannon	гармата (f)	[ɣarˈmata]
to lay (a gun)	навести	[naˈwɛstı]
shell (projectile)	снаряд (m)	[snaˈrʲad]
mortar bomb	міна (f)	[ˈmina]
mortar	мінomet (m)	[minoˈmɛt]
splinter (shell fragment)	осколок (m)	[osˈkolok]
submarine	підводний човен (m)	[pidˈwɔdnıj ˈʧɔwɛn]
torpedo	торпеда (f)	[torˈpɛda]
missile	ракета (f)	[raˈkɛta]
to load (gun)	заряджати	[zarʲaˈdʒatı]
to shoot (vi)	стріляти	[striˈʎatı]
to point at (the cannon)	цілитися	[ˈʦilıtısʲa]
bayonet	багнет (m)	[baɣˈnɛt]
epee	шпага (f)	[ˈʃpaɣa]
saber (e.g., cavalry ~)	шабля (f)	[ˈʃabʎa]
spear (weapon)	спис (m)	[spıs]
bow	лук (m)	[luk]
arrow	стріла (f)	[striˈla]
musket	мушкет (m)	[muʃˈkɛt]
crossbow	арбалет (m)	[arbaˈlɛt]

187. Ancient people

primitive (prehistoric)	первісний	[pɛrˈwisnıj]
prehistoric (adj)	доісторичний	[doistoˈrıʧnıj]
ancient (~ civilization)	стародавній	[staroˈdawnij]
Stone Age	Кам'яний вік (m)	[kamʲjaˈnıj wik]
Bronze Age	Бронзовий вік (m)	[ˈbrɔnzowıj wik]
Ice Age	льодовиковий період (m)	[lʲadowıˈkɔwıj pɛˈriod]
tribe	плем'я (n)	[ˈplɛmʲja]
cannibal	людоїд (m)	[lydoˈjıd]
hunter	мисливець (m)	[mısˈlıwɛʦ]
to hunt (vi, vt)	полювати	[polyˈwatı]
mammoth	мамонт (m)	[ˈmamont]
cave	печера (f)	[pɛˈʧɛra]
fire	вогонь (m)	[woˈɣɔɲ]
campfire	багаття (n)	[baˈɣattʲa]
rock painting	наскальний малюнок (m)	[nasˈkaʎnıj maˈlynok]
tool (e.g., stone ax)	знаряддя (n) праці	[znaˈrʲaddʲa ˈpratsi]
spear	спис (m)	[spıs]

stone ax	кам'яна сокира (f)	[kamʰjaˈna soˈkɪra]
to be at war	воювати	[wojuˈwatɪ]
to domesticate (vt)	приручати	[prɪruˈʧatɪ]

idol	ідол (m)	[ˈidol]
to worship (vt)	поклонятися	[pokloˈɲatɪsʲa]
superstition	забобони (pl)	[zaboˈbɔnɪ]

evolution	еволюція (f)	[ɛwoˈlytsija]
development	розвиток (m)	[ˈrɔzwɪtok]
disappearance (extinction)	зникнення (n)	[ˈznɪknɛɲa]
to adapt oneself	пристосовуватися	[prɪstosowuˈwatɪsʲa]

archeology	археологія (f)	[arhɛoˈloɣija]
archeologist	археолог (m)	[arhɛˈɔloɣ]
archeological (adj)	археологічний	[arhɛoloˈɣiʧnɪj]

excavation site	розкопки (pl)	[rozˈkɔpkɪ]
excavations	розкопки (pl)	[rozˈkɔpkɪ]
find (object)	знахідка (f)	[znaˈhidka]
fragment	фрагмент (m)	[fraɣˈmɛnt]

188. Middle Ages

people (ethnic group)	народ (m)	[naˈrɔd]
peoples	народи (pl)	[naˈrɔdɪ]
tribe	плем'я (n)	[ˈplɛmʰja]
tribes	племена (pl)	[plɛmɛˈna]

barbarians	варвари (pl)	[ˈwarwarɪ]
Gauls	гали (m)	[ˈɣalɪ]
Goths	готи (pl)	[ˈɣɔtɪ]
Slavs	слов'яни (pl)	[slowʰˈjanɪ]
Vikings	вікінги (pl)	[ˈwikiŋɪ]

| Romans | римляни (pl) | [rɪmˈʎanɪ] |
| Roman (adj) | Римський Папа | [ˈrɪmsʲkɪj ˈpapa] |

Byzantines	візантійці (pl)	[wizanˈtijtsi]
Byzantium	Візантія (f)	[wizanˈtija]
Byzantine (adj)	візантійський	[wizanˈtijsʲkɪj]

emperor	імператор (m)	[impɛˈrator]
leader, chief	вождь (m)	[wɔʒdʲ]
powerful (~ king)	могутній	[moˈɣutnij]
king	король (m)	[koˈrɔʎ]
ruler (sovereign)	правитель (m)	[praˈwitɛʎ]

| knight | лицар (m) | [ˈlɪtsar] |
| feudal lord | феодал (m) | [fɛoˈdal] |

feudal (adj)	**феодальний**	[fɛo'daʎnɪj]
vassal	**васал** (m)	[wa'sal]
duke	**герцог** (m)	['ɣɛrʦoɣ]
earl	**граф** (m)	[ɣraf]
baron	**барон** (m)	[ba'rɔn]
bishop	**єпископ** (m)	[ɛ'pɪskop]
armor	**лати** (pl)	['latɪ]
shield	**щит** (m)	[ɕɪt]
sword	**меч** (m)	[mɛʧ]
visor	**забрало** (n)	[zab'ralo]
chainmail	**кольчуга** (f)	[koʎ'ʧuɣa]
crusade	**хрестовий похід** (m)	[hrɛs'tɔwɪj po'hid]
crusader	**хрестоносець** (m)	[hrɛsto'nɔsɛʦ]
territory	**територія** (f)	[tɛrɪ'tɔrija]
to attack (invade)	**нападати**	[napa'datɪ]
to conquer (vt)	**завоювати**	[zawoju'watɪ]
to occupy (invade)	**захватити**	[zahwa'tɪtɪ]
siege (to be under ~)	**облога** (f)	[ob'lɔɣa]
besieged (adj)	**обложений**	[ob'lɔʒɛnɪj]
to besiege (vt)	**облягати**	[obʎa'ɣatɪ]
inquisition	**інквізиція** (f)	[iŋkwi'zɪtsija]
inquisitor	**інквизитор** (m)	[iŋkwi'zɪtor]
torture	**катування** (n)	[katu'wanja]
cruel (adj)	**жорстокий**	[ʒors'tɔkɪj]
heretic	**єретик** (m)	[ɛ'rɛtɪk]
heresy	**єресь** (f)	['ɛrɛsʲ]
seafaring	**мореплавання** (n)	[morɛp'lawanja]
pirate	**пірат** (m)	[pi'rat]
piracy	**піратство** (n)	[pi'ratstwo]
boarding (attack)	**абордаж** (m)	[abor'daʒ]
loot, booty	**здобич** (f)	['zdɔbɪʧ]
treasures	**скарби** (pl)	[skar'bɪ]
discovery	**відкриття** (n)	[widkrɪt'tʲa]
to discover (new land, etc.)	**відкрити**	[widk'rɪtɪ]
expedition	**експедиція** (f)	[ɛkspɛ'dɪʦija]
musketeer	**мушкетер** (m)	[muʃkɛ'tɛr]
cardinal	**кардинал** (m)	[kardɪ'nal]
heraldry	**геральдика** (f)	[ɣɛ'raʎdɪka]
heraldic (adj)	**геральдичний**	[ɣɛraʎ'dɪʧnɪj]

189. Leader. Chief. Authorities

king	**король** (m)	[koˈrɔʎ]
queen	**королева** (f)	[koroˈlɛwa]
royal (adj)	**королівський**	[koroˈliwsʲkɪj]
kingdom	**королівство** (n)	[koroˈliwstwo]
prince	**принц** (m)	[prɪnʦ]
princess	**принцеса** (f)	[prɪnˈʦɛsa]
president	**президент** (m)	[prɛzɪˈdɛnt]
vice-president	**віце-президент** (m)	[ˈwiʦɛ prɛzɪˈdɛnt]
senator	**сенатор** (m)	[sɛˈnɑtor]
monarch	**монарх** (m)	[moˈnɑrh]
ruler (sovereign)	**правитель** (m)	[praˈwɪtɛʎ]
dictator	**диктатор** (m)	[dɪkˈtɑtor]
tyrant	**тиран** (m)	[tɪˈrɑn]
magnate	**магнат** (m)	[mɑɣˈnɑt]
director	**директор** (m)	[dɪˈrɛktor]
chief	**шеф** (m)	[ʃɛf]
manager (director)	**управляючий** (m)	[uprawˈʎɑjutʃɪj]
boss	**бос** (m)	[bos]
owner	**господар** (m)	[ɣosˈpodar]
head (~ of delegation)	**голова** (f)	[ɣoloˈwa]
authorities	**влада** (f)	[ˈwlada]
superiors	**керівництво** (n)	[kɛriwˈnɪʦtwo]
governor	**губернатор** (m)	[ɣubɛrˈnɑtor]
consul	**консул** (m)	[ˈkɔnsul]
diplomat	**дипломат** (m)	[dɪploˈmɑt]
mayor	**мер** (m)	[mɛr]
sheriff	**шериф** (m)	[ʃɛˈrɪf]
emperor	**імператор** (m)	[impɛˈrɑtor]
tsar, czar	**цар** (m)	[ʦar]
pharaoh	**фараон** (m)	[faraˈɔn]
khan	**хан** (m)	[han]

190. Road. Way. Directions

road	**дорога** (f)	[doˈrɔɣa]
way (direction)	**шлях** (m)	[ʃʎah]
freeway	**шосе** (n)	[ʃoˈsɛ]
highway	**автомагістраль** (f)	[awtomaɣistˈraʎ]
interstate	**національна дорога** (f)	[natsioˈnɑʎna doˈrɔɣa]

main road	**головна дорога** (f)	[ɣolow'na do'roɣa]
dirt road	**польова дорога** (f)	[polɜ'wa do'roɣa]
pathway	**стежка** (f)	['stɛʒka]
footpath (troddenpath)	**стежина** (f)	[stɛ'ʒɪna]
Where?	**Де?**	[dɛ]
Where (to)?	**Куди?**	[ku'dɪ]
Where … from?	**Звідки?**	['zwidkɪ]
direction (way)	**напрямок** (m)	['naprʲamok]
to point (~ the way)	**вказати**	[wka'zatɪ]
to the left	**ліворуч**	[liʲworuʧ]
to the right	**праворуч**	[pra'woruʧ]
straight ahead (adv)	**прямо**	['prʲamo]
back (e.g., to turn ~)	**назад**	[na'zad]
bend, curve	**поворот** (m)	[powo'rot]
to turn (~ to the left)	**повертати**	[powɛr'tatɪ]
to make a U-turn	**розвертатися**	[rozwɛr'tatɪsʲa]
to be visible	**виднітися**	[wɪd'nitɪsʲa]
to appear (come into view)	**з'явитися**	[zʲja'wɪtɪsʲa]
stop, halt (in journey)	**зупинка** (f)	[zu'pɪŋka]
to rest, to halt (vi)	**відпочити**	[widpo'ʧɪtɪ]
rest (pause)	**відпочинок** (m)	[widpo'ʧɪnok]
to lose one's way	**заблукати**	[zablu'katɪ]
to lead to … (ab. road)	**вести до**	['wɛstɪ do]
to arrive at …	**вийти до …**	['wɪjtɪ do]
stretch (of road)	**відрізок** (m)	[wid'rizok]
asphalt	**асфальт** (m)	[as'faʎt]
curb	**бордюр** (m)	[bor'dyr]
ditch	**канава** (f)	[ka'nawa]
manhole	**люк** (m)	[lyk]
roadside (shoulder)	**узбіччя** (n)	[uz'biʧʲa]
pit, pothole	**яма** (f)	['jama]
to go (on foot)	**йти**	[jtɪ]
to pass (overtake)	**обігнати**	[obiɣ'natɪ]
step (footstep)	**крок** (m)	[krok]
on foot (adv)	**пішки**	['piʃkɪ]
to block (road)	**перегородити**	[pɛrɛɣoro'dɪtɪ]
boom barrier	**шлагбаум** (m)	[ʃlaɣ'baum]
dead end	**глухий кут** (m)	[ɣlu'hɪj kut]

191. Breaking the law. Criminals. Part 1

bandit	бандит (m)	[ban'dɪt]
crime	злочин (m)	['zlɔtʃin]
criminal (person)	злочинець (m)	[zlo'tʃinɛts]
thief	злодій (m)	['zlɔdij]
to steal (vi, vt)	красти	['krastɪ]
stealing (larceny)	крадеж (m)	['kradɛʃ]
theft	крадіжка (f)	[kra'diʒka]
to kidnap (vt)	викрадення	['wɪkradɛnja]
kidnapping	викрадення (n)	['wɪkradɛnja]
kidnapper	викрадач (m)	[wɪkra'datʃ]
ransom	викуп (m)	['wɪkup]
to demand ransom	вимагати викуп	[wɪma'ɣatɪ 'wɪkup]
to rob (vt)	грабувати	[ɣrabu'watɪ]
robber	грабіжник (m)	[ɣra'biʒnɪk]
to extort (vt)	вимагати	[wɪma'ɣatɪ]
extortionist	вимагач (m)	[wɪma'ɣatʃ]
extortion	вимагання (n)	[wɪma'ɣanja]
to murder, to kill	вбити	['wbɪtɪ]
murder	вбивство (n)	['wbɪwstwo]
murderer	вбивця (m)	['wbɪwtsʲa]
gunshot	постріл (m)	['pɔstril]
to fire a shot	вистрілити	['wɪstrilɪtɪ]
to shoot to death	застрелити	[zast'rɛlɪtɪ]
to shoot (vi)	стріляти	[stri'ʎatɪ]
shooting	стрілянина (f)	[striʎa'nɪna]
incident (fight, etc.)	подія (f)	[po'dija]
fight, brawl	бійка (f)	['bijka]
victim	жертва (f)	['ʒɛrtwa]
to damage (vt)	пошкодити	[poʃ'kɔdɪtɪ]
damage	шкода (f)	['ʃkɔda]
dead body	труп (m)	[trup]
grave (~ crime)	важкий	[waʒ'kɪj]
to attack (vt)	напасти	[na'pastɪ]
to beat (dog, person)	бити	['bɪtɪ]
to beat up	побити	[po'bɪtɪ]
to take (rob of sth)	забрати	[zab'ratɪ]
to stab to death	зарізати	[za'rizatɪ]
to maim (vt)	покалічити	[poka'litʃitɪ]
to wound (vt)	поранити	[po'ranɪtɪ]

blackmail	шантаж (m)	[ʃɑnˈtɑʒ]
to blackmail (vt)	шантажувати	[ʃɑntɑʒuˈwɑtɪ]
blackmailer	шантажист (m)	[ʃɑntɑˈʒɪst]

protection racket	рекет (m)	[ˈrɛkɛt]
racketeer	рекетир (m)	[rɛkɛˈtɪr]
gangster	гангстер (m)	[ˈɣɑŋstɛr]
mafia, Mob	мафія (f)	[ˈmɑfijɑ]

pickpocket	кишеньковий злодій (m)	[kɪʃɛnˈkɔwɪj ˈzlɔdij]
burglar	зломщик (m)	[ˈzlɔmɕɪk]
smuggling	контрабанда (f)	[kɔntrɑˈbɑndɑ]
smuggler	контрабандист (m)	[kɔntrɑbɑnˈdɪst]

forgery	підробка (f)	[pidˈrɔbkɑ]
to forge (counterfeit)	підробляти	[pidrɔbˈʎɑtɪ]
fake (forged)	фальшивий	[fɑʎˈʃɪwɪj]

192. Breaking the law. Criminals. Part 2

rape	зґвалтування (n)	[zgwɑltuˈwɑnjɑ]
to rape (vt)	зґвалтувати	[zgwɑltuˈwɑtɪ]
rapist	ґвалтівник (m)	[gwɑltiwˈnɪk]
maniac	маніяк (m)	[mɑniˈjɑk]

prostitute (fem.)	проститутка (f)	[prɔstɪˈtutkɑ]
prostitution	проституція (f)	[prɔstɪˈtutsijɑ]
pimp	сутенер (m)	[sutɛˈnɛr]

| drug addict | наркоман (m) | [nɑrkɔˈmɑn] |
| drug dealer | наркоторгівець (m) | [nɑrkɔtɔrˈɣiwɛʦ] |

to blow up (bomb)	підірвати	[pidirˈwɑtɪ]
explosion	вибух (m)	[ˈwɪbuh]
to set fire	підпалити	[pidpɑˈlɪtɪ]
incendiary (arsonist)	підпалювач (m)	[pidˈpɑlywɑʧ]

terrorism	тероризм (m)	[tɛrɔˈrɪzm]
terrorist	терорист (m)	[tɛrɔˈrɪst]
hostage	заручник (m)	[zɑˈruʧnɪk]

to swindle (vt)	обманути	[ɔbmɑˈnutɪ]
swindle	обман (m)	[ɔbˈmɑn]
swindler	шахрай (m)	[ʃɑhˈrɑj]

to bribe (vt)	підкупити	[pidkuˈpɪtɪ]
bribery	підкуп (m)	[ˈpidkup]
bribe	хабар (m)	[hɑˈbɑr]
poison	отрута (f)	[ɔtˈrutɑ]
to poison (vt)	отруїти	[ɔtruˈjitɪ]

to poison oneself	отруїтись	[otru'jıtısʲ]
suicide (act)	самогубство (n)	[samo'ɣubstwo]
suicide (person)	самовбивця (m)	[samow'bıwtsʲa]

to threaten (vt)	погрожувати	[poɣ'rɔʒuwatı]
threat	погроза (f)	[poɣ'rɔza]
to make an attempt	вчинити замах	[wtʃı'nıtı 'zamah]
attempt (attack)	замах (m)	['zamah]

| to steal (a car) | украсти | [uk'rastı] |
| to hijack (a plane) | викрасти | ['wıkrastı] |

| revenge | помста (f) | ['pɔmsta] |
| to revenge (vt) | мстити | ['mstıtı] |

to torture (vt)	катувати	[katu'watı]
torture	катування (n)	[katu'wanja]
to torment (vt)	мучити	['mutʃıtı]

pirate	пірат (m)	[pi'rat]
hooligan	хуліган (m)	[huli'ɣan]
armed (adj)	озброєний	[ozb'rɔɛnıj]
violence	насильство (n)	[na'sıʎstwo]

| spying (n) | шпигунство (n) | [ʃpı'ɣunstwo] |
| to spy (vi) | шпигувати | [ʃpıɣu'watı] |

193. Police. Law. Part 1

| justice | правосуддя (n) | [prawo'suddʲa] |
| court (court room) | суд (m) | [sud] |

judge	суддя (m)	[sud'dʲa]
jurors	присяжні (pl)	[prı'sʲaʒni]
jury trial	суд (m) присяжних	[sud prı'sʲaʒnıh]
to judge (vt)	судити	[su'dıtı]

lawyer, attorney	адвокат (m)	[adwo'kat]
accused	підсудний (m)	[pid'sudnıj]
dock	лава (f) підсудних	['lawa pid'sudnıh]

| charge | обвинувачення (n) | [obwınu'watʃɛnja] |
| accused | обвинувачений (m) | [obwınu'watʃɛnıj] |

| sentence | вирок (m) | ['wırok] |
| to sentence (vt) | присудити | [prısu'dıtı] |

guilty (culprit)	винуватець (m)	[wınu'watɛts]
to punish (vt)	покарати	[poka'ratı]
punishment	покарання (n)	[poka'ranja]

fine (penalty)	штраф (m)	[ʃtraf]
life imprisonment	довічне ув'язнення (n)	[do'witʃnɛ uwʰ'jaznɛnja]
death penalty	смертна кара (f)	['smɛrtna 'kara]
electric chair	електричний стілець (m)	[ɛlɛkt'rɪtʃnɪj sti'lɛts]
gallows	шибениця (f)	['ʃibɛnɪtsʲa]
to execute (vt)	стратити	['stratɪtɪ]
execution	страта (f)	['strata]
prison, jail	в'язниця (f)	[wʰjaz'nɪtsʲa]
cell	камера (f)	['kamɛra]
escort	конвой (m)	[kon'wɔj]
prison guard	наглядач (m)	[naɣʎa'datʃ]
prisoner	в'язень (m)	['wʰjazɛɲ]
handcuffs	наручники (pl)	[na'rutʃnɪkɪ]
to handcuff (vt)	надіти наручники	[na'ditɪ na'rutʃnɪkɪ]
prison break	втеча (m)	['wtɛtʃa]
to break out (vi)	утекти	[utɛk'tɪ]
to disappear (vi)	зникнути	['znɪknutɪ]
to release (from prison)	звільнити	[zwiʎ'nɪtɪ]
amnesty	амністія (f)	[am'nistija]
police	поліція (f)	[po'litsija]
police officer	поліцейський (m)	[poli'tsɛjsʲkɪj]
police station	поліцейський відділок (m)	[poli'tsɛjsʲkɪj 'widdilok]
billy club	гумовий кийок (m)	['ɣumowɪj kɪ'jɔk]
bullhorn	рупор (m)	['rupor]
patrol car	патрульна машина (f)	[pat'ruʎna ma'ʃɪna]
siren	сирена (f)	[sɪ'rɛna]
to turn on the siren	увімкнути сирену	[uwimk'nutɪ sɪ'rɛnu]
siren call	виття (n) сирени	[wɪt'tʲa sɪ'rɛnɪ]
crime scene	місце (n) події	['mistsɛ po'dijɪ]
witness	свідок (m)	['swidok]
freedom	воля (f)	['wɔʎa]
accomplice	спільник (m)	['spiʎnɪk]
to flee (vi)	зникнути	['znɪknutɪ]
trace (to leave a ~)	слід (m)	[slid]

194. Police. Law. Part 2

search (investigation)	розшук (m)	['rozʃuk]
to look for ...	розшукувати	[roz'ʃukuwatɪ]
suspicion	підозра (f)	[pi'dɔzra]
suspicious (suspect)	підозрілий	[pidoz'rilɪj]

to stop (cause to halt)	**зупинити**	[zupɪ'nɪtɪ]
to detain (keep in custody)	**затримати**	[zat'rɪmatɪ]
case (lawsuit)	**справа** (f)	['sprawa]
investigation	**слідство** (n)	['slidstwo]
detective	**детектив** (m)	[dɛtɛk'tɪw]
investigator	**слідчий** (m)	['slidtʃɪj]
hypothesis	**версія** (f)	['wɛrsija]
motive	**мотив** (m)	[mo'tɪw]
interrogation	**допит** (m)	['dɔpɪt]
to interrogate (vt)	**допитувати**	[do'pɪtuwatɪ]
to question (vt)	**опитувати**	[o'pɪtuwatɪ]
check (identity ~)	**перевірка** (f)	[pɛrɛ'wirka]
round-up	**облава** (f)	[ob'lawa]
search (~ warrant)	**обшук** (m)	['ɔbʃuk]
chase (pursuit)	**погоня** (f)	[po'ɣɔɲa]
to pursue, to chase	**переслідувати**	[pɛrɛs'liduwatɪ]
to track (a criminal)	**слідкувати**	[slidku'watɪ]
arrest	**арешт** (m)	[a'rɛʃt]
to arrest (sb)	**заарештувати**	[za:rɛʃtu'watɪ]
to catch (thief, etc.)	**зловити**	[zlo'wɪtɪ]
capture	**затримання** (n)	[zat'rɪmaɲa]
document	**документ** (m)	[doku'mɛnt]
proof (evidence)	**доказ** (m)	['dɔkaz]
to prove (vt)	**доводити**	[do'wodɪtɪ]
footprint	**слід** (m)	[slid]
fingerprints	**відбитки** (pl) **пальців**	[wid'bɪtkɪ 'paʎtsiw]
piece of evidence	**доказ** (m)	['dɔkaz]
alibi	**алібі** (n)	['alibi]
innocent (not guilty)	**невинний**	[nɛ'wɪnɪj]
injustice	**несправедливість** (f)	[nɛsprawɛd'lɪwistʲ]
unjust, unfair (adj)	**несправедливий**	[nɛsprawɛd'lɪwɪj]
criminal (adj)	**кримінальний**	[krɪmi'naʎnɪj]
to confiscate (vt)	**конфіскувати**	[konfisku'watɪ]
drug (illegal substance)	**наркотик** (m)	[nar'kɔtɪk]
weapon, gun	**зброя** (f)	['zbrɔja]
to disarm (vt)	**обеззброїти**	[obɛzzbr'ɔjitɪ]
to order (command)	**наказувати**	[na'kazuwatɪ]
to disappear (vi)	**зникнути**	['znɪknutɪ]
law	**закон** (m)	[za'kɔn]
legal, lawful (adj)	**законний**	[za'kɔɲɪj]
illegal, illicit (adj)	**незаконний**	[nɛza'kɔɲɪj]
responsibility (blame)	**відповідальність** (f)	[widpowi'daʎnistʲ]
responsible (adj)	**відповідальний**	[widpowi'daʎnɪj]

NATURE

The Earth. Part 1

195. Outer space

cosmos	космос (m)	['kɔsmos]
space (as adj)	космічний	[kos'mitʃnɪj]
outer space	космічний простір (m)	[kos'mitʃnɪj 'prostir]
universe	всесвіт (m)	['wsɛswit]
galaxy	галактика (f)	[ɣɑ'lɑktɪkɑ]
star	зірка (f)	['zirkɑ]
constellation	сузір'я (n)	[su'zirʰjɑ]
planet	планета (f)	[plɑ'nɛtɑ]
satellite	супутник (m)	[su'putnɪk]
meteorite	метеорит (m)	[mɛtɛo'rɪt]
comet	комета (f)	[ko'mɛtɑ]
asteroid	астероїд (m)	[astɛ'rɔjɪd]
orbit	орбіта (f)	[or'bitɑ]
to revolve (~ around the Earth)	обертатися	[obɛr'tɑtɪsʲɑ]
atmosphere	атмосфера (f)	[atmos'fɛrɑ]
the Sun	Сонце (n)	['sɔntsɛ]
solar system	Сонячна система (f)	['sɔnɑtʃnɑ sɪs'tɛmɑ]
solar eclipse	сонячне затемнення (n)	['sɔnɑtʃnɛ zɑ'tɛmnɛnjɑ]
the Earth	Земля (f)	[zɛm'ʎɑ]
the Moon	Місяць (f)	['misʲɑts]
Mars	Марс (m)	[mɑrs]
Venus	Венера (f)	[wɛ'nɛrɑ]
Jupiter	Юпітер (m)	[ju'pitɛr]
Saturn	Сатурн (m)	[sɑ'turn]
Mercury	Меркурій (m)	[mɛr'kurij]
Uranus	Уран (m)	[u'rɑn]
Neptune	Нептун (m)	[nɛp'tun]
Pluto	Плутон (m)	[plu'tɔn]
Milky Way	Чумацький Шлях (m)	[tʃu'mɑtskɪj ʃʎɑh]
Great Bear	Велика Ведмедиця (f)	[wɛ'likɑ wɛd'mɛdɪtsʲɑ]

North Star	**Полярна Зірка** (f)	[poˈʎarna ˈzirka]
Martian	**марсіанин** (m)	[marsiˈanɪn]
extraterrestrial (n)	**інопланетянин** (m)	[inoplanɛˈtʲanɪn]
alien	**прибулець** (m)	[prɪˈbulɛts]
flying saucer	**літальна тарілка** (f)	[liˈtaʎna taˈrilka]
spaceship	**космічний корабель** (m)	[kosˈmitʃnɪj koraˈbɛʎ]
space station	**орбітальна станція** (f)	[orbiˈtaʎna ˈstantsija]
blast-off	**старт** (m)	[start]
engine	**двигун** (m)	[dwɪˈɣun]
nozzle	**сопло** (n)	[ˈsɔplo]
fuel	**паливо** (n)	[ˈpalɪwo]
cockpit, flight deck	**кабіна** (f)	[kaˈbina]
antenna	**антена** (f)	[anˈtɛna]
porthole	**ілюмінатор** (m)	[ilymiˈnator]
solar battery	**сонячна батарея** (f)	[ˈsɔnʲatʃna bataˈrɛja]
spacesuit	**скафандр** (m)	[skaˈfandr]
weightlessness	**невагомість** (f)	[nɛwaˈɣɔmistʲ]
oxygen	**кисень** (m)	[ˈkɪsɛɲ]
docking (in space)	**стикування** (n)	[stɪkuˈwanʲa]
to dock (vi, vt)	**здійснювати**	[ˈzdijsnywatɪ
	стикування	stɪkuwanʲa]
observatory	**обсерваторія** (f)	[obsɛrwaˈtorija]
telescope	**телескоп** (m)	[tɛlɛsˈkɔp]
to observe (vt)	**спостерігати**	[spostɛriˈɣatɪ]
to explore (vt)	**досліджувати**	[dosˈlidʒuwatɪ]

196. The Earth

the Earth	**Земля** (f)	[zɛmˈʎa]
globe (the Earth)	**земна куля** (f)	[zɛmˈna ˈkuʎa]
planet	**планета** (f)	[plaˈnɛta]
atmosphere	**атмосфера** (f)	[atmosˈfɛra]
geography	**географія** (f)	[ɣɛoɣˈrafija]
nature	**природа** (f)	[prɪˈrɔda]
globe (table ~)	**глобус** (m)	[ˈɣlɔbus]
map	**карта** (f)	[ˈkarta]
atlas	**атлас** (m)	[ˈatlas]
Europe	**Європа** (f)	[ɛwˈrɔpa]
Asia	**Азія** (f)	[ˈazija]
Africa	**Африка** (f)	[ˈafrɪka]
Australia	**Австралія** (f)	[awstˈralija]

America	**Америка** (f)	[a'mɛrɪka]
North America	**Північна Америка** (f)	[piw'nitʃna a'mɛrɪka]
South America	**Південна Америка** (f)	[piw'dɛna a'mɛrɪka]

| Antarctica | **Антарктида** (f) | [antark'tɪda] |
| the Arctic | **Арктика** (f) | ['arktɪka] |

197. Cardinal directions

north	**північ** (f)	['piwnitʃ]
to the north	**на північ**	[na 'piwnitʃ]
in the north	**на півночі**	[na 'piwnotʃi]
northern (adj)	**північний**	[piw'nitʃnɪj]

south	**південь** (m)	['piwdɛɲ]
to the south	**на південь**	[na 'piwdɛɲ]
in the south	**на півдні**	[na 'piwdni]
southern (adj)	**південний**	[piw'dɛnɪj]

west	**захід** (m)	['zahid]
to the west	**на захід**	[na 'zahid]
in the west	**на заході**	[na 'zahodi]
western (adj)	**західний**	['zahidnɪj]

east	**схід** (m)	[shid]
to the east	**на схід**	[na 'shid]
in the east	**на сході**	[na 'shɔdi]
eastern (adj)	**східний**	['shidnɪj]

198. Sea. Ocean

sea	**море** (n)	['mɔrɛ]
ocean	**океан** (m)	[okɛ'an]
gulf (bay)	**затока** (f)	[za'tɔka]
straits	**протока** (f)	[pro'tɔka]

continent (mainland)	**материк** (m)	[matɛ'rɪk]
island	**острів** (m)	['ɔstriw]
peninsula	**півострів** (m)	[pi'wɔstriw]
archipelago	**архіпелаг** (m)	[arhipɛ'laɣ]

bay, cove	**бухта** (f)	['buhta]
harbor	**гавань** (f)	['ɣawaɲ]
lagoon	**лагуна** (f)	[la'ɣuna]
cape	**мис** (m)	[mɪs]

| atoll | **атол** (m) | [a'tɔl] |
| reef | **риф** (m) | [rɪf] |

coral	корал (m)	[ko'ral]
coral reef	кораловий риф (m)	[ko'ralowıj rıf]
deep (adj)	глибокий	[ɣlı'bɔkıj]
depth (deep water)	глибина (f)	[ɣlıbı'nɑ]
abyss	безодня (f)	['bɛzdnɑ]
trench (e.g., Mariana ~)	западина (f)	[zɑ'padınɑ]
current, stream	течія (f)	['tɛtʃijɑ]
to surround (bathe)	омивати	[omı'watı]
shore	берег (m)	['bɛrɛɣ]
coast	узбережжя (n)	[uzbɛ'rɛzʲɑ]
high tide	приплив (m)	[prıp'lıw]
low tide	відплив (m)	[widp'lıw]
sandbank	обмілина (f)	[ob'milınɑ]
bottom	дно (n)	[dno]
wave	хвиля (f)	['hwıʎɑ]
crest (~ of a wave)	гребінь (m) хвилі	['ɣrɛbiɲ 'hwıli]
froth (foam)	піна (f)	[pi'nɑ]
storm	буря (f)	['burʲɑ]
hurricane	ураган (m)	[urɑɣɑn]
tsunami	цунамі (n)	[tsu'nami]
calm (dead ~)	штиль (m)	[ʃtıʎ]
quiet, calm (adj)	спокійний	[spo'kijnıj]
pole	полюс (m)	['pɔlys]
polar (adj)	полярний	[po'ʎarnıj]
latitude	широта (f)	[ʃıro'tɑ]
longitude	довгота (f)	[dowɣo'tɑ]
parallel	паралель (f)	[parɑ'lɛʎ]
equator	екватор (m)	[ɛk'wator]
sky	небо (n)	['nɛbo]
horizon	горизонт (m)	[ɣorı'zɔnt]
air	повітря (n)	[po'witrʲɑ]
lighthouse	маяк (m)	[mɑ'jak]
to dive (vi)	пірнати	[pir'natı]
to sink (ab. boat)	затонути	[zato'nutı]
treasures	скарби (pl)	[skar'bı]

199. Seas' and Oceans' names

Atlantic Ocean	Атлантичний океан (m)	[atlan'tıtʃnıj okɛ'an]
Indian Ocean	Індійський океан (m)	[in'dijsʲkıj okɛ'an]

Pacific Ocean	**Тихий океан** (m)	['tıhıj okɛ'an]
Arctic Ocean	**Північний**	[piw'nitʃnıj
	Льодовитий океан (m)	ɪ̃do'wıtıj okɛ'an]
Black Sea	**Чорне море** (n)	['tʃɔrnɛ 'mɔrɛ]
Red Sea	**Червоне море** (n)	[tʃɛr'wɔnɛ 'mɔrɛ]
Yellow Sea	**Жовте море** (n)	['ʒɔwtɛ 'mɔrɛ]
White Sea	**Біле море** (n)	['bilɛ 'mɔrɛ]
Caspian Sea	**Каспійське море** (n)	[kas'pijsʲkɛ 'mɔrɛ]
Dead Sea	**Мертве море** (n)	['mɛrtwɛ 'mɔrɛ]
Mediterranean Sea	**Середземне море** (n)	[sɛrɛ'dzɛmnɛ 'mɔrɛ]
Aegean Sea	**Егейське море** (n)	[ɛ'ɣɛjsʲkɛ 'mɔrɛ]
Adriatic Sea	**Адріатичне море** (n)	[adria'tıtʃnɛ 'mɔrɛ]
Arabian Sea	**Аравійське море** (n)	[ara'wijsʲkɛ 'mɔrɛ]
Sea of Japan	**Японське море** (n)	[ja'pɔnsʲkɛ 'mɔrɛ]
Bering Sea	**Берингове море** (n)	['bɛrıŋɔwɛ 'mɔrɛ]
South China Sea	**Південно-Китайське море** (n)	[piw'dɛŋɔ kı'tajsʲkɛ 'mɔrɛ]
Coral Sea	**Коралове море** (n)	[ko'ralowɛ 'mɔrɛ]
Tasman Sea	**Тасманове море** (n)	[tas'manowɛ 'mɔrɛ]
Caribbean Sea	**Карибське море** (n)	[ka'rıbsʲkɛ 'mɔrɛ]
Barents Sea	**Баренцове море** (n)	['barɛntsowɛ 'mɔrɛ]
Kara Sea	**Карське море** (n)	['karsʲkɛ 'mɔrɛ]
North Sea	**Північне море** (n)	[piw'nitʃnɛ 'mɔrɛ]
Baltic Sea	**Балтійське море** (n)	[bal'tijsʲkɛ 'mɔrɛ]
Norwegian Sea	**Норвезьке море** (n)	[nor'wɛzʲkɛ 'mɔrɛ]

200. Mountains

mountain	**гора** (f)	[ɣo'ra]
mountain range	**гірське пасмо** (n)	[ɣirsʲ'kɛ 'pasmo]
mountain ridge	**гірський хребет** (m)	[ɣirsʲ'kıj hrɛ'bɛt]
summit, top	**вершина** (f)	[wɛr'ʃına]
peak	**шпиль** (m)	[ʃpıʎ]
foot (of mountain)	**підніжжя** (n)	[pid'nizʲa]
slope (mountainside)	**схил** (m)	[shıl]
volcano	**вулкан** (m)	[wul'kan]
active volcano	**діючий вулкан** (m)	['dijutʃıj wul'kan]
dormant volcano	**згаслий вулкан** (m)	['zɣaslıj wul'kan]
eruption	**виверження** (n)	['wıwɛrʒɛŋja]
crater	**кратер** (m)	['kratɛr]

magma	**магма** (f)	['maɣma]
lava	**лава** (f)	['lawa]
molten (~ lava)	**розжарений**	[roz'ʒarɛnɪj]
canyon	**каньйон** (m)	[kaɲ'jɔn]
gorge	**ущелина** (f)	[u'ɕɛlɪna]
crevice	**ущелина** (n)	[u'ɕɛlɪna]
pass, col	**перевал** (m)	[pɛrɛ'wal]
plateau	**плато** (n)	['plato]
cliff	**скеля** (f)	['skɛʎa]
hill	**горб** (m)	[ɣorb]
glacier	**льодовик** (m)	[lзdo'wɪk]
waterfall	**водоспад** (m)	[wodos'pad]
geyser	**гейзер** (m)	['ɣɛjzɛr]
lake	**озеро** (n)	['ɔzɛro]
plain	**рівнина** (f)	[riw'nɪna]
landscape	**краєвид** (m)	[kraɛ'wɪd]
echo	**луна** (f)	[lu'na]
alpinist	**альпініст** (m)	[aʎpi'nist]
rock climber	**скелелаз** (m)	[skɛlɛ'laz]
to conquer (in climbing)	**підкоряти**	[pidko'ri̯atɪ]
climb (an easy ~)	**піднімання** (n)	[pidni'manja]

201. Mountains names

Alps	**Альпи** (pl)	['aʎpɪ]
Mont Blanc	**Монблан** (m)	[monb'lan]
Pyrenees	**Піренеї** (pl)	[pirɛ'nɛjɪ]
Carpathians	**Карпати** (pl)	[kar'patɪ]
Ural Mountains	**Уральські гори** (pl)	[u'raʎsʲki 'ɣorɪ]
Caucasus	**Кавказ** (m)	[kaw'kaz]
Elbrus	**Ельбрус** (m)	[ɛʎb'rus]
Altai	**Алтай** (m)	[al'taj]
Tien Shan	**Тянь-Шань** (pl)	[tʲaɲ 'ʃaɲ]
Pamir Mountains	**Памір** (m)	[pa'mir]
Himalayas	**Гімалаї** (pl)	[ɣima'lajɪ]
Everest	**Еверест** (m)	[ɛwɛ'rɛst]
Andes	**Анди** (pl)	['andɪ]
Kilimanjaro	**Кіліманджаро** (f)	[kiliman'dʒaro]

202. Rivers

river	**ріка** (f)	[ˈrikɑ]
spring (natural source)	**джерело** (n)	[dʒɛrɛˈlɔ]
riverbed	**річище** (n)	[ˈritʃɪɕɛ]
basin	**басейн** (m)	[bɑˈsɛjn]
to flow into …	**упадати**	[upɑˈdɑtɪ]
tributary	**притока** (f)	[prɪˈtɔkɑ]
bank (of river)	**берег** (m)	[ˈbɛrɛɣ]
current, stream	**течія** (f)	[ˈtɛtʃɪjɑ]
downstream (adv)	**вниз за течією** (f)	[wnɪz zɑ ˈtɛtʃɪɛju]
upstream (adv)	**уверх по течії**	[uˈwɛrh po ˈtɛtʃɪjɪ]
inundation	**повінь** (f)	[ˈpɔwɪɲ]
flooding	**повінь** (f)	[ˈpɔwɪɲ]
to overflow (vi)	**розливатися**	[rozlɪˈwɑtɪsʲɑ]
to flood (vt)	**затоплювати**	[zɑˈtɔplywɑtɪ]
shallows (shoal)	**мілина** (f)	[milɪˈnɑ]
rapids	**поріг** (m)	[poˈriɣ]
dam	**гребля** (f)	[ˈɣrɛbʎɑ]
canal	**канал** (m)	[kɑˈnɑl]
artificial lake	**водосховище** (n)	[wodosˈhɔwɪɕɛ]
sluice, lock	**шлюз** (m)	[ʃlyz]
water body (pond, etc.)	**водоймище** (n)	[woˈdɔjmɪɕɛ]
swamp, bog	**болото** (n)	[boˈlɔto]
marsh	**трясовина** (f)	[trʲɑsowɪˈnɑ]
whirlpool	**вир** (m)	[wɪr]
stream (brook)	**струмок** (m)	[struˈmɔk]
drinking (ab. water)	**питний**	[ˈpɪtnɪj]
fresh (~ water)	**прісний**	[ˈprisnɪj]
ice	**крига** (f)	[ˈkrɪɣɑ]
to freeze (ab. river, etc.)	**замерзнути**	[zɑˈmɛrznutɪ]

203. Rivers' names

Seine	**Сена** (f)	[ˈsɛnɑ]
Loire	**Луара** (f)	[luˈɑrɑ]
Thames	**Темза** (f)	[ˈtɛmzɑ]
Rhine	**Рейн** (m)	[rɛjn]
Danube	**Дунай** (m)	[duˈnɑj]
Volga	**Волга** (f)	[ˈwɔlɣɑ]

| Don | **Дон** (m) | [don] |
| Lena | **Лена** (f) | ['lɛna] |

Yellow River	**Хуанхе** (f)	[huɑn'hɛ]
Yangtze	**Янцзи** (f)	[jɑnʦ'zɪ]
Mekong	**Меконг** (m)	[mɛ'kɔŋ]
Ganges	**Ганг** (m)	[ɣɑŋ]

Nile River	**Ніл** (m)	[nil]
Congo	**Конго** (f)	['kɔŋo]
Okavango	**Окаванго** (f)	[oka'waŋo]
Zambezi	**Замбезі** (f)	[zam'bɛzi]
Limpopo	**Лімпопо** (f)	[limpo'pɔ]
Mississippi River	**Міссісіпі** (f)	[misi'sipi]

204. Forest

| forest | **ліс** (m) | [lis] |
| forest (as adj) | **лісовий** | [liso'wɪj] |

thick forest	**хаща** (f)	['haɕɑ]
grove	**гай** (m)	[ɣaj]
forest clearing	**галявина** (f)	[ɣa'ʎawɪna]

| thicket | **хащі** (pl) | ['haɕi] |
| scrubland | **чагарник** (m) | [ʧa'ɣarnɪk] |

| footpath (troddenpath) | **стежина** (f) | [stɛ'ʒɪna] |
| gully | **яр** (m) | [jar] |

tree	**дерево** (n)	['dɛrɛwo]
leaf	**листок** (m)	[lɪs'tɔk]
leaves	**листя** (n)	['lɪstʲa]

fall of leaves	**листопад** (m)	[lɪsto'pad]
to fall (ab. leaves)	**опадати**	[opa'datɪ]
top (of the tree)	**верхівка** (f)	[wɛr'hiwka]

branch	**гілка** (f)	['ɣilka]
bough	**сук** (m)	[suk]
bud (on shrub, tree)	**брунька** (f)	['bruɲka]
needle (of pine tree)	**голка** (f)	['ɣɔlka]
pine cone	**шишка** (f)	['ʃɪʃka]

hollow (in a tree)	**дупло** (n)	[dup'lɔ]
nest	**гніздо** (n)	[ɣniz'dɔ]
burrow (animal hole)	**нора** (f)	[no'ra]

| trunk | **стовбур** (m) | ['stɔwbur] |
| root | **корінь** (m) | ['kɔriɲ] |

| bark | кора (f) | [ko'ra] |
| moss | мох (m) | [moh] |

to uproot (vt)	корчувати	[kortʃu'watɪ]
to chop down	рубати	[ru'batɪ]
to deforest (vt)	вирубувати	[wɪ'rubuwatɪ]
tree stump	пень (m)	[pɛɲ]

campfire	багаття (n)	[ba'ɣattʲa]
forest fire	пожежа (f)	[po'ʒɛʒa]
to extinguish (vt)	тушити	[tu'ʃitɪ]

forest ranger	лісник (m)	[lis'nɪk]
protection	охорона (f)	[oho'rɔna]
to protect (~ nature)	охороняти	[ohoro'ɲatɪ]
poacher	браконьєр (m)	[brako'ɲjɛr]
trap (e.g., bear ~)	пастка (f)	['pɑstka]

| to gather, to pick (vt) | збирати | [zbɪ'ratɪ] |
| to lose one's way | заблукати | [zablu'katɪ] |

205. Natural resources

natural resources	природні ресурси (pl)	[prɪ'rɔdni rɛ'sursɪ]
minerals	корисні копалини (pl)	['kɔrɪsni ko'palɪnɪ]
deposits	поклади (pl)	['pɔkladɪ]
field (e.g., oilfield)	родовище (n)	[ro'dɔwɪɕɛ]

to mine (extract)	добувати	[dobu'watɪ]
mining (extraction)	добування (n)	[dobu'waɲja]
ore	руда (f)	[ru'da]
mine (e.g., for coal)	копальня (f)	[ko'paʎɲa]
mine shaft, pit	шахта (f)	['ʃahta]
miner	шахтар (m)	[ʃah'tar]

| gas | газ (m) | [ɣaz] |
| gas pipeline | газопровід (m) | [ɣazopro'wid] |

oil (petroleum)	нафта (f)	['nafta]
oil pipeline	нафтопровід (m)	[naftop'rɔwid]
oil well	нафтова вишка (f)	['naftowa 'wɪʃka]
derrick	свердлова вежа (f)	[swɛrd'lɔwa 'wɛʒa]
tanker	танкер (m)	['taŋkɛr]

sand	пісок (m)	[pi'sɔk]
limestone	вапняк (m)	[wap'ɲak]
gravel	гравій (m)	['ɣrawij]
peat	торф (m)	[torf]
clay	глина (f)	['ɣlɪna]
coal	вугілля (n)	[wu'ɣiʎa]

iron	**залізо** (n)	[zɑ'lizo]
gold	**золото** (n)	['zɔloto]
silver	**срібло** (n)	['sriblo]
nickel	**нікель** (m)	['nikɛʎ]
copper	**мідь** (f)	[midʲ]
zinc	**цинк** (m)	[tsɪŋk]
manganese	**марганець** (m)	['mɑrɣɑnɛts]
mercury	**ртуть** (f)	[rtutʲ]
lead	**свинець** (m)	[swɪ'nɛts]
mineral	**мінерал** (m)	[minɛ'rɑl]
crystal	**кристал** (m)	[krɪs'tɑl]
marble	**мармур** (m)	['mɑrmur]
uranium	**уран** (m)	[u'rɑn]

The Earth. Part 2

206. Weather

weather	погода (f)	[poˈɣɔdɑ]
weather forecast	прогноз (m) погоди (f)	[proˈɣnɔz poˈɣɔdɪ]
temperature	температура (f)	[tɛmpɛrɑˈturɑ]
thermometer	термометр (m)	[tɛrˈmɔmɛtr]
barometer	барометр (m)	[bɑˈrɔmɛtr]

humidity	вологість (f)	[wɔlɔɣistʲ]
heat (extreme ~)	спека (f)	[ˈspɛkɑ]
hot (torrid)	гарячий	[ɣɑˈrʲɑtʃɪj]
it's hot	спекотно	[spɛˈkɔtnɔ]

| it's warm | тепло | [ˈtɛplɔ] |
| warm (moderately hot) | теплий | [ˈtɛplɪj] |

it's cold	холодно	[ˈhɔlɔdnɔ]
cold (adj)	холодний	[hɔˈlɔdnɪj]
sun	сонце (n)	[ˈsɔntsɛ]
to shine (vi)	світити	[swiˈtɪtɪ]
sunny (day)	сонячний	[ˈsɔnʲɑtʃnɪj]
to come up (vi)	зійти	[zijˈtɪ]
to set (vi)	сісти	[ˈsistɪ]

cloud	хмара (f)	[ˈhmɑrɑ]
cloudy (adj)	хмарний	[ˈhmɑrnɪj]
rain cloud	хмара (f)	[ˈhmɑrɑ]
somber (gloomy)	похмурний	[pohˈmurnɪj]

rain	дощ (m)	[dɔɕ]
it's raining	йде дощ	[jdɛ dɔɕ]
rainy (day)	дощовий	[dɔɕɔˈwɪj]
to drizzle (vi)	накрапати	[nɑkrɑˈpɑtɪ]

pouring rain	проливний дощ (m)	[prolɪwˈnɪj dɔɕ]
downpour	злива (f)	[ˈzlɪwɑ]
heavy (e.g., ~ rain)	сильний	[ˈsɪʎnɪj]
puddle	калюжа (f)	[kɑˈlʲuʒɑ]
to get wet (in rain)	мокнути	[ˈmɔknutɪ]

fog (mist)	туман (m)	[tuˈmɑn]
foggy	туманний	[tuˈmɑŋɪj]
snow	сніг (m)	[sniɣ]
it's snowing	йде сніг (m)	[jdɛ sniɣ]

207. Severe weather. Natural disasters

thunderstorm	гроза (f)	[ɣro'za]
lightning (~ strike)	блискавка (f)	['blıskawka]
to flash (vi)	блискати	['blıskatı]
thunder	грім (m)	[ɣrim]
to thunder (vi)	гриміти	[ɣrı'mitı]
it's thundering	гримить грім	[ɣrı'mıtʲ ɣrim]
hail	град (m)	[ɣrad]
it's hailing	йде град	[jdɛ ɣrad]
to flood (vt)	затопити	[zato'pıtı]
flood, inundation	повінь (f)	['powiɲ]
earthquake	землетрус (m)	[zɛmlɛt'rus]
tremor, quake	поштовх (m)	['poʃtowh]
epicenter	епіцентр (m)	[ɛpi'tsɛntr]
eruption	виверження (n)	['wıwɛrʒɛɲja]
lava	лава (f)	['lawa]
twister	смерч (m)	[smɛrtʃ]
tornado	торнадо (m)	[tor'nado]
typhoon	тайфун (m)	[taj'fun]
hurricane	ураган (m)	[ura'ɣan]
storm	буря (f)	['burʲa]
tsunami	цунамі (n)	[tsu'nami]
cyclone	циклон (m)	[tsık'lɔn]
bad weather	негода (f)	[nɛ'ɣɔda]
fire (accident)	пожежа (f)	[po'ʒɛʒa]
disaster	катастрофа (f)	[katast'rofa]
meteorite	метеорит (m)	[mɛtɛo'rıt]
avalanche	лавина (f)	[la'wına]
snowslide	обвал (m)	[ob'wal]
blizzard	заметіль (f)	[zamɛ'tiʎ]
snowstorm	завірюха (f)	[zawi'ryha]

208. Noises. Sounds

silence (quiet)	тиша (f)	['tıʃa]
sound	звук (m)	[zwuk]
noise	шум (m)	[ʃum]
to make noise	шуміти	[ʃu'mitı]
noisy (adj)	гучний	[ɣutʃ'nıj]

loudly (to speak, etc.)	голосно	[ˈɣɔlosno]
loud (voice, etc.)	гучний	[ɣutʃˈnɪj]
constant (continuous)	постійний	[posˈtijnɪj]
shout (n)	крик (m)	[krɪk]
to shout (vi)	кричати	[krɪˈtʃatɪ]
whisper	шепіт (m)	[ˈʃɛpit]
to whisper (vi, vt)	шепотіти	[ʃɛpoˈtitɪ]
barking (of dog)	гавкіт (m)	[ˈɣawkit]
to bark (vi)	гавкати	[ˈɣawkatɪ]
groan (of pain)	стогін (m)	[ˈstoɣin]
to groan (vi)	стогнати	[stoɣˈnatɪ]
cough	кашель (m)	[ˈkaʃɛʎ]
to cough (vi)	кашляти	[ˈkaʃʎatɪ]
whistle	свист (m)	[swɪst]
to whistle (vi)	свистіти	[swɪsˈtitɪ]
knock (at the door)	стукіт (m)	[ˈstukit]
to knock (at the door)	стукати	[ˈstukatɪ]
to crack (vi)	тріщати	[triˈɕatɪ]
crack (plank, etc.)	тріск (m)	[trisk]
siren	сирена (f)	[sɪˈrɛna]
whistle (factory ~)	гудок (m)	[ɣuˈdok]
to whistle (ship, train)	гудіти	[ɣuˈditɪ]
honk (signal)	сигнал (m)	[sɪɣˈnal]
to honk (vi)	сигналити	[sɪɣˈnalɪtɪ]

209. Winter

winter (n)	зима (f)	[zɪˈma]
winter (as adj)	зимовий	[zɪˈmɔwɪj]
in winter	взимку	[ˈwzɪmku]
snow	сніг (m)	[sniɣ]
it's snowing	йде сніг (m)	[jdɛ sniɣ]
snowfall	снігопад (m)	[sniɣoˈpad]
snowdrift	замет (m)	[zaˈmɛt]
snowflake	сніжинка (f)	[sniˈʒɪŋka]
snowball	сніжка (f)	[ˈsniʒka]
snowman	сніговик (m)	[sniɣoˈwɪk]
icicle	бурулька (f)	[buˈruʎka]
December	грудень (m)	[ˈɣrudɛɲ]
January	січень (m)	[ˈsitʃɛɲ]
February	лютий (m)	[ˈlytɪj]

severe frost	**мороз** (m)	[mo'rɔz]
frosty (weather, air)	**морозний**	[mo'rɔznıj]
below zero (adv)	**нижче нуля**	['nıʒʧɛ nu'ʎa]
first frost	**заморозки** (pl)	['zamorozkı]
hoarfrost	**паморозь** (f)	['pamorozʲ]
cold (cold weather)	**холод** (m)	['hɔlod]
it's cold	**холодно**	['hɔlodno]
fur coat	**шуба** (f)	['ʃuba]
mittens	**рукавиці** (pl)	[ruka'wıʦi]
to get sick	**захворіти**	[zahwo'ritı]
cold (illness)	**застуда** (f)	[zas'tuda]
to catch a cold	**застудитися**	[zastu'dıtısʲa]
ice	**крига** (f)	['krıɣa]
black ice	**ожеледиця** (f)	[oʒɛ'lɛdıtsʲa]
to freeze (ab. river, etc.)	**замерзнути**	[za'mɛrznutı]
ice floe	**крижина** (f)	[krı'ʒına]
skis	**лижі** (pl)	['lıʒi]
skier	**лижник** (m)	['lıʒnık]
to ski (vi)	**кататися на лижах**	[ka'tatısʲa na 'lıʒah]
to skate (vi)	**кататися на ковзанах**	[ka'tatısʲa na kowza'nah]

Fauna

210. Mammals. Predators

predator	хижак (m)	[hɪ'ʒak]
tiger	тигр (m)	[tɪɣr]
lion	лев (m)	[lɛw]
wolf	вовк (m)	[wowk]
fox	лисиця (f)	[lɪ'sɪt͡sʲa]
jaguar	ягуар (m)	[jaɣu'ɑr]
leopard	леопард (m)	[lɛo'pard]
cheetah	гепард (m)	[ɣɛ'pard]
black panther	пантера (f)	[pan'tɛra]
puma	пума (f)	['puma]
snow leopard	сніговий барс (m)	[sniɣo'wɪj bɑrs]
lynx	рись (f)	[rɪsʲ]
coyote	койот (m)	[kɔjɔt]
jackal	шакал (m)	[ʃa'kal]
hyena	гієна (f)	[ɣi'ɛna]

211. Wild animals

animal	тварина (f)	[twa'rɪna]
beast (animal)	звір (m)	[zwir]
squirrel	білка (f)	['bilka]
hedgehog	їжак (m)	[jɪ'ʒak]
hare	заєць (m)	['zaɛt͡s]
rabbit	кріль (m)	[kriʎ]
badger	борсук (m)	[bor'suk]
raccoon	єнот (m)	[ɛ'nɔt]
hamster	хом'як (m)	[homʰ'jak]
marmot	бабак (m)	[ba'bak]
mole	кріт (m)	[krit]
mouse	миша (f)	['mɪʃa]
rat	щур (m)	[ɕur]
bat	кажан (m)	[ka'ʒan]
ermine	горностай (m)	[ɣornos'taj]
sable	соболь (m)	['sɔboʎ]

marten	куниця (f)	[ku'nɪtsʲa]
weasel	ласка (f)	['laska]
mink	норка (f)	['nɔrka]

| beaver | бобер (m) | [bo'bɛr] |
| otter | видра (f) | ['wɪdra] |

horse	кінь (m)	[kiɲ]
moose	лось (m)	[losʲ]
deer	олень (m)	['ɔlɛɲ]
camel	верблюд (m)	[wɛrb'lyd]

bison	бізон (m)	[bi'zɔn]
aurochs	зубр (m)	[zubr]
buffalo	буйвіл (m)	['bujwil]

zebra	зебра (f)	['zɛbra]
antelope	антилопа (f)	[antɪ'lɔpa]
roe deer	косуля (f)	[ko'suʎa]
fallow deer	лань (f)	[laɲ]
chamois	сарна (f)	['sarna]
wild boar	вепр (m)	[wɛpr]

whale	кит (m)	[kɪt]
seal	тюлень (m)	[ty'lɛɲ]
walrus	морж (m)	[mɔrʒ]
fur seal	котик (m)	['kɔtɪk]
dolphin	дельфін (m)	[dɛʎ'fin]

bear	ведмідь (m)	[wɛd'midʲ]
polar bear	білий ведмідь (m)	['bilɪj wɛd'midʲ]
panda	панда (f)	['panda]

monkey	мавпа (f)	['mawpa]
chimpanzee	шимпанзе (m)	[ʃɪmpan'zɛ]
orangutan	орангутанг (m)	[oraŋu'taŋ]
gorilla	горила (f)	[ɣo'rɪla]
macaque	макака (f)	[ma'kaka]
gibbon	гібон (m)	[ɣi'bɔn]

elephant	слон (m)	[slon]
rhinoceros	носоріг (m)	[noso'riɣ]
giraffe	жирафа (f)	[ʒɪrafa]
hippopotamus	бегемот (m)	[bɛɣɛ'mɔt]

| kangaroo | кенгуру (m) | [kɛŋu'ru] |
| koala (bear) | коала (m) | [ko'ala] |

mongoose	мангуст (m)	[ma'ŋust]
chinchilla	шиншила (f)	[ʃɪn'ʃila]
skunk	скунс (m)	[skuns]
porcupine	дикобраз (m)	[dɪkob'raz]

212. Domestic animals

cat	кішка (f)	['kiʃka]
tomcat	кіт (m)	[kit]
horse	коняка (f)	[ko'ɲaka]
stallion	жеребець (m)	[ʒɛrɛ'bɛts]
mare	кобила (f)	[ko'bɪla]
cow	корова (f)	[ko'rɔwa]
bull	бик (m)	[bɪk]
ox	віл (m)	[wil]
sheep	вівця (f)	[wiw'tsʲa]
ram	баран (m)	[ba'ran]
goat	коза (f)	[ko'za]
billy goat, he-goat	козел (m)	[ko'zɛl]
donkey	осел (m)	[o'sɛl]
mule	мул (m)	[mul]
pig	свиня (f)	[swɪ'ɲa]
piglet	порося (n)	[poro'sʲa]
rabbit	кріль (m)	[kriʎ]
hen (chicken)	курка (f)	['kurka]
rooster	півень (m)	['piwɛɲ]
duck	качка (f)	['katʃka]
drake	качур (m)	['katʃur]
goose	гусак (m)	[ɣu'sak]
tom turkey	індик (m)	[in'dɪk]
turkey (hen)	індичка (f)	[in'dɪtʃka]
domestic animals	домашні тварини (pl)	[do'maʃni twa'rɪnɪ]
tame (e.g., ~ hamster)	ручний	[rutʃ'nɪj]
to tame (vt)	приручати	[prɪru'tʃatɪ]
to breed (vt)	вирощувати	[wɪ'rɔɕuwatɪ]
farm	ферма (f)	['fɛrma]
poultry	свійські птахи (pl)	['swijsʲki pta'hi]
cattle	худоба (f)	[hu'dɔba]
herd (cattle)	стадо (n)	['stado]
stable	конюшня (f)	[ko'nyʃna]
pigsty	свинарник (m)	[swɪ'narnɪk]
cowshed	корівник (m)	[ko'riwnɪk]
rabbit hutch	крільчатник (m)	[kriʎ'tʃatnɪk]
hen house	курник (m)	[kur'nɪk]

213. Dogs. Dog breeds

dog	собака (m)	[so'baka]
sheepdog	вівчарка (f)	[wiw'tʃarka]
poodle	пудель (m)	['pudɛʎ]
dachshund	такса (f)	['taksa]
bulldog	бульдог (m)	[buʎ'dɔɣ]
boxer	боксер (m)	[bok'sɛr]
mastiff	мастиф (m)	[mas'tɪf]
rottweiler	ротвейлер (m)	[rot'wɛjlɛr]
Doberman	доберман (m)	[dobɛr'man]
basset	басет (m)	[ba'sɛt]
bobtail	бобтейл (m)	[bob'tɛjl]
Dalmatian	далматинець (m)	[dalma'tɪnɛts]
cocker spaniel	кокер-спанієль (m)	['kɔkɛr spani'ɛʎ]
Newfoundland	ньюфаундленд (m)	[njyfaund'lɛnd]
Saint Bernard	сенбернар (m)	[sɛnbɛr'nar]
husky	хаскі (m)	[haski]
Chow Chow	чау-чау (m)	[tʃau tʃau]
spitz	шпіц (m)	[ʃpits]
pug	мопс (m)	[mops]

214. Sounds made by animals

barking (n)	гавкіт (m)	['ɣawkit]
to bark (vi)	гавкати	['ɣawkatɪ]
to meow (vi)	нявкати	['ɲawkatɪ]
to purr (vi)	муркотіти	[murko'titɪ]
to moo (vi)	мукати	['mukatɪ]
to bellow (bull)	ревіти	[rɛ'witɪ]
to growl (vi)	ричати	[rɪ'tʃatɪ]
howl (n)	виття (n)	[wɪt'tʲa]
to howl (vi)	вити	['wɪtɪ]
to whine (vi)	скиглити	['skɪɣlɪtɪ]
to bleat (sheep)	бекати	['bɛkatɪ]
to oink, to grunt (pig)	рохкати	['rɔhkatɪ]
to squeal (vi)	вищати	[wɪ'ɕatɪ]
to croak (vi)	кумкати	['kumkatɪ]
to buzz (insect)	дзижчати	[dʑɪʒ'tʃatɪ]
to stridulate (vi)	стрекотати	[strɛko'tatɪ]

215. Young animals

cub	дитинча (n)	[dɪtɪn'tʃa]
kitten	кошеня (n)	[koʃɛ'ɲa]
baby mouse	мишеня (n)	[mɪʃɛ'ɲa]
pup, puppy	цуценя (n)	[tsutsɛ'ɲa]
leveret	зайченя (n)	[zajtʃɛ'ɲa]
baby rabbit	кроленя (n)	[krolɛ'ɲa]
wolf cub	вовченя (n)	[wowtʃɛ'ɲa]
fox cub	лисеня (n)	[lɪsɛ'ɲa]
bear cub	ведмежа (n)	[wɛdmɛ'ʒa]
lion cub	левеня (n)	[lɛwɛ'ɲa]
tiger cub	тигреня (n)	[tɪɣrɛ'ɲa]
elephant calf	слоненя (n)	[slonɛ'ɲa]
piglet	порося (n)	[poro'sʲa]
calf (young cow, bull)	теля (n)	[tɛ'ʎa]
kid (young goat)	козеня (n)	[kozɛ'ɲa]
lamb	ягня (n)	[jaɣ'ɲa]
fawn (young deer)	оленя (n)	[olɛ'ɲa]
young camel	верблюденя (n)	[wɛrblydɛ'ɲa]
baby snake	змієня (n)	[zmiɛ'ɲa]
baby frog	жабеня (n)	[ʒabɛ'ɲa]
nestling	пташеня (n)	[ptaʃɛ'ɲa]
chick (of chicken)	курча (n)	[kur'tʃa]
duckling	каченя (n)	[katʃɛ'ɲa]

216. Birds

bird	птах (m)	[ptah]
pigeon	голуб (m)	['ɣolub]
sparrow	горобець (m)	[ɣoro'bɛts]
tit	синиця (f)	[sɪ'nɪtsʲa]
magpie	сорока (f)	[so'rɔka]
raven	ворон (m)	['woron]
crow	ворона (f)	[wo'rɔna]
jackdaw	галка (f)	['ɣalka]
rook	грак (m)	[ɣrak]
duck	качка (f)	['katʃka]
goose	гусак (m)	[ɣu'sak]
pheasant	фазан (m)	[fa'zan]
eagle	орел (m)	[o'rɛl]
hawk	яструб (m)	['jastrub]

falcon	сокіл (m)	['sɔkil]
vulture	гриф (m)	[ɣrɪf]
condor (Andean ~)	кондор (m)	['kɔndɔr]

swan	лебідь (m)	['lɛbidʲ]
crane	журавель (m)	[ʒura'wɛʎ]
stork	чорногуз (m)	[ʧɔrno'ɣuz]

parrot	папуга (m)	[pa'puɣa]
hummingbird	колібрі (m)	[ko'libri]
peacock	пава (f)	['pawa]

ostrich	страус (m)	['straus]
heron	чапля (f)	['ʧapʎa]
flamingo	фламінго (n)	[fla'miŋo]
pelican	пелікан (m)	[pɛli'kan]

| nightingale | соловей (m) | [solo'wɛj] |
| swallow | ластівка (f) | ['lastiwka] |

thrush	дрізд (m)	[drizd]
song thrush	співучий дрізд (m)	[spi'wuʧij drizd]
blackbird	чорний дрізд (m)	['ʧɔrnɪj drizd]

swift	стриж (m)	[strɪʒ]
lark	жайворонок (m)	['ʒajworonok]
quail	перепел (m)	['pɛrɛpɛl]

woodpecker	дятел (m)	['dʲatɛl]
cuckoo	зозуля (f)	[zo'zuʎa]
owl	сова (f)	[so'wa]
eagle owl	пугач (m)	[pu'ɣaʧ]
wood grouse	глухар (m)	[ɣlu'har]
black grouse	тетерук (m)	[tɛtɛ'ruk]
partridge	куріпка (f)	[ku'ripka]

starling	шпак (m)	[ʃpak]
canary	канарка (f)	[ka'narka]
hazel grouse	рябчик (m)	['rʲabʧɪk]
chaffinch	зяблик (m)	['zʲablɪk]
bullfinch	снігур (m)	[sni'ɣur]

seagull	чайка (f)	['ʧajka]
albatross	альбатрос (m)	[aʎbat'rɔs]
penguin	пінгвін (m)	[piŋ'win]

217. Birds. Singing and sounds

| to sing (vi) | співати | [spi'watɪ] |
| to call (animal, bird) | кричати | [krɪ'ʧatɪ] |

to crow (rooster)	кукурікати	[kuku'rikatı]
cock-a-doodle-doo	кукуріку	[kukuri'ku]
to cluck (hen)	кудкудакати	[kudku'dakatı]
to caw (vi)	каркати	['karkatı]
to quack (duck)	крякати	['kriakatı]
to cheep (vi)	пищати	[pı'ɕatı]
to chirp, to twitter	цвірінькати	[tswi'rіɲkatı]

218. Fish. Marine animals

bream	лящ (m)	[ʎaɕ]
carp	короп (m)	['kɔrɔp]
perch	окунь (m)	['ɔkuɲ]
catfish	сом (m)	[sɔm]
pike	щука (f)	['ɕuka]
salmon	лосось (m)	[lo'sɔsʲ]
sturgeon	осетер (m)	[osɛ'tɛr]
herring	оселедець (m)	[osɛ'lɛdɛts]
Atlantic salmon	сьомга (f)	['sʲɔmɣa]
mackerel	скумбрія (f)	['skumbrija]
flatfish	камбала (f)	[kamba'la]
zander, pike perch	судак (m)	[su'dak]
cod	тріска (f)	[tris'ka]
tuna	тунець (m)	[tu'nɛts]
trout	форель (f)	[fo'rɛʎ]
eel	вугор (m)	[wu'ɣɔr]
electric ray	електричний скат (m)	[ɛlɛkt'rıtʃnıj skat]
moray eel	мурена (f)	[mu'rɛna]
piranha	піранья (f)	[pi'raɲja]
shark	акула (f)	[a'kula]
dolphin	дельфін (m)	[dɛʎ'fin]
whale	кит (m)	[kıt]
crab	краб (m)	[krab]
jellyfish	медуза (f)	[mɛ'duza]
octopus	восьмініг (m)	[wosʲmı'niɣ]
starfish	морська зірка (f)	[morsʲ'ka 'zirka]
sea urchin	морський їжак (m)	[morsʲ'kıj jı'ʒak]
seahorse	морський коник (m)	[morsʲ'kıj 'kɔnık]
oyster	устриця (f)	['ustrıtsʲa]
shrimp	креветка (f)	[krɛ'wɛtka]
lobster	омар (m)	[o'mar]
spiny lobster	лангуст (m)	[la'ɲust]

219. Amphibians. Reptiles

snake	змія (f)	[zmiˈja]
venomous (snake)	отруйний	[otˈrujnɪj]
viper	гадюка (f)	[ɣaˈdyka]
cobra	кобра (f)	[ˈkɔbra]
python	пітон (m)	[piˈtɔn]
boa	удав (m)	[uˈdaw]
grass snake	вуж (m)	[wuʒ]
rattle snake	гримуча змія (f)	[ɣrɪˈmuʧa zmiˈja]
anaconda	анаконда (f)	[anaˈkɔnda]
lizard	ящірка (f)	[ˈjaɕirka]
iguana	ігуана (f)	[iɣuˈana]
monitor lizard	варан (m)	[waˈran]
salamander	саламандра (f)	[salaˈmandra]
chameleon	хамелеон (m)	[hamɛlɛˈɔn]
scorpion	скорпіон (m)	[skorpiˈɔn]
turtle	черепаха (f)	[ʧɛrɛˈpaha]
frog	жабка (f)	[ˈʒabka]
toad	жаба (f)	[ˈʒaba]
crocodile	крокодил (m)	[krokoˈdɪl]

220. Insects

insect, bug	комаха (f)	[koˈmaha]
butterfly	метелик (m)	[mɛˈtɛlɪk]
ant	мураха (f)	[muˈraha]
fly	муха (f)	[ˈmuha]
mosquito	комар (m)	[koˈmar]
beetle	жук (m)	[ʒuk]
wasp	оса (f)	[oˈsa]
bee	бджола (f)	[bʤoˈla]
bumblebee	джміль (m)	[ʤmiʎ]
gadfly	овід (m)	[ˈɔwid]
spider	павук (m)	[paˈwuk]
spider's web	павутиння (n)	[pawuˈtɪnja]
dragonfly	бабка (f)	[ˈbabka]
grasshopper	коник (m)	[ˈkɔnɪk]
moth (night butterfly)	метелик (m)	[mɛˈtɛlɪk]
cockroach	тарган (m)	[tarˈɣan]
tick	кліщ (m)	[kliɕ]

| flea | блоха (f) | ['bloha] |
| midge | мошка (f) | ['moʃka] |

locust	сарана (f)	[sara'na]
snail	равлик (m)	['rawlık]
cricket	цвіркун (m)	[tswir'kun]
lightning bug	світлячок (m)	[switʎa'tʃɔk]
ladybug	сонечко (n)	['sɔnɛtʃko]
cockchafer	хрущ (m)	[hruɕ]

leech	п'явка (f)	['pʰjawka]
caterpillar	гусениця (f)	['ɣusɛnıtsʲa]
earthworm	черв'як (m)	[tʃɛrwʰ'jak]
larva	личинка (f)	[lı'tʃıŋka]

221. Animals. Body parts

beak	дзьоб (m)	['dzɔb]
wings	крила (pl)	['krıla]
foot (of bird)	лапа (f)	['lapa]

feathering	пір'я (n)	['pirʰja]
feather	перо (n)	[pɛ'rɔ]
crest	чубчик (m)	['tʃubtʃık]

gill	зябра (pl)	['zʲabra]
spawn	ікра (f)	[ik'ra]
larva	личинка (f)	[lı'tʃıŋka]

| fin | плавець (m) | [pla'wɛts] |
| scales (of fish, reptile) | луска (f) | [lus'ka] |

fang (canine)	ікло (n)	['iklo]
paw (e.g., cat's ~)	лапа (f)	['lapa]
muzzle (snout)	морда (f)	['mɔrda]
mouth (of cat, dog)	паща (f)	['paɕa]

| tail | хвіст (m) | [hwist] |
| whiskers | вуса (pl) | ['wusa] |

| hoof | копито (n) | [ko'pıto] |
| horn | ріг (m) | [riɣ] |

carapace	панцир (m)	['pantsır]
shell (of mollusk)	мушля (f)	['muʃʎa]
eggshell	шкаралупа (f)	[ʃkara'lupa]

| animal's hair (pelage) | шерсть (f) | [ʃɛrstʲ] |

| pelt (hide) | шкура (f) | ['ʃkura] |

222. Actions of animals

to fly (vi)	літати	[li'tatı]
to make circles	кружляти	[kruʒ'ʎatı]
to fly away	полетіти	[polɛ'titı]
to flap (~ the wings)	махати	[ma'hatı]
to peck (vi)	клювати	[kly'watı]
to sit on eggs	висиджувати яйця	[wɪ'sɪdʒuwatı 'jajtsʲa]
to hatch out (vi)	вилуплюватися	[wɪ'luplywatısʲa]
to build the nest	мостити	[mos'titı]
to slither, to crawl	повзати	['powzatı]
to sting, to bite (insect)	жалити	['ʒalıtı]
to bite (ab. animal)	кусати	[ku'satı]
to sniff (vt)	нюхати	['nyhatı]
to bark (vi)	гавкати	['ɣawkatı]
to hiss (snake)	шипіти	[ʃı'pitı]
to scare (vt)	лякати	[ʎa'katı]
to attack (vt)	нападати	[napa'datı]
to gnaw (bone, etc.)	гризти	['ɣrıztı]
to scratch (with claws)	дряпати	['drʲapatı]
to hide (vi)	ховатися	[ho'watısʲa]
to play (kittens, etc.)	бавитись	['bawıtısʲ]
to hunt (vi, vt)	полювати	[poly'watı]
to hibernate (vi)	бути в сплячці	['butı w 'spʎatʃsi]
to become extinct	вимерти	['wımɛrtı]

223. Animals. Habitats

habitat	середовище (n)	[sɛrɛ'dowıɕɛ
	проживання	proʒı'wanja]
migration	міграція (f)	[miɣ'ratsija]
mountain	гора (f)	[ɣo'ra]
reef	риф (m)	[rıf]
cliff	скеля (f)	['skɛʎa]
forest	ліс (m)	[lis]
jungle	джунглі (pl)	['dʒuŋli]
savanna	савана (f)	[sa'wana]
tundra	тундра (f)	['tundra]
steppe	степ (m)	[stɛp]
desert	пустеля (f)	[pus'tɛʎa]
oasis	оаза (f)	[o'aza]

sea	море (n)	['mɔrɛ]
lake	озеро (n)	['ɔzɛro]
ocean	океан (m)	[okɛ'an]

swamp	болото (n)	[bo'lɔto]
freshwater (adj)	прісноводний	[prisno'wɔdnıj]
pond	став (m)	[staw]
river	ріка (f)	['rika]

den	барліг (m)	[bar'liɣ]
nest	гніздо (n)	[ɣniz'dɔ]
hollow (in a tree)	дупло (n)	[dup'lɔ]
burrow (animal hole)	нора (f)	[no'ra]
anthill	мурашник (m)	[muraʃ'nık]

224. Animal care

| zoo | зоопарк (m) | [zo:'park] |
| nature preserve | заповідник (m) | [zapo'widnık] |

breeder, breed club	розплідник (m)	[rozp'lidnık]
open-air cage	вольєра (f)	[wo'ʎjɛra]
cage	клітка (f)	['klitka]
kennel	буда (f)	['buda]

dovecot	голубник (m)	[ɣolub'nık]
aquarium	акваріум (m)	[ak'warium]
dolphinarium	дельфінарій (m)	[dɛʎfi'narij]

to breed (animals)	розводити	[roz'wɔdıtı]
brood, litter	потомство (n)	[po'tɔmstwo]
to tame (vt)	приручати	[prıru'tʃatı]
feed (fodder, etc.)	корм (m)	[korm]
to feed (vt)	годувати	[ɣodu'watı]
to train (animals)	дресирувати	[drɛsıru'watı]

pet store	зоомагазин (m)	[zo:maɣa'zın]
muzzle (for dog)	намордник (m)	[na'mɔrdnık]
collar	нашийник (m)	[na'ʃıjnık]
name (of animal)	кличка (f)	['klıtʃka]
pedigree (of dog)	родовід (m)	[rodo'wid]

225. Animals. Miscellaneous

pack (wolves)	зграя (f)	['zɣraja]
flock (birds)	зграя (f)	['zɣraja]
shoal (fish)	зграя (f)	['zɣraja]
herd of horses	табун (m)	[ta'bun]

male (n)	**самець** (m)	[sɑˈmɛʦ]
female	**самка** (f)	[ˈsɑmkɑ]
hungry (adj)	**голодний**	[ɣoˈlɔdnɪj]
wild (adj)	**дикий**	[ˈdɪkɪj]
dangerous (adj)	**небезпечний**	[nɛbɛzˈpɛʧnɪj]

226. Horses

horse	**кінь** (m)	[kiɲ]
breed (race)	**порода** (f)	[poˈrɔdɑ]
foal, colt	**лоша** (n)	[loˈʃɑ]
mare	**кобила** (f)	[koˈbɪlɑ]
mustang	**мустанг** (m)	[musˈtɑŋ]
pony	**поні** (m)	[ˈpɔni]
draft horse	**ваговоз** (m)	[wɑɣoˈwɔz]
mane	**грива** (f)	[ˈɣrɪwɑ]
tail	**хвіст** (m)	[hwist]
hoof	**копито** (n)	[koˈpɪto]
horseshoe	**підкова** (f)	[pidˈkɔwɑ]
to shoe (vt)	**підкувати**	[pidkuˈwɑtɪ]
blacksmith	**коваль** (m)	[koˈwɑʎ]
saddle	**сідло** (n)	[sidˈlɔ]
stirrup	**стремено** (n)	[strɛˈmɛno]
bridle	**вуздечка** (f)	[wuzˈdɛʧkɑ]
reins	**віжки** (pl)	[wiʒˈkɪ]
whip (for riding)	**батіг** (m)	[bɑˈtiɣ]
rider	**наїзник** (m)	[nɑˈjiznɪk]
to break in (horse)	**об'їжджати**	[obʰjiˈʒɑtɪ]
to saddle (vt)	**осідлати**	[osidˈlɑtɪ]
to mount a horse	**сісти в сідло**	[ˈsistɪ w sidˈlɔ]
gallop	**галоп** (m)	[ɣɑˈlɔp]
to gallop (vi)	**скакати галопом**	[skɑˈkɑtɪ ɣɑˈlɔpom]
trot (n)	**клус** (m)	[klus]
at a trot (adv)	**клусом**	[ˈklusom]
racehorse	**скаковий кінь** (m)	[skɑkoˈwɪj kiɲ]
horse racing	**перегони** (pl)	[pɛrɛˈɣɔnɪ]
stable	**конюшня** (f)	[koˈnyʃnɑ]
to feed (vt)	**годувати**	[ɣoduˈwɑtɪ]
hay	**сіно** (n)	[ˈsino]
to water (animals)	**поїти**	[poˈjitɪ]

to wash (horse)	**чистити**	['ʧistıtı]
to hobble (tether)	**стриножити**	[strı'nɔʒıtı]
horse-drawn cart	**віз** (m)	[wiz]
to graze (vi)	**пастися**	['pɑstısʲɑ]
to neigh (vi)	**іржати**	[ir'ʒɑtı]
to kick (horse)	**брикнути**	[brık'nutı]

Flora

227. Trees

tree	**дерево** (n)	['dɛrɛwo]
deciduous (adj)	**модринове**	[mod'rɪnowɛ]
coniferous (adj)	**хвойне**	['hwojnɛ]
evergreen (adj)	**вічнозелене**	[witʃnozɛ'lɛnɛ]
apple tree	**яблуня** (f)	['jabluɲa]
pear tree	**груша** (f)	['ɣruʃa]
sweet cherry tree	**черешня** (f)	[tʃɛ'rɛʃɲa]
sour cherry tree	**вишня** (f)	['wɪʃɲa]
plum tree	**слива** (f)	['slɪwa]
birch	**береза** (f)	[bɛ'rɛza]
oak	**дуб** (m)	[dub]
linden tree	**липа** (f)	['lɪpa]
aspen	**осика** (f)	[o'sɪka]
maple	**клен** (m)	[klɛn]
spruce	**ялина** (f)	[ja'lɪna]
pine	**сосна** (f)	[sos'na]
larch	**модрина** (f)	[mod'rɪna]
fir tree	**ялиця** (f)	[ja'lɪtsʲa]
cedar	**кедр** (m)	[kɛdr]
poplar	**тополя** (f)	[to'pɔʎa]
rowan	**горобина** (f)	[ɣoro'bɪna]
willow	**верба** (f)	[wɛr'ba]
alder	**вільха** (f)	['wiʎha]
beech	**бук** (m)	[buk]
elm	**в'яз** (m)	[wʰjaz]
ash (tree)	**ясен** (m)	['jasɛn]
chestnut	**каштан** (m)	[kaʃtan]
magnolia	**магнолія** (f)	[maɣ'nɔlija]
palm tree	**пальма** (f)	['paʎma]
cypress	**кипарис** (m)	[kɪpa'rɪs]
mangrove	**мангрове дерево** (n)	['maɲrowɛ 'dɛrɛwo]
baobab	**баобаб** (m)	[bao'bab]
eucalyptus	**евкаліпт** (m)	[ɛwka'lipt]
sequoia	**секвоя** (f)	[sɛk'wɔja]

228. Shrubs

bush	кущ (m)	[kuɕ]
shrub	кущі (pl)	[ku'ɕi]
grapevine	виноград (m)	[wɪnoɣ'rɑd]
vineyard	виноградник (m)	[wɪnoɣ'rɑdnɪk]
raspberry bush	малина (f)	[mɑ'lɪnɑ]
redcurrant bush	порічки (pl)	[po'ritʃkɪ]
gooseberry bush	аґрус (m)	['ɑgrus]
acacia	акація (f)	[a'kɑtsija]
barberry	барбарис (m)	[bɑrbɑ'rɪs]
jasmine	жасмин (m)	[ʒɑs'mɪn]
juniper	ялівець (m)	[jɑli'wɛts]
rosebush	трояндовий кущ (m)	[tro'jɑndowɪj kuɕ]
dog rose	шипшина (f)	[ʃɪp'ʃɪnɑ]

229. Mushrooms

mushroom	гриб (m)	[ɣrɪb]
edible mushroom	їстівний гриб (m)	[jis'tiwnɪj ɣrɪb]
toadstool	отруйний гриб (m)	[ot'rujnɪj ɣrɪb]
cap (of mushroom)	шапка (f)	['ʃɑpkɑ]
stipe (of mushroom)	ніжка (f)	['niʒkɑ]
cep (Boletus edulis)	білий гриб (m)	['bilɪj ɣrɪb]
orange-cap boletus	підосичник (m)	[pido'sɪtʃnɪk]
birch bolete	підберезник (m)	[pidbɛ'rɛznɪk]
chanterelle	лисичка (f)	[lɪ'sɪtʃkɑ]
russula	сироїжка (f)	[sɪro'jɪʒkɑ]
morel	зморшок (m)	['zmɔrʃok]
fly agaric	мухомор (m)	[muho'mɔr]
death cap	поганка (f)	[po'ɣɑŋkɑ]

230. Fruits. Berries

apple	яблуко (n)	['jɑbluko]
pear	груша (f)	['ɣruʃɑ]
plum	слива (f)	['slɪwɑ]
strawberry	полуниця (f)	[polu'nɪtsʲɑ]
sour cherry	вишня (f)	['wɪʃnɑ]
sweet cherry	черешня (f)	[tʃɛ'rɛʃnɑ]

grape	виноград (m)	[wɪnoɣˈrad]
raspberry	малина (f)	[maˈlɪna]
blackcurrant	чорна смородина (f)	[ˈtʃɔrna smoˈrɔdɪna]
redcurrant	порічки (pl)	[poˈritʃkɪ]
gooseberry	аґрус (m)	[ˈɑgrus]
cranberry	журавлина (f)	[ʒuraw'lɪna]
orange	апельсин (m)	[apɛʎˈsɪn]
mandarin	мандарин (m)	[mandaˈrɪn]
pineapple	ананас (m)	[anaˈnas]
banana	банан (m)	[baˈnan]
date	фінік (m)	[ˈfinik]
lemon	лимон (m)	[lɪˈmɔn]
apricot	абрикос (m)	[abrɪˈkɔs]
peach	персик (m)	[ˈpɛrsɪk]
kiwi	ківі (m)	[ˈkiwi]
grapefruit	грейпфрут (m)	[ɣrɛjpfˈrut]
berry	ягода (f)	[ˈjaɣoda]
berries	ягоди (pl)	[ˈjaɣodɪ]
cowberry	брусниця (f)	[brusˈnɪtsʲa]
field strawberry	суниця (f)	[suˈnɪtsʲa]
bilberry	чорниця (f)	[tʃorˈnɪtsʲa]

231. Flowers. Plants

flower	квітка (f)	[ˈkwitka]
bouquet (of flowers)	букет (m)	[buˈkɛt]
rose (flower)	троянда (f)	[troˈjanda]
tulip	тюльпан (m)	[tyʎˈpan]
carnation	гвоздика (f)	[ɣwozˈdɪka]
gladiolus	гладіолус (m)	[ɣladiˈɔlus]
cornflower	волошка (f)	[woˈlɔʃka]
bluebell	дзвіночок (m)	[dʒwiˈnɔtʃok]
dandelion	кульбаба (f)	[kuʎˈbaba]
camomile	ромашка (f)	[roˈmaʃka]
aloe	алое (m)	[aˈlɔɛ]
cactus	кактус (m)	[ˈkaktus]
rubber plant, ficus	фікус (m)	[ˈfikus]
lily	лілея (f)	[liˈlɛja]
geranium	герань (f)	[ɣɛˈraɲ]
hyacinth	гіацинт (m)	[ɣiaˈtsɪnt]
mimosa	мімоза (f)	[miˈmɔza]
narcissus	нарцис (m)	[narˈtsɪs]

nasturtium	настурція (f)	[nasˈturtsija]
orchid	орхідея (f)	[orhiˈdɛja]
peony	півонія (f)	[piˈwɔnija]
violet	фіалка (f)	[fiˈalka]

pansy	братки (pl)	[bratˈkɪ]
forget-me-not	незабудка (f)	[nɛzaˈbudka]
daisy	стокротки (pl)	[stokˈrɔtkɪ]

poppy	мак (m)	[mak]
hemp	коноплі (pl)	[koˈnɔpli]
mint	м'ята (f)	[ˈmʰjata]

| lily of the valley | конвалія (f) | [konˈwalija] |
| snowdrop | пролісок (m) | [ˈprɔlisok] |

nettle	кропива (f)	[kropɪˈwa]
sorrel	щавель (m)	[ɕaˈwɛʎ]
water lily	латаття (n)	[laˈtattʲa]
fern	папороть (f)	[ˈpaporotʲ]
lichen	лишайник (m)	[lɪˈʃajnɪk]

tropical greenhouse	оранжерея (f)	[oranʒɛˈrɛja]
grass lawn	газон (m)	[ɣaˈzɔn]
flowerbed	клумба (f)	[ˈklumba]

plant	рослина (f)	[rosˈlɪna]
grass, herb	трава (f)	[traˈwa]
blade of grass	травинка (f)	[trawɪŋka]

leaf	листок (m)	[lɪsˈtɔk]
petal	пелюстка (f)	[pɛˈlystka]
stem	стебло (n)	[stɛbˈlɔ]
tuber	бульба (f)	[ˈbuʎba]

| young plant (shoot) | паросток (m) | [ˈparostok] |
| thorn | колючка (m) | [koˈlytʃka] |

to blossom (vi)	цвісти	[tsvisˈtɪ]
to fade, to wither	в'янути	[ˈwʰjanutɪ]
smell (odor)	запах (m)	[ˈzapah]
to cut (flowers)	зрізати	[ˈzrizatɪ]
to pick (a flower)	зірвати	[zirˈwatɪ]

232. Cereals, grains

grain	зерно (n)	[zɛrˈnɔ]
cereal crops	зернові рослини (pl)	[zɛrnoˈwi rosˈlɪnɪ]
ear (of barley, etc.)	колос (m)	[ˈkɔlos]
wheat	пшениця (f)	[pʃɛˈnɪtsʲa]

rye	жито (n)	['ʒɪto]
oats	овес (m)	[o'wɛs]
millet	просо (n)	['prɔso]
barley	ячмінь (m)	[jaʧ'mɪɲ]

corn	кукурудза (f)	[kuku'ruʤa]
rice	рис (m)	[rɪs]
buckwheat	гречка (f)	['ɣrɛʧka]

pea plant	горох (m)	[ɣo'rɔh]
kidney bean	квасоля (f)	[kwa'sɔʎa]
soy	соя (f)	['sɔja]
lentil	сочевиця (f)	[soʧɛ'wɪʦʲa]
beans (pulse crops)	боби (pl)	[bo'bɪ]

233. Vegetables. Greens

| vegetables | овочі (pl) | ['ɔwoʧi] |
| greens | зелень (f) | ['zɛlɛɲ] |

tomato	помідор (m)	[pomi'dɔr]
cucumber	огірок (m)	[oɣi'rɔk]
carrot	морква (f)	['mɔrkwa]
potato	картопля (f)	[kar'tɔpʎa]
onion	цибуля (f)	[ʦɪ'buʎa]
garlic	часник (m)	[ʧas'nɪk]

cabbage	капуста (f)	[ka'pusta]
cauliflower	кольорова капуста (f)	[kolʲ'rɔwa ka'pusta]
Brussels sprouts	брюссельська капуста (f)	[brʲ'sɛʎsʲka ka'pusta]

beetroot	буряк (m)	[bu'rʲak]
eggplant	баклажан (m)	[bakla'ʒan]
zucchini	кабачок (m)	[kaba'ʧɔk]
pumpkin	гарбуз (m)	[ɣar'buz]
turnip	ріпа (f)	['ripa]

parsley	петрушка (f)	[pɛt'ruʃka]
dill	кріп (m)	[krip]
lettuce	салат (m)	[sa'lat]
celery	селера (f)	[sɛ'lɛra]
asparagus	спаржа (f)	['sparʒa]
spinach	шпинат (m)	[ʃpɪ'nat]

pea	горох (m)	[ɣo'rɔh]
beans	боби (pl)	[bo'bɪ]
corn (maize)	кукурудза (f)	[kuku'ruʤa]
kidney bean	квасоля (f)	[kwa'sɔʎa]
pepper	перець (m)	['pɛrɛʦ]

| radish | **редька** (f) | [ˈrɛdʲka] |
| artichoke | **артишок** (m) | [ɑrtɪˈʃɔk] |

REGIONAL GEOGRAPHY

Countries. Nationalities

234. Western Europe

Europe	**Європа** (f)	[ɛw'rɔpɑ]
European Union	**Європейський Союз** (m)	[ɛwro'pɛjsʲkɪj so'juz]
European (n)	**європеєць** (m)	[ɛwro'pɛ:ts]
European (adj)	**європейський**	[ɛwro'pɛjsʲkɪj]
Austria	**Австрія** (f)	['ɑwstrijɑ]
Austrian (masc.)	**австрієць** (m)	[ɑwst'riɛts]
Austrian (fem.)	**австрійка** (f)	[ɑwst'rijkɑ]
Austrian (adj)	**австрійський**	[ɑwst'rijsʲkɪj]
Great Britain	**Великобританія** (f)	[wɛlɪkobrɪ'tɑnijɑ]
England	**Англія** (f)	['ɑŋlijɑ]
British (masc.)	**англієць** (m)	[ɑŋ'liɛts]
British (fem.)	**англійка** (f)	[ɑŋ'lijkɑ]
English, British (adj)	**англійський**	[ɑŋ'lijsʲkɪj]
Belgium	**Бельгія** (f)	['bɛʎijɑ]
Belgian (masc.)	**бельгієць** (m)	[bɛʎ'ɣiɛts]
Belgian (fem.)	**бельгійка** (f)	[bɛʎ'ɣijkɑ]
Belgian (adj)	**бельгійський**	[bɛʎ'ɣijsʲkɪj]
Germany	**Німеччина** (f)	[ni'mɛtʃɪnɑ]
German (masc.)	**німець** (m)	['nimɛts]
German (fem.)	**німкеня** (f)	[nim'kɛɲɑ]
German (adj)	**німецький**	[ni'mɛtskɪj]
Netherlands	**Нідерланди** (f)	[nidɛr'lɑndɪ]
Holland	**Голландія** (f)	[ɣo'lɑndijɑ]
Dutchman	**голландець** (m)	[ɣo'lɑndɛts]
Dutchwoman	**голландка** (f)	[ɣo'lɑndkɑ]
Dutch (adj)	**голландський**	[ɣo'lɑndsʲkɪj]
Greece	**Греція** (f)	['ɣrɛtsijɑ]
Greek (masc.)	**грек** (m)	[ɣrɛk]
Greek (fem.)	**грекиня** (f)	[ɣrɛ'kɪɲɑ]
Greek (adj)	**грецький**	['ɣrɛtskɪj]
Denmark	**Данія** (f)	['dɑnijɑ]
Dane (masc.)	**данець** (m)	['dɑnɛts]

Dane (fem.)	**данка** (f)	['daŋka]
Danish (adj)	**данський**	['dansʲkıj]
Ireland	**Ірландія** (f)	[irˈlandija]
Irishman	**ірландець** (m)	[irˈlandɛʦ]
Irishwoman	**ірландка** (f)	[irˈlandka]
Irish (adj)	**ірландський**	[irˈlandsʲkıj]
Iceland	**Ісландія** (f)	[isˈlandija]
Icelander (masc.)	**ісландець** (m)	[isˈlandɛʦ]
Icelander (fem.)	**ісландка** (f)	[isˈlandka]
Icelandic (adj)	**ісландський**	[isˈlandsʲkıj]
Spain	**Іспанія** (f)	[ispanija]
Spaniard (masc.)	**іспанець** (m)	[ispanɛʦ]
Spaniard (fem.)	**іспанка** (f)	[ispaŋka]
Spanish (adj)	**іспанський**	[ispansʲkıj]
Italy	**Італія** (f)	[iˈtalija]
Italian (masc.)	**італієць** (m)	[itaˈliɛʦ]
Italian (fem.)	**італійка** (f)	[itaˈlijka]
Italian (adj)	**італійський**	[itaˈlijsʲkıj]
Cyprus	**Кіпр** (f)	[kipr]
Cypriot (masc.)	**кіпріот** (m)	[kipriˈɔt]
Cypriot (fem.)	**кіпріотка** (f)	[kipriˈɔtka]
Cypriot (adj)	**кіпрський**	[ˈkiprsʲkıj]
Malta	**Мальта** (f)	[ˈmaʎta]
Maltese (masc.)	**мальтієць** (m)	[maʎˈtiɛʦ]
Maltese (fem.)	**мальтійка** (f)	[maʎˈtijka]
Maltese (adj)	**мальтійський**	[maʎˈtijsʲkıj]
Norway	**Норвегія** (f)	[norˈwɛɣija]
Norwegian (masc.)	**норвежець** (m)	[norˈwɛʒɛʦ]
Norwegian (fem.)	**норвежка** (f)	[norˈwɛʒka]
Norwegian (adj)	**норвезький**	[norˈwɛzʲkıj]
Portugal	**Португалія** (f)	[portuˈɣalija]
Portuguese (masc.)	**португалець** (m)	[portuˈɣalɛʦ]
Portuguese (fem.)	**португалка** (f)	[portuˈɣalka]
Portuguese (adj)	**португальський**	[portuˈɣaʎsʲkıj]
Finland	**Фінляндія** (f)	[finˈʎandija]
Finn (masc.)	**фін** (m)	[fin]
Finn (fem.)	**фінка** (f)	[ˈfiŋka]
Finnish (adj)	**фінський**	[ˈfinsʲkıj]
France	**Франція** (f)	[ˈfranʦija]
Frenchman	**француз** (m)	[franˈʦuz]
Frenchwoman	**французка** (f)	[franˈʦuzka]
French (adj)	**французький**	[franˈʦuzʲkıj]

Sweden	**Швеція** (f)	[ˈʃwɛtsija]
Swede (masc.)	**швед** (m)	[ʃwɛd]
Swede (fem.)	**шведка** (f)	[ˈʃwɛdka]
Swedish (adj)	**шведський**	[ˈʃwɛdsʲkij]

Switzerland	**Швейцарія** (f)	[ʃwɛjˈtsarija]
Swiss (masc.)	**швейцарець** (m)	[ʃwɛjˈtsarɛts]
Swiss (fem.)	**швейцарка** (f)	[ʃwɛjˈtsarka]
Swiss (adj)	**швейцарський**	[ʃwɛjˈtsarsʲkij]

Scotland	**Шотландія** (f)	[ʃotˈlandija]
Scottish (masc.)	**шотландець** (m)	[ʃotˈlandɛts]
Scottish (fem.)	**шотландка** (f)	[ʃotˈlandka]
Scottish (adj)	**шотландський**	[ʃotˈlandsʲkij]

Vatican	**Ватикан** (m)	[watɪˈkan]
Liechtenstein	**Ліхтенштейн** (m)	[lihtɛnʃˈtɛjn]
Luxembourg	**Люксембург** (m)	[lyksɛmˈburɣ]
Monaco	**Монако** (n)	[moˈnako]

235. Central and Eastern Europe

Albania	**Албанія** (f)	[alˈbanija]
Albanian (masc.)	**албанець** (m)	[alˈbanɛts]
Albanian (fem.)	**албанка** (f)	[alˈbaŋka]
Albanian (adj)	**албанський**	[alˈbansʲkij]

Bulgaria	**Болгарія** (f)	[bolˈɣarija]
Bulgarian (masc.)	**болгарин** (m)	[bolˈɣarɪn]
Bulgarian (fem.)	**болгарка** (f)	[bolˈɣarka]
Bulgarian (adj)	**болгарський**	[bolˈɣarsʲkij]

Hungary	**Угорщина** (f)	[uˈɣorɕɪna]
Hungarian (masc.)	**угорець** (m)	[uˈɣorɛts]
Hungarian (fem.)	**угорка** (f)	[uˈɣorka]
Hungarian (adj)	**угорський**	[uˈɣorsʲkij]

Latvia	**Латвія** (f)	[ˈlatwija]
Latvian (masc.)	**латвієць** (m)	[latˈwiɛts]
Latvian (fem.)	**латвійка** (f)	[latˈwijka]
Latvian (adj)	**латиський**	[laˈtɪsʲkij]

Lithuania	**Литва** (f)	[lɪtˈwa]
Lithuanian (masc.)	**литовець** (m)	[lɪˈtɔwɛts]
Lithuanian (fem.)	**литовка** (f)	[lɪˈtɔwka]
Lithuanian (adj)	**литовський**	[lɪˈtɔwsʲkij]

Poland	**Польща** (f)	[ˈpɔʎɕa]
Pole (masc.)	**поляк** (m)	[poˈʎak]
Pole (fem.)	**полька** (f)	[ˈpɔʎka]

Polish (adj)	польський	['poʎsʲkɪj]
Romania	Румунія (f)	[ru'munija]
Romanian (masc.)	румун (m)	[ru'mun]
Romanian (fem.)	румунка (f)	[ru'muŋka]
Romanian (adj)	румунський	[ru'munsʲkɪj]

Serbia	Сербія (f)	['sɛrbija]
Serbian (masc.)	серб (m)	[sɛrb]
Serbian (fem.)	сербка (f)	['sɛrbka]
Serbian (adj)	сербський	['sɛrbsʲkɪj]

Slovakia	Словаччина (f)	[slo'watʃina]
Slovak (masc.)	словак (m)	[slo'wak]
Slovak (fem.)	словачка (f)	[slo'watʃka]
Slovak (adj)	словацький	[slo'watskɪj]

Croatia	Хорватія (f)	[hor'watija]
Croatian (masc.)	хорват (m)	[hor'wat]
Croatian (fem.)	хорватка (f)	[hor'watka]
Croatian (adj)	хорватський	[hor'watsʲkɪj]

Czech Republic	Чехія (f)	['tʃɛhija]
Czech (masc.)	чех (m)	[tʃɛh]
Czech (fem.)	чешка (f)	['tʃɛʃka]
Czech (adj)	чеський	['tʃɛsʲkɪj]

Estonia	Естонія (f)	[ɛs'tonija]
Estonian (masc.)	естонець (m)	[ɛs'tonɛts]
Estonian (fem.)	естонка (f)	[ɛs'toŋka]
Estonian (adj)	естонський	[ɛs'tonsʲkɪj]

Bosnia-Herzegovina	Боснія (f) і Герцеговина (f)	['bɔsnija і ɣɛrtsɛɣo'wɪna]
Macedonia	Македонія (f)	[makɛ'dɔnija]
Slovenia	Словенія (f)	[slo'wɛnija]
Montenegro	Чорногорія (f)	[tʃorno'ɣɔrija]

236. Former USSR countries

Azerbaijan	Азербайджан (m)	[azɛrbaj'dʒan]
Azerbaijani (masc.)	азербайджанець (m)	[azɛrbaj'dʒanɛts]
Azerbaijani (fem.)	азербайджанка (f)	[azɛrbaj'dʒaŋka]
Azerbaijani (adj)	азербайджанський	[azɛrbaj'dʒansʲkɪj]

Armenia	Вірменія (f)	[wir'mɛnija]
Armenian (masc.)	вірменин (m)	[wirmɛ'nɪn]
Armenian (fem.)	вірменка (f)	[wir'mɛŋka]
Armenian (adj)	вірменський	[wir'mɛnsʲkɪj]
Belarus	Білорусь (f)	[bilo'rusʲ]
Belarusian (masc.)	білорус (m)	[bilo'rus]

| Belarusian (fem.) | білоруска (f) | [bilo'ruska] |
| Belarusian (adj) | білоруський | [bilo'rusʲkɪj] |

Georgia	Грузія (f)	[ˈɣruzija]
Georgian (masc.)	грузин (m)	[ɣru'zɪn]
Georgian (fem.)	грузинка (f)	[ɣru'zɪŋka]
Georgian (adj)	грузинський	[ɣru'zɪnsʲkɪj]

Kazakhstan	Казахстан (m)	[kazahs'tan]
Kazakh (masc.)	казах (m)	[ka'zah]
Kazakh (fem.)	казашка (f)	[ka'zaʃka]
Kazakh (adj)	казахський	[ka'zahsʲkɪj]
Kirghizia	Киргизстан (m)	[kɪrɪzs'tan]
Kirghiz (masc.)	киргиз (m)	[kɪr'ɣɪz]
Kirghiz (fem.)	киргизка (f)	[kɪr'ɣɪzka]
Kirghiz (adj)	киргизький	[kɪr'ɣɪzʲkɪj]

Moldavia	Молдова (f)	[mol'dɔwa]
Moldavian (masc.)	молдованин (m)	[moldo'wanɪn]
Moldavian (fem.)	молдаванка (f)	[molda'waŋka]
Moldavian (adj)	молдавський	[mol'dawsʲkɪj]

Russia	Росія (f)	[ro'sija]
Russian (masc.)	росіянин (m)	[rosi'janɪn]
Russian (fem.)	росіянка (f)	[rosi'jaŋka]
Russian (adj)	російський	[ro'sijskɪj]
Tajikistan	Таджикистан (m)	[taʤɪkɪs'tan]
Tajik (masc.)	таджик (m)	[ta'ʤɪk]
Tajik (fem.)	таджичка (f)	[ta'ʤɪʧka]
Tajik (adj)	таджицький	[ta'ʤɪʦkɪj]

Turkmenistan	Туркменістан (m)	[turkmɛnis'tan]
Turkmen (masc.)	туркмен (m)	[turk'mɛn]
Turkmen (fem.)	туркменка (f)	[turk'mɛŋka]
Turkmenian (adj)	туркменський	[turk'mɛnsʲkɪj]

Uzbekistan	Узбекистан (m)	[uzbɛkɪs'tan]
Uzbek (masc.)	узбек (m)	[uz'bɛk]
Uzbek (fem.)	узбечка (f)	[uz'bɛʧka]
Uzbek (adj)	узбецький	[uz'bɛʦkɪj]

Ukraine	Україна (f)	[ukra'jina]
Ukrainian (masc.)	українець (m)	[ukra'jinɛʦ]
Ukrainian (fem.)	українка (f)	[ukra'jiŋka]
Ukrainian (adj)	український	[ukra'jinsʲkɪj]

237. Asia

| Asia | Азія (f) | [ˈazija] |
| Asian (adj) | азіатський | [azi'atsʲkɪj] |

Vietnam	**В'єтнам** (m)	[wʰɛt′nɑm]
Vietnamese (masc.)	**в'єтнамець** (m)	[wʰɛt′nɑmɛʦ]
Vietnamese (fem.)	**в'єтнамка** (f)	[wʰɛt′nɑmkɑ]
Vietnamese (adj)	**в'єтнамський**	[wʰɛt′nɑmsʲkɪj]

India	**Індія** (f)	[′indijɑ]
Indian (masc.)	**індієць** (m)	[in′diɛʦ]
Indian (fem.)	**індійка** (f)	[in′dijkɑ]
Indian (adj)	**індійський**	[in′dijsʲkɪj]

Israel	**Ізраїль** (m)	[iz′rɑjɪʎ]
Israeli (masc.)	**ізраїльтянин** (m)	[izrɑjɪʎ′tʲɑnɪn]
Israeli (fem.)	**ізраїльтянка** (f)	[izrɑjɪʎ′tʲɑŋkɑ]
Israeli (adj)	**ізраїльський**	[iz′rɑjɪʎsʲkɪj]

Jew (n)	**єврей** (m)	[ɛw′rɛj]
Jewess (n)	**єврейка** (f)	[ɛw′rɛjkɑ]
Jewish (adj)	**єврейський**	[ɛw′rɛjsʲkɪj]

China	**Китай** (m)	[kɪ′tɑj]
Chinese (masc.)	**китаєць** (m)	[kɪ′tɑɛʦ]
Chinese (fem.)	**китаянка** (f)	[kɪtɑ′jɑŋkɑ]
Chinese (adj)	**китайський**	[kɪ′tɑjsʲkɪj]

Korean (masc.)	**кореєць** (m)	[ko′rɛːʦ]
Korean (fem.)	**кореянка** (f)	[korɛ′jɑŋkɑ]
Korean (adj)	**корейський**	[ko′rɛjsʲkɪj]

Lebanon	**Ліван** (m)	[li′wɑn]
Lebanese (masc.)	**ліванець** (m)	[li′wɑnɛʦ]
Lebanese (fem.)	**ліванка** (f)	[li′wɑŋkɑ]
Lebanese (adj)	**ліванський**	[li′wɑnsʲkɪj]

Mongolia	**Монголія** (f)	[mo′ŋɔlijɑ]
Mongolian (masc.)	**монгол** (m)	[mo′ŋɔl]
Mongolian (fem.)	**монголка** (f)	[mo′ŋɔlkɑ]
Mongolian (adj)	**монгольський**	[mo′ŋɔʎsʲkɪj]

Malaysia	**Малайзія** (f)	[mɑ′lɑjzijɑ]
Malaysian (masc.)	**малаєць** (m)	[mɑ′lɑɛʦ]
Malaysian (fem.)	**малайка** (f)	[mɑ′lɑjkɑ]
Malaysian (adj)	**малайський**	[mɑ′lɑjsʲkɪj]

Pakistan	**Пакистан** (m)	[pɑkɪs′tɑn]
Pakistani (masc.)	**пакистанець** (m)	[pɑkɪs′tɑnɛʦ]
Pakistani (fem.)	**пакистанка** (f)	[pɑkɪs′tɑŋkɑ]
Pakistani (adj)	**пакистанський**	[pɑkɪs′tɑnsʲkɪj]

Saudi Arabia	**Саудівська Аравія** (f)	[sɑ′udiwsʲkɑ ɑ′rɑwijɑ]
Arab (masc.)	**араб** (m)	[ɑ′rɑb]
Arab (fem.)	**арабка** (f)	[ɑ′rɑbkɑ]
Arabian (adj)	**арабський**	[ɑ′rɑbsʲkɪj]

Thailand	**Таїланд** (m)	[tɑjɪˈlɑnd]
Thai (masc.)	**таєць** (m)	[ˈtɑɛts]
Thai (fem.)	**тайка** (f)	[ˈtɑjkɑ]
Thai (adj)	**тайський**	[ˈtɑjsʲkɪj]

Taiwan	**Тайвань** (m)	[tɑjˈwɑɲ]
Taiwanese (masc.)	**тайванець** (m)	[tɑjˈwɑnɛts]
Taiwanese (fem.)	**тайванка** (f)	[tɑjˈwɑŋkɑ]
Taiwanese (adj)	**тайванський**	[tɑjwɑnsʲkɪj]

Turkey	**Туреччина** (f)	[tuˈrɛtʃɪnɑ]
Turk (masc.)	**турок** (m)	[ˈturok]
Turk (fem.)	**туркеня** (f)	[turˈkɛɲɑ]
Turkish (adj)	**турецький**	[tuˈrɛtskɪj]

Japan	**Японія** (f)	[jɑˈponijɑ]
Japanese (masc.)	**японець** (m)	[jɑˈponɛts]
Japanese (fem.)	**японка** (f)	[jɑˈpoŋkɑ]
Japanese (adj)	**японський**	[jɑˈponsʲkɪj]

Afghanistan	**Афганістан** (m)	[ɑfɣanisˈtɑn]
Bangladesh	**Бангладеш** (m)	[bɑŋlɑˈdɛʃ]
Indonesia	**Індонезія** (f)	[indoˈnɛzijɑ]
Jordan	**Йорданія** (f)	[jorˈdanijɑ]

Iraq	**Ірак** (m)	[iˈrɑk]
Iran	**Іран** (m)	[iˈrɑn]
Cambodia	**Камбоджа** (f)	[kɑmˈbɔʤɑ]
Kuwait	**Кувейт** (m)	[kuˈwɛjt]

Laos	**Лаос** (m)	[lɑˈɔs]
Myanmar	**М'янма** (f)	[ˈmʲjɑnmɑ]
Nepal	**Непал** (m)	[nɛˈpɑl]
United Arab Emirates	**Об'єднані Арабські емірати**	[obʰˈɛdnani aˈrɑbsʲki ɛmiˈrɑtɪ]

Syria	**Сирія** (f)	[ˈsɪrijɑ]
Palestine	**Палестинська автономія** (f)	[pɑlɛsˈtɪnsʲkɑ ɑwtoˈnɔmijɑ]
South Korea	**Південна Корея** (f)	[piwˈdɛŋɑ koˈrɛjɑ]
North Korea	**Північна Корея** (f)	[piwˈnitʃnɑ koˈrɛjɑ]

238. North America

United States of America	**Сполучені Штати Америки**	[spoˈlutʃɛni ˈʃtɑtɪ ɑmɛrɪkɪ]
American (masc.)	**американець** (m)	[ɑmɛrɪˈkɑnɛts]
American (fem.)	**американка** (f)	[ɑmɛrɪˈkɑŋkɑ]
American (adj)	**американський**	[ɑmɛrɪˈkɑnsʲkɪj]
Canada	**Канада** (f)	[kɑˈnɑdɑ]

Canadian (masc.)	канадець (m)	[kɑˈnɑdɛts]
Canadian (fem.)	канадка (f)	[kɑˈnɑdkɑ]
Canadian (adj)	канадський	[kɑˈnɑdsʲkɪj]

Mexico	Мексика (f)	[ˈmɛksɪkɑ]
Mexican (masc.)	мексиканець (m)	[mɛksɪˈkɑnɛts]
Mexican (fem.)	мексиканка (f)	[mɛksɪˈkɑŋkɑ]
Mexican (adj)	мексиканський	[mɛksɪˈkɑnsʲkɪj]

239. Central and South America

Argentina	Аргентина (f)	[ɑrɣɛnˈtɪnɑ]
Argentinian (masc.)	аргентинець (m)	[ɑrɣɛnˈtɪnɛts]
Argentinian (fem.)	аргентинка (f)	[ɑrɣɛnˈtɪŋkɑ]
Argentinian (adj)	аргентинський	[ɑrɣɛnˈtɪnsʲkɪj]

Brazil	Бразилія (f)	[brɑˈzɪlijɑ]
Brazilian (masc.)	бразилець (m)	[brɑˈzɪlɛts]
Brazilian (fem.)	бразилійка (f)	[brɑzɪˈlijkɑ]
Brazilian (adj)	бразильський	[brɑˈzɪʎsʲkɪj]

Colombia	Колумбія (f)	[koˈlumbijɑ]
Colombian (masc.)	колумбієць (m)	[kolumˈbiɛts]
Colombian (fem.)	колумбійка (f)	[kolumˈbijkɑ]
Colombian (adj)	колумбійський	[kolumˈbijsʲkɪj]

Cuba	Куба (f)	[ˈkubɑ]
Cuban (masc.)	кубинець (m)	[kuˈbɪnɛts]
Cuban (fem.)	кубинка (f)	[kuˈbɪŋkɑ]
Cuban (adj)	кубинський	[kuˈbɪnsʲkɪj]

Chile	Чилі (f)	[ˈtʃɪli]
Chilean (masc.)	чилієць (m)	[tʃɪˈliɛts]
Chilean (fem.)	чилійка (f)	[tʃɪˈlijkɑ]
Chilean (adj)	чилійський	[tʃɪˈlijsʲkɪj]

Bolivia	Болівія (f)	[boˈliwijɑ]
Venezuela	Венесуела (f)	[wɛnɛsuˈɛlɑ]
Paraguay	Парагвай (m)	[pɑrɑɣˈwɑj]
Peru	Перу (f)	[pɛˈru]
Suriname	Суринам (m)	[surɪˈnɑm]
Uruguay	Уругвай (m)	[uruɣˈwɑj]
Ecuador	Еквадор (m)	[ɛkwɑˈdɔr]

The Bahamas	Багамські острови (pl)	[bɑˈɣɑmsʲki ostroˈwɪ]
Haiti	Гаїті (m)	[ɣɑˈjiti]
Dominican Republic	Домініканська республіка (f)	[domiˈkɑnsʲkɑ rɛsˈpublikɑ]
Panama	Панама (f)	[pɑˈnɑmɑ]
Jamaica	Ямайка (f)	[jɑˈmɑjkɑ]

240. Africa

Egypt	**Єгипет** (m)	[ɛ'ɣɪpɛt]
Egyptian (masc.)	**єгиптянин** (m)	[ɛɣɪp'tʲanɪn]
Egyptian (fem.)	**єгиптянка** (f)	[ɛɣɪp'tʲaŋka]
Egyptian (adj)	**єгипетський**	[ɛ'ɣɪpɛtsʲkɪj]
Morocco	**Марокко** (n)	[ma'rɔkko]
Moroccan (masc.)	**марокканець** (m)	[maro'kanɛts]
Moroccan (fem.)	**марокканка** (f)	[maro'kaŋka]
Moroccan (adj)	**марокканський**	[maro'kansʲkɪj]
Tunisia	**Туніс** (m)	[tu'nis]
Tunisian (masc.)	**тунісець** (m)	[tu'nisɛts]
Tunisian (fem.)	**туніска** (f)	[tu'niska]
Tunisian (adj)	**туніський**	[tu'nisʲkɪj]
Ghana	**Гана** (f)	['ɣana]
Zanzibar	**Занзібар** (m)	[zanzi'bar]
Kenya	**Кенія** (f)	['kɛnija]
Libya	**Лівія** (f)	['liwija]
Madagascar	**Мадагаскар** (m)	[madaɣas'kar]
Namibia	**Намібія** (f)	[na'mibija]
Senegal	**Сенегал** (m)	[sɛnɛ'ɣal]
Tanzania	**Танзанія** (f)	[tan'zanija]
South Africa	**Південно-Африканська Республіка** (f)	[piw'dɛŋo afrɪ'kansʲka rɛs'publika]
African (masc.)	**африканець** (m)	[afrɪ'kanɛts]
African (fem.)	**африканка** (f)	[afrɪ'kaŋka]
African (adj)	**африканський**	[afrɪ'kansʲkɪj]

241. Australia. Oceania

Australia	**Австралія** (f)	[awst'ralija]
Australian (masc.)	**австралієць** (m)	[awstra'liɛts]
Australian (fem.)	**австралійка** (f)	[awstra'lijka]
Australian (adj)	**австралійський**	[awstra'lijsʲkɪj]
New Zealand	**Нова Зеландія** (f)	[no'wa zɛ'landija]
New Zealander (masc.)	**новозеландець** (m)	[nowozɛ'landɛts]
New Zealander (fem.)	**новозеландка** (f)	[nowozɛ'landka]
New Zealand (as adj)	**новозеландський**	[nowozɛ'landsʲkɪj]
Tasmania	**Тасманія** (f)	[tas'manija]
French Polynesia	**Французька Полінезія** (f)	[fran'tsuzʲka poli'nɛzija]

242. Cities

Amsterdam	**Амстердам** (m)	[amstɛr'dam]
Ankara	**Анкара** (f)	[aŋka'ra]
Athens	**Афіни** (n)	[a'finɪ]
Baghdad	**Багдад** (m)	[baɣ'dad]
Bangkok	**Бангкок** (m)	[baŋ'kɔk]
Barcelona	**Барселона** (f)	[barsɛ'lɔna]
Beijing	**Пекін** (m)	[pɛ'kin]
Beirut	**Бейрут** (m)	['bɛjrut]
Berlin	**Берлін** (m)	[bɛr'lin]
Bombay, Mumbai	**Бомбей** (m)	[bom'bɛj]
Bonn	**Бонн** (m)	[bon]
Bordeaux	**Бордо** (n)	[bor'dɔ]
Bratislava	**Братислава** (f)	[bratɪs'lawa]
Brussels	**Брюссель** (m)	[bry'sɛʎ]
Bucharest	**Бухарест** (m)	[buha'rɛst]
Budapest	**Будапешт** (m)	[buda'pɛʃt]
Cairo	**Каїр** (m)	[ka'jɪr]
Calcutta	**Калькутта** (f)	[kaʎ'kutta]
Chicago	**Чикаго** (n)	[ʧɪ'kaɣo]
Copenhagen	**Копенгаген** (m)	[kopɛ'ŋaɣɛn]
Dar-es-Salaam	**Дар ес Салам** (m)	[dar ɛs sa'lam]
Delhi	**Делі** (n)	['dɛli]
Dubai	**Дубаї** (n)	[du'bajɪ]
Dublin	**Дублін** (m)	['dublin]
Düsseldorf	**Дюссельдорф** (m)	[dysɛʎ'dɔrf]
Florence	**Флоренція** (f)	[flo'rɛnʦija]
Frankfurt	**Франкфурт** (m)	['fraŋkfurt]
Geneva	**Женева** (f)	[ʒɛ'nɛwa]
The Hague	**Гаага** (f)	[ɣa'aɣa]
Hamburg	**Гамбург** (m)	['ɣamburɣ]
Hanoi	**Ханой** (m)	[ha'nɔj]
Havana	**Гавана** (f)	[ɣa'wana]
Helsinki	**Гельсінкі** (n)	['ɣɛʎsiŋki]
Hiroshima	**Хіросіма** (f)	[hiro'sima]
Hong Kong	**Гонконг** (m)	[ɣo'ŋkɔŋ]
Istanbul	**Стамбул** (m)	[stam'bul]
Jerusalem	**Єрусалим** (m)	[ɛrusa'lɪm]
Kiev	**Київ** (m)	[kɪ'jɪw]
Kuala Lumpur	**Куала-Лумпур** (m)	[ku'ala lum'pur]
Lisbon	**Лісабон** (m)	[lisa'bɔn]
London	**Лондон** (m)	['lɔndon]
Los Angeles	**Лос-Анджелес** (m)	[los 'andʒɛlɛs]

Lyons	**Ліон** (m)	[li'ɔn]
Madrid	**Мадрид** (m)	[mɑd'rɪd]
Marseille	**Марсель** (m)	[mar'sɛʎ]
Mexico City	**Мехіко** (n)	['mɛhiko]
Miami	**Маямі** (n)	[mɑ'jɑmi]
Montreal	**Монреаль** (m)	[monrɛ'ɑʎ]
Moscow	**Москва** (f)	[mosk'wɑ]
Munich	**Мюнхен** (m)	['mynhɛn]

Nairobi	**Найробі** (n)	[nɑj'robi]
Naples	**Неаполь** (m)	[nɛ'ɑpoʎ]
New York	**Нью-Йорк** (m)	[nju 'jork]
Nice	**Ніцца** (f)	['nitsɑ]
Oslo	**Осло** (n)	['ɔslo]
Ottawa	**Оттава** (f)	[ot'tɑwɑ]

Paris	**Париж** (m)	[pɑ'rɪʒ]
Prague	**Прага** (f)	['prɑɣɑ]
Rio de Janeiro	**Ріо-де-Жанейро** (n)	['rio dɛ ʒɑ'nɛjro]
Rome	**Рим** (m)	[rɪm]

Saint Petersburg	**Санкт-Петербург** (m)	[sɑŋkt pɛtɛr'burɣ]
Seoul	**Сеул** (m)	[sɛ'ul]
Shanghai	**Шанхай** (m)	[ʃɑn'hɑj]
Singapore	**Сінгапур** (m)	[siŋɑ'pur]
Stockholm	**Стокгольм** (m)	[stok'ɣoʎm]
Sydney	**Сідней** (m)	['sidnɛj]

Taipei	**Тайбей** (m)	[tɑj'bɛj]
Tokyo	**Токіо** (n)	['tɔkio]
Toronto	**Торонто** (n)	[to'rɔnto]

Venice	**Венеція** (f)	[wɛ'nɛtsijɑ]
Vienna	**Відень** (m)	['widɛɲ]
Warsaw	**Варшава** (f)	[war'ʃɑwɑ]
Washington	**Вашингтон** (m)	[wɑʃɪŋ'tɔn]

243. Politics. Government. Part 1

politics	**політика** (f)	[po'litkɑ]
political (adj)	**політичний**	[poli'tɪtʃnij]
politician	**політик** (m)	[po'litk]

state (country)	**держава** (f)	[dɛr'ʒɑwɑ]
citizen	**громадянин** (m)	[ɣromɑdʲɑ'nin]
citizenship	**громадянство** (n)	[ɣromɑ'dʲɑnstwo]

national emblem	**герб** (m) **національний**	[ɣɛrb nɑtsio'nɑʎnij]
national anthem	**державний гімн** (m)	[dɛr'ʒɑwnij ɣimn]
government	**уряд** (m)	['urʲɑd]

head of state	**керівник** (m) **країни**	[kɛriw'nık kra'jını]
parliament	**парламент** (m)	[par'lamɛnt]
party	**партія** (f)	['partija]
capitalism	**капіталізм** (m)	[kapita'lizm]
capitalist (adj)	**капіталістичний**	[kapitalis'tıʧnıj]
socialism	**соціалізм** (m)	[sotsia'lizm]
socialist (adj)	**соціалістичний**	[sotsialis'tıʧnıj]
communism	**комунізм** (m)	[komu'nizm]
communist (adj)	**комуністичний**	[komunis'tıʧnıj]
communist (n)	**комуніст** (m)	[komu'nist]
democracy	**демократія** (f)	[dɛmok'ratija]
democrat	**демократ** (m)	[dɛmok'rat]
democratic (adj)	**демократичний**	[dɛmokra'tıʧnıj]
Democratic party	**демократична партія** (f)	[dɛmokra'tıʧna 'partija]
liberal (n)	**ліберал** (m)	[libɛ'ral]
liberal (adj)	**ліберальний**	[libɛ'raʎnıj]
conservative (n)	**консерватор** (m)	[konsɛr'wator]
conservative (adj)	**консервативний**	[konsɛrwa'tıwnıj]
republic (n)	**республіка** (f)	[rɛs'publika]
republican (n)	**республіканець** (m)	[rɛspubli'kanɛts]
Republican party	**республіканська партія** (f)	[rɛspubli'kansɪka 'partija]
poll, elections	**вибори** (pl)	['wıborı]
to elect (vt)	**обирати**	[obı'ratı]
elector, voter	**виборець** (m)	['wıborɛts]
election campaign	**виборча компанія** (f)	['wıborʧa kom'panija]
voting (n)	**голосування** (n)	[ɣolosu'wanja]
to vote (vi)	**голосувати**	[ɣolosu'watı]
suffrage, right to vote	**право** (n) **голосу** (m)	['prawo 'ɣolosu]
candidate	**кандидат** (m)	[kandı'dat]
to be a candidate	**балотуватися**	[balotu'watısɪa]
campaign	**кампанія** (f)	[kam'panija]
opposition (as adj)	**опозиційний**	[opozı'ʦijnıj]
opposition (n)	**опозиція** (f)	[opo'zıʦija]
visit	**візит** (m)	[wi'zıt]
official visit	**офіційний візит** (m)	[ofi'ʦijnıj wi'zıt]
international (adj)	**міжнародний**	[miʒna'rodnıj]
negotiations	**переговори** (pl)	[pɛrɛɣo'worı]
to negotiate (vi)	**вести переговори**	['wɛstı pɛrɛɣo'worı]

244. Politics. Government. Part 2

society	**суспільство** (n)	[susˈpiʎstwo]
constitution	**конституція** (f)	[konstɪˈtutsɪljɑ]
power (political control)	**влада** (f)	[ˈwlɑdɑ]
corruption	**корупція** (f)	[koˈruptsijɑ]
law (justice)	**закон** (m)	[zɑˈkɔn]
legal (legitimate)	**законний**	[zɑˈkɔnɪj]
justice (fairness)	**справедливість** (f)	[sprɑwɛdˈlɪwistʲ]
just (fair)	**справедливий**	[sprɑwɛdˈlɪwɪj]
committee	**комітет** (m)	[komiˈtɛt]
bill (draft law)	**законопроект** (m)	[zɑkonoproˈɛkt]
budget	**бюджет** (m)	[byˈʤɛt]
policy	**політика** (f)	[poˈlitɪkɑ]
reform	**реформа** (f)	[rɛˈfɔrmɑ]
radical (adj)	**радикальний**	[rɑdɪˈkɑʎnɪj]
power (strength, force)	**сила** (f)	[ˈsɪlɑ]
powerful (adj)	**сильний**	[ˈsɪʎnɪj]
supporter	**прибічник** (m)	[prɪˈbiʧnɪk]
influence	**вплив** (m)	[wplɪw]
regime (e.g., military ~)	**режим** (m)	[rɛˈʒɪm]
conflict	**конфлікт** (m)	[konfˈlikt]
conspiracy (plot)	**змова** (f)	[ˈzmɔwɑ]
provocation	**провокація** (f)	[prowoˈkɑtsijɑ]
to overthrow (regime, etc.)	**скинути**	[ˈskɪnutɪ]
overthrow (of government)	**скинення** (n)	[ˈskɪnɛnjɑ]
revolution	**революція** (f)	[rɛwoˈlʲutsijɑ]
coup d'état	**переворот** (m)	[pɛrɛwoˈrɔt]
military coup	**військовий переворот** (m)	[wijsʲˈkɔwɪj pɛrɛwoˈrɔt]
crisis	**криза** (f)	[ˈkrɪzɑ]
economic recession	**економічний спад** (m)	[ɛkonoˈmiʧnɪj spɑd]
demonstrator (protester)	**демонстрант** (m)	[dɛmonstˈrɑnt]
demonstration	**демонстрація** (f)	[dɛmonstˈrɑtsijɑ]
martial law	**воєнний стан** (m)	[woˈɛnɪj stɑn]
military base	**військова база** (f)	[wijsʲˈkɔwɑ ˈbɑzɑ]
stability	**стабільність** (f)	[stɑˈbiʎnistʲ]
stable (adj)	**стабільний**	[stɑˈbiʎnɪj]
exploitation	**експлуатація** (f)	[ɛkspluɑˈtɑtsijɑ]
to exploit (workers)	**експлуатувати**	[ɛkspluɑtuˈwɑtɪ]
racism	**расизм** (m)	[rɑˈsɪzm]

racist	**расист** (m)	[rɑ'sɪst]
fascism	**фашизм** (m)	[fɑ'ʃɪzm]
fascist	**фашист** (m)	[fɑ'ʃɪst]

245. Countries. Miscellaneous

foreigner	**іноземець** (m)	[ino'zɛmɛts]
foreign (adj)	**іноземний**	[ino'zɛmnɪj]
abroad (adv)	**за кордоном**	[zɑ kor'dɔnom]

emigrant	**емігрант** (m)	[ɛmiɣ'rɑnt]
emigration	**еміграція** (f)	[ɛmiɣ'rɑtsijɑ]
to emigrate (vi)	**емігрувати**	[ɛmiɣru'wɑtɪ]

the West	**Захід** (m)	['zɑhid]
the East	**Схід** (m)	[shid]
the Far East	**Далекий Схід** (m)	[dɑ'lɛkɪj shid]

| civilization | **цивілізація** (f) | [tsɪwili'zɑtsijɑ] |
| humanity (mankind) | **людство** (n) | ['lydstwo] |

world (earth)	**світ** (m)	[swit]
peace	**мир** (m)	[mir]
worldwide (adj)	**світовий**	[swito'wɪj]

homeland	**батьківщина** (f)	[bɑtʲkiw'ɕɪnɑ]
people (population)	**народ** (m)	[nɑ'rɔd]
population	**населення** (n)	[nɑ'sɛlɛnjɑ]
people (a lot of ~)	**люди** (pl)	['lydɪ]
nation (people)	**нація** (f)	['nɑtsijɑ]
generation	**покоління** (n)	[poko'linjɑ]

territory (area)	**територія** (f)	[tɛrɪ'tɔrijɑ]
region	**регіон** (m)	[rɛɣi'ɔn]
state (part of a country)	**штат** (m)	[ʃtɑt]

tradition	**традиція** (m)	[trɑ'dɪtsijɑ]
custom (tradition)	**звичай** (m)	['zwɪtʃɑj]
ecology	**екологія** (f)	[ɛko'lɔɣijɑ]

Indian (Native American)	**індіанець** (m)	[indi'ɑnɛts]
Gipsy (masc.)	**циган** (m)	[tsɪ'ɣɑn]
Gipsy (fem.)	**циганка** (f)	[tsɪ'ɣɑŋkɑ]
Gipsy (adj)	**циганський**	[tsɪ'ɣɑnsʲkɪj]

empire	**імперія** (f)	[im'pɛrijɑ]
colony	**колонія** (f)	[ko'lɔnijɑ]
slavery	**рабство** (n)	['rɑbstwo]
invasion	**навала** (f)	[nɑ'wɑlɑ]
famine	**голодомор** (m)	[ɣolodo'mɔr]

246. Major religious groups. Confessions

religion	релігія (f)	[rɛ'liɣija]
religious (adj)	релігійний	[rɛli'ɣijnɪj]
faith, belief	віра (f)	['wira]
to believe (in God)	вірити	['wirɪtɪ]
believer	віруючий	['wirujuʧɪj]
atheism	атеїзм (m)	[atɛ'jɪzm]
atheist	атеїст (m)	[atɛ'jɪst]
Christianity	християнство (n)	[hrɪstɪ'janstwo]
Christian (n)	християнин (m)	[hrɪstɪ'janɪn]
Christian (adj)	християнський	[hrɪstɪ'jansʲkɪj]
Catholicism	Католицизм (m)	[katolɪ'ʦɪzm]
Catholic (n)	католик (m)	[ka'tolɪk]
Catholic (adj)	католицький	[kato'lɪʦkɪj]
Protestantism	Протестантство (n)	[protɛs'tanʦtwo]
Protestant Church	Протестантська церква (f)	[protɛs'tanʦʲka 'ʦɛrkwa]
Protestant	протестант (m)	[protɛs'tant]
Orthodoxy	Православ'я (n)	[prawos'lawʰja]
Orthodox Church	Православна церква (f)	[prawos'lawna 'ʦɛrkwa]
Orthodox	православний	[prawos'lawnɪj]
Presbyterianism	Пресвітеріанство (n)	[prɛswitɛri'anstwo]
Presbyterian Church	Пресвітеріанська церква (f)	[prɛswitɛri'ansʲka 'ʦɛrkwa]
Presbyterian (n)	пресвітеріанин (m)	[prɛswitɛri'anɪn]
Lutheranism	Лютеранська церква (f)	[lytɛ'ransʲka 'ʦɛrkwa]
Lutheran (n)	лютеранин (m)	[lytɛ'ranɪn]
Baptist Church	Баптизм (m)	[bap'tɪzm]
Baptist (n)	баптист (m)	[bap'tɪst]
Anglican Church	Англіканська церква (f)	[aŋli'kansʲka 'ʦɛrkwa]
Anglican (n)	англіканин (m)	[aŋli'kanɪn]
Mormonism	Мормонство (n)	[mor'mɔnstwo]
Mormon (n)	мормон (m)	[mor'mɔn]
Judaism	Іудаїзм (m)	[iuda'jɪzm]
Jew (n)	іудей (m)	[iu'dɛj]
Buddhism	Буддизм (m)	[bud'dɪzm]
Buddhist (n)	буддист (m)	[bud'dɪst]
Hinduism	Індуїзм (m)	[indu'jɪzm]

Hindu (n)	індуїст (m)	[indu'jɪst]
Islam	Іслам (m)	[is'lam]
Muslim (n)	мусульманин (m)	[musuʎ'manɪn]
Muslim (adj)	мусульманський	[musuʎ'mansʲkɪj]

Shiah Islam	Шиїзм (m)	[ʃi'jɪzm]
Shiite (n)	шиїт (m)	[ʃi'jɪt]
Sunni Islam	Сунізм (m)	[su'nizm]
Sunnite (n)	суніт (m)	[su'nit]

247. Religions. Priests

| priest | священик (m) | [swʲa'ɕɛnɪk] |
| the Pope | Папа Римський | ['papa 'rɪmsʲkɪj] |

monk, friar	чернець (m)	[tʃɛr'nɛts]
nun	черниця (f)	[tʃɛr'nɪtsʲa]
pastor	пастор (m)	['pastor]

abbot	абат (m)	[a'bat]
vicar (parish priest)	вікарій (m)	[wi'karij]
bishop	єпископ (m)	[ɛ'pɪskop]
cardinal	кардинал (m)	[kardɪ'nal]

preacher	проповідник (m)	[propo'widnɪk]
preaching	проповідь (m)	['prɔpowidʲ]
parishioners	парафіяни (pl)	[parafi'janɪ]

| believer | віруючий (m) | ['wirujutʃɪj] |
| atheist | атеїст (m) | [atɛ'jɪst] |

248. Faith. Christianity. Islam

| Adam | Адам (m) | [a'dam] |
| Eve | Єва (f) | ['ɛwa] |

God	Бог (m)	[boɣ]
the Lord	Господь (m)	[ɣos'pɔdʲ]
the Almighty	Всесильний (m)	[wsɛ'sɪʎnɪj]

sin	гріх (m)	[ɣrih]
to sin (vi)	грішити	[ɣri'ʃɪtɪ]
sinner (masc.)	грішник (m)	['ɣriʃnɪk]
sinner (fem.)	грішниця (f)	['ɣriʃnɪtsʲa]

hell	пекло (n)	['pɛklo]
paradise	рай (m)	[raj]
Jesus	Ісус (m)	[i'sus]

Jesus Christ	Ісус Христос (m)	[iˈsus hrisˈtɔs]
the Holy Spirit	Святий Дух (m)	[swʲaˈtij duh]
the Savior	Спаситель (m)	[spaˈsitɛʎ]
the Virgin Mary	Богородиця (f)	[boɣoˈrɔditsʲa]

the Devil	диявол (m)	[dɪˈjawol]
devil's (adj)	диявольський	[dɪˈjawoʎsʲkɪj]
Satan	Сатана (m)	[sataˈna]
satanic (adj)	сатанинський	[sataˈninsʲkɪj]

angel	ангел (m)	[ˈaŋɛl]
guardian angel	ангел-охоронець (m)	[ˈaŋɛl ohoˈrɔnɛts]
angelic (adj)	ангельський	[ˈaŋɛʎsʲkɪj]

apostle	апостол (m)	[aˈpɔstol]
archangel	архангел (m)	[arˈhaŋɛl]
the Antichrist	антихрист (m)	[anˈtɪhrist]

Church	церква (f)	[ˈtsɛrkwa]
Bible	Біблія (f)	[ˈbiblija]
biblical (adj)	біблійний	[bibˈlijnɪj]

Old Testament	Старий Завіт (m)	[staˈrɪj zaˈwit]
New Testament	Новий Завіт (m)	[noˈwɪj zaˈwit]
Gospel	Євангеліє (n)	[ɛˈwaŋɛliɛ]
Holy Scripture	Священне Писання (n)	[swʲaˈɕɛŋɛ pɪˈsaŋja]
heaven	Небо (n)	[ˈnɛbo]

Commandment	заповідь (f)	[ˈzapowidʲ]
prophet	пророк (m)	[proˈrɔk]
prophecy	пророцтво (n)	[proˈrɔtstwo]

Allah	Аллах (m)	[aˈlah]
Mohammed	Магомет (m)	[maɣoˈmɛt]
the Koran	Коран (m)	[koˈran]

mosque	мечеть (f)	[mɛˈʧɛtʲ]
mullah	мула (m)	[muˈla]
prayer	молитва (f)	[moˈlɪtwa]
to pray (vi, vt)	молитися	[moˈlɪtɪsʲa]

pilgrimage	паломництво (n)	[paˈlɔmnɪtstwo]
pilgrim	паломник (m)	[paˈlɔmnɪk]
Mecca	Мекка (f)	[ˈmɛkka]

church	церква (f)	[ˈtsɛrkwa]
temple	храм (m)	[hram]
cathedral	собор (m)	[soˈbɔr]
Gothic (adj)	готичний	[ɣoˈtɪʧnɪj]
synagogue	синагога (f)	[sɪnaˈɣɔɣa]
mosque	мечеть (f)	[mɛˈʧɛtʲ]
chapel	каплиця (f)	[kapˈlɪtsʲa]

abbey	**абатство** (n)	[aˈbɑtstwo]
convent	**монастир** (m)	[monɑsˈtɪr]
monastery	**монастир** (m)	[monɑsˈtɪr]
bell (in church)	**дзвін** (m)	[dzwin]
bell tower	**дзвіниця** (f)	[dzwiˈnɪtsʲɑ]
to ring (ab. bells)	**дзвонити**	[dzwoˈnɪtɪ]
cross	**хрест** (m)	[hrɛst]
cupola (roof)	**купол** (m)	[ˈkupol]
icon	**ікона** (f)	[iˈkɔnɑ]
soul	**душа** (f)	[duˈʃɑ]
fate (destiny)	**доля** (f)	[ˈdɔʎɑ]
evil (n)	**зло** (n)	[zlo]
good (n)	**добро** (n)	[dobˈrɔ]
vampire	**вампір** (m)	[wɑmˈpir]
witch (sorceress)	**відьма** (f)	[ˈwidʲmɑ]
demon	**демон** (m)	[ˈdɛmon]
devil	**чорт** (m)	[tʃort]
spirit	**дух** (m)	[duh]
redemption (giving us ~)	**спокута** (f)	[spoˈkutɑ]
to redeem (vt)	**спокутувати**	[spoˈkutuwɑtɪ]
church service, mass	**меса** (f)	[ˈmɛsɑ]
to say mass	**служити**	[sluˈʒɪtɪ]
confession	**сповідь** (f)	[ˈspowidʲ]
to confess (vi)	**сповідатися**	[spowiˈdɑtɪsʲɑ]
saint (n)	**святий** (m)	[swʲɑˈtɪj]
sacred (holy)	**священний**	[swʲɑˈɕɛɲɪj]
holy water	**свята вода** (f)	[swʲɑˈtɑ woˈdɑ]
ritual (n)	**ритуал** (m)	[rɪtuˈɑl]
ritual (adj)	**ритуальний**	[rɪtuˈɑʎnɪj]
sacrifice	**жертвування** (n)	[ˈʒɛrtwuwɑnjɑ]
superstition	**забобони** (pl)	[zaboˈbɔnɪ]
superstitious (adj)	**забобонний**	[zaboˈbɔnɪj]
afterlife	**загробне життя** (n)	[zaɣˈrɔbnɛ ʒɪtˈtʲɑ]
eternal life	**вічне життя** (n)	[ˈwitʃnɛ ʒɪtˈtʲɑ]

MISCELLANEOUS

249. Various useful words

background (green ~)	**фон** (m)	[fon]
balance (of situation)	**баланс** (m)	[ba'lans]
barrier (obstacle)	**перешкода** (f)	[pɛrɛʃ'kɔda]
base (basis)	**база** (f)	['baza]
beginning	**початок** (m)	[po'ʧatok]
category	**категорія** (f)	[katɛ'ɣorija]
cause (reason)	**причина** (f)	[prɪ'ʧɪna]
choice	**вибір** (m)	['wɪbir]
coincidence	**збіг** (m)	[zbiɣ]
comfortable (~ chair)	**зручний**	[zruʧ'nɪj]
comparison	**порівняння** (n)	[poriw'ɲaɲa]
compensation	**компенсація** (f)	[kompɛn'satsija]
degree (extent, amount)	**ступінь** (m)	['stupiɲ]
development	**розвиток** (m)	['rɔzwɪtok]
difference	**різниця** (f)	[riz'nɪtsɪa]
effect (e.g., of drugs)	**ефект** (m)	[ɛ'fɛkt]
effort (exertion)	**зусилля** (n)	[zu'sɪʎa]
element	**елемент** (m)	[ɛlɛmɛnt]
end (finish)	**закінчення** (n)	[za'kinʧɛɲa]
example (illustration)	**приклад** (m)	['prɪklad]
fact	**факт** (m)	[fakt]
frequent (adj)	**приватний**	[prɪ'watnɪj]
growth (development)	**зростання** (n)	[zros'taɲa]
help	**допомога** (f)	[dopo'mɔɣa]
ideal	**ідеал** (m)	[idɛ'al]
kind (sort, type)	**вид** (m)	[wɪd]
labyrinth	**лабіринт** (m)	[labi'rɪnt]
mistake, error	**помилка** (f)	[po'mɪlka]
moment	**момент** (m)	[mo'mɛnt]
object (thing)	**об'єкт** (m)	[obʰ'ɛkt]
obstacle	**перешкода** (f)	[pɛrɛʃ'kɔda]
original (original copy)	**оригінал** (m)	[orɪɣi'nal]
part (~ of sth)	**частина** (f)	[ʧas'tɪna]
particle, small part	**частка** (f)	['ʧastka]
pause (break)	**пауза** (f)	['pauza]

position	позиція (f)	[poˈzɪtsija]
principle	принцип (m)	[ˈprɪntsɪp]
problem	проблема (f)	[probˈlɛma]

process	процес (m)	[proˈtsɛs]
progress	прогрес (m)	[proɣˈrɛs]
property (quality)	властивість (f)	[wlasˈtɪwistʲ]
reaction	реакція (f)	[rɛˈɑktsija]
risk	ризик (m)	[ˈrɪzɪk]

secret	таємниця (f)	[taɛmˈnɪtsʲa]
section (sector)	секція (f)	[ˈsɛktsija]
series	серія (f)	[ˈsɛrija]
shape (outer form)	форма (f)	[ˈfɔrma]
situation	ситуація (f)	[sɪtuˈɑtsija]

solution	рішення (n)	[ˈriʃɛnja]
standard (adj)	стандартний	[stanˈdartnɪj]
standard (level of quality)	стандарт (m)	[stanˈdart]
stop (pause)	перерва (f)	[pɛˈrɛrwa]
style	стиль (m)	[stɪʎ]
system	система (f)	[sɪsˈtɛma]

table (chart)	таблиця (f)	[tabˈlitsʲa]
tempo, rate	темп (m)	[tɛmp]
term (word, expression)	термін (m)	[ˈtɛrmin]
thing (object, item)	річ (f)	[ritʃ]
truth	істина (f)	[ˈistɪna]
turn (please wait your ~)	черга (f)	[ˈtʃɛrɣa]
type (sort, kind)	тип (m)	[tɪp]

urgent (adj)	терміновий	[tɛrmiˈnɔwɪj]
urgently (adv)	терміново	[tɛrmiˈnɔwo]
utility (usefulness)	користь (f)	[ˈkɔrɪstʲ]

variant (alternative)	варіант (m)	[wariˈant]
way (means, method)	спосіб (m)	[ˈspɔsib]
zone	зона (f)	[ˈzɔna]

250. Modifiers. Adjectives. Part 1

additional (adj)	додатковий	[dodatˈkɔwɪj]
ancient (~ civilization)	давній	[ˈdawnij]
artificial (adj)	штучний	[ˈʃtutʃnɪj]
back, rear (adj)	задній	[ˈzadnij]
bad (adj)	поганий	[poˈɣanɪj]

beautiful (~ palace)	гарний	[ˈɣarnɪj]
beautiful (person)	гарний	[ˈɣarnɪj]
big (in size)	великий	[wɛˈlɪkɪj]

bitter (taste)	гіркий	[ɣir'kɪj]
blind (sightless)	сліпий	[sli'pɪj]
calm, quiet (adj)	спокійний	[spo'kijnɪj]
careless (negligent)	недбалий	[nɛd'balɪj]
caring (~ father)	турботливий	[tur'botlɪwɪj]
central (adj)	центральний	[ʦɛnt'raʎnɪj]
cheap (adj)	дешевий	[dɛ'ʃɛwɪj]
cheerful (adj)	веселий	[wɛ'sɛlɪj]
children's (adj)	дитячий	[dɪ'tʲatʃɪj]
civil (~ law)	громадянський	[ɣroma'dʲansʲkɪj]
clandestine (secret)	підпільний	[pid'piʎnɪj]
clean (free from dirt)	чистий	['tʃɪstɪj]
clear (explanation, etc.)	зрозумілий	[zrozu'milɪj]
clever (smart)	розумний	[ro'zumnɪj]
close (near in space)	близький	[blɪzi'kɪj]
closed (adj)	закритий	[zak'rɪtɪj]
cloudless (sky)	безхмарний	[bɛzh'marnɪj]
cold (drink, weather)	холодний	[ho'lɔdnɪj]
compatible (adj)	сумісний	[su'misnɪj]
contented (adj)	задоволений	[zado'wɔlɛnɪj]
continuous (adj)	тривалий	[trɪ'walɪj]
continuous (incessant)	безперервний	[bɛzpɛ'rɛrwnɪj]
convenient (adj)	придатний	[prɪ'datnɪj]
cool (weather)	прохолодний	[proho'lɔdnɪj]
dangerous (adj)	небезпечний	[nɛbɛz'pɛtʃnɪj]
dark (room)	темний	['tɛmnɪj]
dead (not alive)	мертвий	['mɛrtwɪj]
dense (fog, smoke)	щільний	['ɕiʎnɪj]
difficult (decision)	важкий	[waʒ'kɪj]
difficult (problem, task)	складний	[sklad'nɪj]
dim, faint (light)	тьмяний	['tʲmʲanɪj]
dirty (not clean)	брудний	[brud'nɪj]
distant (faraway)	далекий	[da'lɛkɪj]
distant (in space)	далекий	[da'lɛkɪj]
dry (clothes, etc.)	сухий	[su'hɪj]
easy (not difficult)	легкий	[lɛɣ'kɪj]
empty (glass, room)	пустий	[pus'tɪj]
exact (amount)	точний	['tɔtʃnɪj]
excellent (adj)	добрий	['dɔbrɪj]
excessive (adj)	надмірний	[nad'mirnɪj]
expensive (adj)	дорогий	[doro'ɣɪj]
exterior (adj)	зовнішній	['zɔwniʃnij]
fast (quick)	швидкий	[ʃwɪd'kɪj]

fatty (food)	**жирний**	['ʒɪrnɪj]
fertile (land, soil)	**родючий**	[ro'dytʃɪj]
flat (~ panel display)	**плаский**	['plaskɪj]
even (e.g., ~ surface)	**рівний**	['riwnɪj]
foreign (adj)	**іноземний**	[ino'zɛmnɪj]
fragile (china, glass)	**крихкий**	[krɪh'kɪj]
free (at no cost)	**безкоштовний**	[bɛzkoʃ'townɪj]
free (unrestricted)	**вільний**	['wiʎnɪj]
fresh (~ water)	**прісний**	['prisnɪj]
fresh (e.g., ~ bread)	**свіжий**	['swiʒɪj]
frozen (food)	**заморожений**	[zamo'roʒɛnɪj]
full (completely filled)	**повний**	['pownɪj]
good (book, etc.)	**хороший**	[ho'roʃɪj]
good (kindhearted)	**добрий**	['dobrɪj]
grateful (adj)	**вдячний**	['wdʲatʃnɪj]
happy (adj)	**щасливий**	[ɕas'lɪwɪj]
hard (not soft)	**твердий**	[twɛr'dɪj]
heavy (in weight)	**важкий**	[waʒ'kɪj]
hostile (adj)	**ворожий**	[wo'roʒɪj]
hot (adj)	**гарячий**	[ɣa'rʲatʃɪj]
huge (adj)	**величезний**	[wɛlɪ'tʃɛznɪj]
humid (adj)	**вологий**	[wo'lɔɣɪj]
hungry (adj)	**голодний**	[ɣo'lɔdnɪj]
ill (sick, unwell)	**хворий**	['hwɔrɪj]
immobile (adj)	**нерухомий**	[nɛru'hɔmɪj]
important (adj)	**важливий**	[waʒ'lɪwɪj]
impossible (adj)	**неможливий**	[nɛmoʒ'lɪwɪj]
incomprehensible	**незрозумілий**	[nɛzrozu'milɪj]
indispensable (adj)	**необхідний**	[nɛob'hidnɪj]
inexperienced (adj)	**недосвідчений**	[nɛdos'widtʃɛnɪj]
insignificant (adj)	**незначний**	[nɛznatʃ'nɪj]
interior (adj)	**внутрішній**	['wnutriʃnɪj]
joint (~ decision)	**спільний**	['spiʎnɪj]
last (e.g., ~ week)	**минулий**	[mɪ'nulɪj]
last (final)	**останній**	[os'tanɪj]
left (e.g., ~ side)	**лівий**	['liwɪj]
legal (legitimate)	**законний**	[za'kɔnɪj]
light (in weight)	**легкий**	[lɛɣ'kɪj]
light (pale color)	**світлий**	['switlɪj]
limited (adj)	**обмежений**	[ob'mɛʒɛnɪj]
liquid (fluid)	**рідкий**	[rid'kɪj]
long (e.g., ~ way)	**довгий**	['dɔwɣɪj]
loud (voice, etc.)	**гучний**	[ɣutʃ'nɪj]
low (voice)	**тихий**	['tɪhɪj]

251. Modifiers. Adjectives. Part 2

main (principal)	головний	[ɣolow'nɪj]
matt (paint)	матовий	['matowɪj]
meticulous (job)	охайний	[o'hajnɪj]
mysterious (adj)	загадковий	[zaɣad'kɔwɪj]
narrow (street, etc.)	вузький	[wuzʲ'kɪj]
native (of country)	рідний	['ridnɪj]
nearby (adj)	ближній	['blɪʒnij]
near-sighted (adj)	короткозорий	[korotko'zɔrɪj]
necessary (adj)	потрібний	[pot'ribnɪj]
negative (~ response)	негативний	[nɛɣa'tɪwnɪj]
neighboring (adj)	сусідній	[su'sidnij]
nervous (adj)	нервовий	[nɛr'wɔwɪj]
new (adj)	новий	[no'wɪj]
next (e.g., ~ week)	наступний	[nas'tupnɪj]
nice (kind)	милий	['mɪlɪj]
nice (voice)	приємний	[prɪ'ɛmnɪj]
normal (adj)	нормальний	[nor'maʎnɪj]
not big (adj)	невеликий	[nɛwɛ'lɪkɪj]
unclear (adj)	неясний	[nɛ'jasnɪj]
not difficult (adj)	неважкий	[nɛwaʒ'kɪj]
obligatory (adj)	обов'язковий	[obowʲjaz'kɔwɪj]
old (house)	старий	[sta'rɪj]
open (adj)	відкритий	[widk'rɪtɪj]
opposite (adj)	протилежний	[protɪ'lɛʒnɪj]
ordinary (usual)	звичайний	[zwɪ'ʧajnɪj]
original (unusual)	оригінальний	[orɪɣi'naʎnɪj]
past (recent)	минулий	[mɪ'nulɪj]
permanent (adj)	постійний	[pos'tijnɪj]
personal (adj)	персональний	[pɛrso'naʎnɪj]
polite (adj)	ввічливий	['wwiʧlɪwɪj]
poor (not rich)	бідний	['bidnɪj]
possible (adj)	можливий	[moʒ'lɪwɪj]
destitute (extremely poor)	жебрак (m)	[ʒɛb'rak]
present (current)	справжній	['sprawʒnij]
principal (main)	основний	[osnow'nɪj]
private (~ jet)	особистий	[oso'bɪstɪj]
probable (adj)	імовірний	[imo'wirnɪj]
public (open to all)	громадський	[ɣro'madsʲkɪj]
punctual (person)	пунктуальний	[puŋktu'aʎnɪj]
quiet (tranquil)	тихий	['tɪhɪj]
rare (adj)	рідкісний	['ridkisnɪj]

raw (uncooked)	сирий	[sı'rıj]
right (not left)	правий	['prawıj]
right, correct (adj)	вірний	['wirnıj]

ripe (fruit)	дозрілий	[doz'rilıj]
risky (adj)	ризикований	[rızı'kowanıj]
sad (~ look)	сумний	[sum'nıj]
sad (depressing)	сумний	[sum'nıj]
safe (not dangerous)	безпечний	[bɛz'pɛtʃnıj]

salty (food)	солоний	[so'lɔnıj]
satisfied (customer)	задоволений	[zado'wɔlɛnıj]
second hand (adj)	уживаний	[u'ʒıwanıj]
shallow (water)	мілкий	[mil'kıj]

sharp (blade, etc.)	гострий	['ɣɔstrıj]
short (in length)	короткий	[ko'rɔtkıj]
short, short-lived (adj)	короткочасний	[korotko'tʃasnıj]
significant (notable)	значний	[znatʃ'nıj]
similar (adj)	схожий	['shɔʒıj]

simple (easy)	простий	[pros'tıj]
skinny	худий	[hu'dıj]
thin (person)	худий	[hu'dıj]

smooth (surface)	гладкий	['ɣladkıj]
soft (to touch)	м'який	[mʰja'kıj]
solid (~ wall)	міцний	[mits'nıj]
somber, gloomy (adj)	похмурий	[poh'murıj]
sour (flavor, taste)	кислий	['kıslıj]

spacious (house, etc.)	просторий	[pros'tɔrıj]
special (adj)	спеціальний	[spɛtsi'aʎnıj]
straight (line, road)	прямий	[prʲa'mıj]
strong (person)	сильний	['sıʎnıj]

stupid (foolish)	дурний	[dur'nıj]
sunny (day)	сонячний	['sɔnatʃnıj]
superb, perfect (adj)	чудовий	[tʃu'dowıj]
swarthy (adj)	смаглявий	[smaɣ'ʎawıj]
sweet (sugary)	солодкий	[so'lɔdkıj]

tan (adj)	засмаглий	[zas'maɣlıj]
tasty (adj)	смачний	[smatʃ'nıj]
tender (affectionate)	ніжний	['niʒnıj]
the highest (adj)	вищий	['wıɕıj]

the most important	найважливіший	[najwaʒlı'wiʃıj]
the nearest	найближчий	[najb'lıʒtʃıj]
the same, equal (adj)	однаковий	[od'nakowıj]
thick (e.g., ~ fog)	густий	[ɣus'tıj]
thick (wall, slice)	товстий	[tows'tıj]

tired (exhausted)	**втомлений**	[ˈwtɔmlɛnɪj]
tiring (adj)	**утомливий**	[uˈtɔmlɪwɪj]
transparent (adj)	**прозорий**	[prɔˈzɔrɪj]
unique (exceptional)	**унікальний**	[uniˈkɑʎnɪj]
warm (moderately hot)	**теплий**	[ˈtɛplɪj]
wet (e.g., ~ clothes)	**мокрий**	[ˈmɔkrɪj]
whole (entire, complete)	**цілий**	[tsiˈlɪj]
wide (e.g., ~ road)	**широкий**	[ʃɪˈrɔkɪj]
young (adj)	**молодий**	[moloˈdɪj]

MAIN 500 VERBS

252. Verbs A-C

to accompany (vt)	супроводжувати	[supro'wodʒuwatɪ]
to accuse (vt)	звинувачувати	[zwɪnu'watʃuwatɪ]
to acknowledge (admit)	визнавати	[wɪzna'watɪ]
to act (take action)	діяти	['dijatɪ]
to add (supplement)	додавати	[doda'watɪ]
to address (speak to)	звертатися	[zwɛr'tatɪsʲa]
to admire (vi)	захоплюватися	[za'hoplywatɪsʲa]
to advertise (vt)	рекламувати	[rɛklamu'watɪ]
to advise (vt)	радити	['radɪtɪ]
to affirm (insist)	стверджувати	['stwɛrdʒuwatɪ]
to agree (say yes)	погоджуватися	[po'ɣodʒuwatɪsʲa]
to allow (sb to do sth)	дозволяти	[dozwo'ʎatɪ]
to allude (vi)	натякати	[natʲa'katɪ]
to amputate (vt)	ампутувати	[amputu'watɪ]
to answer (vi, vt)	відповідати	[widpowi'datɪ]
to apologize (vi)	вибачатися	[wɪba'tʃatɪsʲa]
to appear (come into view)	з'являтися	[zʰjaw'ʎatɪsʲa]
to applaud (vi, vt)	аплодувати	[aplodu'watɪ]
to appoint (assign)	призначати	[prɪzna'tʃatɪ]
to approach (come closer)	підходити	[pid'hodɪtɪ]
to arrive (ab. train)	прибувати	[prɪbu'watɪ]
to ask (~ sb to do sth)	просити	[pro'sɪtɪ]
to aspire to …	прагнути	['praɣnutɪ]
to assist (help)	асистувати	[asɪstu'watɪ]
to attack (mil.)	атакувати	[ataku'watɪ]
to attain (objectives)	досягати	[dosʲa'ɣatɪ]
to revenge (vt)	мстити	['mstɪtɪ]
to avoid (danger, task)	уникати	[unɪ'katɪ]
to award (give medal to)	нагородити	[naɣo'rodɪtɪ]
to battle (vi)	битися	['bɪtɪsʲa]
to be (~ on the table)	лежати	[lɛ'ʒatɪ]
to be (vi)	бути	['butɪ]
to be afraid	боятися	[bo'jatɪsʲa]
to be angry (with …)	гніватися	['ɣniwatɪsʲa]

to be at war	воювати	[wɔju'watɪ]
to be based (on …)	базуватися	[bazu'watɪsʲa]
to be bored	нудьгувати	[nudʲɣu'watɪ]
to be convinced	переконуватися	[pɛrɛ'kɔnuwatɪsʲa]
to be enough	вистачати	[wɪsta'ʧatɪ]
to be envious	заздрити	['zazdrɪtɪ]
to be indignant	обурюватися	[o'burywatɪsʲa]
to be interested in …	цікавитися	[tsi'kawɪtɪsʲa]
to be lying down	лежати	[lɛ'ʒatɪ]
to be needed	бути потрібним	['butɪ pot'ribnɪm]
to be perplexed	не розуміти	[nɛ rozu'mitɪ]
to be preserved	зберігатися	[zbɛri'ɣatɪsʲa]
to be required	бути необхідним	['butɪ nɛob'hidnɪm]
to be surprised	дивуватись	[dɪwu'watɪsʲ]
to be worried	хвилюватися	[hwɪlʲu'watɪsʲa]
to beat (dog, person)	бити	['bɪtɪ]
to become (e.g., ~ old)	ставати	[sta'watɪ]
to become pensive	замислитися	[za'mɪslɪtɪsʲa]
to behave (vi)	поводитися	[po'wɔdɪtɪsʲa]
to believe (think)	вірити	['wirɪtɪ]
to belong to …	належати	[na'lɛʒatɪ]
to berth (moor)	причалювати	[prɪ'ʧalywatɪ]
to blind (other drivers)	осліплювати	[os'liplywatɪ]
to blow (wind)	дути	['dutɪ]
to blush (vi)	червоніти	[ʧɛrwo'nitɪ]
to boast (vi)	хвастатися	['hwastatɪsʲa]
to borrow (money)	позичати	[pozɪ'ʧatɪ]
to break (branch, toy, etc.)	ламати	[la'matɪ]
to breathe (vi)	дихати	['dɪhatɪ]
to bring (sth)	привозити	[prɪ'wɔzɪtɪ]
to burn (paper, logs)	палити	[pa'lɪtɪ]
to buy (purchase)	купляти	[kup'ʎatɪ]
to call (for help)	кликати	['klɪkatɪ]
to call (with one's voice)	покликати	[pok'lɪkatɪ]
to calm down (vt)	заспокоювати	[zaspo'kɔjuwatɪ]
can (v aux)	могти	[moɣ'tɪ]
to cancel (call off)	скасувати	[skasu'watɪ]
to cast off	відчалювати	[wid'ʧalywatɪ]
to catch (e.g., ~ a ball)	ловити	[lo'wɪtɪ]
to catch sight (of …)	побачити	[po'baʧɪtɪ]
to cause …	бути причиною	['butɪ prɪ'ʧɪnoju]
to change (~ one's opinion)	поміняти	[pomi'ɲatɪ]
to change (exchange)	міняти	[mi'ɲatɪ]
to charm (vt)	зачаровувати	[zaʧa'rɔwuwatɪ]

to choose (select)	вибирати	[wɪbɪˈratɪ]
to chop off (with an ax)	відрубати	[wɪdruˈbatɪ]
to clean (from dirt)	чистити	[ˈʧɪstɪtɪ]
to clean (shoes, etc.)	очищати	[oʧɪˈɕatɪ]
to clean (tidy)	прибирати	[prɪbɪˈratɪ]
to close (vt)	закривати	[zakrɪˈwatɪ]
to comb one's hair	причісувати	[prɪˈʧisuwatɪ]
to come down (the stairs)	спускатися	[spusˈkatɪsʲa]
to come in (enter)	увійти	[uwijˈtɪ]
to come out (book)	вийти	[ˈwɪjtɪ]
to compare (vt)	зрівнювати	[ˈzriwnywatɪ]
to compensate (vt)	компенсувати	[kompɛnsuˈwatɪ]
to compete (vi)	конкурувати	[koŋkuruˈwatɪ]
to compile (~ a list)	складати	[sklaˈdatɪ]
to complain (vi, vt)	скаржитися	[ˈskarʒɪtɪsʲa]
to complicate (vt)	ускладнювати	[uskˈladnywatɪ]
to compose (music, etc.)	створити	[stwoˈritɪ]
to compromise (reputation)	компрометувати	[komprometuˈwatɪ]
to concentrate (vi)	концентруватися	[konʦɛntruˈwatɪsʲa]
to confess (criminal)	признаватися	[prɪznaˈwatɪsʲa]
to confuse (mix up)	помилятися	[pomɪˈʎatɪsʲa]
to congratulate (vt)	вітати	[wiˈtatɪ]
to consult (doctor, expert)	консультуватися з …	[konsuʎtuˈwatɪsʲa z]
to continue (~ to do sth)	продовжувати	[proˈdɔwʒuwatɪ]
to control (vt)	контролювати	[kontroˈlywatɪ]
to convince (vt)	переконувати	[pɛrɛˈkɔnuwatɪ]
to cooperate (vi)	співробітничати	[spiwroˈbitnɪʧatɪ]
to coordinate (vt)	координувати	[koːrdɪnuˈwatɪ]
to correct (an error)	виправляти	[wɪprawˈʎatɪ]
to cost (vt)	коштувати	[ˈkɔʃtuwatɪ]
to count (money, etc.)	лічити	[liˈʧitɪ]
to count on …	розраховувати на …	[rozraˈhɔwuwatɪ na]
to crack (ceiling, wall)	тріскатися	[ˈtriskatɪsʲa]
to create (vt)	створити	[stwoˈritɪ]
to cry (weep)	плакати	[ˈplakatɪ]
to cut off (with a knife)	відрізати	[wɪdriˈzatɪ]

253. Verbs D-G

to dare (~ to do sth)	насмілюватися	[nasˈmilywatɪsʲa]
to date from …	датуватися	[datuˈwatɪsʲa]
to deceive (vi, vt)	обманювати	[obˈmanywatɪ]

to decide (~ to do sth)	**вирішувати**	[wɪ'riʃuwatɪ]
to decorate (tree, street)	**прикрашати**	[prɪkra'ʃatɪ]
to dedicate (book, etc.)	**присвячувати**	[prɪs'wiɑtʃuwatɪ]
to defend (a country, etc.)	**захищати**	[zahɪ'ɕatɪ]
to defend oneself	**захищатись**	[zahɪ'ɕatɪsʲ]
to demand (request firmly)	**вимагати**	[wɪma'ɣatɪ]
to denounce (vt)	**доносити**	[do'nɔsɪtɪ]
to deny (vt)	**заперечувати**	[zapɛ'rɛtʃuwatɪ]
to depend on …	**залежати**	[za'lɛʒatɪ]
to deprive (vt)	**позбавляти**	[pozbaw'ʎatɪ]
to deserve (vt)	**заслуговувати**	[zaslu'ɣɔwuwatɪ]
to design (machine, etc.)	**проектувати**	[proɛktu'watɪ]
to desire (want, wish)	**бажати**	[ba'ʒatɪ]
to despise (vt)	**зневажати**	[znɛwa'ʒatɪ]
to destroy (documents, etc.)	**знищувати**	['znɪɕuwatɪ]
to differ (from sth)	**відрізнятися**	[widriz'ɲatɪsʲa]
to dig (tunnel, etc.)	**рити**	['rɪtɪ]
to direct (point the way)	**направляти**	[napraw'ʎatɪ]
to disappear (vi)	**зникнути**	['znɪknutɪ]
to discover (new land, etc.)	**відкривати**	[widkrɪ'watɪ]
to discuss (vt)	**обговорювати**	[obɣo'wɔrywatɪ]
to distribute (leaflets, etc.)	**поширювати**	[po'ʃɪrywatɪ]
to disturb (vt)	**заважати**	[zawa'ʒatɪ]
to dive (vi)	**пірнати**	[pir'natɪ]
to divide (math)	**ділити**	[di'lɪtɪ]
to do (vt)	**робити**	[ro'bɪtɪ]
to do the laundry	**прати**	['pratɪ]
to double (increase)	**подвоювати**	[pod'wɔjuwatɪ]
to doubt (have doubts)	**сумніватися**	[sumni'watɪsʲa]
to draw a conclusion	**робити висновок**	[ro'bɪtɪ 'wɪsnowok]
to dream (daydream)	**мріяти**	['mrijatɪ]
to dream (in sleep)	**бачити сни**	['batʃɪtɪ snɪ]
to drink (vi, vt)	**пити**	['pɪtɪ]
to drive a car	**вести машину**	['wɛstɪ ma'ʃɪnu]
to drive away (scare away)	**прогнати**	[proɣ'natɪ]
to drop (let fall)	**упускати**	[upus'katɪ]
to drown (ab. person)	**тонути**	[to'nutɪ]
to dry (clothes, hair)	**сушити**	[su'ʃɪtɪ]
to eat (vi, vt)	**їсти**	['jistɪ]
to eavesdrop (vi)	**підслухати**	[pids'luhatɪ]
to emit (give out - odor, etc.)	**наповнювати запахом**	[na'pɔwnywatɪ 'zapahom]
to enter (on the list)	**уписувати**	[u'pɪsuwatɪ]

to entertain (amuse)	розважати	[rozwaˈʒatɪ]
to equip (fit out)	обладнати	[obladˈnatɪ]
to examine (proposal)	розглянути	[rozɣˈʎanutɪ]
to exchange (sth)	обмінюватися	[obˈminywatɪsʲa]

to exclude, to expel	виключати	[wɪklyˈʧatɪ]
to excuse (forgive)	вибачати	[wɪbaˈʧatɪ]
to exist (vi)	існувати	[isnuˈwatɪ]
to expect (anticipate)	очікувати	[oˈʧikuwatɪ]
to expect (foresee)	передбачити	[pɛrɛdˈbatʃitɪ]

to explain (vt)	пояснювати	[poˈjasnywatɪ]
to express (vt)	виразити	[ˈwɪrazɪtɪ]
to extinguish (a fire)	тушити	[tuˈʃitɪ]
to fall in love (with …)	закохатися	[zakoˈhatɪsʲa]

to feed (provide food)	годувати	[ɣoduˈwatɪ]
to fight (against the enemy)	боротися	[boˈrɔtɪsʲa]
to fight (vi)	битися	[ˈbɪtɪsʲa]
to fill (glass, bottle)	наповнювати	[naˈpownywatɪ]
to find (~ lost items)	знаходити	[znaˈhɔdɪtɪ]

to finish (vt)	закінчувати	[zaˈkinʧuwatɪ]
to fish (angle)	ловити рибу	[loˈwɪtɪ ˈrɪbu]
to fit (ab. dress, etc.)	пасувати	[pasuˈwatɪ]
to flatter (vt)	лестити	[ˈlɛstɪtɪ]

to fly (bird, plane)	літати	[liˈtatɪ]
to follow … (come after)	іти слідом	[iˈtɪ ˈslidom]
to forbid (vt)	забороняти	[zaboroˈɲatɪ]
to force (compel)	примушувати	[prɪˈmuʃuwatɪ]
to forget (vi, vt)	забувати	[zabuˈwatɪ]

to forgive (pardon)	прощати	[proˈɕatɪ]
to form (constitute)	складати	[sklaˈdatɪ]
to get dirty (vi)	забруднитися	[zabrudˈnɪtɪsʲa]
to get infected (with …)	заразитися	[zaraˈzɪtɪsʲa]

to get irritated	дратуватися	[dratuˈwatɪsʲa]
to get married	одружуватися	[odˈruʒuwatɪsʲa]
to get rid of …	позбавлятися	[pozbawˈʎatɪsʲa]
to get tired	втомлюватися	[ˈwtomlywatɪsʲa]
to get up (arise from bed)	підводитися	[pidˈwɔdɪtɪsʲa]

to give (vt)	давати	[daˈwatɪ]
to give a bath	купати	[kuˈpatɪ]
to give a hug, to hug (vt)	обіймати	[obijˈmatɪ]
to give in (yield to)	поступатися	[postuˈpatɪsʲa]

| to go (by car, etc.) | їхати | [ˈjihatɪ] |
| to go (on foot) | йти | [jtɪ] |

to go for a swim	купатися	[ku'patɪsʲa]
to go out (for dinner, etc.)	вийти	['wɪjtɪ]
to go to bed	лягати спати	[ʎa'ɣatɪ 'spatɪ]

to greet (vt)	вітати	[wi'tatɪ]
to grow (plants)	вирощувати	[wɪ'rɔɕuwatɪ]
to guarantee (vt)	гарантувати	[ɣarantu'watɪ]
to guess right	відгадати	[widɣa'datɪ]

254. Verbs H-M

to hand out (distribute)	роздати	[roz'datɪ]
to hang (curtains, etc.)	вішати	['wiʃatɪ]
to have (vt)	мати	['matɪ]
to have a try	спробувати	['sprɔbuwatɪ]
to have breakfast	снідати	['snidatɪ]

to have dinner	вечеряти	[wɛ'ʧɛrʲatɪ]
to have fun	веселитися	[wɛsɛ'lɪtɪsʲa]
to have lunch	обідати	[o'bidatɪ]
to head (group, etc.)	очолювати	[o'ʧɔlywatɪ]

to hear (vt)	чути	['ʧutɪ]
to heat (vt)	нагрівати	[naɣri'watɪ]
to help (vt)	допомагати	[dopoma'ɣatɪ]
to hide (vt)	ховати	[ho'watɪ]
to hire (e.g., ~ a boat)	наймати	[naj'matɪ]

to hire (staff)	наймати	[naj'matɪ]
to hope (vi, vt)	сподіватися	[spodi'watɪsʲa]
to hunt (for food, sport)	полювати	[poly'watɪ]
to hurry (sb)	квапити	['kwapɪtɪ]

to hurry (vi)	поспішати	[pospi'ʃatɪ]
to imagine (to picture)	уявляти собі	[ujaw'ʎatɪ so'bi]
to imitate (vt)	імітувати	[imitu'watɪ]
to implore (vt)	благати	[bla'ɣatɪ]
to import (vt)	імпортувати	[importu'watɪ]

to increase (vi)	збільшуватися	['zbiʎʃuwatɪsʲa]
to increase (vt)	збільшувати	['zbiʎʃuwatɪ]
to infect (vt)	заражати	[zara'ʒatɪ]
to influence (vt)	впливати	[wplɪ'watɪ]

to inform (~ sb about ...)	повідомляти	[powidom'ʎatɪ]
to inform (vt)	інформувати	[informu'watɪ]
to inherit (vt)	успадкувати	[uspadku'watɪ]
to inquire (about ...)	довідуватись	[do'widuwatɪsʲ]
to insist (vi, vt)	наполягати	[napoʎa'ɣatɪ]
to inspire (vt)	надихати	[ujaw'ʎatɪ]

to instruct (teach)	інструктувати	[instruktu'watı]
to insult (offend)	ображати	[obra'ʒatı]
to interest (vt)	цікавити	[ʦi'kawıtı]
to intervene (vi)	втручатися	[wtru'ʧatısʲa]
to introduce (present)	знайомити	[zna'jomıtı]
to invent (machine, etc.)	винаходити	[wına'hodıtı]
to invite (vt)	запрошувати	[zap'roʃuwatı]
to iron (laundry)	прасувати	[prasu'watı]
to irritate (annoy)	дратувати	[dratu'watı]
to isolate (vt)	ізолювати	[izoly'watı]
to join (political party, etc.)	приєднуватися	[prı'ɛdnuwatısʲa]
to joke (be kidding)	жартувати	[ʒartu'watı]
to keep (old letters, etc.)	зберігати	[zbɛri'ɣatı]
to keep silent	мовчати	[mow'ʧatı]
to kill (vt)	убивати	[ubı'watı]
to knock (at the door)	стукати	['stukatı]
to know (sb)	знати	['znatı]
to know (sth)	знати	['znatı]
to laugh (vi)	сміятися	[smi'jatısʲa]
to launch (start up)	запускати	[zapus'katı]
to leave (~ for Mexico)	їхати	['jihatı]
to leave (spouse)	покидати	[pokı'datı]
to leave behind (forget)	залишати	[zalı'ʃatı]
to liberate (city, etc.)	звільняти	[zwiʎ'ɲatı]
to lie (tell untruth)	брехати	[brɛ'hatı]
to light (campfire, etc.)	запалити	[zapa'lıtı]
to light up (illuminate)	освітлювати	[os'witlywatı]
to love (e.g., ~ dancing)	любити	[ly'bıtı]
to like (I like ...)	подобатися	[po'dobatısʲa]
to limit (vt)	обмежувати	[ob'mɛʒuwatı]
to listen (vi)	слухати	['sluhatı]
to live (~ in France)	проживати	[proʒı'watı]
to live (exist)	існувати	[isnu'watı]
to load (gun)	заряджати	[zarʲa'ʤatı]
to load (vehicle, etc.)	вантажити	[wan'taʒıtı]
to look (I'm just ~ing)	дивитися	[dı'wıtısʲa]
to look for ... (search)	шукати	[ʃu'katı]
to look like (resemble)	бути схожим	['butı 'shoʒım]
to lose (umbrella, etc.)	губити	[ɣu'bıtı]
to love (sb)	кохати	[ko'hatı]
to lower (blind, head)	опускати	[opus'katı]
to make (~ dinner)	готувати	[ɣotu'watı]
to make a mistake	помилятися	[pomı'ʎatısʲa]

to make angry	гнівити	[ɣni'wɪtɪ]
to make copies	розмножити	[rozm'nɔʒɪtɪ]
to make easier	полегшити	[po'lɛɣʃɪtɪ]
to make the acquaintance	знайомитися	[zna'jɔmɪtɪsʲa]
to make use (of …)	користуватися	[korɪstu'watɪsʲa]

to manage, to run	керувати	[kɛru'watɪ]
to mark (make a mark)	зазначити	[zaz'natʃɪtɪ]
to mean (signify)	значити	['znatʃɪtɪ]
to memorize (vt)	запам'ятати	[zapamʰja'tatɪ]
to mention (talk about)	згадувати	['zɣaduwatɪ]

to miss (school, etc.)	пропускати	[propus'katɪ]
to mix (combine, blend)	змішувати	['zmiʃuwatɪ]
to mock (make fun of)	насміхатися	[nasmi'hatɪsʲa]
to move (to shift)	пересувати	[pɛrɛsu'watɪ]
to multiply (math)	множити	['mnɔʒɪtɪ]
must (v aux)	бути винним	['butɪ 'wɪŋɪm]

255. Verbs N-S

to name, to call (vt)	називати	[nazɪ'watɪ]
to negotiate (vi)	вести переговори	['wɛstɪ pɛrɛɣo'wɔrɪ]
to note (write down)	позначити	[poz'natʃɪtɪ]
to notice (see)	помічати	[pomi'tʃatɪ]

to obey (vi, vt)	підкорятися	[pidko'rʲatɪsʲa]
to object (vi, vt)	заперечувати	[zapɛ'rɛtʃuwatɪ]
to observe (see)	спостерігати	[spostɛri'ɣatɪ]
to offend (vt)	ображати	[obra'ʒatɪ]
to omit (word, phrase)	пропускати	[propus'katɪ]

to open (vt)	відчинити	[widtʃɪ'nɪtɪ]
to order (in restaurant)	замовляти	[zamow'ʎatɪ]
to order (mil.)	наказувати	[na'kazuwatɪ]
to organize (concert, party)	організовувати	[orɣani'zɔwuwatɪ]

to overestimate (vt)	переоцінювати	[pɛrɛo'ʦinywatɪ]
to own (possess)	володіти	[wolo'ditɪ]
to participate (vi)	брати участь	['bratɪ 'utʃastʲ]
to pass (go beyond)	минути	[mɪ'nutɪ]
to pay (vi, vt)	платити	[pla'tɪtɪ]

to peep, spy on	підглядати	[pidɣʎa'datɪ]
to penetrate (vt)	проникати	[pronɪ'katɪ]
to permit (vt)	дозволяти	[dozwo'ʎatɪ]
to pick (flowers)	рвати	['rwatɪ]

| to place (put, set) | розташовувати | [rozta'ʃowuwatɪ] |
| to plan (~ to do sth) | планувати | [planu'watɪ] |

to play (actor)	грати	[ˈɣratɪ]
to play (children)	грати	[ˈɣratɪ]
to point (~ the way)	указати	[ukaˈzatɪ]

to pour (liquid)	наливати	[nalɪˈwatɪ]
to pray (vi, vt)	молитися	[moˈlɪtɪsʲa]
to predominate (vi)	переважати	[pɛrɛwaˈʒatɪ]
to prefer (vt)	воліти	[woˈlitɪ]

to prepare (~ a plan)	підготувати	[pidɣotuˈwatɪ]
to present (sb to sb)	рекомендувати	[rɛkomɛnduˈwatɪ]
to preserve (peace, life)	зберігати	[zbɛriˈɣatɪ]
to progress (move forward)	просуватися	[prosuˈwatɪsʲa]
to promise (vt)	обіцяти	[obiˈtsʲatɪ]

to pronounce (vt)	вимовляти	[wɪmowˈʎatɪ]
to propose (vt)	пропонувати	[proponuˈwatɪ]
to protect (e.g., ~ nature)	охороняти	[ohoroˈɲatɪ]
to protest (vi)	протестувати	[protɛstuˈwatɪ]

to prove (vt)	доводити	[doˈwɔdɪtɪ]
to provoke (vt)	провокувати	[prowokuˈwatɪ]
to pull (~ the rope)	тягти	[tʲaɣˈtɪ]
to punish (vt)	покарати	[pokaˈratɪ]
to push (~ the door)	штовхати	[ʃtowˈhatɪ]

to put away (vt)	сховати	[shoˈwatɪ]
to put in (insert)	вставляти	[wstawˈʎatɪ]
to put in order	привести до ладу	[prɪˈwɛstɪ do ˈladu]
to put, to place	класти	[ˈklastɪ]

to quote (cite)	цитувати	[tsɪtuˈwatɪ]
to reach (arrive at)	досягати	[dosʲaˈɣatɪ]
to read (vi, vt)	читати	[tʃɪˈtatɪ]
to realize (a dream)	здійснювати	[ˈzdijsnywatɪ]
to recall (~ one's name)	згадувати	[ˈzɣaduwatɪ]

to recognize (identify sb)	узнавати	[uznaˈwatɪ]
to recommend (vt)	рекомендувати	[rɛkomɛnduˈwatɪ]
to recover (~ from flu)	видужувати	[wɪˈduʒuwatɪ]
to redo (do again)	переробляти	[pɛrɛrobˈʎatɪ]

to reduce (speed, etc.)	зменшувати	[ˈzmɛnʃuwatɪ]
to refuse (~ sb)	відмовляти	[widmowˈʎatɪ]
to regret (be sorry)	жалкувати	[ʒalkuˈwatɪ]
to reinforce (vt)	зміцнювати	[ˈzmitsnywatɪ]
to remember (vt)	пам'ятати	[pamʲjaˈtatɪ]

to remind of …	нагадувати	[naˈɣaduwatɪ]
to remove (~ a stain)	виводити	[wɪˈwɔdɪtɪ]
to remove (~ an obstacle)	усувати	[usuˈwatɪ]

to rent (sth from sb)	**наймати**	[naj'matı]
to repair (mend)	**ремонтувати**	[rɛmontu'watı]
to repeat (say again)	**повторювати**	[pow'torywatı]
to report (make a report)	**доповідати**	[dopowi'datı]
to reproach (vt)	**докоряти**	[doko'rʲatı]
to reserve, to book	**бронювати**	[brony'watı]

to restrain (hold back)	**утримувати**	[ut'rımuwatı]
to return (come back)	**повертатися**	[powɛr'tatısʲa]
to risk, to take a risk	**ризикувати**	[rızıku'watı]
to rub off (erase)	**стерти**	['stɛrtı]

to run (move fast)	**бігти**	['biɣtı]
to satisfy (please)	**задовольняти**	[zadowoʎ'ɲatı]
to save (rescue)	**рятувати**	[rʲatu'watı]
to say (~ thank you)	**сказати**	[ska'zatı]
to scold (vt)	**лаяти**	['lajatı]

to scratch (with claws)	**дряпати**	['drʲapatı]
to select (to pick)	**вибрати**	['wıbratı]
to sell (goods)	**продавати**	[proda'watı]
to send (a letter)	**відправляти**	[widpraw'ʎatı]

to send back (vt)	**відправити назад**	[widp'rawıtı na'zad]
to sense (danger)	**почувати**	[potʃu'watı]
to sentence (vt)	**присуджувати**	[prı'sudʒuwatı]
to serve (in restaurant)	**обслуговувати**	[obslu'ɣowuwatı]
to settle (a conflict)	**залагоджувати**	[zala'ɣodʒuwatı]

to shake (vt)	**трясти**	[trʲas'tı]
to shave (vi)	**голитися**	[ɣo'lıtısʲa]
to shine (gleam)	**блищати**	[blı'ɕatı]
to shiver (with cold)	**тремтіти**	[trɛm'titı]

to shoot (vi)	**стріляти**	[stri'ʎatı]
to shout (vi)	**кричати**	[krı'tʃatı]
to show (to display)	**показувати**	[po'kazuwatı]
to shudder (vi)	**здригатися**	[zdrı'ɣatısʲa]
to sigh (vi)	**зітхнути**	[zith'nutı]

to sign (document)	**підписувати**	[pid'pısuwatı]
to signify (mean)	**означати**	[ozna'tʃatı]
to simplify (vt)	**спрощувати**	['sproɕuwatı]
to sin (vi)	**грішити**	[ɣri'ʃıtı]

to sit (be sitting)	**сидіти**	[sı'ditı]
to sit down (vi)	**сісти**	['sistı]
to smash (~ a bug)	**розчавити**	[roz'tʃawıtı]
to smell (scent)	**пахнути**	['pahnutı]
to smell (sniff at)	**нюхати**	['nyhatı]
to smile (vi)	**посміхатися**	[posmi'hatısʲa]
to snap (vi, ab. rope)	**розірватися**	[rozir'watısʲa]

to solve (problem)	розв'язувати	[rozwʰʲjazuwatɪ]
to sow (seed, crop)	сіяти	[ˈsijatɪ]
to spill (liquid)	проливати	[prolɪˈwatɪ]
to spit (vi)	плювати	[plyˈwatɪ]
to stand (toothache, cold)	терпіти	[tɛrˈpitɪ]
to start (begin)	починати	[potʃɪˈnatɪ]
to steal (money, etc.)	красти	[ˈkrastɪ]
to stop (please ~ calling me)	припиняти	[prɪpɪˈɲatɪ]
to stop (for pause, etc.)	зупинятися	[zupɪˈɲatɪsʲa]
to stop talking	замовчати	[zamowˈtʃatɪ]
to stroke (caress)	гладити	[ˈɣladɪtɪ]
to study (vt)	вивчати	[wɪwˈtʃatɪ]
to suffer (feel pain)	страждати	[straʒˈdatɪ]
to support (cause, idea)	підтримати	[pidtˈrɪmatɪ]
to suppose (assume)	припускати	[prɪpusˈkatɪ]
to surface (ab. submarine)	спливати	[splɪˈwatɪ]
to surprise (amaze)	дивувати	[dɪwuˈwatɪ]
to suspect (vt)	підозрювати	[piˈdɔzrywatɪ]
to swim (vi)	плавати	[ˈplawatɪ]
to turn on (computer, etc.)	вмикати	[wmɪˈkatɪ]

256. Verbs T-W

to take (get hold of)	брати	[ˈbratɪ]
to take a bath	митися	[ˈmɪtɪsʲa]
to take a rest	відпочивати	[widpotʃɪˈwatɪ]
to take aim (at ...)	цілитися	[ˈtsilɪtɪsʲa]
to take away	відносити	[widˈnɔsɪtɪ]
to take off (airplane)	злітати	[zliˈtatɪ]
to take off (remove)	знімати	[zniˈmatɪ]
to take pictures	фотографувати	[fotoɣrafuˈwatɪ]
to talk to ...	розмовляти з ...	[rozmowˈʎatɪ z]
to teach (give lessons)	навчати	[nawˈtʃatɪ]
to tear off (vt)	відірвати	[widirˈwatɪ]
to tell (story, joke)	розповідати	[rozpowiˈdatɪ]
to thank (vt)	дякувати	[ˈdʲakuwatɪ]
to think (believe)	вважати	[wwaˈʒatɪ]
to think (vi, vt)	думати	[ˈdumatɪ]
to threaten (vt)	погрожувати	[poɣˈrɔʒuwatɪ]
to throw (stone)	кидати	[kɪˈdatɪ]
to tie to ...	прив'язувати	[prɪwʰʲjazuwatɪ]

to tie up (prisoner)	зв'язувати	['zwʰjazuwatı]
to tire (make tired)	стомлювати	['stɔmlywatı]
to touch (one's arm, etc.)	торкатися	[tor'katısʲa]
to tower (over ...)	підноситися	[pid'nɔsıtısʲa]
to train (animals)	дресирувати	[drɛsıru'watı]
to train (sb)	тренувати	[trɛnu'watı]
to train (vi)	тренуватися	[trɛnu'watısʲa]
to transform (vt)	трансформувати	[transformu'watı]
to translate (vt)	перекладати	[pɛrɛkla'datı]
to treat (patient, illness)	лікувати	[liku'watı]
to trust (vt)	довіряти	[dowi'rʲatı]
to try (attempt)	намагатися	[nama'ɣatısʲa]
to turn (~ to the left)	повертати	[powɛr'tatı]
to turn away (vi)	відвертатися	[widwɛr'tatısʲa]
to turn off (the light)	гасити	[ɣa'sıtı]
to turn over (stone, etc.)	перевернути	[pɛrɛwɛr'nutı]
to underestimate (vt)	недооцінювати	[nɛdɔː'ʦinywatı]
to underline (vt)	підкреслити	[pidk'rɛslıtı]
to understand (vt)	розуміти	[rozu'mitı]
to undertake (vt)	здійснювати	['zdijsnywatı]
to unite (vt)	об'єднувати	[obʰ'ɛdnuwatı]
to untie (vt)	відв'язувати	[widwʰ'jazuwatı]
to use (phrase, word)	уживати	[uʒı'watı]
to vaccinate (vt)	робити щеплення	[ro'bıtı 'ɕɛplɛnja]
to vote (vi)	голосувати	[ɣolosu'watı]
to wait (vt)	чекати	[ʧɛ'katı]
to wake (sb)	будити	[bu'dıtı]
to want (wish, desire)	хотіти	[ho'titı]
to warn (of the danger)	попереджувати	[popɛ'rɛdʒuwatı]
to wash (clean)	мити	['mıtı]
to water (plants)	поливати	[polı'watı]
to wave (the hand)	махати	[ma'hatı]
to weigh (have weight)	важити	['waʒıtı]
to work (vi)	працювати	[praʦy'watı]
to worry (make anxious)	хвилювати	[hwıly'watı]
to worry (vi)	хвилюватися	[hwıly'watısʲa]
to wrap (parcel, etc.)	загортати	[zaɣor'tatı]
to wrestle (sport)	боротися	[bo'rɔtısʲa]
to write (vt)	писати	[pı'satı]
to write down	записувати	[za'pısuwatı]

Made in the USA
Las Vegas, NV
05 April 2022